GERONTOLOGY SERIES

Sheldon R. Roen, Ph.D., Series Editor

Research Planning and Action for the Elderly:

The Power and Potential of Social Science

Edited by

Donald P. Kent, Ph.D.
The Pennsylvania State University,
University Park, Pennsylvania
Robert Kastenbaum, Ph.D.
Wayne State University,
Detroit, Michigan
and
Sylvia Sherwood, Ph.D.
Hebrew Rehabilitation Center for Aged,
Boston, Massachusetts

 **HUMAN SCIENCES PRESS**
72 Fifth Avenue   3 Henrietta Street
NEW YORK, NY 10011 ● LONDON, WC2E 8LU

MATERIALS PURCHASED
WITH TITLE III FUNDS

Library of Congress Catalog Card Number 72-140049
Standard Book Number 87705-056-2
Copyright © 1972 by Behavioral Publications

Reprinted 1976

Reprinted 1979 by Human Sciences Press
72 Fifth Avenue
New York, N.Y. 10011

BEHAVIORAL PUBLICATIONS, 72 Fifth Avenue,
New York, New York 10011

Printed in the United States of America

CONTRIBUTORS

Malcolm Arth, Ph.D., *Chairman and Curator of Education, Department of Education, American Museum of Natural History, New York.*

Ruth G. Bennett, Ph.D., *Principal Research Scientist, Biometrics, New York Department of Mental Hygiene; Adjunct Associate Professor, Teachers College, Columbia University, New York.*

Robert G. Burnight, Ph.D., *Professor of Sociology, University of North Carolina, Chapel Hill.*

Helen Turner Burr, A.C.S.W., *Visiting Nurse Service of N.Y.; Office on Services to Aged, Washington.*

Stanley H. Cath, M.D., *Boston Psychoanalytic Society; Assistant Clinical Professor, Tufts University Medical School, Boston.*

Joseph R. Cautela, Ph.D., *Professor of Psychology, Boston College, Chestnut Hill.*

Carole Estes, M.A., *University of California, San Diego.*

John F. Galliher, Ph.D., *Department of Sociology, University of Missouri, Columbia.*

Michael W. Gillespie, M.A., *Department of Sociology, University of Alberta, Alberta.*

Alvin I. Goldfarb, M.D., *Associate Attending Psychiatrist, Chief of Geriatric Service, The Mount Sinai Hospital, New York City; Associate Clinical Professor of Psychiatry, Mount Sinai Medical School of the City University of New York, New York.*

Leonard E. Gottesman, Ph.D., *Senior Research Psychologist, Philadelphia Geriatric Center.*

Carl Hirsch, A.M., *Associate Director, Aged Services Project, The Pennsylvania State University, University Park.*

Jacquelyne Johnson Jackson, Ph.D., *Assistant Professor of Medical Sociology, Department of Psychiatry, Duke University Medical Center, Durham.*

Robert Kastenbaum, Ph.D., *Professor of Psychology, Wayne State University, Detroit.*

Donald P. Kent, Ph.D., *Professor of Sociology, The Pennsylvania State University, University Park.*

Louis Lowy, Ph.D., *Professor of Social Work, Boston University School of Social Work, Boston.*

M. Powell Lawton, Ph.D., *Research Psychologist, Philadelphia Geriatric Center, Philadelphia and Norristown State Hospital, Norristown.*

George L. Maddox, Ph.D., *Professor of Sociology, Duke University, Durham.*

Sarah C. Main, B.S., *Assistant to the Provost, Stanford University, Stanford.*

Parker Grimes Marden, Ph.D., *Associate Professor of Sociology and Program Associate, International Population Program, Cornell University, Ithaca.*

Stephen J. Miller, Ph.D., *Associate Dean of the Faculty, Harvard Medical School, Cambridge.*

Theodore Nadelson, M.D., *Instructor in Psychiatry, Harvard Medical School; Associate in Psychiatry, Beth Israel Hospital, Boston.*

Lucille Nahemow, Ph.D., *Graduate Center, City University of New York, New York.*

Kermit K. Schooler, Ph.D., *Brandeis University, Waltham.*

Siroon P. Shahinian, Ph.D., *Professional Examination Service, American Public Health Association, New York.*

Sylvia Sherwood, Ph.D., *Director of Social Gerontological Research, Hebrew Rehabilitation Center for the Aged, Boston.*

Suzanne L. Silverman, M.A., *Department of Sociology, The Pennsylvania State University, University Park.*

Charles Taylor, Ph.D., *Professor of Human Development and Psychology, The Pennsylvania State University, University Park.*

Sheldon S. Tobin, Ph.D., *School of Social Service Administration and Committee on Human Development, University of Chicago, Chicago.*

Avery D. Weisman, M.D., *Associate Professor of Psychiatry, Massachusetts General Hospital; Harvard Medical School, Cambridge.*

Robert L. Wolk, Ph.D., *The Hebrew Home for the Aged, Riverdale.*

CONTENTS

ix

Part III Studies in Research and Theory

INTRODUCTION

DONALD P. KENT, ROBERT KASTENBAUM, and SYLVIA SHERWOOD

Like the framers of the Great Declaration, editors of books are required by "a decent respect to the opinions of mankind" to "declare the causes which impel them" to their work. The motivations for this book are several.

One of the major stimulants is its subject population, the aged. Their rapid increase in number has been more than matched by the increased need for new programs and approaches and, consequently, new knowledge. The proliferation of services together with the rapid increase in the number of professionals have created a situation where the demand for knowledge greatly exceeds supply.

While these needs have prompted a marked increase in both research and action programs, the field of gerontology is still young. This in itself offers special opportunities and requires special efforts. Included in the latter are the needs for frequent assessments of the field and broad diffusion of extant knowledge. The vernal nature of gerontology in turn both permits and demands the kind of eclectic generalizing manifest in this collection of papers. The sharp distinctions between theory and practice, between basic and applied research, and between specialists and generalists have not yet developed in gerontology to the degree that they have in the more mature sciences. While there is no large body of verified knowledge that provides systematic directives for intervention, neither are there many entrenched traditional service

Some parts of this introduction originally appeared in a paper written by Sylvia Sherwood, "A Demonstration Program in a Home for the Aged: Observation, Research and Practice" which was published by the Duke University Council on Aging and Human Development, *Proceedings of Seminars 1965-69.*

programs based on the historical development of a given type of clinical experience that might well resist change and hinder the development of an integrated action-research emphasis.

Deeply rooted in the philosophy of science is the conviction that theory and practice are integral to the full development of a discipline. Theory, research methodology, and practice suffer in isolation; in concert, they reinforce one another. It is this belief that has prompted the selection of papers and the organization of this book. While each paper has been judged to have individual merit, the editors also look to the broader context and objectives.

The editors hold an action-research frame of reference. We begin with the belief that programs of services for, and participation by, the elderly are needed and desirable. To live is to act, and all action is purposeful. The problem with much social action is that the purpose is not often made explicit. It is incumbent upon all of us to try to define as sharply as possible the intended outcome of our actions.

At the same time we must avoid the fallacy of assuming that good intentions automatically yield good results; or the correlative error of assuming good process inevitably yields good results. In short, efforts must be made to assess the effects of actions—the consequences of intervention. If we are to judge our programs, adequate evaluative research must accompany our practical efforts.

Faith in good "practice"—appropriately labelled the "success cult" or the "rose-colored glasses syndrome"—is not enough. While the training and experience of the professionals involved, as well as the number of persons reached may be important, they are not adequate criteria for measuring "success." To illustrate, in the past there have been medical programs for the cure of typhoid that employed specialized techniques for bloodletting. The better the training and the greater the experience of the physician, presumably the more proficient and the greater his facility in the bleeding procedures. This was a very highly developed and, during the era of its popularity, a well intentioned practice. But frequently the patient died. The usefulness of programs of service must ultimately be measured not in terms of whether they were designed by "experts" and are being offered in a professional manner by qualified persons, but rather in terms of outcome—whether the program is producing the desired change in the target population.

Unfortunately, in many of the current rehabilitation demonstration projects attempting new and expanded rehabilitative procedures, positive program impact is *assumed*. Some of the methodologically more sophisticated projects do attempt to analyze the changes that occur in the actual population being reached by the rehabilitation program. But even here, it is usually in the form of follow-up investigation rather than "impact" research. Changes in the clients served are traced but there is little effort to provide for controlled comparisons. Change over time, however, is not synonymous with impact. In order to draw conclusions about impact we must first have a basis to say that observed changes *would not have taken place anyway* without the particular intervention. From this point of view, "no change" may, in fact, represent impact. An intervention program may be halting a debilitative process. If we looked at change measurements alone, it would seem as if nothing had happened. But if we had a sound basis to estimate that the condition would have deteriorated and then found that, at the second point in time, it had not become worse, there would then be reason to conclude that the intervention had impact.

It may be obvious that, without evaluation research, programs that do not have the desired impact may appear successful. What is probably less obvious is that, without evaluation research, a program may be considered a failure when in reality it is highly successful. This is especially true in the case of rehabilitation studies for the elderly. Very often the best we may expect to achieve is a slowdown in degenerative processes. If we merely study the "before and after" behavior of elderly persons being served by a rehabilitation program, we may be observing a downward pattern and assume failure.

The best way of measuring impact is through experimental intervention using randomly allocated control groups. Random allocation provides a basis for making statistical inferences concerning whether observed differences among the groups after intervention are due to chance or to the intervention. Developments in the lives of persons in the control groups—those not being reached by the program—provide estimates of what would have happened without the intervention. "Demonstration" projects offer excellent opportunities to study impact of services within such an experimental framework. Unfortunately, in many if not most cases, these opportunities have been passed by.

There are circumstances, however, in which random allocation is not possible. Statistical techniques have been developed (the analysis of co-variance, in particular) that make it possible to draw reasonably valid conclusions from comparisons between groups receiving services and those not, even when the groups are somewhat dissimilar prior to the intervention. But there are times when it is not feasible to utilize "control" groups. The problem of studying the impact of changes in legal statutes, for instance, presents a real challenge to the methodologist. If we merely recorded observations at a point in time prior to a change in statute and again at a point some time after its implementation, insights could be derived for hypothesis formulation but there would be no "evidence" regarding impact. Based on investigations of conditions *over time* during the preceding years, however, it may be possible to establish trend lines concerning areas of behavior that may be affected by a new legal statute. By extrapolating from these trends, predictions can then perhaps be made concerning *what would have happened in the natural course of events without the intervening change,* and knowledge of impact would be possible.

The action-research framework envisioned is not limited to impact analysis alone. It can function on many levels in the pursuit of knowledge. It is rather a point of view that advocates a questioning stance. It searches for possibilities of learning from the unique situation, from collections of descriptive data and from controlled studies designed to test hypotheses or gain specific kinds of knowledge —such as the impact of intervention programs. Its analytic framework demands a systematic recording of relevant data and a specification of the method of operation so that the procedures are "repeatable."

The very nature of the data being gathered and the inquiring approach within which services are provided set the stage for the multitude of possible contributions of action-research. To begin with, the action component of such a venture, as in any service program, provides an immediate service designed to meet some recognized need. At the same time, the demand of the research component to make explicit the relationship between the input variables (the treatments) and the desired outcomes enables a clarification of goals against which treatment strategies can be viewed by the practitioner. A statement of goals can lessen difficulty in communication among clinicians as well as differentiate the outcome goals from the treatment process. Furthermore, the necessity for specifying the impact model—logically interrelating the treatment process to the outcome goals—can stimulate more thoughtful analyses of the problem than might ordinarily occur under the pressure of "doing" when the charge is to provide service only.

Process research can serve still another function. Viewed as case history material, hypotheses and directions for future research may be suggested that can contribute not only to theories of therapeutic intervention but to a more general understanding of behavior—in this case, problems of the aged and the aging process.

Action-research can also serve a "fact-finding" function. Descriptive characteristics of the population being served, diagnoses of needs, and the recommendations made provide the raw data necessary for planning purposes. Such data can answer the *who, where, when,* and *how much* type of questions concerning needs and recommended services. Analysis of this kind of information can help identify problems and differentiate among them in terms of relative importance and community need.

Finally, contributions to methodology and basic research potentialities of action-research should not be overlooked. For example, by using and developing promising research tools from other studies, an appraisal of the utility of these tools in a variety of contexts is made possible. It will also result in increasing the fund of comparable data from a broad array of populations. Furthermore, research findings and postulations concerning behavior—the principles used to describe or explain some phenomena—should apply, if they are valid, to these same phenomena when and where they occur. Therefore, the data being collected and the action setting itself provide excellent opportunities to check previous findings and test theories of behavior.

Like most statements of piety, the preceding comments mean little unless we develop adequate avenues of implementation. In the case of science, this means the development of generalized theory, specific research strategies, communicative systems, and links among the various individuals engaged in their separate but complementary activities.

This conceptual approach has been the organizing principle for this book. Part I focuses upon theory, concepts and the broad issues of social research and social action; Part II upon research strategies and techniques, and Part III upon case studies, substantive findings, and research reports with implications for practice.

Implicit in this approach is the belief that there are no sharp dividing lines, and this is reflected in the choice of papers and in their ordering. Many do not fit neatly. Other editors would make different decisions not only with regard to the inclusion of individual papers but also to their categorizing. No brief is held for this as the only approach; however, it is our conviction that these papers do indeed contribute to the integration of research and practice.

Throughout the book the emphasis is upon utility. For example, the section on techniques presents a smorgasbord. This is deliberate. All are judged to be useful, and their application in any one article is of less moment than their repeatability. Each was judged to have potential. In some papers reproduced here the size of the sample makes the study in itself of little value; others obviously are pilot studies; yet in these, as in other papers in this book, their importance lies not in their content alone but in their potential for other researchers. Given this orientation we have endeavored to present scales and other details in a manner that permit replication.

The editors believe that planners, researchers, and practitioners often labor with a lack of understanding at best and even some mutual contempt at worst. Mutual understanding is both essential and possible. For this to occur it is necessary for each to understand the assumptions made, the rationales employed, the techniques used, and the goals desired.

All the papers selected for inclusion have at least one thing in common. All directly concern older people. Therefore, we have a built-in bias that there should be some interrelation between what is reported here and what actually can be applied to older people. We are not attempting to generalize among older people by studying rats in a maze or naive undergraduates. This is not to say that the latter approaches are to be eschewed, particularly when it is often difficult to study the target population. However, the assumption is that only under special circumstances would the study of "substitute" populations be considered desirable when it is possible to study the target population itself.

While the populations involved here are the aged, it should nevertheless be pointed out that the viewpoints of perspectives brought to bear are not necessarily narrowly gerontologic. Many represent the broadest viewpoints in the field of social science, the application of general theories of behavior to the aging process. We have such varied viewpoints as Pavlovian theory applied to aged, disengagement theory, developmental-field theory, as well as psychoanalysis applied to the aging process. This by no means exhausts all possibilities, but an unusually varied range of viewpoints has been covered, with each of the authors making an attempt to apply his concepts seriously to the aged. Secondly, well beyond the immediate goal of this book, there may be some contribution not only to linking theory, research, and action for the aged, but theory, research, and action for people.

It is customary for editors to issue modest disclaimers; and we also hasten to do so less out of reverence for custom than for our own awareness of deficient execution of a lofty conception. The nature of the latter impels us to the effort, however imperfect.

Many of the papers offered here were presented at a symposium organized by the editors, hence both the frequent cross-referencing and some obvious gaps. Most of those participating in the symposium came from the world of research rather than that of practice, and the consequent emphasis is upon research. However, all of the participants were oriented to action and all had at least some appreciation of the constraints under which practitioners work.

The present knowledge available does not provide an adequate base for sound practice; nor can the practitioner delay action pending the development of such knowledge. The needs for action are so immediate and so pressing that the practitioner must act utilizing the best available knowledge and his common sense. This condition imposes obligations upon all involved in the gerontologic enterprise. From the practitioner the researcher can derive issues and leads; to the practitioner the researcher can give new knowledge and an assessment of the relative effectiveness of varying approaches. The theoreticians, who may be either researchers or practitioners, not only can carry their joint efforts to a higher level of analysis but also provide new insights.

This book does not in itself represent a massive survey that integrates these three viewpoints. Rather, it is a sampling of what we hope are some promising works of gerontologists that either fit directly into this framework or can be useful in an integration of theory, research, and action.

These papers either embody some attempt to reach out from their own perspective to embrace one or another perspective, or they embody potentialities for doing so. To some degree we are looking at the state of the art. How far are we from being able to have an integrated system of theories, research and action? The reader might judge for himself that in some ways we are very close and in some ways we may seem to be far apart. We hope that this book will have the purpose, first, of presenting papers that may be of interest in themselves, most of which have not appeared elsewhere; and secondly, to enable all of us to judge whether we wish to find closer integration among these perspectives and how we may best proceed to accomplish it.

PART I

SOCIAL SCIENCE AND SOCIAL ACTION

1:: SOCIAL POLICY AND PROGRAM CONSIDERATIONS IN PLANNING FOR THE AGING

DONALD P. KENT

This paper is concerned basically with the relationships between social policy and social research as they relate to program planning for the aged. The subject is an important one and, like most important subjects, a complex one. Consequently, it will be necessary to oversimplify, and it would be misleading to pretend to have answers where none exist. The scope of this paper is more modest; it hopes to outline some problem areas, to raise some issues and questions, and to point to some of our dilemmas.

The topic is complex partly because the aging process itself is complex. There is no agreement as to when aging begins; even though one might find general agreement on the definition of aging "as a process of physical and psychological decrements that occur with the passing of time." Put in these terms, aging begins when growth and maturation stop.

This definition and approach may adhere too closely to the biological model where decrement is very apparent. In the psychological and social spheres, decrement is often visible and measurable but is by no means inevitable. All of us know individuals who have remained psychologically intact and brilliant until death at an old age; and history is replete with examples of old men who have performed

Based on a paper presented to the Faculty of the School of Social Work, University of Pennsylvania, Philadelphia, Pennsylvania, February 18, 1966.

difficult social tasks with consummate wisdom, not in spite of old age, but because of a long life of rich experience.

It is necessary to think in terms of at least three types of growth processes: biological, psychological, and social. The curves of maturation and aging in each differ considerably.

We must again be cautious in applying the biological model to the social realm. While individuals age biologically at different rates, it seems likely that individual variations from the average are far less in a biological than social sense. There are individuals who show no significant diminution in social functioning across several decades of living—a statement that one cannot make regarding biological aging. This fact, however, should not obscure the fact that for *most* individuals there are pronounced changes with age both in social expectations and social performance. There is no blinking the fact that most elderly persons suffer some decrements in the performance of social roles. It is still further complicated by the fact that while we talk about biological or sociological aging, in actuality any part of the system has its own rate of aging. Thus the sensory organs age more rapidly than the visceral, etc.

An added factor making for complexity is that the process of aging itself is poorly understood. We just lack knowledge; and our confusion is confounded when we interject the additional factors incident to the relationship of social research to social policy.

As one reviews present relationships between the university and the political worlds, two sharply opposed views are advanced. It is contended that the differences noted between the university and the political worlds reflect the differences in general between the areas of social research and social practice. The ethos of these spheres is respectively alike and different. On the one hand, there is fear that social research will not be used; and on the other hand there is fear that social research will be used in a way that compromises the integrity and impairs the function of both the scholar and the policy maker. Let me offer two quotes that point up this dilemma.

Dr. Kalman Silvert (1965) has said that "American social science is in a crisis of ethics." Basic to our problem, Dr. Silvert feels, is the nature of "the proper ties between the political and the academic worlds (p. 9)." In the physical sciences, this problem was faced some time ago and formalized procedures have been developed defining the relationship of the scientist to his past, to the public, and to his profession. But, as Dr. Silvert (1965, p. 9) points out:

> No such clarity exists in the social sciences. We have no National Science Foundation discharging a brokerage function between the two worlds. We have had no such consistent public debates on academic objectivity and public commitment as have, say, the atomic physicists. No broadly accepted statement of ethics has come from our professional associations, and very few university administrations have concerned themselves with the problem. The result has been that social scientists have generally crossed and recrossed the lines separating their functions from governmental policy making, the only inhibitions being their personally held standards of conduct.

From a somewhat different vantage point, Dr. Donald Hornig (1965), one-time director of the Office of Science and Technology and Chairman of the President's Science Advisory Committee, notes:

> Despite the fact that the behavioral sciences affect every aspect of our lives and interact with every function of the government, I believe we would all agree that they have not been applied to government problems in the same systematic way as the natural sciences nor has a clear picture emerged as to how their development should be fostered. It is my view that we must move to remedy both these problems.

These two views, one pleading for more and closer contacts between the social researcher and the policy maker and the other warning of the dangers of such relationships, highlight the complexity of the area.

The thesis of this paper is relatively simple. It is that government has grown enormously, and with this growth have come changes of focus and function. Some part of governmental activities today are frankly related to the area of social reconstruction, and basic to this area is social research. If society is to be reordered, and if this reconstruction is to be based on something other than conventional wisdom or practical experience, there must be some connection between the policy maker and the social researcher. It is contended here that at present we have inadequate bridges (both institutional and informal) between the two. There is a need for the construction of bridges to insure a free flow of information between the policy maker and the scholar without the loss of integrity and purpose of either one.

Ideally, as Dr. Robert Blum (1964, p. 1) has pointed out, such interrelationships may be viewed "as a kind of cross-fertilization in which the results of scholarship are made available to the makers of public policy and in which the scholars are made more aware of the relevance of their studies."

Dr. Blum (1964, p. 1) also notes from such relationships there may develop a "kind of homogenization, as a result of which the scholar and the policy maker become somewhat inter-distinguishable . . . There is a danger that the efforts of both may be somewhat dulled as a result."

Implicit in the views presented in this paper are a number of considerations that are not widely shared.

In the first place, a question may be raised about consensus. Walter Lippman has said that "when all men agree it's a sign that someone is not thinking." Popular folk wisdom has it that "a few fleas is good for a dog;" and it is possible that a few disagreements are good for a group—be it a family, community, university, or nation. An experiment within a governmental agency can be cited where a team of inter-disciplinary scholars was assembled and molded into a single frame of reference, hopefully to scale the heights. The results were a great disappointment. All thought alike, but this thought was at the level where there was a common denominator which unfortunately was not a high one. While there are areas of articulation between social research and social policy, there are also areas of disagreement which we cannot ignore. Our concern is not to eliminate the differences or to gloss over them, but to explore ways of making these inherent differences useful to each activity and to the society.

One cannot understand the interrelationships of social research and social policy without first understanding the changes that have occurred in government over the past several decades.

The enormous growth of government is readily apparent. In the mid-nineteenth century, the entire Federal budget totaled only 35 million dollars, considerably less than that of an average good-sized city today. By 1940 this had grown to 9 billion dollars. In the two and a half decades since then, almost 200 billion dollars have been added to the annual Federal budget.

Federal civilian employment has seen a corresponding growth in the past two decades. The number of civilian employees has almost trebled, going from one to three million persons.

Less amenable to statistical treatment have been the changes in function. Initially the basic, and almost sole, function of the Federal Government was that of protecting the national security. The Federal establishment embraced the areas of defense, conduct of foreign affairs, and protection. To this was soon added the function of regulation (initially of interstate affairs), but expanding across time to a multiplicity of activities that have been judged to impinge upon the well-being of the citizen and our national security. In turn, this function has been designed to promote the general welfare. And in recent times a new function has been added—that of social reconstruction.

The programs of housing for older people, urban renewal, development of community action programs, construction of hospitals and nursing homes, the training of professional personnel; all are closely related to social reconstruction.

This social renewal is based upon a rationale first enunciated by

President Kennedy (February, 1961) in a special message to the Congress on health needs of the American people. In it he said there were four elements to sound governmental programs. The first of these is research, for we must have sound knowledge in order to plan well and build wisely. The second is trained personnel, for without adequately trained people, the knowledge is useless. The third is providing the services and facilities necessary for the effective transmission of research findings to the people. The fourth is a means of paying for it.

This rationale can be seen in the development of programs for the health care for older people. In recent years there have been large increases in the amount spent for gerontological research. Between 50 and 75 million dollars is spent annually on health research in the area of gerontology. While this seems a sizable sum, it is a very small portion of our total research and development budget which exceeds 15 billion dollars.

The impact of this investment in gerontological research can be seen in a variety of ways. If one looks at the *Journal of Gerontology* during the first eight years of its existence from 1946-53, one discovers that there were only three articles which note support from Federal funds. In the next eight years, between 1954 and 1962, there were 169 articles indicating by footnote that they were supported, either in whole or in part, by Federal funds. Today virtually all large-scale research efforts in gerontology carry a footnote of this kind.

One can see the fruits of this in another regard. In 1940 it is estimated that there were something less than one hundred articles per year published in the area of gerontology. The National Institutes of Health now estimate that some five thousand articles a year are published in this area. There can be little doubt that through government support research in the area of gerontology has markedly increased.

To create a reservoir of trained personnel the Congress has enacted the Health Professions Education Act and given support for the construction of medical schools, loans to medical students, scholarships and grants for nurses and for other health personnel.

In 1961 the Congress passed the Community Health Services Facilities Program which was designed to meet in part the demands of the third element in the rationale—the provision of services and facilities by which research could be translated into services for individuals and communities. And, of course, the passage of Medicare in 1965 was designed to provide a means of paying for these services and facilities.

This Federal approach to meeting health needs stands in marked contrast to earlier conceptions of the role of government; and it is obvious that in this approach there is a need for social and behavioral scientists. This too can be seen by looking at Federal employment. Federal records in 1965 indicated that there were some 20,000 employees in the category of social science, psychology, and social welfare; approximately 15,000 in mathematics and statistics; and about 20,000 more in the general area of education. These figures in themselves do not indicate the full extent of influence. Consultants are widely used and, in fact, today nearly every committee needs to have its sociologist, psychologist, and social worker. It would be misleading to assume that these people are mere window dressing. They obviously exert great influence. In fact, the influence extends beyond the individual to subject matter, and the Supreme Court's decision with reference to school desegregation stands as a monument to social science and social research.

At a level somewhat less spectacular than the 1954 Supreme Court decision, one detects the influence of social research upon social policy. For example, the Public Housing Administration has made a multi-billion dollar investment in housing specifically designed for the elderly. Guidelines for such housing have been developed and embodied in a manual called *The Architect's Checklist* (1962). Even a cursory examination of this checklist reveals the influence of research. For example, physiologists have noted that with aging comes a drop at the heel and change in foot structure. This leads to a tendency to scuff along and the greater chance of tripping over door risers and ledges. As a consequence, the checklist indiciates that housing for the elderly should be designed without such hindrances.

Similarly, one could look at the requirements with regard to the tone of the doorbell, the amount of illumination, the location of electric fixtures, the composition of floors, the location of doors, etc., and see that each one of these is rooted in some bit of research indicating limitations on physical activity that come with age.

Such examples should not mislead us into thinking that most social policy is rooted in research or that the contributions of the social scientist have no bounds. Dr. Silvert (1962, p. 12) has noted that under the "very best conditions," there are limits to the functioning of the social researcher. He suggests that the researcher can do the following:

a. He can generate and make available new data.
b. He can order these data to permit informed guessing about the nature of the lacunae.
c. He can indicate relevant theoretical patterns for the interpretation of the data.
d. He can—explaining himself carefully—indicate the probabilities of effectiveness of various selected courses of action.
e. He can indicate which choices are foreclosed by the adoption of given courses of action.
f. He can indicate which new choices will be made available by the adoption of given courses of action.

One can cite examples of behavioral scientists influencing social policies vis-à-vis the aging in each of the ways listed above.

The generation of new data has played an important part in shaping public policies. The special report, *Senior Citizens and How They Live* (1962), was an analysis of 1960 census data focusing upon the housing conditions of older people. It noted: "Over 19% of the 16 million housing units in which senior citizens live may be characterized as substandard in that they lack private bath, toilet or running water, or were structurally deficient." The report went on to show that "nearly one half of the renter households with incomes of less than $1000 live in substandard units (p. 7)." These data played an important part in persuading to Congress to markedly expand the program of housing for older people.

There are many areas in which new data are needed for the development of sound public policy. For example, we know very little about what happens to persons who are denied old age assistance.

Each year departments of welfare are forced to turn away applicants for assistance who just do not meet the eligibility requirements. Yet the applying individuals were motivated by feelings of need. We do not know how, or if, these individuals meet these real or imagined needs. While we know that almost half of the persons 65 and over are living alone without spouse, we know very little about the specifics of the single person family. We know that among the females in the 70 to 74 year bracket more than 60% are living alone and in the 85 and up age group almost 90% are without living spouse; yet we know little of widowhood.

The social researcher can order data to permit informed guessing. It is very easy to demonstrate that the retired person has an enormous amount of free time. How this time is used and how it can best be used can be inferred from studies that have already been made. The social researcher has the freedom to make some imaginative suggestions of alternatives to our present pattern. For example, it would make more sense to this writer to spread leisure throughout the working life rather than having a highly concentrated work period followed by early retirement and many years of concentrated leisure.

The social researcher knows, for example, that activity centers reach only a very small portion of older people. This is only partly because of unavailability. Even when available, they are not widely used. Researchers estimate that in New York City only about one out of every one hundred persons has ever used an activity center, notwithstanding the fact that they are municipally sponsored. In Syracuse about five out of one hundred use the centers. The highest use of activity centers of which we have record is in London where, after an all-out drive, some 12% of the older people used the facilities.

On the other hand we have data indicating that for some people educational opportunities similar to those that are being fostered by the Institute for Retired Professionals at the New School for Social Research, or volunteer activities, or opportunities for civic service have far greater appeal. Here again there is a role for the social researcher in suggesting alternatives to existing patterns.

Social researchers can also indicate relevant theoretical patterns for the interpretation of data. One might cite as an example of social research being used in this manner a study of Yonina Talmon-Garber (1962). Dr. Talmon-Garber has studied aging in collective settlements in Israel. She notes:

> The collectives have solved many of the basic and most persistent problems of aging. Aging members enjoy full economic security. Communal services care for them in case of ill health or infirmity. Retirement from work is gradual and does not entail an abrupt and complete break from work routines. Aging members are not cut off from community life. What is most important of all, grown-up children are expected to live in the community founded by their parents. Parents are able to maintain close and constant relations with their children without losing their independence. Elderly and old people are thus spared much of the insecurity and isolation, the futile inactivity, and dependence entailed in aging. Yet in spite of the many safeguards and advantages, growing old is by no means a smooth process in the collectives. On the personal level it is experienced as a difficult, sad, and painful process of reorientation [p. 462].

Dr. Talmon-Garber has gone further and tried to isolate some of the foci of strain. She notes for example that the aged are living in a future-oriented society. The kibbutz, an outgrowth of revolutionary movement, glorifies youth as full of potentialities, free, and creative. It emphasizes discontinuity. This youth-centered ideology instills a feeling that aging, in the words of Dr. Talmon-Garber, is "a gradual fall from grace."

Dr. Talmon-Garber also notes the central position of work. Within the collective, work is invested with an almost religious quality. And absence from work creates feelings of guilt. It is also apparent that one who lives in the kibbutz is taught to give generously of himself but is not taught to receive. One is taught to be independent, rather than knowing how to accept dependence. The kibbutz is also oriented toward progress with the consequence that old knowledge and experience is soon outmoded.

As a consequence of the work of Dr. Talmon-Garber, in many of the collective settlements efforts have been made to organize life in a somewhat different manner.

Social researchers can provide a theoretical rationale of programs and operations. For example, Walter Beattie in a paper entitled "Matching Services to Individual Needs of the Aging" (1965) has develped a model that can be used by social policy makers in the ordering of programs and the development of structures. To oversimplify Mr. Beattie's model, he developed a program that operates on two axes. On one is a level of service and on the other a level of operation. Beattie lists five levels going from basic services (those needed by all people), adjustment and integrated services (designed to permit older people to participate in the community), support services (to keep the older person in his own habitat), level of congregate and shelter care (where the older person is protected from hazards of an open environment), to the level of protective services (where the individual's civil rights and personal well-being are protected). On the axis of level of operation, Beattie identifies general goals, followed by specific goals, then conditions to which these are related, and finally details specific services at each level.

The social researcher can of course indicate the effectiveness of selective courses of action. The extensive work on personality and patterns of adjustment that have been done by Dr. Suzanne Reichard and her associates (1962), Dr. Bernice Neugarten (1964) and her associates, and Dr. Irving Rosow (1967) are yielding marked similarities in identifying basic personality types.

The characteristics of each "personality type" or the ways in which they were identified will not be described here. The importance of these studies is that they have relevance to developing balanced programs. Policy makers are necessarily concerned with objective programs. It is important to remember that such programs must be evaluated not only in terms of what they are intended to do (or can do for some groups) but also in terms of how they will be defined subjectively.

The researcher can provide both a rationale to aid in understanding behavior and guidelines for the development of specific programs. The practitioner can test research findings in the "real world" and give a feedback that is invaluable. Each serves to check the other, and each enhances the other.

Research noted above reinforces the observation of practitioners that no amount of friendly visiting will satiate the person who has an insatiable appetite for sociability. We know of no activity program that will turn the phlegmatic, "rocking chair person" into the behavior patterns of the "mature person." The significance here for policy makers is that *specific* programs must be developed for *specific* types of situations and personalities.

Another important function of the social researcher is to indicate the choices and consequences of courses of action. For example the Department of Housing and Urban Development has long puzzled over the question: Should it encourage age-segregated housing or should it foster age-integrated housing? Within the agency there are proponents for each point of view. The question, of course, is one of basic social policy. As so often happens with the absence of evidence, the policy that has developed is one of "let's do both." On the one hand, large retirement villages, such as Leisure World in Laguna Beach where some

30,000 older people will eventually live together, are supported by Federal programs. At the same time, Federal support is being given to communities and groups which are trying to bring about an integrated age structure.

One reason for this lack of clarity is the fact that there is very little social research that bears upon this question. One study that does is the five-year study conducted at Western Reserve University by Dr. Irving Rosow (1964).

This study is basically concerned with the effects of environment upon the social integration of individuals. Integration may be viewed from different vantage points. Social integration refers to the articulation of various institutional structures, and personal integration is concerned with the manner and ways in which a person is tied into the beliefs and activities of his society. It is the latter with which Rosow was concerned.

Integration has, Dr. Rosow (1964, p. 8) notes, three dimensions: (1) the sharing of social values; (2) having meaningful roles; and (3) participating in formal and informal groups.

Most research so far conducted indicates that the social values of the aged do not differ markedly from those held by others in the society. In fact this is one source of the problem of the aged (cf. Sherwood, 1962). Given a youth-centered society and a set of social values that favor youth, the aged frequently possess an unfavorable self-image. The values which they have incorporated are antithetical to accepting their present conditions.

We also know that for most individuals a progressive loss in roles comes with age. Marital roles decline, work roles diminish, and most of the aged live in a contracting social world.

Dr. Rosow was concerned primarily with the dimension of personal integration, group living, and friendship patterns. More specifically, he was concerned with the effects of residential density upon these. His method was first to classify apartment houses in Cleveland by the percentage of older occupants. If the percentage was from 1-15% aged, he classified this as a "normal" concentration of elderly. If it was between 33-49%, he classed it a "concentrated type." And if the percentage of older people was 50% or more, it was considered to be "densely populated" by older people. A random sample of some twelve hundred older people was then studied. They were divided into middle class and working class groups and viewed under housing conditions of the normal, concentrated and dense environments.

From this study certain conclusions became clear. As we would expect, middle class persons generally have more friends than do the working class. For example, 16% of the working class indicated that they had no good friends, while only 6% of the middle class so indicated. At the other extreme, 44% of the middle class indicated that they had ten or more good friends in contrast to only 25% of the working class. It is obvious that one of the policy implications here is that isolation and need for friends is more a working class than middle class problem.

Dr. Rosow was concerned about the influence of residential density upon making friends. He discovered that if you took people who had made four new friends in a year and looked at the environment in which they lived, density of aged was the single most significant factor. Among the working class only 19% who had made four or more new friends were living in a normal environment, while 56% who were living in a dense concentration of older people made four new friends in a year. The same pattern obtains for the middle class but the difference is less striking. Twenty-six percent of those living in a normal environment, and 31% who were living in the dense environment made four new friends in a year.

The policy implications here are very clear. Among older people, density is a significant factor in the promotion of friendships.

From this study one finds that generally the working class person is more dependent upon friends *within* the neighborhood setting than is the middle class person. It also became apparent that with respect to help patterns, older people depend chiefly upon *other older people*.

Even older people living in this normal environment turn to their peers for help.

This study is cited in detail because it throws into relief some of the problems and differences between social policy makers and social researchers. In the first instance, researchers are nearly always concerned with a higher level of abstraction than are policy makers. The latter are concerned with providing an environment that provides maximum life satisfactions for older people consistent with the economic resources that the society has allocated. The social researcher, on the other hand, is interested in basic knowledge. These two functions are not necessarily the same, but the end result can be a complementary one if either the practitioner and/or the researcher can forge the connecting links.

Another difference, (which does not show in the above), was present. Some years ago the Congress was concerned with a basic policy issue and asked a social scientist what the answer was. He replied he did not know, but that it could be studied. Congress said in effect, "This is wonderful, go study it. And how soon will we have our answer?" In asking this question, the Congress was thinking in terms of perhaps three months, six months, or at the most a year. They were shocked to discover that the social scientist thought it would take four to five years.

Public policy can rarely wait until all the evidence is in. Conversely, good research takes time. Public policy obviously must be formulated at times without the infra-structure of research. It is equally obvious that it should be modifiable in the light of social research. Even more than that, it should have built in the research component that will yield the knowledge necessary for a rational social policy.

Professor George E. Taylor, Director of the Far Eastern and Russian Institute at the University of Washington, spoke to the State Department on the relationship of the scholar in making national policy and said this:

The main business that we should be in, I think, is fundamental research and here we have as much to gain as to give because it is very often from the practical problems of politics that research can begin. You may start from the same problem and do a job on it for the policy maker by tomorrow morning at 10 o'clock. You may start from that problem and look at it from the scholarly point of view and let it take you wherever it will to build up theoretical systems that you can use for related problems as a basis, ultimately we hope, for decision making. Fundamental research is a university responsibility, but it can best be done in the sciences if we are in touch with political problems and if we see how creative politics can be.

Some years ago *Science* magazine said, "The Scientific community has not responded adequately to the high trust placed in it by the Nation. Perhaps if our role were better understood we would search more diligently for ways of discharging our responsibilities."

Research, policy and practice are surely not the same, but surely they are not unrelated. Practice that is not rooted in broad policy is apt to be worthless; and policy that is not informed by knowledge may well be worse than worthless; it may be dangerous. One could begin at the other end of the chain. Research that is unrelated to some need and utility is likely to be trivial in conception and hardly likely to attract the keen imagination and personal dedication indispensable to great discovery.

REFERENCES

Beattie, W. Matching services to individual needs of the aging. Unpublished manuscript, Gerontological Society, St. Louis, Mo., 1965.

Blum, R. The scholar and the policy maker. In United States Department of State, External Research Staff, *External research.* Washington, D.C.: U.S. Department of State, 1964.

Hornig, D. F. Challenges before the behavioral sciences. Address at the dedication of the new building of the American Psychological Association, Washington, D.C., 1965.

Housing and Home Finance Agency, Office of the Administrator, Office of Program Policy. *Senior citizens and how they live: Part I, The national scene.* Washington, D.C.: U.S. Government Printing Office, July 1962.

Neugarten, B. L. & Associates (Eds.). *Personality in middle and late life.* New York: Atherton Press, 1964.

Public Housing Administration, Housing and Home Finance Agency. *Architect's check list.* Washington, D.C.: U.S. Government Printing Office, 1962.

Reichard, S., Livson, R., & Petersen, P. G. *Aging and personality.* New York: Wiley, 1962.

Rosow, I. *Housing and social integration of the aged.* Cleveland: Western Reserve University, 1964.

Sherwood, S. Conservatism and age—A re-examination. *Indian Journal of Social Research,* 1962, *2,* 39-44.

Silvert, K. H. American academic ethics and social research abroad. *American Universities Field Staff Reports Service,* West Coast South America Series, 1965, *12* (3), entire issue.

Talmon-Garber, Y. Aging in collective settlements in Israel. In C. Tibbitts, & W. Donahue (Eds.), *Social and psychological aspects of aging.* New York: Columbia University Press, 1962.

2:: THE ROLE OF SOCIAL GERONTOLOGY IN THE DEVELOPMENT OF SOCIAL SERVICES FOR OLDER PEOPLE

LOUIS LOWY

The definition of social gerontology provided by Clark Tibbits (1963, p. 19) serves as an anchoring point for this presentation: "Social gerontology may be seen as a striving to establish a body of verified propositions and systematic hypotheses with reference to the aging process in the individual following early adulthood, to the societal factors in aging and to the adaptations of society to older people. It represents a cross-sectional approach to the study of those aspects of the individual, the group and the culture which have reference to aging." Social gerontology provides the scientific foundation to guide the activist in planning, developing, and implementing programs in the field of aging. This is a reciprocal relationship and the knowledge gained by the activist may be converted into new testable proportions and will contribute to the fund of gerontological knowledge.

Robert Binstock (1966, p. 157) has stated: "The responsibility for converting basic knowledge in the field of gerontology into actual benefits for older persons lies with the 'action people'—those who are developing policies and programs and arranging for their implementation." Unfortunately there is considerable time lag between completion of studies and their assimilation into programs of application. In spite

Based on a paper presented at the 19th Annual Meeting of the Gerontological Society, New York, N.Y., November, 1966.

of the lag, however, it is clear that once systematic studies are undertaken within a field, practice moves steadily forward. These preliminary thoughts serve as a theme pervading this paper. More specifically this paper will focus on the contribution which social gerontology can make in (1) determining the types of social services needed by older persons; (2) developing of social services and their organization; and (3) staffing of these services.

Determination of the Type of Social Services Needed by Older Persons

At the White House Conference on Aging in 1961 (U.S. Department of Health, Education and Welfare Special Staff on Aging, p. 171) social services were defined as a flexibly organized system of activities and institutions to help individuals attain satisfying standards of life and health, while at the same time helping them develop their full capacities in personal and social relationships. For older persons they are those organized and practical activities which conserve, protect, and improve human resources. These programs include: financial assistance, casework and counselling, information and referral, friendly visiting, group activities and protective services.

This definition has been widely accepted, and it has been used in the design of programs for the aging. It is based on assumptions of "common human needs," on a residual conception of social welfare, and on experiences rooted in the practice wisdom of the helping professions. This definition does not take into account the emerging hypotheses and propositions relative to differential stages of later life and varying adaptations which are made to these stages. Nor does it embrace the developmental hypotheses and theories based on personality types.

Social gerontological theories of behavior which have been developed by Reichard and her associates (Reichard, Livson & Peterson, 1962) and by the Committee of Human Development in Chicago (Tobin,

1966) can provide us with more differentiated guidelines as to the types of social services needed. Reichard and her associates have differentiated five patterns of maladjustment to aging at retirement. What types of differential social services are needed for these five "types" of men? The "mature," well-integrated men probably require different types of service from the "angry" and "self-hating" group of men who face particular crises upon retirement.

Customarily social services have been divided into those that provide support for the functioning of older people in their own homes and those that provide institutional care and support. With regard to the first category of services, we have yet to learn to differentiate the type of services that are appropriate for various types of housing arrangements for older people. All too often it is assumed that housing for the elderly follows one distinctive pattern and the only issue is one of age-segregated versus age-integrated housing. Empirical studies reveal the complex of factors that are involved. Elias S. Cohen (1966) lists nine possible arrangements ranging from "independent housing in the community" to "retirement-villages." A number of questions arise: What use can be made by research findings in ecology, relating the spatial arrangements of living to the development of social relationships? How do we test such hypotheses as those of Rosow (1961), who points out that the segregated pattern concentrates older people, but insulates them rather than isolates them from the community environment? His suggestion that segregated housing assists social integration of older people deserves replication since its verification or refutation would be a better guide to housing policy for older persons than presumed needs and folkloric assumptions.

We now group services for older persons into five major categories: (1) medically oriented services; (2) services to enhance a person's ability to participate in the activities of daily living such as homemaker services, food services; (3) services to maintain social contact and participation which include friendly visiting, group services, day center programs; (4) problem-solving and socially supportive services, e.g., counselling, information and referral, protective services; and (5) financial assistance services. To list such services is not enough. We need to know when and where to utilize them most effectively. For this we need data derived from research developed in practice and/or explanations of empirical relationships. We need to know the effect of certain personality types of homemakers upon certain types of older persons. We need to know what activities in the homemaker role can be generalized to develop into a "social role." The list of knowledge "needs" is great and its answers depends upon research.

We have tended to assume that older people should be maintained in their own homes as long as possible—preferably with social and medical services available to make this feasible. Institutionalization has been stigmatized. To a large extent this has been due in part to the type of institutional arrangements in which older people have been placed, and in part to the "psychology" inherent in considering institutions as terminal stations. The use of institutions either as rehabilitation centers or as appropriate living arrangements can be better determined if, and when, gerontological research gives guidelines to policy planners and decision-makers as to: (1) the nature of conditions which makes the use of an institution preferable to keeping older people in their own homes; and (2) the types of institutional services that are essential to meet the criteria of a healthful living arrangement for the older person.

From this we can conclude that the exploration of tested theories, the use of empirical studies, and the design of intervention programs have to be directed toward learning more about the five categories of social services in reference to older people with different needs and in different circumstances. We might therefore differentiate at least three major types of social services: (1) those to be provided to *all* older persons as a "social utility" regardless of "need" but as a right; (2) those supplementary services needed by older people with particular problems in adjustment to aging that are temporary; (3) those to be offered as special services necessitated by social or personal conditions that are more permanent and lasting.

If we adopt this approach to the provision of social services we have indeed moved to embrace the institutional or developmental conception of social welfare, at least with regard to the older population. This conception, while basic, is not sufficient. We have to be able to translate it to make possible the effective organization and delivery of services. And to do so requires more knowledge, and therefore more research.

Development and Organization of Social Services for Older People

Most of the existing social services do not meet the basic criteria of comprehensiveness, coordination, continutiy, and differentiation. The literature is replete with references to this, and testimonies given to the United States Senate Special Committee on Aging (1966) during its hearings about the effect of the War on Poverty on the older American attest to the widespread nature of these problems.

Certain theoretical formulations have been developed in the field of community planning that provide helpful conceptual tools to approach the development of social services in a more rational way. Robert Morris and Robert Binstock (Morris & Binstock, 1965; Binstock, 1966) state that the development of services needs an appropriate stance and frame of reference. They indicate that development or expansion of social services requires changes in community and agency policy, in budget allocations, and in community attitudes. They specify three basic processes to do this: (1) goal setting; (2) assessing feasibility of goal implementation, which includes an assessment of resistance and the resources available to overcome this resistance; (3) balance-striking between goal and feasibility. If social services for the elderly are to be expanded and developed along dimensions pointed out earlier in this paper, we need to know more about the process of goal formulation in agencies and/or institutions. We need answers to such questions as: What kinds of organizations or agencies resist what kinds of plans for changes in their policies? What is the nature of the resistance which prevails in certain types of organizations against the inclusion of new programs? What do theories of organizational behavior tell us about goal displacement that could shed light on the resistance of certain types of institutions to introduction of a new service? What do we know from Lewinian field theory about dynamics of change in small groups that can be utilized when we work with the board of directors of a community institution of the aged? In short, if we want to initiate, expand, and develop social services for older people, we need to know upon which kind of available theories and research findings we may draw that can provide us with guideposts for action.

The "trial and error methods" to which we are accustomed can still yield valuable data and major contributions if we utilize measures for testing the effectiveness of action programs. We must begin to evaluate the procedures used against the outcomes desired. This means that when we plan to initiate a new service for older people, we must build in a method for evaluation. Careful evaluative studies may yield answers to such questions as: How do we formulate goals? How do we marshall support for these goals? How do we overcome resisting forces in the community? Which interventive strategies have been most successful in overcoming resistance? What methods have been most productive in getting social agencies to cooperate? What principles can we relate to hypotheses that have been developed regarding agency cooperation and coordination in the literature (Lippitt, Watson and Weatley, 1958)? If we make an attempt to build such testing into the development process itself, then we are not only able to learn from what we are doing, but also we add to the knowledge-building process which can be tested further through experimental studies. Thus we contribute to that branch of social gerontology which concerns itself with the nature of social institutions for the aged and their possible impact upon our social structure.

Once social services are developed, our concern shifts to the ways in which they are organized. Three major questions require consideration here and the field of social gerontology may be in a position to turn its attention to these questions:

1. How can social services be available where and when older people need them?

2. What causes older people to use, or not to use, social services?
3. How does the internal structure of the organization affect the delivery of social services to older people?

Availability of services

An examination of demographic factors shows that the highest proportion of older people lives in the smaller urban areas some distance removed from large metropolitan centers (Cowgill, 1965). Further demographic analyses is needed to determine the significance of this as well as the effects of climate, economic opportunity, cost of living, attitudes of the populace, proximity to children, and to other relatives. Such analyses are basic for the development and organization of social services.

Knowledge about prevalent usage of services during day and night time is necessary for the proper allotment of service functions. Especially needed is knowledge concerning the ecology of services.

Utilization of social services

A corollary to the questions regarding the availability of services center about their utilization: We need urgent answers to the question since it has often been assumed—if not hypothesized—that geographic proximity is a function of usage. But the questions are much more complex. Is non-use related to the perceived stigma of certain social services, notably in relation to income maintenance? Is it related to differential sex roles? Is use or non-use of centers and Golden Age clubs related to perception of play and leisure? Is the use or non-use of social services a function of self-image of old-age? Is is related to discomfort within bureaucratic structure and formal organization? Is use or non-use based on availability of information? Who among the elderly are the more frequent users of social services? What kinds of social services are being used in institutional settings? Do multi-service centers for older people attract a cross-section of the elderly by ethnic origin, religion, race, level of education, income division? A finding just completed by the Family Counseling and Guidance Centers, Inc. (1966) in Boston, "The Utilization of Volunteers to Promote the Well-Being of Older People" has again confirmed the hypothesis that among a group of older persons, whom they identified as "isolates." many cannot reach out and make their needs known. They recommend that more intensive "recruitment" through agencies, the clergy, and housing authorities should be attempted. But here we need to specify again what the variables are. What do we know about this segment of the older population? To what kind of outreach do they respond? Social gerontology can contribute to our understanding by bringing together relevant knowledge and theoretical formulations about the isolated elderly who have been deprived of object relationships (Berezin and Cath, 1965), the ways in which they can be reached, and knowledge about their past use of community resources. In the area of mental health our efforts have been placed increasingly on providing prevention services through non-hospital facilities. Ethel Shanas (1964, p. 85) puts it this way:

> If we are serious about our desire to reduce the older patient-load of mental hospitals in this country . . . We need to make a new start in community services for the aged. Older people, whether socially isolated or not, need to have readily available to them home medical care, homemaker and housekeeping services, visiting nurse services and home chirpody services, among others.

While granting the need to have services available, we still need to know under what conditions certain groups of older persons use or do not use certain types of social services. A number of studies give us insight into some of the factors relative to use of social services. These include the studies of adjustment (Havighurst, Neugarten and Bengston, 1966), self perception relative to social position (Rosow, 1962), attitudes toward non-work roles and leisure (Miller, 1965), and the older person's role in a family context (Streib and Thompson, 1960).

Delivery of services

Social services are generally administered through bureaucratic organizations. While the essential characteristics of formal organizations are designed to facilitate the giving of service in an impartial and fair way to all "clients," they often have the opposite effect on people who come in contact with bureaucracies. They feel compartmentalized, subordinated, confused, and "left out." Often the services offered are subject to considerable delay and the agency assumes an image of a formidable "machine" that cannot easily be moved. Older people who have not grown up with such formidable bureaucracies may find them bewildering.

In becoming clients or patients in an institution, they are expected to learn new social roles. While carefully controlled laboratory studies have shown that the primary ability of the individual to learn is not age-bound, there are observable behavioral differences between old and young learners (Donahue, 1966). It would therefore appear that if an older person is expected to learn the role of client, group member, or patient in a long-term care facility, then his attitudes toward agency, staff, and service must be assessed and taken into consideration. Increase in cautiousness and need for self-protection of the elderly will have to be taken into account by the dispensers of service. Emphasis on rules and procedures will have to be tempered and the concomitants of an impersonal approach will need modification.

While these ideas are based on evidence culled from social science research findings, these findings do not as yet tell us how to modify an impersonal approach or how to structure services so that clients' attitudes toward the agency or staff can be taken into account. We do not know yet really how to de-emphasize rules and procedures; nor do we know how to provide an informal atmosphere, guarantee impartiality, remove authority obstacles or coordinate services. Our objective is to deliver services to people in such a way that they consider them as their right and can accept them with dignity and utilize them to their maximum advantage. We do not know how to do this; and what is more, we do not know what the effect for the older person would be if the services were indeed delivered in this fashion.

The number of questions and issues which highlight the need for further knowledge from social gerontological research is almost limitless. I have not touched upon questions of cost (Corson & McConnell, 1956) and the contributions of economics in helping social welfare planners assess the economic factors in developing social services. Needless to say, the economist in gerontology has an important function in the development of social services that goes beyond the assessment of how our economy can shoulder the cost of supplying adequate incomes required to maintain the growing number of older people in a state of economic well-being.

The effective delivery of quality social services to older persons on a differential basis depends not only on the clarity of our goals, or the commitment to humanitarian values, but also on available knowledge of *how* to bring dispensers and consumers of services together.

Staffing of social services for older people

Without adequately trained personnel, the services themselves will be jeopardized. No amount of scientific knowledge will be of help unless we have personnel of high quality and in sufficient quantity to work with older people. Personnel to staff social services may be drawn not only from the profession of social work, but also from other professions such as nursing, teaching, psychology, psychiatry, and home economics. In fact, the multi-service orientation necessitates a multi-occupational staffing pattern. This staffing arrangement requires both professional personnel and subprofessionals. Any of these categories may and should include older persons themselves.

Three major questions need to be answered in order to plan for appropriate staffing of social services in a variety of settings:

1. What are the personnel requirements based on a projection of needs?
2. How can appropriate personnel be recruited, selected, and retained?
3. What type of training is essential for such personnel?

Projections of manpower needs long have been a concern of economists and labor experts. In a recent study by the Departmental Task Force on Social Work Education and Manpower (1965, pp. 41-42), U.S. Department of Health, Education, and Welfare, projections of needs for one source of manpower have been made.

> The estimates from agencies within the Department of Health, Education and Welfare suggest a need in their programs alone of approximately 100,000 social workers with full education by 1970, a vast increase in the numbers of social workers with baccalaureate level of education, and development of several categories of technical and auxiliary personnel. The problem increases in geometric proportion if to these totals are added the expanding needs for the same categories of personnel in the voluntary agencies, in progress of service to special groups such as the aged, the retarded and the physically handicapped and in the new programs to combat poverty, delinquency and ignorance.

What needs to be done now is to develop more accurate projections of manpower needs based on a differentiation of social services for older persons as defined in this paper. What types of social services require what kind of staff functions and on what level? How many social planners, caseworkers, groupworkers, coordinators of services, homemakers, medical aides, foster grandparents, legal aides, administrators, etc. are needed to provide the projected services? How will these services be distributed over the land and how can we facilitate an appropriate distribution process in a society that operates under the principle of individual freedom of vocational choice and of geographic location?

This leads to questions of recruitment, selection, and retention of personnel. Apart from a universally recognized need to step up recruitment efforts in the helping professions, it has become increasingly evident that research in career choices and in the utilization and deployment of personnel is of major importance if we are to move toward a solution to the manpower problem on a more rational basis.

The Center of Research in Careers at the Harvard Graduate School of Education has developed a series of studies that sheds light on the complexities of career choice and moves toward a theory of career development. Findings of studies conducted by the Council on Social Work Education (Pins, 1963; Berengarten, 1968) and the National Opinion Research Center of the University of Chicago (Gockel, 1965), point toward the need for: (1) providing high school and undergraduate students with observation and working experience in health and welfare agencies and (2) raising the salary and status levels of the profession of social work.

While studies yield valuable data in general, we must develop research projects that provide us with clues to the characteristics of social workers and other helping professionals who choose to work with the elderly. We have to find out why people choose, or choose not, to work with older persons and which variables account for these decisions. Is such choice, or non-choice, a function of attitudes toward older people, or is it a fear of the "Reluctant Therapist" as Kastenbuam (1964) calls him, to face the decline of life associated with older people? Is resistance to work with older people on the part of many helping professionals related to a mispercpetion that potentials for growth in later life are not present (Wilensky and Barmark, 1966)? Exploratory studies investigating these kinds of questions are the subject of group M.S.W. theses at Boston University School of Social Work. Hopefully some of the clues obtained will be helpful in designing larger studies. Knowledge gained about the process of career choice related to the field of aging hopefully will lead to a more rational and productive approach to the recruitment and retention of personnel.

Carefully conducted studies alone are not sufficient to deal with the manpower situation. "Without concomitant and drastic overhauling of the social welfare structure including systems of job classification and methods of administration and provision of services, the manpower gap will not be closed" (U.S. Department of Health, Education and Welfare, Departmental Task Force on Social Work Education and Manpower, 1965, p.57). Research on the utilization and deployment of personnel in social work has started with a number of studies conducted by the N.A.S.W. (1965), Columbia University School of Social Work (Firestone, 1964), the Veterans Administration (U.S. Department of Health, Education and Welfare, Departmental Task Force on Social Work Education and Manpower, 1965, p. 60), and other agencies and schools. Their attempts to delineate specific functions which require distinctive types of education and training are directed toward developing uniform criteria for several levels and types of personnel. In addition they have attempted to define and delineate functions of auxiliary and technical personnel. It goes without saying that these developments have significant implications for the practitioners in the field of gerontology.

The major questions in education and training for workers with older persons are not only concerned with the nature and types of training for a variety of job levels but also with content. What knowledge and skill areas should be included in a generic curriculum for gerontological practitioners? What knowledge and skill areas should be included in a curriculum for specific practitioners? In order to deal with the generic-specific dimension issue we need to dig into educational theories, design studies and experiment with training programs that have built into them rigorous research components.

A large number of national, state, and local training programs are in progress (e.g., The Training Institute for Public Welfare Specialists on Aging in Cleveland, in 1965; training institutes sponsored by the National Jewish Welfare Board and and the Benjamin Rose Institute, the University of Michigan's Annual Institutes, the conference sponsored by the Community Research and Services Branch of the National

Institute of Mental Health in Bethesda, and training courses sponsored by the National Council on Aging). In addition to content areas that have been communicated to the participants of these training programs, we need information about the impact of the educational aspects of such training so that new programs may be soundly conceived. In short, we need to draw on the discipline of education as well as feed back into it what we have learned.

No discussion of social services can be complete without taking into account the fact that their development or non-development depends to a large extent upon our social policy with respect to the aging. Our present policy reflects a good deal of confusion as evidenced by our program approach. "Do we want to remove older people from full participation in society? This goal would prompt the use of congregate institutions, the growth of retirement villages, and increased legal constraints against participation by older people. As an alternative goal, do we wish to provide humane care for the needy aged, while minimizing the cost to society? . . . Is it our primary goal to rehabilitate older people, socially and physically? . . ." (Taber, 1965, p. 378). Is it our goal to provide substitute provisions as exemplified by the Social Security system with its emphasis on income maintenance? Or do we consider as a goal the inclusion of older people in the present existing social structure and maximize their social utility (Taber, 1965)? Such questions need discussion and eventually some resolution. According to Robert Binstock (1966, p. 160):

> Perhaps the most important areas for researchers to actively engage themselves are national, state and local policy developments in the field of aging . . . But unless researchers begin to take an active role, it will be a long time before policy in the field of social gerontology becomes sophisticated and comprehensive enough to have the greatest possible impact in enhancing the lives of older persons.

To this should be added: Not only must the researcher engage

himself, but also the practitioner, the administrator, and the teacher
whose experiences and knowledge will supply important ingredients
"through the advocacy of conflicting views" in shaping clearer goals for
social policy for our aging population and thereby effect a more
creative development of social services.

REFERENCES

Berengarten, S. *Admissions predictions and student performance in
    social work education.* New York: Council on Social Work Educa-
    tion, 1968.
Berezin, M. A., & Cath, S. H. (Eds.) *Geriatric psychiatry: Grief, loss and
    emotional disorders in the aging process.* New York: International
    Universities Press, 1965.
Binstock, R., Some deficiencies of gerontological research in social
    welfare. *Journal of Gerontology,* 1966, *21,* 175-160.
Burgess, E. W. (Ed.) *Retirement villages.* Ann Arbor: University of
    Michigan, Division of Gerontology, 1961.
Cohen, E. The range of having to meet the needs of older people. In
    U.S. Department of Health, Education and Welfare, *Planning welfare
    services of older people.* Washington, D.C.: U.S. Government
    Printing Office, 1966.
Corson, J., & McConnell, J. W. *Economic needs of older people.* New
    York: Twentieth Century Fund, 1956.
Cowgill, D. The demography of aging in the midwest. In A. M. Rose
    and W. A. Peterson (Eds.), *Older people and their social world.*
    Philadelphia: F. A. Davis, 1965.
Donahue, W. Psychological changes with advancing age. In U.S.
    Department of Health, Education and Welfare, *Planning welfare
    services for older people.* Washington, D.C.: U.S. Government
    Printing Office, 1966.
Family Counseling and Guidance Centers, Inc. *The utilization of
    volunteers to promote the well-being of older people.* Boston: 1966.
Finestone, S. *Differential utilization of casework staff in public welfare.*
    New York: Columbia University School of Social Work, 1964.
Gockel, G. *Career choices of undergraduate and graduate students: The
    case of social work.* Unpublished manuscript, University of Chicago,
    1965.

Havighurst, R., Neugarten, B., & Bengston, V. A cross national study of adjustment to retirement. *The Gerontologist,* 1966, *6,* 137-138.

Kastenbaum, R. The reluctant therapist. In R. Kastenbaum (Ed.), *New thoughts on old age.* New York: Springer, 1964.

Lippitt, R., Watson, J., & Weatley, B. *The dynamics of planned change: A comparative study of principles and techniques.* Harcourt, Brace and World, 1958.

Miller, S. The social dilemma of the aging leisure participant. In A. M. Rose, & W. A. Peterson (Eds.), *Older people and their social world.* Philadelphia: F. A. Davis, 1965.

Morris, R., & Binstock, R. Comprehending the social planning process—Toward a theory of social planning. Unpublished manuscript, Brandeis University, 1965.

National Association of Social Workers. Utilization of social work personnel in mental health hospitals project. Unpublished manuscript, 1965.

Pins, A. *Who chooses social work, when and why.* New York: Council on Social Work Education, 1963.

Reichard, S., Livson, F. & Peterson, P. *Aging and personality.* New York: Wiley, 1962.

Rosow, I. Retirement housing and social integration, *The Gerontologist,* 1961, *1,* 85-91.

Rosow, I. Old age: One moral dilemma of an affluent society. *The Gerontologist,* 1962, *2,* 182-191.

Ross, M. *Community organization: Theory and principles.* New York: Harper and Row, 1955.

Shanas, E. The older person at home—A potential isolate or participant. In National Institute of Mental Health, Community Research and Services Branch, *Research utilization in aging: An exploration.* (Public Health Service Publication No. 1211.) Bethesda, Md.: U.S. Public Health Service, 1964.

Streib, G., & Thompson, W. The older person in a family context. In C. Tibbitts (Ed.), *Handbook of social gerontology.* Chicago: University of Chicago Press, 1960.

Taber, M. Application of research findings to the issues of social policy. In A. M. Rose, & W. A. Peterson (Eds.), *Older people and their social world.* Philadelphia: F. A. Davis, 1965.

Tibbitts, C. Social gerontology. In C. Vedder (Ed.), *Gerontology; A book of readings.* Springfield, Ill.: C. C. Thomas, 1963.

Tobin, S. Basic needs of all older people. In U.S. Department of Health, Education and Welfare, *Planning welfare services of older people.* Washington, D.C.: U.S. Government Printing Office, 1966.

Townsend, P. *The last refuge: A survey of residential institutions and homes for the aged in England and Wales.* London: Routledge and Kegan Paul, 1964.

United States Department of Health, Education and Welfare, Special Staff on Aging. *The nation and its older people; Report of the White House Conference on Aging, 1961.* Washington, D.C.: U.S. Government Printing Office, 1961.

United States Department of Health, Education and Welfare, Department Task Force on Social Work Education and Manpower. *Closing the gap in social work man power.* Washington, D.C.: U.S. Government Printing Office, 1965.

United States Senate, Special Committee on Aging. *The war on poverty as it affects older Americans.* Hearings before the Special Committee on Aging, U.S. Senate, 89th Congress, Second Session, 1966.

Wilensky, H., & Barmark, T. Interest of doctoral students in clinical psychology in work with older adults. *Journal of Gerontology,* 1966, *21,* 410-414.

Zander, A., Cohen, A., & Stotland, E. *Role relations in the mental health professions.* Ann Arbor: University of Michigan, 1957.

3:: A DEVELOPMENTAL-FIELD APPROACH TO AGING AND ITS IMPLICATIONS FOR PRACTICE

ROBERT KASTENBAUM

The caretaker of an office building in downtown Cleveland was sharpening his ice skates when he was invited for a helicopter ride as a birthday present.

A Mormon bishop in Layton, Ohio returned from an important three-day conference in time to watch a good fight on television. Although he had received very little schooling, and was one of fourteen siblings, this man had risen to become the president of a bank.

After once again passing his examination for a driver's license, a farmer in Milford, Illinois inspected his two farms to determine how the modernization programs he had designed were progressing. When a visitor at his home inquired into his health, the farmer kicked his foot over his head and then reached over and touched the palms of both hands to the floor.

The caretaker enjoyed his first helicopter ride on the occasion of his hundredth birthday, and continued in full employment for almost five more years. At age 101, the bishop no longer broke wild horses or undertook missionary assignments, but did remain an active consultant to his church. He was proud of being its oldest living patriarch. The farmer had attained his ambition of reaching his hundredth birthday,

Based on a paper presented to the 1966 meetings of the Gerontological Society (New York, N.Y.), and a Short-term Conference on Social Work with the Aged (Boston University, 1966). Much of the research experience from which this presentation derives was supported by the USPHS grants MHO-4818 and MHO-1520 at Cushing Hospital, Framingham, Massachusetts.

37

and since then had been too busy with his farms and family life to form any new ambitions; although he rewarded himself by purchasing a new car every year (Social Security Administration, 1964).

People such as these are not very common, nor are they likely to be found on the case loads of social workers, psychologists, or psychiatrists. Nevertheless, enough men and women do continue to function well in advanced age to raise fundamental questions for both scientists and practitioners. I mean the scientist and practitioner within each of us; for it is rare to find a practitioner who does not wish to extend his basic knowledge of aging and the aged, or a researcher who does not want to find some useful application for his work.

In this exploratory paper I would like to share with you some questions that occur to a developmental psychologist when he turns his attention to the later years of life.

Aging is often assumed to be a negative, universal, and inevitable phase for those of us who survive the middle years of life. Yet some people, such as those mentioned above, seem to find meaning and fulfillment even at the most extreme reaches of the life span. Is it possible that psychological development continues throughout the entire life span—for some people, at least? If development is possible in the later years, what form does it take? Under what conditions is it most likely to occur? How is "development" (by which we generally imply a positively-valued process) to be understood in relation to "aging" (by which we generally imply a negatively-valued process)? Questions such as these cannot be answered with a few choice words; several generations of skillful research and enlightened experience will be necessary. Right now we might limit our objectives to acquiring some sensitivity to the theoretical issues and to their potential application in daily life.

How we regard the relationship between aging and development has great significance for our decisions and our actions, both in our own lives and in our professional contacts with the elderly. One set of implications comes from the conclusion that human development necessarily terminates or even reverses itself in the later years of life. There is a very different set if we assume that human development continues, or, at least, *might* continue under favorable circumstances throughout the entire life span.

Facts and opinions from the biological sciences tend to support the first proposition; namely, that aging is a negative, deteriorative process or set of processes which not only bring about intrinsic changes, but also make the individual more vulnerable to external stress. It is difficult to elicit a kind word about aging from our colleagues in biology! The second proposition, that development might maintain itself, or even advance during the later years, tends to be supported mostly by our fond hopes or wishful thinking, bolstered by occasional observations of flourishing elders. Frankly, we would like to discover some solid basis for assuming that positive as well as negative processes may be at work in advanced age. It is important that our values and wishes be clearly acknowledged so that they can be controlled; otherwise, we might be lured into the habit of ignoring negative findings or over-emphasizing the positive.

Developmental Psychology

The developmental approach in psychology should be particularly informative in exploring potentials for personal growth in later life. Students of human development should be in a position to determine when we are actually in the presence of developmental processes, and when we are dealing with behavior that merely gives the impression of constituting a new developmental phenomenon. However, we are not yet equipped to deal adequately with such questions. The main reason is that developmental psychologists, like most other people, have given precious little attention to old age. Unlike most other people, however, the developmental psychologist has had to cultivate a genius for avoiding this topic since aging is so closely intertwined with development. One wonders how we have managed to avoid the problem so long.

Development is certainly one of the great concepts in man's intellectual history. It is such a broad idea that it can never become the personal property of any single branch of knowledge or art. Principles of development are significant not only in biology, but also in music, psychology, philosophy, and so forth. When we say that development is taking place, we usually mean that we are witnessing not simply a sequence of events, but a systematic change. Furthermore, the change is qualitative, or emergent, as well as quantitative. The adult is not simply larger and heavier than the child. In a developmental sequence something really different is happening in the second stage than that which happened in the first—yet there is an intrinsic relationship between the phases. Most theories in psychology make some use of this developmental model. Indeed, it is very difficult to think at all without some concern for development.

Traditionally, developmental psychology has been closely associated with childhood, the early years of life. This is probably an accident of cultural history, for there is no fundamental reason to limit developmental considerations to such a narrow age range. Perhaps it is just that most of us are more interested in children than the aged, and that the speed and flamboyancy with which developmental processes occur in the early years of life make them more difficult to ignore than those changes which occur later.

While most psychological theorists have something to say about development, there are some approaches which are more purely or exclusively developmental (e.g., Piaget, 1960; Werner, 1948). These approaches usually share a common set of assumptions. It is assumed that the individual moves from a relatively global, undifferentiated state to a more highly differentiated condition. This applies not only to the total functioning of the person, but also to his specific perceptions and behaviors. It is also assumed that we function on a number of qualitatively distinct levels. A level is defined in terms of the processes that a person uses to interpret his experience and guide his behavior. The fact that two people show the same behavior in a given situation does not conclusively establish that they are functioning on the same developmental level; for each individual may have arrived at his response through different processes. Similarly, the fact that two people give a different response in a particular situation does not necessarily prove that they are functioning on different levels. It may be that the same process has led to different responses because of differences in the individuals' previous experiences, the amount of vigor they brought into the present situation, etc. This viewpoint has some important implications for our work with the aged, as will be suggested later.

The concept of level is most frequently introduced by investigators who are studying basic psychological processes under controlled conditions. Those who are mostly concerned with general personality and social development are more likely to speak of stages. A developmental stage is defined by the set of life-tasks that challenge the individual at a particular time. Adolescence, for example, is regarded by many observers as a developmental stage because a distinctive set of challenges arises for most individuals within this age range. The same individual in pre-puberty and early adulthood is regarded as participating in different stages of his developmental career. It is often assumed that successful transition to a new stage requires competent management of the preceding stage. Adolescent-type problems that are not resolved "on schedule" would thus be expected to interfere with the individual's attempt to master the new tasks of young adulthood.

Unfortunately, both concepts—level and stage—often are formulated with too little precision and rigor, and almost no attempt has been made to integrate these two somewhat different developmental approaches into a single, coherent framework. Despite these problems, and many others that might be mentioned, the developmental approach should be expected to improve our understanding of aging and the aged as developmentalists move their own interests further along the life span.

The notions sketched in the balance of this paper have been snatched—prematurely no doubt—from one particular developmental approach that I have called the developmental-field theory (cf. Kastenbaum, 1965, 1966; Costa & Kastenbaum, 1967). This is one of the newer conceptual approaches in the social sciences, and one of the relatively few that begins with an emphasis upon the second half of life. Rather than burden the reader with an exposition of the general theory, let me simply make use of a few concepts and findings that are relevant to our immediate purposes.

The One and Only Way to Grow Old

"There is, of course, only one way to grow old." This assumption fulfills the requirements of the principle of least effort—perhaps that is why it has become popular. We might simplify our task even further by adding that there is only one to *grow*—one way to grow "up," and one way to grow "old." The proposition that both development and aging proceed along a single, universal pathway is quite appealing. It permits us to theorize, offer therapy, legislate, and administer with the serene confidence that we have all the basic phenomena well within our sights. We can devise "master plans" to cope with the problem of old age. Precisely what we take to be the one and only way to grow old is less important than the assumption that there is just one reality, one pathway.

May I suggest that this assumption is not justified on the basis of present knowledge. Daily observation, clinical and experimental studies suggest that there is a tremendous *variety* of behavior and experience at all age levels. We are likely to make more errors and fewer discoveries if we permit ourselves to visualize old age as though it were a fixed, monolithic element in nature. Both our theoretical models and our action programs must respect the important differences within the general population of the elderly, although this approach tends to complicate our traditional quest for unitary theories and unitary programs.

For now, let us make a few rather crude distinctions within the ranks of the elderly. These distinctions pertain to developmental status and direction. We are not minimizing the significance of biological, ethnic, personality, and contextual factors, but simply are taking development as the handle. Consider if you will the following "types" of older people.

Mr. A. is ill, weary, uncomfortable. "His body is on his mind," to coin an improbable metaphor. His experience of daily life and his behavior are conditioned by aches, pains, and a sense of reduced energy and limited physical functioning. He is suffering, in short, from the so-called "miseries of old age."

Mr. B. is of an age with Mr. A. However, his health is adequate and his appearance relatively youthful. His outlook is also that of a younger person. Mr. B. seems to regard himself as still being a participant in general adult society rather than an elder. He seems to have "held on" to the values and attributes of youth and early middle age.

Mr. C. is most forlorn and stricken. Not only does he suffer from physical ills and impairments, as does Mr. A., but his life is also disrupted in the mental, emotional, and social spheres. He does not think right, may even appear totally disoriented. His emotional responses tend to be primitive. Irritability, pleadings for support, and profound apathy are among his characteristic emotional orientations. He does not hold his own in personal and social relations. Such terms as "senile" and "regressed" seem appropriate.

Mr. D. is in relatively good health or at least has not been inundated by ailments and infirmities. In contrast with Mr. B., he looks and acts his age. One would not characterize him as either a young man in an old man's skin or a miserable old man. Mr. D.'s viewpoint and actions suggest that he has moved psychologically beyond youth and middle age. He seems to have attuned himself to this advanced stage of life, meeting the new challenges by developing a new orientation.

The unitary model of old age would lead us to regard each of these age-mates in a similar manner. It should be obvious, however, that a program which perfectly suits the needs and resources of any one of these elders would most likely be inappropriate for the others. From a developmental-field perspective, we would suggest that these four individuals represent three different developmental situations.

Mr. A. is probably at the same developmental level as you and I. He is different from us chiefly in that he is sicker and has less psychobiologic energy available to him. Because this sick man happens to be aged, we might make the error of regarding him as fundamentally different from ourselves. "Of course, he's that way—he's on a lower developmental level, you know." Such a misuse of developmental terminology would foster the already existent tendency to regard elderly people as "special cases."

Mr. B.: Chances are he is also developmentally on a par with us. Here we can make the error of assuming that he has developed into a fine old chap, when it might be nearer the truth to say that he has successfully resisted "aging" or "development" (your choice).

Mr. C. probably is functioning on a lower developmental level than the others. It is likely that this represents a regression or drop from a higher level of maturation, although in some cases the elderly person who seems "regressed" actually has been functioning on an arrested level of development for many years. It is important to recognize that a plunge to a lower level of development can be temporary. Whether Mr. C. remains at his present, relatively primitive level may depend in large part upon how he is treated by others in his environment.

Of this elderly quartet, Mr. D. is the only person who appears to have attained a new phase of development. Assuming that we know Mr. D. very well, we might say that he has oriented his life around a somewhat different set of values or tasks than those which had been of primary importance to him at mid-life. Because Mr. D. has accepted his place in the psychosocial world of the elderly, we might consider that he is in a new developmental stage. It also would appear that he is developing new strategies, new processes to cope with his life-tasks—and so it might be said that Mr. D. has entered upon a new developmental level. It is possible, of course, that he might recognize the challenges specific to later life (new developmental stage), yet continue to rely upon his previous strategies and processes to cope with the new challenges (no change in developmental level). But let's try to keep things reasonably simple for now, and just consider that some people, such as Mr. D., move on to a new developmental phase in their later years.

A Few Implications

The preceding suggests that psychological development may occur in the later years of life, but that it is just one of several alternatives. Further, it is implied that we could be more helpful to our elders if we improved our ability to discriminate among the alternatives. Let us explore this topic a bit—in capsule form.

Example 1

Imagine a person who seems to have changed very little with the years. His behavior and attitudes yield the impression that both developmental level and stage have remained constant in approximately the middle-adulthood range. We look more closely now: yes, the form of his behavior is relatively unchanged, but it is being maintained by a rather desperate injection of extra energy. He is working very hard to stay the same. The underlying instability could derive from several sources. He might, for example, be "ripe" to move on to a phase of true developmental aging. Yet this development might be hindered by his anticipation that he would be admitting failure to give up his middle-aged, socially-valued orientation. Or he might be experiencing the first serious premonitions of impending decline and death. Lacking adequate resources in his own background and adequate resources in his present environment, he faces the apparent choice of holding on grimly or dissolving, regressing. After a careful, holistic exploration of his situation we should be able to determine what pressures can be alleviated, where we can intervene, so that he does not have to expend so much of his life's energy to maintain a fragile stability. We should be able to help him either to maintain his present developmental phase with less desperation, or to make a gentle transition to a phase that is more in keeping with his actual psychobiological status.

Example 2

Imagine an elderly person who is no longer "with it." His behavior seems random, purposeless, bootless. Energy is at a low ebb. The physical appearance is sickly and hollow. Except for occasional flashes of near-normal functioning, this individual seems to be approaching psychological and social death. One of our first concerns here is to distinguish between two alternative explanations for this dismal picture. Most often, perhaps, this person would be regarded as "regressed," and the regression interpreted as a permanent and "natural" outcome of the aging process. However, it is also possible that we have here a person who is suffering from a multiple stress syndrome that has exceeded his adaptive capacity. In other words, this is a "Mr. A.," not a "Mr. C." The sources of stress might well include several specific diseases and infirmities, multiple bereavement, social rejection, gross discontinuity with previous life patterns and supports, etc. Viewed in this light, we would not assume that his present condition must also be his permanent condition.

In actual practice it is too often the case that inadequate diagnostic and therapeutic attention is directed to each of the sources of stress. Even symptomatic relief of physical ailments, modest efforts at rehabilitation of infirmities, and provision of prosthetic devices can sometimes bring about a remarkable "return to life." But such a program would not be initiated if we assumed that a psychobiological setback is identical to an intrinsic, inevitable process of regression. And even relatively simple interventions by members of the helping professions can often produce most gratifying results. Once the monolithic concept of "inevitable (developmental) regression" is overcome, the helper is free to use his own sensitivity in finding the appropriate modes of assistance (e.g., bereavement counseling, finding one or two confidants, mending some of the mendable social discontinuities, etc.).

The assumption that a miserable-looking elderly person necessarily is regressed is all too likely to act as a self-fulfilling prophecy. Even the elder who *is* regressed (Mr. C.) can be helped to remain a human being—again, often with relatively simple procedures (e.g., Cautela, Part I; Kastenbaum, Part III). Occasionally an aged person who gives a most convincing picture of regression will "snap out of it" when a conducive environment is provided. But we need not tantalize ourselves with the prospect of such dramatic outcomes. It is also a worthwhile goal to improve the life situation of a person who will probably remain somewhat regressed.

Appropriate goals and methods of intervention are easier to formulate when we learn to differentiate between the older person who is beleaguered by a variety of stresses, some of which are modifiable, and his peer who has actually entered fully into the pattern of "negative aging" or intrinsic decline.

Example 3

About ten years ago this man was beset by multiple stresses, with his enforced retirement being perhaps the "last straw." (He was then Mr. A.). Unable to cope with the onslaughts from all directions, he went into a regressive episode (became Mr. C.). However, sympathetic attention was given to his plight and his specific problem areas were identified. As some of the stress became alleviated, he returned to a life adjustment that was more in keeping with his previous style (became Mr. B.). Now he is moving in another direction. He seems to be shedding some of his past activities and responsibilities as though they are now excess baggage. He is developing a strategy of simplification or essentialization. This is quite different from having still-valued activities, objects, etc., wrenched away from him. He has less energy, but it is under more efficient control. Without turning his back on life, he is beginning to orient himself toward death, and yet not in what could be called a "morbid" way. Friends and relations have observed this direction of change. Appreciating that he is entering appropriately into a new and final phase of life, they offer him continued support without forcing him to remain within the confines of previous relationships. They are willing to develop their relationships with Mr. D. just as he is working out developmental tasks within himself. And those close to this elder choose to suspend their stereotyped expectations about how an old man should behave—instead they observe and learn from him. As he completes his own development, he serves as a mentor to those who eventually will confront the same challenges. In this idealized example, both the aging individual and those around him are able to understand and cherish a certain core or invariance that does not change through the years, but they also allow sufficient room for new development. He is not forced into the bind of either keeping up a facade of youthfulness, or being rejected as a has-been.

Both development and aging occur within the context of human relationships. Just as the child's development is shaped to advantage or disadvantage by the interpersonal network in which he lives, so the developmental career of the aging person is contingent upon his social context. Over the years, many people have adopted a rigid, peevish, apathetic and somewhat paranoid attitude toward their elders whom they characterized as: rigid, peevish, apathetic, and somewhat paranoid. Perhaps the place to start is "at home," developing more adequate orientations toward aging ourselves so that we can offer liberating rather than hobbling relationships to our elders.

REFERENCES

Costa, P. T. & Kastenbaum, R. Some aspects of memories and ambitions in centenarians. *Journal of Genetic Psychology*, 1967, *110* 3-16.

Kastenbaum, R. Engrossment and perspective in later life: a developmental-field approach. In R. Kastenbaum (Ed.), *Contributions to the psychobiology of aging*. New York: Springer, 1965, 3-18.

Kastenbaum, R. Developmental-field theory and the aged person's inner experience. *The Gerontologist*, 1966, *6*, 10-13.

Piaget, J. *The psychology of intelligence*. New York: Littlefield, 1960.

Social Security Administration. *America's centenarians: Reports of interviews with Social Security beneficiaries who have lived to be 100*. Washington, D.C.: Social Security Administration, 1964.

Werner, H. *Comparative psychology of mental development*. Chicago: Follett, 1948.

4:: APPLICATIONS OF PSYCHOLOGICAL RESEARCH TO SOCIAL ACTION

LEONARD E. GOTTESMAN

For many years growth in the field of gerontology has been closely tied to the "Problems of the Aging." It has been responsive to the large growth in the number of old people in the last century, to their sickness, to their loss of roles, and to their poverty. Many studies published in gerontological journals have dealt either directly or indirectly with attempts to ameliorate the serious and real problems of older people in our society. These studies have sought new understanding and new programs to enrich the life of the elderly. In this paper I shall express a few thoughts on the role of psychology in achieving these new understandings and programs. In doing so it will be of some value to make a distinction between the striving for new understandings and the implementation of them in programs.

Recently a number of scientists have distinguished between invention, defined as new understanding or discovery or creation, and innovation, defined as the introduction into a situation of a means or an end that is new to that situation (Friedmann, Mohr, & Northrop, 1966). An invention thus conceived is a newly created product, discovery or understanding—whether it is widely used or not. Thus Louis Pasteur had made an invention in his discovery of pasteurization before it became an accepted procedure in most parts of the world. By the same

Based on a paper given at the Gerontological Society meeting, New York, November 4, 1966.

token, each new nation which uses pasteurization is innovating, even though the process was invented many years before.

Typically the psychologist, like other scientists, is viewed as an inventor, while the practitioner is seen as an innovator. The psychologist is responsible for new insights, while the practitioner expresses these in new programs. From a professional group as large as in the field of psychology, the number of new insights should be great. Last year (Garvey & Belver, 1965) the American Psychological Association had 22,000 members, and it has been estimated that there are 30,000 psychologists in the United States. About a thousand presentations are made at each annual meeting and an equal number at regional meetings. One month's issues of the twenty key journals serving psychology contain 500 to 600 articles. In addition, there are innumerable technical reports and between 200 and 300 books published each year.

Of course not all 22,000 psychologists are inventors. From within the larger association Garvey estimates about two thousand psychologists to be extremely active in scientific communication, producing most of the papers, articles, and books and holding most major research grants. Certainly not all these products can fairly be called inventive. But irrespective of the number actually active in general psychology, it is clear that psychologists' interest in aging and the aged is small. The Division of Maturity and Old Age with 291 members in 1965 comprised less than two percent of the A. P. A. membership and was significantly larger than only one other A. P. A. division. I have not counted the members of this division who may be called inventive, but using the average for the Association they would be fewer than fifty.

The future does not promise a significant increase in the ranks of psychologists interested directly in the field of aging. Wilensky and Barmack (1966) found that among 165 graduate students returning questionnaires from six New York City-area schools having doctoral programs in clinical psychology, the aged were rated as least attractive as clinical subjects, geriatric problems were least preferred of all diagnostic categories, and institutions for the aged were next to least popular (next to the Army) as work settings. I have found no similar record of student's interests in research on the aged; however, my own experience at the University of Michigan leads me to believe that while such interest is not absent, it is small.

Despite the meager pickings when one searches among psychologists directly interested in the field of aging, there have been important insights relevant to the aged made both by those working with the aged and by investigators in other areas of psychology.

An exploration of the major areas within psychology, as reviewed in Birren's recent *Psychology of Aging*, (1964) shows that the aged have a generalized deficit in almost all sense organs, a slowing of reactions, decreased abilities in complex motor skills, and impaired ability to learn new skills. This review also shows a breakdown of those intellectual functions requiring motor response or new learning, but maintenance and perhaps even gains in those aspects of intelligence which are enhanced by experience.

Studies of social activity among the aged suggest that friends decrease in number and distance from home and that the elderly turn inward to egocentric concerns. Studies of personality show a generalized movement toward interest in more passive pursuits and at least some softening of attitudes toward usually negatively valenced objects like minority groups, and even perhaps an acceptance of the inevitability of death. Psychopathology among the aged, while more prevalent than in younger groups, and to some extent related to a deterioration of neural mechanisms, has been found to be manifest in the same varieties that are known among younger persons. The aged can be neurotic, psychosomatic, psychopathic, or functionally or organically psychotic. In much the same vein studies of personality have shown that there is no single "personality of the aged" but rather a widely varied number of configurations which range from almost complete withdrawal, to compulsive holding on, to continuous readjustment and involvement in the face of shifting social demands. Perhaps most prominent of all the general findings of psychology regarding the aging is the lateness in life at which many of the age-related changes appear and the great dispersion of behavior found at any given old age.

Both the variety of behaviors and their wide dispersion suggest the presence of variables beyond the aging of the organism as influencing age-related changes. Thus the true significance of psychological insights can be understood only in the context of other disciplines. The failing sensory, perceptual, and motor responses of the aged achieve meaning only in the light of an understanding of a changing biology. Changing social behavior has meaning only in the context of chronic disease statistics and a knowledge of the economic disadvantage of the elderly. Likewise, social withdrawal of the aged takes on more complex meaning when one considers the withdrawal of society from the aged. All of the above have new meaning when the psychiatric term depression is applied as an underlying affective response.

Each of these complicating factors, when introduced into the realm of psychology, calls forth still other disciplines which are needed to understand *them,* and the total of the various disciplines frequently defies the stipulation of clear cause and effect relationships. Thus, the closer psychology tries to come to applications in real life, the more it, like other scientific disciplines, becomes immersed in a net of multidisciplinary, multicausality relationships. And yet it is just at this level that psychology, the inventor, is asked to contribute. "Tell me," says the practitioner, "what your truths about the aged would have me do for them." Or even more likely, "Tell me that what I am doing is new, effective and true."

Typically the psychological researcher is unhappy with these kinds of requests. Some psychologists have retreated to the laboratory where they can do careful and controlled research precisely to avoid the complexities and uncontrollable variables of real life. But they have paid the price frequently of doing little studies on inconsequential questions; the results of which cannot even be generalized to other college sophomores than those they tested. Even where they have used careful controls and achieved satisfactory levels of significance for their findings, the possibilities for inférence based on their data are frequently so small as to be of little interest to the practitioner (Dunnette, 1966).

Other psychologists stouter of heart have entered the arena of research on reality. Rein and Miller (1966) point acidly to the disappointment of expectations that results will be definite, clear-cut, and dramatic. Changers of social policy are frequently unwilling or unable to wait for the findings to come in; for frequently the same *Zeitgeist* which made possible the funding of research calls for an immediate push to change social policy while the time is ripe. Often in a search for rigor, the researchers lose sight of the goals of the research. Even with good research, the goals of social action are usually not clearly enough defined to be tested; and the time and money available for an adequate test are insufficient. Rein and Miller (1966, p. 36) suggest that perhaps as a result research findings are "more likely to show that expectations were unrealistic, than to prove them worthwhile." They conclude that "present-day research methodology is simply inadequate for evaluating comprehensive demonstration programs which are subject to the vagaries of political expediency."

But would we then accept the obverse of their argument and suggest that the practitioner go it alone without evaluation, relying only on the insights which he can form in the field? I would share neither Rein and Miller's pessimism about research nor the expectation that psychology will either point the way for the activist or prove him right. The exigencies of working in the field usually preclude stepping back to evaluate existing programs or to formulate new ones. The activist because of his orientation to complex reality, generally has neither the skills nor the stylistic bent to consider in an organized fashion whether his program is having its desired impact or what the broad implications of his endeavor may be. The researcher, on the other hand, is trained in, and comfortable with, asking questions. He has the time to step back, observe, describe and evaluate. He can seek the inter-disciplinary ties that make complex realities understandable and point out their implications. He can, therefore, help understand reality, conceptualize it, and point to new directions.

But note that this role—the psychologist researcher as conceptualizer—requires several conditions. First, he must be trained and inclined to consider practical questions in their multi-dimensional complexity. Just as the insights of psychology in the field of aging have little relevance unless considered together with findings from other perspectives, so also purely psychological findings would have restricted relevance to the activist. Studies of attitudes toward retirement, for example, have little value unless considered along with the social role of the retiree, his economic status, and his health status. Second, the psychologist researcher must have freedom to ask questions beyond the obvious scope of the action program. In mental hospitals, outcomes of programs to improve patient's mental health may relate to their physical health, their family situation, and also to the organization of the sercices themselves and to the attitudes of the servers. The psychologist-researcher must also play the sometimes schizophrenic role of being involved in the action while at the same time being free to distance himself from it. Carl Rogers, who pioneered research on psychotherapy, frequently spoke of his need to have two hats in his closet—one which he could wear when doing therapy, but the other—equally important—to wear when evaluating therapy. In most action programs the distinction between these two hats is not, cannot, and should not be complete. The researcher depends on involvement in reality for his insight. Finally, the researcher must have resources of time, money, and personnel. The kinds of contributions that the psychologist should be expected to make and can make, cannot mature in an hour here and there. In our current research on milieu treatment for the geriatric mentally ill we have a full-time research team of several scientists, who work together with practitioners, attempting to describe, evaluate, and understand a complex program. The program team, deeply committed to treating patients, would be unable to evaluate their treatment in the time they have.

The output that can be expected if these conditions are met should not be viewed in terms of statistical significance alone. Because of the complexities of reality, the likelihood of strong statistical findings will not be the rule, although such findings can be and have been strengthened not by retreat into the less complex unreality of the laboratory, but by adding to the research consideration of a number of variables from many perspectives. Hays (1964) and others have strongly stated the need for psychologists to concern themselves more with the strength of inference possible from their data and not only with their statistical significance. This is one direction in which research in the future must move. But in addition to finding statistical relationships, the psychologist-researcher can make a significant contribution to action by his ability to put together the scattered pieces of a multi-disciplinary problem from the research and activists' point of view. He can be a conceptualizer of the action program.

As an example, in one aspect of our milieu treatment study we have used data gathered from a social psychology perspective to gain insight into the effects of transfer and the effects of treatment on geriatric mental patients. Dr. Sherwood (Social Science and Action Research, Part I of this volume), in her incisive analysis of several studies relating to the effects of environmental change on the aged, raises important questions including the possibility of sample selection influencing the findings that shifts in residential arrangements are related to increased mortality, morbidity and psychological disability.

An important additional question may be inferred from some data presented recently by Shaughnessey (1964). In a description of patients in twenty-five Massachusetts nursing homes, among 612 patients the median length of stay (by which I read life expectancy) was twenty-two months. Less than three percent of the patients expected to ever leave the home alive. Yet among these patients, twenty-two percent required only social supervision and had no "medical or nursing requirements." The patients in that study were found to have few visitors or visitors who came only out of obligation; they formed few friends when surrounded by many others who could not talk sensibly; and they had few opportunities for meaningful use of them. In such settings one must raise the question, as have many others, of the long-term influence of the environment on the geriatric patient.

Shaughnessey's data cannot be examined for such effects, but data derived from the University of Michigan-Ypsilanti State Hospital studies of older mental patients can (Ciarlo & Gottesman, 1966). In this study a carefully selected sample of patients averaging sixty years of age and thirteen years of hospitalization was divided randomly into four groups with each group transferred to a ward with a different program. The data from systematic biweekly observations of ward behavior show clearly that on a ward having only regular staff and nothing other than the hospital's usual custodial program a fairly steady 50% to 60% of patients will be inactive, i.e., sleeping or just sitting around. On a ward with an augmented staff and offering an occupational therapy program, this figure is decreased to about 40%; while on either regularly-staffed or augmented wards offering a sheltered workshop the number of patients observed in null behavior is about halved.

This difference by itself might be seen only as a direct program effect and therefore of little meaning, although even the sheer difference in the use of time is by many standards an important indicator of mental health. Further indication of the impact of the programs on these patients may, however, be gained from inspection of the amount of pathology observed manifest by the patients during these same observations. Before the experiment began one ward had housed a fairly disturbed group of younger patients. As new patients were transferred to this ward a few at a time to replace the previous residents, about 35% of the new patients exhibited observable pathology. As the previous residents were transferred out pathology in the new group decreased steadily, leveling off at about 22% on this highly staffed occupational therapy ward. On the regularly staffed ward with a sheltered workshop new patients replaced others who had been deeply involved in a sheltered workshop program for some time and many of whom were awaiting discharge. On this ward initially observed pathology was only 18%, half that on the previous ward. Pathology rose slightly as more and more former residents left, but peaked at 22% and then decreased steadily to a low of about 15% after twenty-two weeks. On the other two wards newly arriving patients replaced physically sick but psychiatrically stabilized elderly residents. Beginning roughly equal at about 22% observed pathology, the augmented-staff ward with a workshop showed a slight decrease in pathology while the regularly staffed hospital ward remained steady or showed a slight rise in pathology. By the twenty-second week all four wards, composed of similar patients as you recall, were much closer together than they had been at the beginning when influenced by different already present populations, but the two workshop wards had the least pathology. These findings suggest two conclusions regarding the influence of environment on pathological behavior: first, that a patient's behavior will be influenced by the kinds of people he joins in a new setting; secondly, that even with identical cohorts, program differences do affect patients' behavior.

In this instance the orderliness and system applied to observing a well-known technique of the practitioner has made possible the understanding of trends and relationships in patient behavior which might not have been easily seen in the midst of operating a program.

Obviously this suggestion from the data is not an end point, but for both the researcher and the programmer, a beginning. From this point we must raise many questions regarding other characteristics of the original resident populations on each ward. What was the influence of the age of the original residents? How did the discharging of many patients from one ward influence its new patients? What patient attitudes influenced the behavioral differences found? Were the staffs equally effective? And so on. In spite of many questions remaining we have begun to understand at least one aspect of a complex issue which has great import for practice.

Recently psychology as a field has begun to turn more in the direction of studying and conceptualizing action programs. At the University of Michigan, the Center for Research on the Utilization of Knowledge, the Center for Conflict Resolution, and the Center for Research on Learning and Teaching are all multidisciplinary endeavors which are committed to both research and its application. Throughout the country the burgeoning new specialty of community psychology has already left its origin in clinical psychology and begun to consider the psychologist as a research activist who with others, will participate in the process of environmental change in schools, neighborhoods, mental hospitals, and elsewhere.

The Gerontological Society has long held this multi-disciplinary research-action view. Shortly after its beginning the basic medical scientists, who were its founders, felt the need to include researchers from other disciplines, as well as practitioners working with the aging. Although there have been several times in its history when relationships among these groups have been strained, it has successfully held together so that the Society still serves as a forum where I can talk to and, more important, work with colleagues in clinical medicine, in the biological sciences, in the social sciences, and in applied social research. The existence of such a forum is of central importance to the furtherance of good research and good social action in gerontology.

REFERENCES

Birren, J.E. (Ed.). *The psychology of aging.* Englewood Cliffs, N.J.: Prentice-Hall, 1964.

Ciarlo, J. A., & Gottesman, L. E. The effects of differing treatment milieus upon the ward behavior of geriatric mental patients. Paper presented at the meeting of the American Psychological Association, New York, 1966.

Dunnette, M. D. Fads, fashions, and folderol in psychology. *American Psychologist,* 1966, *21,* 343-351.

Freidman, R. S., Mohr, L. B., & Northrop, R. M. Innovation in state and local bureaucracies. Paper presented at the meeting of the

American Political Science Association, New York, 1966.

Garvey, W. D., & Belver, C. G. Scientific communication: The dissemination system in psychology and a theoretical framework for planning innovations. *American Psychologist,* 1965, *20,* 157-164.

Hays, W. L. *Statistics for psychologists.* New York: Holt, Rinehart and Winston, 1964.

Rein, M., & Miller, S. W. Social action on the installment plan. *Transactions,* 1966 *3,* 31-48.

Shaughnessey, M. E. Implications of research in geriatric nursing home care. In National Institute of Mental Health, Community Research and Services Branch, *Research utilization in aging: An exploration.* (Public Health Service Publication No. 1211.) Bethesda, Md.: U.S. Public Health Service, 1964.

Wilensky, H., & Barmack, J. E. Interests of doctoral students in clinical psychology in work with older adults. *Journal of Gerontology,* 1966, *21,* 410-414.

5:: MANIPULATION OF THE PSYCHOSOCIAL ENVIRONMENT OF THE GERIATRIC PATIENT

JOSEPH R. CAUTELA

In studying cortical processes by means of the conditioned reflex, Pavlov (1928, p. 250) and his co-workers observed that sometimes a dog would become drowsy and fall asleep. Since the drowsy or sleeping dog interrupted the ongoing experiment, and because Pavlov saw this as an interesting phenomenon in its own right, he set out to systematically investigate sleep during the experimental session.

During the course of his investigations, Pavlov (1928) discovered certain conditions influential in developing drowsiness and sleep in the experimental animal. He states: "The animal (dog) was usually put on a stand on a table fastened by loops suspended from a beam of the stand, and his head held up by a cork around his neck (p. 305)." The stand and dog were confined in a special room while the experimenter was stationed in an outside chamber to present the stimuli and the reactions of the dog by a specially arranged apparatus. By manipulating the above conditions, Pavlov concluded that confinement and isolation played an important role in the phenomena of sleep which took place during the experimental session. He also concluded that monotonous and continuous stimulation leads to drowsiness and sleep (p. 307). A long delay (thirty seconds or more) caused the animal to become drowsy and go to sleep, or become quite motionless (p. 309). Pavlov also found to his surprise, that dogs which were lively outside of the experimental room

Paper read at the American Psychological Association meetings in New York, September, 1966.

61

proved to be especially susceptible to sleep, and animals which were considered stolid and inactive were not as susceptible to sleep for a long time during the experimental sessions, even under the most favorable conditions for sleep (p. 306).

Factors That Delayed or Prevented Sleep
During the Experimental Session

After carefully studying the conditions that led to sleep, Pavlov set about to discover ways of preventing sleep in the experimental session. Some of these were:

1. Beginning the experiment as soon as the animal was put in the experimental stand tended to prevent the occurrence of sleep (p. 251).

2. Reinforcing the animal by food delayed and sometimes prevented sleep, but this was not always true if the experimental session was a long one and the trials were close together (p. 253).

3. Calling, stroking, and slapping the dog during the experimental session tended to prevent sleep (p. 252).

Pavlov's physiological speculations on why certain conditions tended to encourage sleep and others tended to prevent sleep are presented in the paper "The Pavlovian Basis of Old Age" in Part III of this book. For the purposes of this paper it is sufficent to present only the important observable conditions involved.

Before we turn to the relevance of Pavlov's work in relation to the geriatric patient, it is important to note that Das (1958) was able to produce a state of drowsiness and sleep in humans analogous to that observed in Pavlov's dogs. He was able to accomplish this by presenting some conditions to the Ss similar to those used by Pavlov (monotonous stimulus while the Ss sat in a confined dentist-type chair).

Geriatric Patients in Institutional Settings

Almost anyone who has observed geriatric patients in institutional settings has probably noted similarities between the conditions and behavior of these patients and the conditions and behaviors of Pavlov's dogs reported above.

The patients are often confined to a bed, room or ward under conditions of isolation where stimulus variability is minimal. There is little or no reinforcement presented to the patient other than that which may occur accidentally by the staff or that which is generated by the patient's own behavior. The geriatric patients are often observed to be lethargic, drowsy, asleep, or in a coma. They often seem to have a hypnotic-like stare. (Pavlov called the states of inhibition or drowsiness that occurred between normal wakefulness and sleep "hypnotic trances.")

For the most part, this lack of activity and sleep-like behavior is attributed to the patient's old age or some kind of brain damage. It is the contention of this paper that such behaviors as "lack of enthusiasm" or "aimless talking, walking, and moving" are primarily due to lack of adequate stimulus variability and reinforcement of activity. Besides the usual isolating and monotonous situations in geriatric institutions, isolation is enhanced by the poor sensory acuity often found in the geriatric patient. Also, there are some patients with brain damage, and according to Pavlov, these individuals are apt to develop faster and longer-lasting inhibitory states. Even in these individuals, however, proper manipulation of environmental stimuli can often reduce inactive behavior.

METHODS OF INTRODUCING STIMULUS VARIABILITY TO DEVELOP ADAPTIVE BEHAVIOR

Teaching Machines

Geriatric patients are regarded as slow learners (Botwinick & Kornetsky, 1960), fast forgetters, (Gilbert, 1941), poorly motivated individuals (Birren, 1964). It is surprising that little or no use has been made of teaching machines to overcome these disabilities (so far as the author can determine, nothing has been published in this area). Teaching machines are so programmed that the individual can progress from point to point by small increments. The learner can proceed at his own pace. If the aged individual gets tired, he can stop and come back to the material later when he is rested. Self-motivation will be generated once he has had beginning exposure to programmed instruction. The material learned can lead to the desire for further knowledge by means of other programs or by actively engaging in the activity (e.g., gardening).

The teaching machine can be used to get the person out of bed or a particular room in order to engage in new interactions. It can further be utilized to provide positive reinforcement for the new behaviors. Special programs will have to be developed for the aged population in general and the aged individual in particular.

Through a study of each patient's case history, or through interview procedures, one can ascertain significant events that will arouse interest in the aged individual. Individual programs may also be used to present relevant information in the individual's past that has been lost. This material can increase self-identity and perhaps decrease the psychological process of deterioration.

Programmed instruction need not be limited to the patients themselves, but can be developed for the staff and relatives of the patient to provide a background of better interaction with the patient. The research potential in the use of the teaching machine in geriatric institutions is a great one. Perhaps this research will lead to a new model for understanding geriatric patients.

Shaping Desirable Behavior by Reinforcement

Lack of reinforcement may have extinguished much of the previously adaptive behavior of the aged person. This is especially true of the aged individual's social behavior. As an individual gets older, he usually suffers declines in his ability to converse with others. He has trouble keeping up with current events and seems to dwell on the past a great deal. Besides this, he is often not especially pleasing to look at when judged by the cultural standards of our society. He often presents somatic complaints that are boring to the average younger individual. These behaviors of the geriatric patient do not lead to social reinforcement by others. This is especially true in geriatric settings where nurses and attendants discourage, often unwittingly, behavior such as asking questions, seeking attention, and requesting help. It is easier for the staff if the patient exhibits a minimum of behavior. The author has observed this even in some of our better hospitals.

It is therefore crucial that a concerted effort be made to save previously adaptive social behavior and develop new behaviors whenever necessary. This is done by reinforcing any behavior that approaches the final behavior you want to achieve. By a reinforcing stimulus I mean a stimulus which, when presented, increases the possibility of response, and when removed, reduces the probability of a response.

In practice, one finds that there are some classes of stimuli which are reinforcing to many individuals (e.g., smiling, paying attention). These are what we can call "general reinforcers." Also there are stimuli that are especially reinforcing to some individuals and not to others. For one person jazz music may have reinforcing value; for another person it may be classical music. Talking about sports may be reinforcing for one individual and not another. The reinforcing stimuli which are especially reinforcing for one individual but perhaps not for many others can be designated as "idiosyncratic reinforcers." Many times it is necessary to discover the idiosyncratic reinforcers for efficient behavior shaping.

Dr. Kastenbaum and I (1967) have developed the Reinforcing Survey Schedule (RRS) for the purpose of identifying this type of reinforcing stimuli for particular individuals. The scale can be administered to the geriatric patient orally, or if he is able, by having the patient fill out the schedule himself. Once these stimuli can be identified, they can be used in a number of ways to benefit the patient: to help establish rapport; to counter-condition fear responses and to shape certain desired behavior. For example, let us say the desired behavior is eating in the dining room. A particular patient will not leave his room under any circumstances though he is physically capable of doing so. Suppose we found that this patient likes classical music. The approach would then be to play classical music for a few moments whenever he makes a response toward the threshold leading out of his room. This is done until that behavior is shaped to that point. Then the music will be played only if he puts a foot over the threshold, and so on, until he is in the dining room. A combination of reinforcers can be used to shape the desired behavior, of course, and once the desired behavior occurs, that behavior may lead to other reinforcers (e.g., once the patient gets to the dining room, he gets attention, or has an opportunity to watch television.

Token Economy

When previous investigators have attempted to alter behavior in an institutional setting, they have found it cumbersome to rely on the actual presentation of the reinforcing stimuli whenever the desirable behavior occurs. Also, there is often a delay in reinforcement. Such problems have led these investigators to develop what has been called "a token economy" in an institutional setting. In this arrangement, the patients are reinforced by tokens that can later be exchanged for goods bought at a specially run store. This token economy has been quite effective in getting efficient ward management (Ayllon & Michael, 1959) with chronic schizophrenics. Whether a token economy program can work as effectively with geriatric patients remains to be seen. The procedure takes a long time to set up, however, and special training is needed for the staff. Administration also has to be convinced of the value of this type of program.

Desensitization

For many people, institutional confinement is often due to the fact that they are controlled by anxiety-producing stimuli (Wolpe, 1958). Wolpe has developed a procedure known as "Systematic Desensitization Based on Relaxation," which appears to be an efficient means of eliminating unadaptive anxiety. In this procedure the patient is taught to relax. A hierarchy is then constructed according to the degree of anxiety elicited by different aspects of the fear-provoking stimulus. These stimuli are then gradually presented to the S in imagination until the thought of the stimulus no longer leads to an anxiety response.

Direct transfer usually occurs from the imagined situation, which is accompanied by a calm response in the therapist's office, to the real-life situation. As previously indicated, some of the confined behavior of geriatric patients may be due to lack of reinforcement or to anxiety-provoking stimuli. A patient may not want to go to the dining room to eat because he is afraid of being poisoned or assaulted. Such patients can be taught to relax: A heirarchy can be constructed concerning the poison or the possibility of assault; then the desensitization procedure can be applied. In practice, one may want to use both desensitization and reinforcement procedures to produce a particular behavior.

One of the possible uses of the desensitization procedure which has been developed involves the training of nursing and attendant personnel. Almost everyone feels uncomfortable with the appearance of certain aged persons and with some of their behavior. The antisocial reactions of personnel then become evident to the patients, who in turn feel uncomfortable. This is not a reinforcing situation. As a possible way of eliminating this problem, we could have the nurses rank-order a series of pictures of geriatric patients in terms of their likes or dislikes. The nurses can then be desensitized to the certain kinds of physical characteristics of aged individuals which they find repugnant. This can also be done with the certain kinds of behaviors they find repulsive.

What the Methods Accomplish

The methods presented here are designed to eliminate inattention to the environment. Taking the Pavlovian findings as guidelines, stimulus variability can be maintained by the use of teaching machines and by reinforcing responses to a spectrum of stimulation. The reinforcements themselves (as Pavlov found) can be used to maintain an alert state in the geriatric patient. The use of desensitization whenever indicated can release the aged from psychological confinement so that they will be free to interact with a greater part of the environment.

Studies in sensory deprivation (Bexton, Heron, & Scott, 1954; Heron, Doane & Scott, 1956) and Pavlov's work (1928) indicate that a minimum of sensory stimulation and stimulus variability is needed for normal functioning. If the stimulation is not supplied from outside, the person tends to supply his own stimulation in terms of thoughts, fantasies, and imagery.

The aged individual's constant preoccupation with past events can be explained in this manner. The past experiences act as sources of stimulation and stimulus variability. Since these experiences are often pleasant ones, they also act as reinforcers. As conditions for monotonous stimulation and isolation continue, there is more preoccupation with one's own sources of stimulation which are reinforcing. This leads to further inattention to the environment, which, of course, leads to more isolation and stimulus constancy. The spiral can continue upward until such behavior as talking out loud and "senseless movements" are made to increase stimulus variability and self-reinforcement. By this time, the patient is said to be "out of it" and probably suffering from senile deterioration.

In summary, I am saying that the usual geriatric institution provides a Pavlovian-like experimental chamber where there is a kind of isolation, repetition of stimuli, and lack of reinforcement. This often leads to lethargic and comatose behavior. The methods presented here are suggested in addition to other methods that may be already in use to provide stimulus variability to shape the behavior which will lead to a more fruitful existence for the aged individual.

REFERENCES

Ayllon, T., & Michael, J. The psychiatric nurse as a behavioral engineer. *Journal of the Experimental Analysis of Behavior,* 1959, *2,* 323-334.

Bexton, W. H., Heron, W., & Scott, T. H. Effects of decreased variations in the sensory environment. *Canadian Journal of Psychology,* 1954, *8,* 70-76.

Birren, J. E. *The pyschology of aging.* Englewood Cliffs, N.J.: Prentice-Hall, 1964.

Botwinick, J., & Kornetsky, C. Age differences in the acquisition and extinction of the GSR. *Journal of Gerontology,* 1960, *15,* 83-84.

Cautela, J. R., & Kastenbaum, R. A reinforcement survey schedule for use in therapy, training and research. *Psychological Reports,* 1967, *20,* 115-130.

Das, J. P. The Pavlovian theory of hypnosis: An evaluation. In R. E. Shor & M. T. Orne (Eds.), *The nature of hypnosis.* New York: Holt, Rinehart and Winston, 1965.

Gilbert, T. G. Memory loss in senesence. *Journal of Abnormal and Social Psychology,* 1941, *36,* 73-86.

Heron, W., Doane, B. K., & Scott, T. H. Visual disturbance after prolonged perceptual isolation. *Canadian Journal of Psychology,* 1956, *10,* 13-16.

Pavlov, I. P. *Lectures on conditioned reflexes.* New York: International Publishers, 1928.

Wolpe, J. *Psychotherapy by reciprocal inhibition.* Stanford: Stanford University Press, 1958.

6:: SOCIAL SCIENCE AND ACTION RESEARCH

SYLVIA SHERWOOD

The underlying assumption of this paper is that there is a need to formulate policies and social action programs on the basis of relevant social science knowledge, and further that this calls for ongoing social research aimed at the application of social science to human problems. This position, while perhaps not sufficiently understood or accepted by some or even many practitioners, is by no means new, nor am I alone among gerontologists in holding it. (National Institute of Mental Health, 1964; Donahue, 1964; Morris, 1964)

Social science knowledge can have a number of functions. It can identify problems; differentiate among them in terms of degree of importance and community need; suggest alternative action approaches; and in some highly developed areas, predict that a given type of action program is likely to work for appropriate persons serviced by it.

To point to problems and differentiate among them, bits of knowledge are often all that may be needed. These are known as descriptive data, defined here as the raw data accumulated from the objective collection of "facts." Case histories, statistical summaries, depiction of trends, etc. are examples of descriptive data. But much as descriptive data may suggest that a given kind of action is needed in a community, they contain no specific directives concerning the program

Based on a paper presented at the Nineteenth Annual Meeting of the Gerontological Society, New York, New York, November, 1966 (joint symposium of the Psychological and Social Sciences and Social Welfare Sections, Nov. 4). Supported in part by U.S. Public Health Service Grant CH 23-26.

steps that should be taken. If, for example, it is found that a large number of aged individuals in a community have caries, this item of descriptive data reveals a need calling for an action program to help persons with their dental problems. But it does not provide us with the technical knowhow for preventing caries or for motivating individuals to make use of services in existence that might deal with the established need. Other levels of knowledge are necessary to suggest the specific action steps that can effectively solve the problem.

This paper will focus attention on three approaches that may well advance applicable levels of social science knowledge: 1) attempting to explain observed *empirical relationships* having to do with the aging process and/or the aged; 2) exploring social scientific *theories of behavior* for action implications; and 3) designing *intervention programs* and *testing their effectiveness.*

Attempting to Explain Observed Empirical Relationships

By empirical relationships I am referring to empirical associations between two or more conditions, including patterns of variation, correlations, etc., accumulated through "controlled" studies of the statistical connections between or among them. They are observed uniformities describing statistical connections between categories of facts, considered as variables. The findings that women tend to live to an older age than men, or that married men tend to live to an older age than single men are examples of empirical "relationships" discovered when controlled studies were made of differences in age-specific death rates among these categories of individuals.

Empirical relationships to some extent suggest specifics concerning the content of action programs but, without further analysis, very often contain little in the way of specifying the program steps for action. For example, Bennett and Nahemow (1964) found in a study of individuals in a home for the aged that aged individuals who are socially isolated prior to admission tend to have more difficulty in adjusting to life in an old age home than those who are not socially isolated prior to admission. Prock (1965), in a study comparing applicants to an old age home with residents of the home found that individuals on a waiting list to a home for the aged are more likely to be anxious, despondent, exhibit greater excitability, etc. than individuals residing in an old age home. Although such findings are valuable in focusing attention on particular aspects of a problem and in making practitioners more sensitive to possible causal connections, they contain little in the way of specific implications for action. However, to the extent that they direct attention to meaningful questions concerning possible causal connections and explanations, they may be instrumental in providing specific directives for program procedures. Indirectly, therefore, relationship findings contain implications for action programs.

At this point, perhaps, it may be wise to caution social scientists examining an "observed" relationship for possible explanations leading to social action to analyze critically the research evidence claimed in its support. Formulating theories of behavior on the basis of a non-valid relationship or on the basis of improperly controlled studies is not likely to be an efficient procedure for adding significantly to the storehouse of scientific knowledge.

Empirical relationships can contribute to the advancement of levels of knowledge applicable to social action. However, the analysis must probe beyond the superficial level. For example, consider the consistent finding that significant changes in residential arrangements of the aged are related to "increased mortality, morbidity, and psychological disability" (Miller & Lieberman, 1965, p. 492; Farrar, Ryder, &. Blenkner, 1964; Aldrich & Mendkoff, 1963; Camargo & Preston, 1945; Kay, Norris, & Post, 1956; Lieberman, 1961).

At the very outset, the question arises whether those experiencing environmental change constituted sicker groups to begin with than the groups to which they were being compared. If the answer is "yes," the studies cannot be considered properly controlled for state of health (mental or physical). It is fairly safe to predict that the more vulnerable are more likely to experience adverse developments than the less healthy (almost by definition), *with or without* environmental change. Therefore, unless it can be ascertained that the groups being compared were equated on state of health or that the persons experiencing environmental change (the groups for whom greater adverse reactions were found) were healthier to begin with than the persons with whom they are being compared, it cannot be asserted that there is scientific evidence to support any relationship between environmental change and adverse reactions in the elderly.

However, it is suggested here that under certain circumstances it may be possible to assert a relationship between residential change and adverse reactions even if the groups being compared are not initially strictly comparable. Specifically it may be possible under certain conditions to assert a relationship between the two variables if the elderly experiencing both environmental change and adverse reactions *were the more healthy.* Under ordinary circumstances, it can be expected that the group, alike on salient characteristics except that it consists of initially more healthy persons, will be less likely to experience adverse developments than the sicker group. Should it appear that, in spite of lesser initial vulnerability, the healthier group subjected to environmental change is experiencing greater adverse reactions than the environmentally stable and initially sicker group, logically this lends greater support for the relationship under investigation. The position taken here is that it is possible to claim empirical support for propositions even when groups being compared are not comparable on a salient characteristic if it can be ascertained that the groups differentially exposed to a sitmulus *are comparable prior to exposure on other salient features and that in spite of the fact that the bias introduced would tend to hide it, the relationship still appears to be statistically significant.*

Even assuming that studies had proper sampling controls—that the groups being compared were in fact similar in mental and physical health and other salient characteristics prior to the shift in residential arrangements—for program as well as for scientific purposes it is appropriate to raise a question concerning the overall complexion of the samples of persons under investigation. Were a variety of types of elderly persons studied or did the samples tend to consist of a particular type of person? In other words, does this finding pertain to aged groups in general, or does this hold only for certain categories of older persons?

What is being suggested here is that perhaps the association between adverse reactions and environmental change found so consistently *can be accounted for by sample selection.* For example, in a study reported in this volume (Part III) by Goldfarb, Shihinian, & Turner, relocation of the very sick elderly in nursing homes was associated with increased death rate, *but relocation of persons with remaining vitality was associated with decreased death rate.* For both sets of findings to be valid—the association previously found between residential change and increased adverse conditions *and* the Goldfarb et al. findings—it should be found that the samples utilized in the earlier studies consisted by and large of the more vulnerable aged; thus the consistency in results.

It may be, however, that the groups being compared were not controlled properly for health (mental or physical) conditions and that those experiencing environmental change were, in fact, a sicker group to begin with than the group of persons with whom they were compared. Under these sampling conditions, if the Goldfarb et al. findings are valid, the relationship between environmental change and adverse conditions should appear even more striking than if the entire study population consisted of the more vulnerable aged. However, as already pointed out, if the groups subject to environmental change were initially less healthy than the groups with whom they were compared, it is not possible on this evidence scientifically to assert support for any relationship between residential change and experiencing adverse effects even if greater adverse conditions are subsequently found among those subjected to environmental change.

For the purpose of this analysis, however, let us assume that the relationship between environmental change and an increase in adverse conditions for aged persons holds whether pertaining to the aged population in general or to specific categories of the aged. Questions concerning possible explanations of this finding can then be raised: Do significant changes in residential arrangements and other life patterns and daily routines lead to—i.e., cause—increased mortality, morbidity, and other disabilities? Or, in other words, does the maturational process render an individual less capable of handling extensive changes in life patterns and daily routines when he grows old? Is it suddenness of change, the extent, the type, change itself, or, rather than change, some other concurrent factor that is crucial in adversely affecting the aged individual? Does perception concerning whether this is a permanent "premortuary" change from which there is no return enter into whether an elderly person will experience adverse reactions to such a change? Does ambiguity and uncertainty of what these new arrangements are like affect whether he will be affected adversely? Does non-participation in and/or nonconcurrence with decisions concerning change in residential arrangements adversely affect his reaction to change? We might continue with similar queries.

These possible causal connections between change in the sociophysical environment of aged persons and increased mortality, morbidity, and psychological disability contain a variety of directives for action programs. Indeed, of these directives a number represent distinct alternatives for social action. For example, if it is the suddenness of the change that is adversely affecting the individual, one program directive suggested is to initiate educational efforts aimed at gradually enlightening the individual as to the kind of change he will be likely to face, well in advance of the anticipated change. Another program directive suggested by this theory is to allow the aged person an opportunity to experience either short trial periods simulating the conditions of the anticipated change or to allow for a number of intermittent "step" changes in the residential arrangements for the aged person, each in the direction of, and coming closer to, the eventual change anticipated.

But what if it is not the suddenness or the extent of the change that adversely affects aged persons, but a decreasing ability per se to handle change itself as one grows older? The fact that studies to date have concentrated on the relationship between extensive change and mortality, disability, etc. does not preclude the possiblity that the significant relationship is between change itself—even relatively small change (as, for example, changing the room of an elderly person in a nursing home from one floor to another)—and these adverse outcomes. Then several small changes may indeed be more detrimental to an aged person than one sudden, extensive change. Furthermore, if such is the case, informing the aged person of the expected change—the anticipation of change—may itself be experienced as change and start the adverse reaction. And, on this assumption, even if it is considered that a specified change in residential arrangements or other living conditions of an individual would give him more opportunity to engage in activities and to form meaningful social relationships, the risks involved in changing an individual from an environment to which he has become accustomed to a new situation with new activities would certainly have to be weighed carefully against any possible advantages seemingly offered by this new environment.

To establish which, if any, of the postulated causal connections is likely to produce effective program directives, an important first step is to analyze the implications of each of these theories both for other general behavioral predictions as well as for action implications. With these predictions and action directives in mind, a valuable next step is to review the available literature for studies which yield evidence pertaining either to any of the general behavioral predictions or to the degree to which any of the implied action directives have proved effective. Evidence from scientifically controlled "evaluation" studies of program efforts is especially valuable for these purposes. The findings can then be analyzed to determine the extent to which research evidence already gathered tends to support one explanation over others.

If evidence of this nature does not appear to exist, research studies are called for to test the derived hypotheses. In particular, to establish which set of implied action directives is the more or most rewarding, a demonstration project is called for in which alternate approaches are attempted for comparable groups of persons who are carefully observed and compared over time in terms of impact—mortality, morbidity, and psychological disabilities being negative "outcome variables." Not only would such a study provide conclusions concerning the relative effectiveness of the programs being compared for changing the environment of elderly persons and the advisability of continuing or initiating such programs elsewhere, but also it would test alternate explanations of behavior with other practical implications for the care of the elderly. To cite examples, there would be practical implications for specific policy decisions concerning: placing individuals living in the community into old age homes, nursing homes, etc.; the conditions under which it would be best to make radical changes in the environment of an aged person—for example, whether it would be better to treat certain kinds of conditions at home as compared with a hospital or other environment; the shifting of the aged from one to another relative's home; movement of an individual within an institution from one room to another or from one activity to an unfamiliar one; the types of programs to initiate in different types of institutions; and even the physical location of an institution for which building is contemplated.

Exploring Theories of Behavior for Action Implications

By "theories" I am referring to explanations which put order into observed descriptive data and empirical relationships. In other words, theories provide an understanding for observed phenomena. To be counted as "scientific knowledge" a theory must be reasonably supported through empirical test—one for which the evidence has been, for the most part, consistently supportive with little or no negative evidence.

In essence, the questions asked earlier concerning possible explanations of the relationship between changes in residential arrangements of the aged and increased mortality and disability suggested propositions which can be described as theoretical formulations (simple though they may be). However, the emphasis in the previous section was on the attempt to arrive at reasonably plausible explanations (which in turn lead to action directives) by building upon observed uniformities. The emphasis in this section is on exploring theories currently being developed in the literature for implications for social action. Moreover, while the focus previously was on formulations specifically related to the aged, the emphasis here will be on the analysis of theories of behavior not necessarily developed as explanations of the behavior of the aged.

The goal of science is the development of inclusive "verified" theories, those which systematize many more limited propositions. The key property of "general" theoretical propositions is their power to imply other propositions—both on factual and relationship levels. The greater the number and variety of deductions, the more powerful the theory. A general theory of behavior, then, may in fact provide many more implications for social action than a highly specific theory. At the present time in social science there are no general theories of behavior which can properly be classified as well-verified. But there are a number of general theories of behavior that have generated much analysis and for which there is a growing body of research. Rather than focusing on theories of behavior centered exclusively, or almost exclusively, on the aged, the position taken here is that an important way in which to advance applicable knowledge is to put some of these more general theories to work.

From such explanations of behavior, established or not as "supported" theories, productive sets of specific directives for social action programs can be derived. The more a theory has been subjected to test by measuring deduced implications—predictions from the theory— against empirical reality and the evidence has consistently supported its validity, the more confident we can be of the theory and, in turn, the likelihood of success of a social action program based upon it.

But if we wish to have more than confidence—by this I mean "evidence"—concerning the likelihood that a program will have the desired impact, it is important, initially at least, to include a research component to determine its effectiveness. It goes without saying that in such a test it must be ascertained that the logic connecting the theory to the social action directives is impeccable and that the program *is in fact* being implemented as specified by these directives.

It is recognized that these are no easy tasks. At the very least the logic behind the program should be made explicit, and records should be kept that describe what, in fact, occurred over time in the course of the development and operation of the program so that checking is possible.

Under these conditions, should the evidence indicate that the program is not having the predicted impact, this would lead to a re-thinking and perhaps modification of some of the postulates of the theory. On the other hand, should the evidence indicate that the program *is* having the predicted impact, this would point to the general value of this type of program for meeting the specific set of needs as well as the value of further exploring the theory for social action implications to meet still other as yet unmet needs.

Recently, an innovative gerontological program has been given nationwide publicity—the practice of serving wine and beer at specified times on the wards at Cushing Hospital, a state-run home for the aged in Massachusetts having, as its name implies, full hospital facilities and being accredited as such (Kastenbaum, Part III). What is not generally known is that this program was instituted as a result of the findings from a small-scale experimental program undertaken by the Psychological Unit of Cushing Hospital under the direction of Dr. Robert Kastenbaum (1965a, Kastenbaum and Slater, 1964). Initially, the introduction of wine to groups of elderly persons at Cushing was conceived as a test of some of the implications of development-field theory opposed to what Kastenbaum refers to as the "Pathology Model."

which views an individual as a medical management problem, extending "... to an implicit substitution of 'pathological specimen' ... identity

as a person (he may even be spoken of as 'a Kidney' or as 'a C.B.S.')."
In the Pathology Model, the therapeutic regime centers around the
disease rather than the overall needs of the person.

If the goal is to act in the best interests of the patients, the
developmental-field approach would suggest a very different way of
thinking about, and behaving toward, them. The developmental-field
approach is an integration of the basic postulates of both developmental and field theories. The basic framework of each of these
theories will be described below.

Developmental theory may be described as a biosocial approach to
human behavior. It visualizes a dynamic interplay of inner (the intrinsic
potential at any given point of time) and outer pressures (the
environmental experiences) in both the biological and social maturation
of an individual. Even heredity is discussed in these terms. According to
Murphy (1947, p. 52):

> . . . the word heredity refers at best to the continuity of certain
> dispositions from one generation to the next . . . There develops
> the paradox that heredity is known only by the liberation of the
> hereditary potentials through specific environmental forces; and
> what is liberated is as much a function of the environing pressures
> as it is of the latent or potential dispositions.

With reference to the biosocial approach and the emphasis upon the
dynamic interplay of inner and outer pressures, Murphy (1947, p. 52)
states: "In the life process, whether studied in embryology or later,
nature is not made up, mosaic fashion, of heredity and environmental
elements . . . What they [the terms heredity and environment] really
denote, if carefully studied, is a dual function; the two always occur
together and are separated only for conceptual convenience."

According to this theory there is a general principle of development
involving three basic stages: 1) diffuseness (undifferentiated mass); 2)
differentiation; and 3) hierarchical integration.[1] Werner (1957) has

---

[1] Again, in the words of Murphy (1947, p. 343), "No problem of development
arises unless a thing changes; a homogeneous thing can only change qualitatively
by breaking up into recognizably distinct parts; and it is only when such a

referred to this sequence as constituting the *orthogenetic principle.* In development theory, particular attention is given to perceptual and cognitive processes. According to Murphy (1947), pp. 342-344):

> The "blur" [diffuseness] stage of perception, stage one of the perceptual development, is replaced by *differentiation.* A third stage is possible: *integration,* the articulation of the differentiated parts. All three stages are manifest in the child or adult whenever he confronts a novel *situation* . . . . The fact seems to be that the adult mind is functioning all the time at all three levels, but that each individual has his own proportion, his own balance of the three.

Through his perceptual and symbolic processes, the individual orders the myriads of experiences to which he is exposed and his learned behaviors into meaningful units on several distinct levels. Moreover, what he extracts from, and how he copes with, new experiences will be a function both of environmental influences and his psychobiological development at the time. For a better understanding of the postulates presented above and a more complete exposition of the scope and description of the propositions embraced by developmental theory, in addition to the sources already cited (Kastenbaum and Murphy), see as examples Harris (1957), Piaget (1960), and Werner (1957).

As in the case for developmental theory, field theory assumes that the boundaries set by the real world of things around him (the "space," in Lewin's [1935, 1938, 1948] terminology of the real world he encounters) are much wider than the boundaries of the world he perceives (his "life space") and within which he operates. But field theory focuses more specifically on behaviors in their situational contexts, field dynamics often being "regarded as a set of interactions occurring simultaneously or within a relatively limited period of time (Kastenbaum, 1965a, p. 6)." Although not dealt with specifically in the

breaking-up has occurred that the heterogeneous elements can be integrated into an articulate whole. Unless individuation follows mass behavior, there can scarcely be behavior units; and unless integration follows, there can scarcely be adjustment to the environment."

discussion above of the implications of development-field theory which led to the experimental program being discussed, it should be pointed out that both developmental and field processes can be regarded as occurring in either a limited or extensive framework. "Microgenesis" is the term applied to developmental processes that occur so rapidly that the situational rather than the longitudinal framework appears appropriate. The term "time perspective" has been used to designate the research area in which field dynamics is studied with reference to a calendar.

For example, one set of propositions developed by field theorists deals with the desire and fear invoking potential of elements perceived in a situation. Field theory postulates that the strength of each of the desire-invoking elements (the "positive valences") and *their effect* at that time on the individual's behavior will depend upon the situational context. This would include: the number of each; how they are seen in relationship to each other; and the physical distance of the desire and fear-invoking elements from the individual.

While only touching upon the postulates integrated within the development-field approach, the foregoing discussion will perhaps suffice as a basis for describing its scope. It should be seen that both longitudinal processes and situational dynamics are being incorporated within the set of postulates and that both psychological development (the inner state, the psychobiological "potential") and behavior of the individual (how he will act) under various situational conditions are the subject matter for which the postulates have implications.

Within this framework, much of Kastenbaum's analysis rests on the basic assumption that early in life human beings develop a need (whether inherited or learned) for mutual gratification, the need for pleasurable interactions with others.

By the time a person reaches adulthood he is likely to play many roles in society—son, husband, father, citizen, neighbor, friend, employee, parishioner—and has learned to differentiate the appropriate sets of behavior for these roles. Each of these role relationships is a potential source for mutual gratification. In addition, his experiences in his role relationships and the reactions of others to him in the various roles he plays are likely to have enabled him to formulate a definite and consistent "picture of self." He builds a more or less stable framework of personal identity. If the young adult suffers a loss in one role relationship, he has many other sources of mutual gratification and his picture of self is not likely to be seriously altered. According to Kastenbaum (1965, p. 269):

> When differentiation occurs within a broad, stable framework of personal identity, one can regard himself as being "the same person" who has nevertheless undergone certain changes. Thus, Mr. Newman, a young, employed, socially involved person, most likely will differentiate myself-as-ill from myself-as-healthy without encountering an identity crisis.

The situation, however, is different for the elderly adult. Through deaths of friends and relatives, meaningful relationships in his interpersonal world are likely to have decreased considerably. Furthermore, the roles of the elderly may be less valued than those of other age groups; role definitions are more ambiguous; there are, indeed, fewer roles to play, multiple lines of discontinuity, and fewer sources both of mutual gratification and of supports for what previously may have been a stable framework of personal identity.

Whatever the extent to which this holds for the aged in general, it is especially descriptive of aged persons requiring institutionalization in a nursing care facility. Contributing further to the loss of his previous framework for personal identity, says Kastenbaum (1965, p. 269):

> Mr. Oldman's admission into an institution confers a new identity, "geriatric patient." This identity serves further to differentiate him from his previous life, and substitutes a highly simplified, generalized identity, one that in most respects is interchangeable with any other "geriatric patient."

Moreover, this generalized identity strongly hampers the geriatric patient's chances of developing new sources for mutual gratification. As Kastenbaum (1965, p. 270) points out:

... Staff members and fellow patients expect neither to receive pleasure from Mr. Oldman nor to give pleasure to him. The staff-patient relationship is focused upon active giving and passive receiving of care-taking services. The patient-patient relationship is virtually non-existent; two passive entities have little to exchange directly with each other.

When the Pathology Model is assumed as the basis for interacting with the geriatric patient, the situational dynamics are likely to accentuate his losses, to add to his confusion, and to increase the identity crisis within him. Developmental-field theory would expect that his resultant psychobiological functioning will be such as to render him less goal-directed and less capable of coping with his problems and meeting new situations. He will tend to be apathetic, unsociable, and to exhibit reduced and primitivized intellectual activity. Therefore, if the above theoretical considerations are valid, a program designed to stimulate interactions with and among geriatric patients on the basis of mutual gratifications should help counteract these trends.

The program of serving wine in a group setting to patients at Cushing Hospital was devised for this purpose. (At a later date, beer was included as well.) Pleasurable interaction between staff and patients was the "intermediate" action goal; lasting increased sociability and activity of the geriatric patient was the "outcome" action goal.

Kastenbaum reasoned that centering a program around the serving of wine should implement the action goals on a number of grounds. On the one hand wine is one of the psychotropic drugs—those which act on the mind, as, for example, tranquilizers. Therefore, the program could be interpreted to, and accepted by, hospital staff in terms of familiar role expectations—the administering of a prescribed medicine by hospital staff to patients requiring psychotropic drug treatment. On the other hand the serving and drinking of wine in a group setting hold pleasurable social connotations that can be expected to have a positive influence in line with the mutual gratification model on both staff and patients.

From the patient's viewpoint, he is not being asked to take a pill, but instead is being offered a drink. Rather than a situational context that points to his impairments and dependency, the geriatric patient is participating in a situation in which he can consider himself "a responsible party capable of enjoying life on an adult level and moving in a mature sphere of interaction (Kastenbaum, 1965a, p. 271)." As a matter of fact, it was hypothesized on this basis that wine might not only encourage the growth of interpersonal relationships through its social connotations, but also operate more effectively on a psychophysiological level than conventional mood-influencing drugs. From the staff's viewpoint, rather than being ordered to be *sociable,* the social atmosphere likely to be engendered in wine-serving and drinking sessions is conducive to encouraging pleasurable interactions between them and the patients. Participation in the program therefore is not likely to be viewed as another "grim duty." Rather, this aspect of the action program should have a good chance of succeeding because the staff member can view himself in a pleasurable role and as personally receiving gratification from the situation. The wine serving and drinking sessions should therefore act as learning experiences for both staff and patients. Here they can see each other as fellow human beings, giving and receiving interpersonal gratification.

The studies undertaken by the Psychological Unit at Cushing in which staff response and patients' behavior were observed over extended periods of time after the initiation of the action program strongly suggest that the practice of serving wine in a geriatric group setting induced a sufficiently pleasurable and lasting reaction "to offer a challenge to the pathology model of aging (Kastenbaum, 1965a, p. 275)." Interestingly enough the nursing service at Cushing has now embodied the concept of mutual gratification in its own program and in fact is using social groups along the general model provided by the wine programs in its recently initiated long-range in-service training program.

In any event the findings reveal that the behavior of patients and staff changed in the direction predicted by the theory. These results indicate the value of the specific action program for increasing sociability and activity levels in geriatric patients and point to the utility of further exploring the developmental-field approach with emphasis on the mutual gratification model for additional social action implications to achieve these and other social welfare goals.

The foregoing perhaps will suffice as an example of the productive application of theory and research for action purposes. Hopefully it illustrates the advantage of exploring general theoretical principles which are being developed and reported in the literature in order to advance knowledge applicable to human problems in general, and in this case to problems of the aged in particular.

Designing Intervention Programs and Testing Their Effectiveness

The social action programs discussed above can be labeled "intervention" programs. The research cited emphasizes the need for testing the effectiveness of the program steps initiated. It is the purpose of this section to discuss in greater detail the necessity for action research, and the ways in which it can advance knowledge relevant to the solution of human problems.

Up to this point, the analysis has centered on the contentions that: 1) meaningful social action implications can be deduced from explicit theoretical formulations concerning human behavior, whether the theoretical formulations are arrived at from attempts to explain specific findings or from the development of general theories of behavior; and 2) there is a need to test these action implications through controlled studies of programs that put into action the implied directives. This does not mean that research is necessary to test the impact of a program only if it is based on an explicitly stated theory of behavior nor that only a program based on an explicitly stated theory can be successful. Certainly it is not being argued that present social efforts are haphazard or poorly conceived if they do not explicitly set down their assumptions or rationalize their goals and methods. It should be understood that all programs operate in terms of some set of assumptions (which may or may not be consistent with each other or uniformly understood by those implementing the program) whether these assumptions are explicit or implicit, valid or invalid. The contention at this time is that, whatever the assumptions upon which a program is based, if we are going to intervene in the solving of human problems, it is important to "test" these interventions. In this way a stockpile of applicable knowledge can be built concerning for whom and the extent to which programs are likely to work.

There have been been relatively few social action programs formulated around a clear and explicit set of social science propositions. There are even fewer programs which have been subjected to scientific evaluation—that is, which have included a bona fide research component designed to test impact from a scientific point of view. Often it is effective public relations—the ability to "sell" the public rather than scientific evidence of success—that keeps specific social action procedures in existence. Moreover, traditionally when evaluation efforts are undertaken, programs are evaluated *not* in terms of "impact" but rather in terms of the size of the professional staff, the educational background of the specialists, or the number of clients serviced by the program. The question used frequently as a basis for evaluating social action programs seems to be: "Are the services offered in a professional manner by qualified persons who in turn are supervised by qualified supervisors?" It is recognized that, for a fair test of effectiveness, it may be necessary that the program be implemented by qualified personnel employing the specified procedures. But the position taken here, the underlying theme of this paper, is that: "*In the final analysis,* success must be viewed in terms of *outcome* rather than in terms of the supposed quality of the procedures used (Freeman & Sherwood, 1966, p. 8)."

It is recognized, of course, that there are major obstacles to moving from evaluation of services in terms of the quality of personnel and procedures to evaluations in terms of program impact. One source of objection to impact research involves reaction to the necessity of selecting scientifically controlled samples, particularly when randomization procedures are used to determine who will be offered and who will be denied program service. The objection centers around the supposition that denial of service violates a basic social service principle. The practitioners taking this position seem to forget that few programs in existence have ever been able to offer service to all applicants in a specified period of time; usually there are long waiting lists. It would be helpful if practitioners could be made to see, since some would-be clients will have to be denied program service anyway, that a sample-controlling procedure such as randomization merely provides a substitute to what very often is a first-come, first-served allocation basis. Moreover the advantage of using such a sampling procedure is that it denies "service" in a systematic way which enables us to learn from what we are doing. Even more to the point, it would be helpful if it were understood that it is surely unfair to claim that service is being denied unless it can be ascertained that the social action in question really "works." The fact of the matter is that in some instances, particularly where there is poorly conceived or poorly implemented programming, it is conceivable that what is being considered "denial of service" is in reality denial of "harm." Be that as it may, in order to obtain evidence to settle the issue, we are back to the need for devising a methodology whereby individuals exposed to program efforts can be compared with a *similar group of individuals who are not so exposed.*

Other obstacles, perhaps more difficult to overcome, are related to attitudinal patterns in our culture. There exists a social climate of resistance to impact research engendered by skepticism about the possibility of applying scientific techniques to the understanding and solution of human problems. Often we are faced with the paradox that the persons who deny the possibility of scientifically studying the impact of social action efforts will demand that we "know" that the program will work before giving financial support. "Knowledge" for them takes the form here of assertion by "experts"—what Cohen and

Nagel (1934, pp. 193-194) refer to as the method of "authority." To "we do not know" or "we are not sure of what will work" is looked upon as a sign of failure and personal incompetence of the professionals willing to make such an assertion.

Another aspect of this reluctance to accept impact research is fear of the ultimate findings. Resistance here is based upon anxiety resulting from potential threats to job security, from ego involvement of action personnel, from challenges to institutionalized procedures, and so on. What is called for here is a transformation in social climate. Discarding program procedures which, upon testing, do not appear to work and attempting new lines of attack must be seen as positive values. In a paper presented at the 1966 National Conference on Social Welfare a major conclusion was that (Sherwood, 1966, p. 9):

> A new set of criteria for judging the performance of public and private officials who have the responsibility for allocating society's resources must be adopted by their publics. They must be judged and rewarded, not in terms of the claims of success which can be made, but in terms of the extent to which they have provided for a feedback of information concerning the performance of programs relative to the goals of those programs and the extent to which they make decisions concerning future allocations of resources on the basis of that information.

Although slow in coming, there are already encouraging signs of change. Increasingly, appearing in professional service-oriented journals (such as *American Journal of Public Health, Social Service Review, Smith College Studies of Social Work* and *Journal of the American Geriatrics Society*) are articles that emphasize the need for applying social science knowledge rather than intuition to policy decisions concerning programs for social action. Even more encouraging, an increasing number of research studies that add to the stockpile of applicable knowledge are being reported in the literature. In the past few years, in fact, a number of experimentally controlled studies of services to the elderly have been reported (Sainsbury & Grad, 1962; Blenkner, Jahn, & Wasser, 1964; Tarpy, O'Donnell & Glynn, 1964; Goldfarb, 1964; Perrow, 1959; Bailey, 1965; Aldrich & Mendkoff, 1963). Additional experimentally controlled intervention programs are known to be under way.

Adding another bright note to the picture, motivation for a number of these studies has come from responsible individuals in policy-making positions, forward-looking (from this point of view) administrators genuinely interested in basing action programs on relevant social science findings rather than on intuitive reasonableness and impressionistic worth. The demonstration project in progress at the Hebrew Rehabilitation Center for Aged in Boston—the one with which I am most familiar—can be cited as a case in point.

This project design is discussed here only insofar as it deals with impact research. The design in its present shape resulted from the interpretation by the author of the plans and goals of community leaders. The immediate participants in the group formulating the details of the proposals included representatives from the Hebrew Rehabilitation Center for Aged; Combined Jewish Philanthropies; Jewish Family and Children's Service; Beth Israel Hospital; and the Jewish Memorial Hospital. Maurice I. May, Executive Director of HRCA, was responsible for describing the envisioned program and the specific project objectives as well as for the other information required in the application submitted for support of the project. The application was submitted and received funding from the Public Health Service (CH-23-26) before the author was invited as principal investigator and project coordinator.

This project developed from a felt need for constructive social action in connection with the long waiting list of applicants to the Hebrew Rehabilitation Center for Aged in Boston. The Center (formerly the Hebrew Home for the Aged) has been in existence for over sixty years; and in response to the pressure of an increasing number of elderly in the community, it moved to a new and expanded facility in the fall of

1963. The new facility placed a greater emphasis on rehabilitation and increased the home's capacity from 264 to 475 beds. It now has an extensive program involving recreation, rehabilitation and medical care designed to maximize the well-being and functional capacity of the residents. The Center is a combination residence, nursing home, and chronic disease hospital.

Prior to the move to the new facility, applications had come in moderate volume. After the move, the new facility was quickly filled and within a year had a waiting list of over five hundred. Since then, rather than decreasing in number, the waiting list has continued to grow. This unexpected development stimulated serious thinking about the problem on the part of the executive director and other leaders at the Center in conjunction with leaders from other health and social agencies in the community. What might be done about the service needs of the applicants during the long waiting period for residency admission? Should the new facility be enlarged? Is institutionalization in this type of facility really the best answer to the problems faced by applicants? Or is it possible to devise a program that can divert the seemingly overwhelming demand for residency in a home for the aged into other appropriate channels of community service resources?

The decision was made to study the problem on a scientific basis. A three-year demonstration project at the Hebrew Rehabilitation Center for Aged was proposed in which applicants would be made the target of a community maintenance program aimed at meeting their needs in the "best possible" fashion. In this proposal the "best possible" fashion was to be determined by an interdisciplinary team including a social worker, a public health nurse, an internist, a physiatrist, and a psychiatrist. The team members were to evaluate individual needs of applicants and, as a group, specify recommendations for meeting assessed needs for each one. The project staff personnel were to be responsible for following through on recommendations. Wherever possible, needs of the aged persons in question were to be met by referrals to existing resources in the community. However, even for those referred to other service agencies, the project staff was to continue coordinating services throughout the demonstration period, taking periodic account of the individual's situation.

The proposal was submitted to and received funding from the Community Health Service of the United States Department of Health, Education and Welfare. In order to ensure that the effectiveness of the program, would be studied from a scientific point of view, the executive director of the Center and the other members of the committee responsible for the proposal sought a social science researcher interested in impact research to take the role of both project coordinator and principal investigator. The person appointed was to be responsible for coordinating program efforts, for developing the details of the research design to coordinate with the program efforts, and for undertaking the research spelled out by the design.

The demonstration program was conceived in the research design subsequently developed as containing two interrelated sub-programs: one, a program for assessing the needs of aged individuals and mapping the necessary services to meet these needs; the second, a program to facilitate the follow-through of services deemed necessary for the group of aged individuals being assessed. Since it is possible that the diagnostic process, especially coming to the Center and being seen by members of an evaluation team, may itself have an impact on applicants, it was considered important to study a sample of applicants who were exposed to the evaluation aspects of the program. This does not mean, however, that the project staff would hinder any applicant from seeking services elsewhere on his own.

Three comparable groups of applicants therefore are now being studied: two "experimental" groups—one being exposed to both the diagnostic process and to follow-through services, another being exposed to the diagnostic process only—and a "control" group, to receive no treatment. To ensure initial comparability of groups, randomization is being used as the basis for allocation. Given the number of applicants with whom the project can reasonably deal within the period of the project grant, it is expected that there will be some one hundred applicants in each group.

For answers concerning impact to be meaningful for policy decisions, it is necessary to be very explicit about the type of intervention being considered. Detailed accounts, therefore, are being kept of the characteristics of the program efforts being "tested." Furthermore, incorporated in the home interview being conducted for program purposes are questions providing comparable measurements to those found in other studies. In addition to the economic and scientific value of using previously developed devices, particularly those that have been tested and found reliable, their use will contribute even more generally to scientific knowledge by facilitating an appraisal of the utility of these devices in a variety of contexts and by adding to the collection of comparable data from many types of samples.

Toward this end the initial home interview includes measurements of the health scale developed by Rosow, Katz's ADL scale, Lawton's morale scale for the elderly, Kastenbaum's VIRO scale, and a variety of items from other studies of the aging and the handicapped. The initial home interview is being administered to all of the applicants whether they are in either of the two "experimental" groups or in the "control" group.

In addition, comprehensive data are being compiled: from the original applications for admission to the Center; from medical records; from social service records; from published vital statistics; from daily checks of the obituary columns; and, toward the end of the demonstration program period, from a post-test home interview with all applicants still in the community. The data obtained in the post-test interview will include the standardized test items being asked in the initial (pre-test) home interview.

From the data collected, it will be possible to compare the two experimental groups, and the control group will be compared in terms of at least the following "outcome" variables: 1) deferment rates for those already offered admission (or for those not yet offered admission, attitude of applicants toward remaining in the community); 2) death and accident rates of the applicants; 3) functional health status of the applicants; 4) participation in "normal" activities; and 5) "morale."

Since motivation for the impact research came in the first place from responsible community individuals in policy-making positions, it is anticipated that the findings of this study will be used for policy decisions concerning the future of the program in the Boston metropolitan area after the demonstration period. Hopefully this change in social climate will continue to spread and increasing numbers of individuals in policy positions will look to action impact research as a necessary guide to decisions on intervention programs. Furthermore it is hoped that social scientists undertaking impact research will feel impelled: 1) to describe carefully the program being "tested"; 2) to investigate and record the extent to which its provisions are being carried out as specified; and 3) to report impact findings *whether or not the program turns out to be successful.* It is important to know what failed as well as to know what succeeded.

In conclusion it should be noted that, when intervention programs include research components to test effectiveness of their procedures, there are rewards over and above impact knowledge itself. As has been pointed out by Freeman & Sherwood (1966, p. 18) impact research:

> ... forces those responsible for program design to clearly specify their objectives, to define what it is they are trying to achieve, what specific changes they are trying to effect. At the very least, it requires them to cooperate in efforts to operationalize what they have in mind. ... It shifts the emphasis from "procedure as an end" to "procedure as a means." Program personnel must then consider the relationship between the procedures it recommends and the defined outcomes that have been chosen.

REFERENCES

Aldrich, C. K. & Mendkoff, E. Relocation of the aged and disabled: A mortality study. *Journal of the American Geriatric Society,* 1963, *11,* 185-194.

Bailey, M. C. Evaluation of public health nursing services through a study of patient progress. *American Journal of Public Health*, 1965, *55*, 892-900.

Bennett, R. & Nahemow, L. The relations between social isolation, socialization and adjustment in residents of a home for aged. In M. P. Lawton & F. Lawton (Eds.), *Mental impairment in the aged.* Philadelphia: Philadelphia Geriatric Center, 1965.

Blenkner, J., Jahn, J., & Wasser, E. *Serving the aging: An experiment in social work and public health nursing.* New York: The Community Service Society of New York, 1964.

Camargo, O., & Preston, G. H. What happens to patients who are hospitalized for the first time when over sixty-five? *American Journal of Psychiatry*, 1945, *102*, 168-173.

Cohen, M. R., & Nagel, E. *An introduction to logic and the scientific methods.* New York: Harcourt, Brace & Company, 1934.

Donahue, W. Aging: A historical perspective. In National Institute of Mental Health, Community Research and Services Branch, *Research utilization in aging: An exploration.* (Public Health Service Publication No. 1211.) Bethesda, Md.: U.S. Public Health Service, 1964.

Farrar, M., Ryder, M. B., & Blenkner, M. Social work responsibility in nursing home care. *Social Casework*, 1964, *45*, 527-533.

Freeman, H. E., & Sherwood, C. C. Research in large-scale intervention programs. *The Journal of Social Issues*, 1966, *21*, 11-28.

Goldfarb, A. I. The evaluation of geriatric patients following treatment. In P. H. Hoch and J. Zubin (Eds.), *Evaluation of psychiatric treatment.* New York: Grune and Stratton, 1964.

Harris, D. B. (Ed.) *The concept of development.* Minneapolis: University of Minnesota Press, 1957.

Kastenbaum, R. Engrossment and perspective in later life: A developmental-field approach. In R. Kastenbaum (Ed.), *Contributions to the psychobiology of aging.* New York: Springer, 1965.

Kastenbaum, R. Wine and fellowship in aging: An exploratory action program. *Journal of Human Relations*, 1965, *13*, 266-276, (a)

Kastenbaum R., & Slater, P. E. Effects of wine on the interpersonal behavior of geriatric patients: An exploratory study. In R. Kastenbaum (Ed.), *New thoughts on old age.* New York: Springer, 1964.

Kay, D. W. K., Norris, V., & Post, F. Prognosis in psychiatric disorders of the elderly. *Journal of Mental Science*, 1956, *102*, 129-140.

Lewin, K. *A dynamic theory of personality.* New York: McGraw-Hill, 1935.

Lewin, K. *The conceptual representation and the measurement of psychological forces.* Durham, N.C.: Duke University Press, 1938.

Lewin, K. *Resolving social conflicts.* New York: Harper & Brothers, 1948.

Lieberman, M. A. Relationship of mortality rates to entrance to a home for the aged. *Geriatrics,* 1961, *16,* 515-519.

Miller, D., & Lieberman, M. A. The relationship of affect state and adaptive capacity to reactions to stress. *Journal of Gerontology,* 1965, *20,* 492-497.

Morris, R. Community planning for development, expansion and coordination of resources. In National Institute of Mental Health, Community Research and Services Branch, *Research utilization in aging: An exploration.* (Public Health Service Publication No. 1211.) Bethesda, Md.: U.S. Public Health Service, 1964.

Murphy, G. *Personality.* New York: Harper & Brothers, 1947.

National Institute of Mental Health, Community Research and Services Branch. *Research utilization in aging: An exploration.* (Public Health Service Publication No. 1211.) Bethesda, Md.: U.S. Public Health Service, 1964.

Piaget, J. *The psychology of intelligence.* New York: Littlefield, 1960.

Prock, V. N. Institutionalization as a stabilizing process. Paper presented at the meeting of the Gerontological Society, Los Angeles, November 1965.

Sainsbury, P., & Grad, J. An evaluation of community care: Some findings on the aged. In C. Tibbits and W. Donahue (Eds.), *Aging around the world: Social and psychological aspects of aging.* New York: Columbia University Press, 1962.

Sherwood, C. C. Issues in the measurement of results of action programs. Paper presented at the National Conference on Social Welfare, Chicago, June 1966.

Tarpy, E. K., O'Donnell, T., & Glynn, J. G. Intensive casework with chronically ill, neuro-psychiatric geriatric patients. *Journal of the American Geriatrics Society,* 1964, *12,* 1077-1082.

Werner, H. *Comparative psychology of mental development.* (Rev. ed.) New York: International Universities Press, 1957.

Werner, H. The concept of development from a comparative and organismic point of view. In D. B. Harris (Ed.), *The concept of development.* Minneapolis: University of Minnesota Press, 1957. (a)

PART II

RESEARCH STRATEGIES AND RESEARCH TECHNIQUES

7:: SOCIAL GERONTOLOGY
AND RESEARCH STRATEGIES

SYLVIA SHERWOOD

A fundamental contention of this paper is that both the subject matter of social gerontology and the fact that "old age" represents a pressing social issue of our time pose special problems which dictate the selection of certain research strategies. Basic both to the development of social gerontology as a body of knowledge and to finding solutions to current problems, there is a need for a much greater understanding than presently exists of: 1) the social and psychological aspects of the aging process—the changes which can be expected to occur in persons over time as part of or as a function of aging and age-related conditions; and 2) the kinds of impacts that given types of intervention are likely to have on this process. Both areas of investigation—the aging process per se and the effects of intervention on this process—involve the notion of *change*. The position taken here is that social gerontologists must study change and deal with the methodological problems associated with its measurement if social gerontology is to advance beyond the realm of the accumulation of isolated uniformities and descriptive knowledge of the historical circumstances of a given generation of individuals who have now reached old age.

"Change" implies knowledge of or estimates of at least two measurements—one at each of two points in time. To test hypotheses

Based on a paper presented at the 7th International Congress of Gerontology, Vienna, Austria, June 26-July 2, 1966.

concerning change, the research procedure selected must in some way satisfy this requirement. A survey of the literature suggests the need for social gerontologists to recognize and deal with the limitations of the assumptions and operations of some of the research techniques being employed in efforts to understand the aging process. These include, in particular, avoiding the logical fallacies in some methodological procedures, implementing the more useful research strategies, and dealing with some of the technical problems involved in the study of behavioral change. In the pages that follow, research strategies will be discussed in terms of three related major types of fallacies; technical problems with which social gerontologists must deal will be explored; and the kinds of impacts that given types of interventions have on the elderly will be briefly noted.

Most gerontological studies to date attempt to draw conclusions about the aging process by comparing different age segments of the population at the same point in time, committing the *cross-sectional fallacy;* that is, drawing conclusions concerning changes in persons over time—the aging process—by comparing different age segments of the population at a given point of time. The position taken here is that findings from cross-sectional studies may be pointing to *between-group* differences rather than to *within-group* changes.

For example, in a study of a sample of adults aged 40-70 (the Kansas City Study of Adult Life,) an inverse association was found between participation in formal associations and age for men (Havighurst, 1961). From this finding it is concluded that "formal associations lose attractiveness as age changes from 40 to 70 (p. 316)." It is assumed that "type of activity" is the dependent variable and chronological age, the independent variable. However, it may be that the differences found among the age groups resulted from different attitudes toward participation in formal groups to which each age group was exposed during its formative years rather than from the aging process. These data may suggest the hypothesis that formal associations lose attractiveness as one grows older, but they do not demonstrate it.

The need for longitudinal studies to understand the dynamic processes of personality change in relationship to aging is further exemplified in the limitations imposed on the findings from the studies of Neugarten and her colleagues by their cross-sectional methodology (Neugarten, 1964; Greun, 1964; Rosen & Neugarten, 1964). Using a sample of community members, efforts were made to determine the realationship between age and a number of personality and adjustment variables. The sample was interviewed and then classified on the basis of age, sex, and social class, and the responses were analyzed by analysis of variance for factor effects (age, sex, and social class) and for interactions among the factors. The aim of the study was to determine whether people's personalities, attitudes, capacity for adjustment, etc., change over time and whether these changes are related to and substantively identifiable with particular age periods derived from Erikson's theoretical formulations. But they attempted to test their hypotheses by comparing people who were of different ages at the same point in time.

An alternate hypothesis can be postulated that differences among age segments found at a given point of time may be a function of the different socio-cultural influences, particularly during childhood and early adulthood, rather than a function of the aging process or even conditions associated with aging. Sociological theory certainly predicts attitudinal and behavioral differences among different segments of the population. If individuals are influenced by experiences, and if experiences are different, we should expect to find differences in attitudes and behavior. This is why we assume and how we explain differences among racial, social, economic, educational, and other categories. Since differences between age groups at a particular point in time are not synonymous with changes over time for particular individuals, clearly there is a need for longitudinal studies to test such hypotheses.

Sometimes an attempt is made to trace the developmental process by the "life review" technique—by asking elderly persons about their past behavior, feelings, and attitudes. Although investigations of past activities and perceptions of past behavior and attitudes are valuable for many purposes, the usefulness of this research strategy for knowledge concerning "change" is questionable. The recall method poses serious problems of validity and difficulties for the interpretation of findings pertaining to any age group. Unless extensive checks are made for validity, this method would appear to be very precarious as a method of studying changes in people as they grow older.

In addition to the problems inherent in the cross-sectional method discussed above, the method forces the commission of another fallacy, which is termed here *the absolutist fallacy.* The data and method of the Kutner, Fanchel, Togo, & Langner (1956) study, *Five Hundred Over Sixty,* will serve as an example to describe this methodological problem. The authors offered the following explanation of their finding that morale gradually decreases with age: ". . . the matter of life adjustment may be affected by the cumulation of the problems of widowhood, declining living standards, and health . . . (p. 5)." This explanation hypothesizes that certain events or changes (e.g., change in status from married to widow) will tend to be followed by certain other changes (e.g., lower morale, increased maladjustment). With a cross-sectional methodology, the only possible way to test such an hypothesis is to compare, for example, the morale scores of the "married" and the "widowed," with the prediction being that a significantly higher proportion of the widowed than of the married will have "low morale." The fallacy committed is that the hypothesis is not that widows will tend to have "low morale," but that their morale will be "lower" after widowhood than before. The post-widowhood morale scores of widows may be anywhere in the range of morale scores—from very low to very high; for the hypothesis to be confirmed it is only necessary that their morale be significantly *lower* (although in many instances perhaps still relatively high) than it was before widowhood. This information cannot be obtained in a cross-sectional study.

The confused causality fallacy is another fallacy easily committed when, based on findings from cross-sectional studies, efforts are made to offer explanations which causally connect sets of changes with one another. It involves the logical fallacy of assuming that, when a relationship is found to exist between two variables, differences in one of the variables are causing the differences found in the other variable. For example, if it is found by cross-sectional comparisons that there is a relationship between the number of activities (as one variable) in which elderly persons participate and adjustment (measured independently and considered as another variable), it is fallacious to assert from this information that increased participation *increases* adjustment in the elderly or conversely that decrease in activities *causes* lack of adjustment.

A study by Pan (1952) perhaps will suffice to illustrate the limitations imposed by the use of a cross-sectional research strategy to study change variables and how they can lead to the commission of the confused causality fallacy. He compared the personal adjustment of old people in Protestant church homes for the aged and old people living outside of institutions as an indication of the influence of institutionalization upon personal adjustment in old age. Although he did regard his results as tentative, he concluded that individuals living in their own homes are more adjusted than those who live in old age institutions. From the explicitly stated purpose of his study, the implication of his findings is that this difference is an indication of a negative influence of institutionalization on adjustment. But by his methodology, even if the relationship is found to hold, it cannot be ascertained whether institutionalization caused the lower adjustment found in the institutionalized elderly, whether individuals who are more poorly adjusted in the first place are more likely to seek institutionalization, or whether poor adjustment and seeking institutionalization are concomitantly related—that is, both sets of phenomena are being caused by another set of factors. Although there are long standing and oft-repeated warnings in the statistical literature against the commission of this logical error—stated in the maxim "correlation is not causation"—its repeated appearance in social gerontological research reports warrants its inclusion here.

Recognition of and attempts to avoid the cross-sectional and absolutist fallacies, in addition to requiring a longitudinal methodology, will lead to the recognition of a technical, methodological problem which does not occur within a cross-sectional approach. This problem relates to the measuring instruments and is termed here "the bottoming-out and topping-out problem." If it is agreed that what we are after is the testing of dynamic hypotheses involving relationships between changes and that it is "lower" or "higher" scores rather than "low" or "high" scores which are predicted and thus to be tested, instruments must be devised which have a sufficiently broad range of possible scores so that insignificantly small (ideally zero) proportions of the population achieve minimum or maximum scores, particularly at pre-test time. This is for the simple reason that a hypothesis which predicts a "lower" score after a change in some independent variable cannot be tested on that part of the population which obtained a minimum score at the outset. Hypotheses predicting "higher" scores encounter instrument problems at the other end of the scale. This instrument problem is not encountered when the cross-sectional route is taken since it fallaciously equates "lower" with "low" and therefore does not require room in the instrument for movement, only for variability. This is why the fallacious cross-sectional method of "measuring" change can utilize three category scales—e.g., "high," "medium," and "low"—since static differences are used as estimates of change. The longitudinal, relationship-between-changes method requires room for movement in both directions for all or nearly all of its study population. If a three-category scale is used in this approach, the members of one of the three categories would be exempt from being tested on every change hypothesis.

Unfortunately, there are no ready answers to this type of problem. As has been pointed out by Webster & Bereiter (1963, p. 39) "only very rudimentary methods for measuring social and psychological change are known, at a time when much more of this kind of knowledge might easily be very useful." However, there is a growing awareness of this and related problems in the study of change and serious and concentrated efforts are being made toward their solution (Harris, 1963).

Although there are other imposing technical problems facing the researcher, one other fundamental problem in studying "change" will be discussed here—the *unreliability* of change measurement. According to Lord (1963, p. 25), a "major source of confusion in studies of change is the presence of errors of measurement." Very often the change differences may be smaller than the error in the measuring instrument.

Dealing with reliability of measurement in general is a major problem of social science. Problems of dealing with reliability of change measurements are even more complex. However, problems of relating the mathematically demonstrated greater unreliability of change scores to the reliability of the scores from which they were derived are currently receiving attention from a number of statisticians and psychometricians (Harris, 1963). According to Webster and Bereiter (1963, p. 40) "The attack on unreliability initiated by Spearman and by Kelly has been sustained, and some notable advances have been made recently, particularly by Lord." They look forward "confidently to a time when measurement in social science will be much more effective and useful (p. 40)."

The reliability problem must be adequately handled if precise tests of change hypotheses are to be achieved via the longitudinal method. Instruments must be devised for social gerontology which are sufficiently sensitive to identify real changes within the magnitude ranges predicted by the change theories or hypotheses. That is, of course, just a reminder of the long standing caution posed by statisticians that a real change in score cannot be determined arbitrarily, but involves a decision-making operation which relates the score changes to the error range of the instrument, as estimated by the responses of some particular population at some particular place and time. It is mentioned here only because it is believed that to the extent that the field of gerontological research relies increasingly on a longitudinal, relationship-between-changes methodology, it is going to have to attack this problem with increasing vigor, and hopefully, success.

REFERENCES

Gruen, W. Adult personality: An empirical study of Erikson's theory of ego development. In B. L. Neugarten & Associates (Eds.), *Personality in middle and late life*. New York: Atherton Press, 1964.

Harris, C. W. (Ed.) *Problems in measuring change*. Madison: University of Wisconsin Press, 1963.

Havinghurst, R. J. The nature and values of meaningul free-time activity. In R. W. Kleemeier (Ed.), *Aging and leisure*. New York: Oxford University Press, 1961.

Kleemeier, R. W. (Ed.) *Aging and leisure*. New York: Oxford University Press, 1961.

Kutner, B., Fanchel, D., Togo, A., & Langner, T. *Five hundred over sixty*. New York: Russell Sage Foundation, 1956.

Lord, F. M. Elementary models for measuring change. In C. W. Harris (Ed.), *Problems in measuring change*. Madison: University of Wisconsin Press, 1963.

Neugarten, B. L. & Associates (Eds.) *Personality in middle and late life*. New York: Atherton Press, 1964.

Pan, J. A comparison of factors in the personal adjustment of old people in the Protestant church homes for the aged and old people living outside of institutions. *The Journal of Social Psychology*, 1952, *35*, 195-203.

Rosen, J. L., & Neugarten, B. L. Ego functions in the middle and later years. in B. L. Neugarten & Associates (Eds.), *Personality in middle and late life*. New York: Atherton Press, 1964.

Webster, H., & Bereiter, C. The reliability of changes measured by mental test scores. In C. W. Harris (Ed.), *Problems in measuring change*. Madison: University of Wisconsin Press, 1963.

8:: DIFFERENCES BETWEEN CURRENT GERONTOLOGICAL THEORIES: IMPLICATIONS FOR RESEARCH METHODOLOGY

K. K. SCHOOLER and C. L. ESTES

The earliest statements of disengagement theory described the aging process as the inevitable mutual withdrawal resulting in decreased interaction between the individual and society (Cumming, Dean, Newell, & McCaffrey, 1960; Cumming & Henry, 1961). Cumming later enlarged upon the theory through a discussion of the differential aspects of disengagement, relating them to differences in biologically determined temperament, differences in societal constraints, and as responses to changing roles (Cumming, 1963). Subsequent to the publication of *Growing Old,* Henry (1964) has also commented on the earlier position of the disengagement theory on the basis of additional analysis. In "The Theory of Intrinsic Disengagement," presented at the Sixth International Congress of Gerontology, he implied that "engagement and disengagement are a general form of personality dynamic and the disengagement of the aged a special case (p. 32)."

The crux of his presentation was his speculation on the question of the extent to which disengagement is an intrinsic process: "The processes of disengagement are intrinsic in the sense that social, environmental events are not sufficient to predict them and that they appear clearly related to various personality processes generally

An earlier version of this paper was presented at the Seventh International Congress of Gerontology, Vienna, June 1966. Its preparation was supported in part by U.S. Public Health Service Grant #EF 00654.

understood to be of long duration (p. 34)." The assumption of the intrinsic nature of the disengagement process thus persists as a keystone of the theory, in spite of the modification suggested previously by Cumming.

Others, using data from the Kansas City Study of Adult Life have addressed themselves to the question of adjustment of the disengaged elderly, and Havighurst, Neugarten, & Tobin (1963) have summarized their analysis of the Kansas City data with the inference that "those older persons who are highly engaged in various social roles generally have greater life satisfaction than those who have lower role levels of engagement. At the same time, the relationship is not a consistent one. Presumably there are certain personality types who, as they age, disengage with relative comfort. Others disengage with great discomfort and show a drop in life satisfaction (p. 422)." Still others, we may believe, for a large part of their lives have been relatively disengaged and are quite satisfied in that state. In this respect, aging brings no noticeable change.

Subsequent research by Neugarten (1964) leads her to suggest that neither the activity theory nor the disengagement theory of successful aging accounts for the empirical findings. In other words, following the inferences of Neugarten as just cited, of Maddox & Eisdorfer (1962) and of others, it would appear that satisfaction or adjustment in later years is positively associated with engagement for some persons and negatively associated for others.

In analyzing a series of studies contributing to a *developmental* theory of adult personality, Neugarten contributes further to the disengagement theory when she shows significant age differences with respect to the intra-psychic aspects of personality. Although there is undoubtedly a circular process between psychological and social elements of disengagement, she says the implication of her findings is that the psychological changes (described in her work as increased inward-orientation and decreased cathexes for outer-world events) seem to precede rather than follow measurable changes in extent of social interaction.

Returning to Cumming's (1963, pp. 378-379) further thoughts on theory of disengagement, "deeply rooted differences in character ... color all of life, including the disengagement process." But what of that which Cumming refers to as societal constraint or response to changing role? And what of the even earlier statements about mutual withdrawal of society and the individual? Where do the intrinsic theorists begin to account for not only the withdrawal of society but also the recent evidence that society may be initiating re-engagement? It requires a considerably different theoretical perspective to account for the phenomena of successful aging in the context of an interactive environment, an environment of people as well as of objects, an environment that can withdraw but that can also re-engage and be re-engaged.

Arnold Rose (Rose & Peterson, 1965) and his collaborators offer such a theoretical perspective in *Older People and Their Social World*. They view the phenomena of the aging process in the context of the emergence of an aging subculture. Rose defines a class of persons he calls the aging group-conscious. They are "those elderly persons aware not merely that they are old but that they are subject to certain deprivations because they are old, and they react to these deprivations with resentment and with some positive effort to overcome the deprivations (p. 19)." They acquire a sense of identification with other elderly persons because of their awareness of these affronts.

Another way of describing the phenomenon is in terms of the enforced loss of roles and enforced acquisition of undesired roles. Rose then goes on to identify several patterns of response to the changing roles. There are, among the elderly, some who experience no deprivation—old age is merely a continuation of a pattern experienced during the early or middle adult years. In terms of disengagement process, these may be persons who have always been more or less disengaged. Others, experiencing loss of roles, resign themselves to the situation and seek no alternatives. A third class of elderly persons consists of two subclasses: Those who succeed in creating new independent roles, that is, who become re-engaged, and those who create new roles for themselves in an aging sub-society which is different from the larger general society.

To summarize, the emphasis of disengagement theory and the personality theorists has been on the intrinsic processes, although lip service has been given to the importance of social interaction. The interactionists, on the other hand, apparently unwilling to acknowledge the possibility of individual differences of personality in accounting for the observed changes in interaction with the environment, emphasize the concepts of self-image, social role, and group support for these self-conceptions. While the fact that disengagement or degree of engagement is explained by Neugarten, Henry and others largely by invoking concepts of egodevelopment, Rose and his associates account for these same phenomena by invoking the concepts of role theory and group identification. It is significant, however, that in summarizing her work *Personality in Middle and Late Life,* Neugarten (1964) states that what are especially needed now are "investigations in which, in delineating the salient dimensions of personality, attention is centered on intimate social networks and subtle aspects of social interaction (p. 199)." Thus, while the position that the processes are intrinsic appears to be softening so as to permit more emphasis on the quality of interaction of the individual with society, it remains to be seen if the interactionists will recognize in their research efforts those individual differences in developmental phenomena that may account for a differential response to social events and which may account for the three classes defined by Rose.

It is not the purpose of this paper to evaluate the merit of any particular theoretical position but rather to suggest that if a particular position is pursued, or more likely, if some rapprochement between the two positions is to be sought, certain aspects of methodology require attention.

First, it is apparent that most of the data in support of either view comes from cross-sectional rather than longitudinal studies. It would be naive to suggest here that this is an original observation: Others have previously suggested that inferences about causal relationships or the temporal sequence of events cannot be derived with assurance from cross-sectional data. Streib (1963) has, moreover, provided a comprehensive description of the problems of longitudinal studies, and Sherwood (Part II) has given a cogent analysis of some of the problems of drawing inferences from cross-sectional data when longitudinal data are required.

What is needed, however, is an appropriate method for the analysis of longitudinal data. Both intrinsic and interactionist theorists are obliged to demonstrate the extent to which characteristics of personality and inner life operate independently of societal events. To make such a convincing demonstration from a longitudinal study, the analyst must employ a model which permits social events to vary and is capable of showing how behavioral and other changes are related to social events, irrespective of the time-lag between the event and the behavioral change.

Conventional procedures do not permit one to differentiate easily between events caused by immediately preceding circumstances and those caused by circumstances a year or two prior to the observation. Some useful analytical procedures for investigating such problems, however, are suggested by the literature on attitude change and psychometrics (Anderson, 1954; Harris, 1967).

One fruitful line of inquiry may be the use of the analysis of Markov chains, relying on a mathematical model involving the probability that a person exhibiting a particular response at one point in time is likely to exhibit a different response at a later point in time. Employing the model of the Markov process, one may determine whether the probabilities of change themselves change over time. Considering that the personality processes are expected to be relatively constant, one would further expect that the transitional probabilities for various classes of individuals would remain constant over time; if such probabilities themselves change, it may then be inferred that external events are responsible for the change. Inspection of the data for various time intervals would permit one to infer which events, at which times, are responsible for behavioral change and the transitional probability.

Other approaches warranting examination are what Campbell calls cross-lagged panel correlation analysis, analogous to Lazarsfeld's "sixteen-fold-table," and the other multivariate models suggested in the volume edited by Harris (1963). In summary, one chief obstacle to the execution of longitudinal studies—unavailability of methods for analysis—can, it seems, be overcome.

A second problem of methodological interest derives from the importance of the concept of interaction for both theoretical positions. In the Kansas City Studies, the interaction index is simply an indication of the saturation of the daily life with interaction, and it says nothing about *variety* of characteristics of roles or numbers performed. It is based on the response to two open-ended questions asking what a typical day is like and what a typical weekend is like. The use of such a measure may be questioned with respect to the way such data are collected, for, even though we may obtain inter-rater reliability with respect to the coding of the responses, it must be admitted that a question in this form, using "a typical day" as a frame of reference, may serve merely as a projective device.

The crux of the matter is that our interest in interaction is in *real* interaction and not in *perceived* interaction. We want to know what, in fact, did the respondent do and not what he thinks is an appropriate response for a person in his status.

Several substitutes are available to the investigator. For example, he might ask, as some others have done, for a report of the interaction for the preceding day. Such a procedure, however, could only be feasible if it were possible to obtain interviews on a random sample of days and on a large random sample of respondents. Another possibility, albeit fraught with hazards for the researcher, is the use of diaries.

However, even if the problems of collecting data on the density or frequency of interaction in daily life were to be overcome, a much more fundamental problem faces the researcher concerned with the concept of interaction; i.e., the issue raised by Lowenthal (1965) in suggesting that *frequency* of interaction appears to be a less meaningful concept than the *quality* of interaction. Lowenthal has been admirably cautious in the presentation of her findings. However, on the assumption that her tentative findings will be substantiated by subsequent research and analysis, the implication for the methodologist is that new measures must be developed, and new procedures for analysis must be derived, in order that we may give appropriate weight to the qualitative aspects of interaction as well as to frequency.

To give a trivial illustration, we need to develop the means for comparing and assigning weights to the relatively frequent-but-insignificant interaction with, say, one's grocer, and the relatively infrequent-but-intense and meaningful interaction with, say, siblings who are geographically distant.

Concern for the methodology of measuring interaction quantitatively and qualitatively leads then to two other problems, one having to do with the dimensions of the life space, and the other with measurement of role behavior. First, it raises the question, "Interaction with whom?" Clearly, the use of diaries and the use of the random-day procedure determine for the investigator who the participants in interaction with the subject are, but ought not the investigator allow himself the possibility or opportunity to study frequency or quality of interaction with some relevant persons who, on a chance basis, would not be mentioned in either of the two preceding procedures? Ought not there to be some procedure by which the dimensions, the limits, or the parameters of the life space are determined? Who are the significant people and institutions in this elderly person's life? The methodological problem is to catalogue all of the relevant or significant others, not only individual but institutional, having in advance some uniform criterion of significance. The methods of obtaining such a list are not altogether clear. However, the importance of obtaining such a list is clear.

If investigators are to concern themselves with interaction and social behavior of the elderly, and if theory is concerned with withdrawal of society from the individual or engagement with him, where society is institutions as well as individuals, the investigator should become able to ask meaningful questions or perform meaningful observations about all levels and types of interaction. At present, either the elements in one's life space are defined haphazardly or concern is limited to a few known significant persons.

The final methodological problem raised by a concern for interaction is that of role analysis. It is apparent that the current research in gerontology making any reference to role behavior is really only half complete. Investigators concern themselves with counting roles and frequently only counting certain specified roles such as housewife or mother or grandparent. However, simply to count the number of roles acted is analogous to simply counting the number of interactions in an average day. The qualitative aspects of role performance are much more meaningful. But in order to study the qualitative aspect of role behavior, at least a conceptual definition of the term "role" ought to be acknowledged, and the reciprocal aspect of role, that which has to do with the mutual expectations of behavior, ought to be recognized.

Whether being old in itself constitutes a role may be questioned; however, the elderly do perform a number of other roles and it is with respect to these, as well as to the role of being old, that the expectations of others with respect to ego's performance must be determined. It should not be assumed that *all* persons have uniform expectations about the performance of roles by the elderly. It follows then that *measures* of the expectations of significant others with respect to specific role behavior should be obtained. To understand fully the elderly person in the role of, say, grandparent, one must have some understanding not only of the older person's perceptions and expectations, but also of the expectations of behavior held by the grandchild and the child.

The number of studies reporting data based on the reports of significant others is sparse and even fewer perform a primary analysis of the reports of the significant others as they pertain to each in the sample of the elderly. Nevertheless, one recent hopeful example, employing the data of the Kansas City studies can be found in Hink's (1966) report on "the perceptions of significant others in the lifespace of the elderly individual." While this particular study does not address itself to the problem of role analysis, the utility of the method of using significant others as informants, as well as the older person himself, is clearly indicated.

Summary

It is suggested here that the current status of theorizing in the field of social gerontology is such that a truly social-psychological theory may emerge but that in order for theory to be tested in the field, at least four problems indicated here ought to be faced. The first is the problem of analysis of longitudinal data; the second, the problem of defining the qualitative aspects of social interaction; the third is the problem of defining limits of the lifespace; and the fourth, the problem of using the reports of significant others in the analysis of the elderly person's role. In the face of the need for so much methodological development prior to the effective test of theory, it is concluded here that, rather than engaging in large-scale survey research studies, gerontologists should now call for extensive support of a series of smaller studies of limited scope designed primarily for the purpose of developing and further refining of these methods.

REFERENCES

Anderson, T. Probability models for analyzing time changes in attitudes. In P. Lazarsfeld (Ed.), *Mathematical thinking in the social sciences*. Glencoe, Ill.: Free Press, 1954.

Cumming, E. Further thoughts on the theory of disengagement. *International Social Science Journal*, 1963, *15*, 377-393.

Cumming, E., Dean, L. R., Newell, D. S., & McCaffrey, I. Disengagement: A tentative theory of aging. *Sociometry*, 1960, *23*, 23-35.

Cumming, E., & Henry, W. E. *Growing old: The process of disengagement.* New York: Basic Books, 1961.

Harris, C. W., (Ed.) *Problems in measuring change.* Madison: University of Wisconsin Press, 1963.

Havighurst, R., Neugarten, B., & Tobin, S. Disengagement, personality and life satisfaction in the later years. In P. F. Hansen (Ed.), *Age with a future; Proceedings of the Sixth International Congress of Gerontology, Copenhagen, 1963.* Copenhagen: Munksgaard, 1964.

Henry, W. E. The theory of intrinsic disengagement. In P. F. Hansen (Ed.), *Age with a future; Proceedings of the 6th International Congress of Gerontology, Copenhagen, 1963.* Copenhagen: Munksgaard, 1964.

Hink, D. L. Interpersonal perception in selected social systems: A study of aging persons. Unpublished doctoral dissertation, University of Chicago, 1966.

Lowenthal, M. F. Social environmental factors in maintaining mental health. Unpublished manuscript, Langley Porter Neuropsychiatric Institute, 1965.

Maddox, G., & Eisdorfer, C. Some correlates of activity and morale among the elderly. *Social Forces,* 1962, *40,* 254-260.

Neugarten, B. L., & Associates (Eds.). *Personality in middle and late life.* New York: Atherton Press, 1964.

Rose, A. M. & Peterson, W. A. *Older people and their social world.* Philadelphia: F. A. Davis, 1965.

Sherwood, S. Social gerontology and research strategies. *Proceedings 7th International Congress of Gerontology,* 1966, *6,* 383-387.

Streib, G. F. Longitudinal studies in social gerontology. In R. H. Williams, C. Tibbitts, & W. Donahue (Eds.), *Processes of aging.* New York: Atherton Press, 1963.

9:: FROM 'N' TO EGO

DONALD P. KENT and SYLVIA K. BARG

The provision of services to help research subjects with their problems results in additional information that is dynamic and multidimensional. Although research strategies vary greatly in design, they are alike in at least two respects: each has been developed to deal with specific problems of inquiry; and each has its individual strengths and weaknesses. The researcher uses the strategy that, among the resources available to him, he thinks will yield the most complete answers to the root questions prompting the study. At the same time he tries to modify his design to compensate for its inherent shortcomings. This article is a report of one such compensatory measure developed in a research project that employed social survey methods.

Despite the manifest advantages and contributions of such survey research, one basic shortcoming is that the individual is often lost. According to Galtung (1967, p. 150), he is "literally torn out of his social context and made to appear in the sample as a society of one person to be compared with other societies of one person." The individual becomes a part of N, the total sample population, and in this process the ego, by which is meant the dynamic self, the individual in his social situation, disappears.

For the past two years the authors of this article have conducted a social survey of the aged population in low income areas of Philadelphia, a study that is still in progress. In an area probability sample,

This article is based on a paper presented at the twenty-first annual meeting of the Gerontological Society, Denver, Colorado, November 1, 1968. Reprinted from *Social Casework*, April 1969. Copyright © by Family Service Association of America, 44 East 23rd Street, New York, N.Y.

1,039 aged persons (approximately 75% Negro and 25% white) were interviewed. The subjects of the research obviously had many problems; and indeed the research was initiated to gain more specific information about their needs and the manner in which they were or were not met. Very early in the project, however, it became apparent that the interviewers not only were going to uncover problems but also were going to be asked to help. Quite apart from the issue of the social responsibility of the investigator was the fact that to ignore justifiable pleas would obviously have a dysphoric effect upon the interviewers; assistance had to be given whenever possible. Interviewers in most studies are not professionally competent to offer help, and this was true of our interviewers, who were, for the most part, neighborhood women who had been trained in interviewing.

Although the need for a social worker was recognized, the Aged Services Project had no funds to employ one. The dilemma was resolved when Jeanette Reis volunteered her professional services. The interviewers were instructed to advise respondents who requested help that their problems would be reported to the main office. No assurance of assistance was given other than that a trained social worker would be alerted to their need. Of the subjects interviewed, 11.4%, or 119 persons, requested immediate help for critical problems. It is our contention that responding to the requests for help adds a dimension to research that is important substantively and methodologically.

Substantive Dimensions

An analysis of the requests showed that the largest number of problems was economic in nature. Forty-five individuals asked for help in areas relating to Social Security benefits and old-age assistance or requested money for special expenditures. Twenty-five persons presented problems in areas related to health. An additional thirteen persons had problems that involved the financing of medical care.

Fourteen respondents raised problems related to housing, and the remainder had a variety of problems including transportation, need for legal advice, and problems of interpersonal relationships. It would be a mistake, however, to view such categories as definitive. In most instances in which requests were made for specific help, the worker found a problem syndrome rather than a single problem. For example, there were financial problems, but they were usually complicated by poor health, inadequate housing, and little familial or community support. The disposition of the problems was perhaps more significant than their nature. In all but a few instances the social worker was able to make a referral to an existing agency. Problems were solvable within the framework of existing health and welfare agencies; the need was not so much for new agencies as for greater accessibility to services.

Methodological Dimensions

While the benefits to the subjects were tangible, the benefits to research of building in a service element were also considerable, although less amenable to empirical verification. Clearly the interviewers felt relieved to know that when help was requested there was a good chance that it would be given. This fact was particularly important in a study in which a single interview often lasted two hours or longer. Inevitably there was a mutual exchange between the interviewer and interviewee—establishing a rapport that yielded in-depth material for the study. This rapport inevitably opened the interviewer to demands that could not be ignored. In the periodic conferences between the interviewers and the project directors, it became clear that without a means for dealing with the critical problems presented by the subjects being interviewed, the interviewers could not have continued.

Illustrative requests

Mrs. A. greeted the interviewer with the statement: "If someone doesn't help me, I will die right here; I can't take it any more." She pleaded for relocation help especially. Mrs. A was partially blind, seventy-two years of age, and lived alone, supported by an old-age assistance grant. Because of defective wiring, her second-floor apartment had no electricity and no cooking facilities. The rental agent had failed to respond to her requests for repairs. The interviewer commented that she could not have probed for responses or asked the questions related to morale at all had she not been able to promise help for the immediate problem confronting Mrs. A.

An extreme example of respondent mistrust was presented by Mr. B who wrote to the office describing his long experience with agencies designed to help. The social worker made an appointment to see him and secured the research interview only after taking a detailed case history and giving assurance of a thorough investigation.

The reverse of a distrustful attitude was also apparent. Interviews were given with obvious candor. Highly personal information was disclosed and fully discussed, partly because of the manifest empathy and understanding of the neighborhood interviewers and partly because there was an effort made to obtain help when a respondent requested it. By dealing with the subjects' immediate needs, it became possible to probe for abeyant needs and feelings.

Mrs. C, although on crutches, was caring for three grandchildren. While giving responses readily, several times she expressed her need for a wheelchair, finally asking whether the interviewer could possibly be of help. Upon being told it was quite likely that help could be given, Mrs. C launched into a recital of what she would then be able to do and described fully her activities in behalf of the "grands," including considerable information regarding other elderly women in the neighborhood who had a similar custodial responsibility.

Conclusion

We have found the provision of social work services equally useful in a community study currently being conducted by Trans Century Associates for the Redevelopment Authority of Philadelphia and the

Grays Ferry Community Council. All respondents have been asked if they wish help from a referral office established for this purpose. In a significant proportion of the sample, additional information has been volunteered following the offer of assistance with problems.

The offer to help research subjects with their problems has other results for applied social research. The information that accompanies the discussion of the problem places the individual in a social context. The subject no longer is "N" but ego; the social context within which he lives is made manifest and the previously static, unidimensional information becomes dynamic and multidimensional. The benefits to the informant and to the interviewer are substantial, and the resulting research data may well be richer and more meaningful.

REFERENCES

Galtung, J. *Theory and methods of social research.* New York: Columbia University Press, 1967.

10:: ASSESSING THE COMPETENCE OF OLDER PEOPLE

M. POWELL LAWTON

This paper will attempt to define "competence" as a behavioral variable at a theoretical level. The empirical manifestations of competence at various levels of functioning germane to the behavior of older people also will be considered. Finally, some old and new ways of assessing the competence of older people will be described.

As a first task, it may be useful to anchor competence within the framework of other efforts to specify optimum human functioning. In particular, one may view competence in terms of Jahoda's criteria of positive mental health (1958). She described three intrapsychic components of mental health: self-attitude, self-actualization, and personality integration. Three other criteria of mental health refer to an interaction between individual and environmental variables: reality perception, autonomy, and environmental mastery. Competence is seen as related primarily to the last two mentioned criteria of positive mental health.

There are five major attributes of competence: 1) Competence refers to external phenomena, to tasks that are to be performed by the individual; 2) The task performance, or behavior, is to be evaluated; evaluation of competence is frequently achieved by reference to incompetence; 3) The behavior to be evaluated occurs in contemporary time. Competence is not an enduring dimension, but it varies over time;

Presented at the Eastern Psychological Association, Boston, April 7, 1967. Parts of this work were supported by Grants MHO 2329 and CD 00137 from the United States Public Health Service.

4) Full definition of competence is possible only when the opportunities and constraints of the environment are specified; and 5) Domains of competence are hierarchically arranged with respect to the degree of complexity of behavior required in each domain.

Competence may be contrasted with other traditional psychological constructs. The more enduring, primarily endopsychic, characteristics of an individual which exist independently of, or across, many tasks, times, and settings are more appropriately referred to as personality traits. Ability is the inner and enduring aspect of competence as applied particularly to cognition and conation. Unlike personality or ability, competence has no inner aspects. Motivation and affect, on the other hand, are both inner phenomena and in themselves cannot be subjected to evaluative procedures, though behavior which is associated with a motive or an affect may be evaluated in terms of its competence.

Levels of Organization by Which Competence May Be Judged

Gerard (1959) has constructed a model of dynamic systems which describes the three major attributes of the system as being, behaving, and becoming—alternatively, structure, function, and development. Organization of the human system proceeds through levels of increasing complexity, beginning with the molecular and proceeding through the cellular, the body organ, the individual, the group, and the social to the macrosocial. The levels are continuous and mutually interdependent and/or autonomous in varying degree. The system may be described from the point of view of being, behaving, or becoming and, concurrently, with respect to any level or combination of levels. Thus, an individual at a given moment may be described as a schizoid individual (being), as retreating into an isolated office during the office party (behaving), and as in the process of dealing with imminent old age (becoming). This example refers to the psychological level, but other levels of organization, such as the cellular, may be viewed equally well from the points of view of being, behaving, and becoming. Descriptions at one level may or may not have obvious relationships with descriptions at other levels. The schizoid person's physiology may or may not vary with his social behavior. Within Gerard's concept, competence is clearly marked as behavior evaluated.

Competent behavior is partially defined by norms for the level under consideration. Norms set gross limits on the appropriateness and relevance of the behavior of the individual in terms of the survival of the individual and the social structures of which he is a part. However, the criteria by which competence is judged are not merely normative, but are also teleological. One might say that the goal of competent behavior is maximum complexity within the limits set by normative considerations.

To take a concrete example, normative and teleological competence is exhibited by the retired carpenter who continues to use his skills in his home workshop to produce cabinetwork, without risk to himself. Lessened normative competence with continued teleological competence is shown when the older person tries to use his tools on demanding tasks in the same manner as he always has despite the empirical result of injury to himself and inability to produce the desired result. Normative competence and lessened teleological competence, finally, would be shown when the carpenter attacks simpler tasks with more appropriate tools, and produces a less complex but acceptable product without injury to himself. Thus, the carpenter's behavior may be evaluated in terms of either normative appropriateness or level of complexity. In practice, this distinction is not always easy to make, and the history of measurement is replete with unsuccessful efforts to combine statistical and value-oriented approaches.

Theorists such as Piaget and Werner have posited a process of differentiation combined with reintegration at higher levels of organization to describe mental growth. The present thoughts about competence share with their concepts the hierarchical ordering of levels and the implication that a "goal" may be ascribed to each behavior in terms of the next highest level of complexity at which that behavior may occur.

On the other hand, the major purpose of this presentation is less an attempt to develop a model for behavior than to sketch an ordered way in which assessment of the older person can take place. Thus, the primarily descriptive approach suggested here may prove to be of some use to the later development of a more sophisticated theory of behavior.

While one could map how one might measure competence at each of the possible levels of organization of the human system, the aim in this discussion is to elaborate the manner in which competence may be measured at the levels which are of interest to the behavioral scientist and social gerontologist. Beginning at the level following Gerard's level of organ function, one may distinguish within the "individual" level a series of sublevels in roughly ascending order of complexity of function:

1. Life maintenance
2. Functional health
3. Perception and cognition
4. Physical self-maintenance
5. Instrumental self-maintenance
6. Effectance
7. Social role performance

Such an attempt to rank human characteristics takes all the usual risks of oversimplification and error. The sublevels vary greatly in the range of complexity of possible behavior within each. Nevertheless, in general, it would appear that as one goes from the functional health to the social role sublevel, 1) increasingly more complex perceptions, cognitions, judgments and finely discriminated behaviors are required for competence at each succeeding sublevel, and 2) an impairment at any given sublevel is more likely to imply impairment at the sublevels above it than at the sublevels below it. Further, within any sublevel statistical criteria of competence may be applied.

A set of ideal measures of competence would possess the following characteristics:

(a) All possible sublevels of organization within the "individual" level, in Gerard's terms, would be represented;

(b) Competence at each sublevel would be operationally defined;

(c) Each sublevel would be distinguished conceptually and operationally from each other sublevel;

(d) The range of discrimination within each sublevel would be wide enough to encompass every degree of competence or incompetence, though the content of the measures could vary through the range. Measures need particularly to be developed to discriminate among degress of excellence; and

(e) Ideal scaling should allow the assessment of both normative and teleological competence. In practice, a compromise between normative and teleological criteria would permit an individual to be classified according to the highest sublevel at which his competence was average, or to be represented by a profile showing his competence at each sublevel. Much work in gerontology has been directed toward measuring competence at these various sublevels.

The remainder of this paper will attempt to specify goals appropriate to each sublevel of competence, review some measures of competence at different sublevels, and briefly describe some measures that are being developed at the Philadelphia Geriatric Center to fill gaps in the spectrum of measurement techniques.

Figure 1 is an attempt to portray schematically the relationship of the individual sublevels to each other. Their hierarchical relationships are indicated primarily by the stepwise lowest positions of the sublevels, though there is some tendency for the "midpoint" of each sublevel to be higher than the one preceding it in the hierarchy. The behaviors within each sublevel are representative, rather than exhaustive, listings. Their positions with respect to other representative behaviors within the same sublevel are at best approximate. In addition to the pictured overlap in complexity between sublevels, a similar overlap in complex-

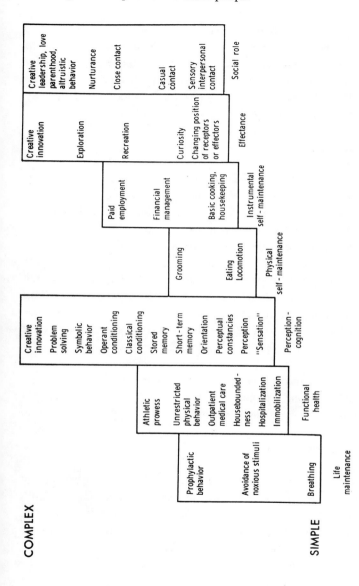

Fig. 1. Schematic diagram of sublevels of individual organization.

ity among behaviors within a sublevel is implicit in the model. The varying heights of the bars representing the sublevels are an attempt to specify roughly the unequal ranges of possible variation in complexity of behavior in the different sublevels. Finally, attention should be called to the fact that there is no sublevel whose behavioral complexity does not overlap at least partially every other sublevel.

1. Life maintenance

Behaviors which keep a person alive are relatively few: eating, sleeping, eliminating, breathing, avoiding noxious stimuli, seeking lifesaving objects. Failure in these life-maintaining behaviors signals death, or is taken as the criterion for legal incompetence. No attempt has been made to scale this type of activity, though it is clear that a continuum of competence, rather than a dichotomy, best describes the reality. Breathing is perhaps the most basic, while sleeping, eating and elimination occupy an intermediate position. The avoidance of noxious stimuli has simple and complex aspects, and the seeking of lifesaving objects such as going to a doctor when one is ill or taking active prophylactic measures (giving up smoking) are the most genetically advanced forms of life-maintenance behavior. Scaling would be useful primarily at the lowest end of this continuum, for instance where differentiation among a group of chronic brain syndrome or regressed schizophrenic patients would be desired.

2. Functional health

Medical competence as represented by the presence or absence of diagnosed diseases properly belongs in the next lowest of Gerard's levels, that is, the body organ or body system level. On the individual level, however, some behavioral consequences of diagnosed disease states may be immobilization, confinement to bed, hospitalization, surgery, taking medicine, or seeking regular medical care. Such data are relatively objective and are among the most frequently used indices of competence in functional health. These indices have among their advantages the fact that they represent only the behavioral aspect of health, rather than intermixing information on competence at several different levels. By contrast, rating scales of functional health designed by Zeman (1946), Waldman and Fryman (1964), Krauss (1963), and the Veterans Administration use competence at several levels—health behavior, self-maintenance, cognition and social behavior—as the criterion. Rosow's scale (1966) similarly uses information from several levels, though the source of his data is the subject, rather than the physician. The factorial complexity of indices of health has been explored by Lawton, Ward and Yaffe (1967). At the upper levels, endurance, robustness, and athletic prowess are representative behaviors.

3. Perception and cognition

The limitations of any attempt to place behavior in a hierarchy become particularly apparent when one considers perception and cognition. One may begin with the problematic "sensation" and go through perception to the simple task of retrieving from memory one's own name to the creation of a theory of matter. Impairment in cognitive behavior usually is reflected in behavior at all higher levels. However, the sublevels of cognitive performance are many, ranging from immediate memory to symbolic thinking and problem solving. As Figure 1 indicates, the widest possible variation occurs at this sublevel. Many of the representative behaviors listed could themselves be subdivided and hierarchically ordered.

In any case, perceptual-cognitive behavior is the most thoroughly worked level, throughout all ranges. While there is no single test that will evaluate the cognitive behavior of the elderly in a culture-free manner through all the ranges of competence, Kaplan's Grade Assessment Questionnaire (Kaplan, Rumbaugh, Mitchell, & Thomas, 1963) and Kahn, Pollack & Goldfarb's Mental Status Questionnaire (1961) are simple tests of orientation, memory, and basic information which differentiate among very low levels of functioning.

Kastenbaum (In press) has suggested schema whereby the cognitive aspects of any test, whether it is primarily a cognitive test or not, can be evaluated in hierarchical fashion. Beginning at the most primitive level, the test response may be scored according to whether it occurs in any relationship with basic dimensions of time, place, and person ("concrete orientation"). The next higher aspect is "testability"— whether the subject can recognize the test as a test and play the game in at least a minimal way. Third is the "quantitative score" aspect, where norms or other scoring methods are used in the traditional psychometric way. Finally there are the "open system functions," where the use of organizing effort, creativity, and high level abstractions may be scored. His approach thus deals with a wide range of cognitive competence and utilizes both teleologic and normative criteria.

Birren (1959) and Botwinick (1967) have treated perception and cognition in their deserved detail.

4. Physical self-maintenance

Physical self-maintenance is the name given by the Langley-Porter group (Lowenthal, 1964) to a Guttman-scaled set of observer ratings of competence in the activities of dressing, grooming, eating, bathing, locomotion, and toileting. Katz *et al.* (1963) have devised a very similar scale. Table 1 shows an adaptation of the Langley-Porter scale used at the author's institution. Dichotomization points are shown by dash lines between points on each scale, while criteria for scalogram analysis are shown in the left- and right-hand columns. This scale has the advantage for communication of having a series of five-point subscales. These activities are motoric behaviors which are genetically early, relate exclusively to the body, and are apt to regress only when impairment at higher levels is gross. This level of behavior appears relatively easy to evaluate, at least in the gross terms of the above rating scales. More refined measures may be necessary for purposes of evaluating change over time, or in response to treatment. It is of interest that even this kind of gross behavior rating scale required rescaling in order to

TABLE 1: Physical self-maintenance *

Mentally impaired				Applicants to home		
Score	%+	% error		Score	%+	% error
			A. Toilet			
			1. Cares for self at toilet completely, no incontinence.	+	89	3
+	70	10	2. Needs to be reminded or needs help in cleaning self, or has rare (weekly at most) accidents.			
			3. Soiling or wetting while asleep more than once a week.			
			4. Soiling or wetting while awake more than once a week.			
			5. No control of bowels or bladder.			
+	58	10	B. Feeding	+	92	6
			1. Eats without assistance.			
			2. Eats with minor assistance at meal times and/or with special preparation of food, or help in cleaning up after meals.			
			3. Feeds self with moderate assistance and is untidy.			
			4. Requires extensive assistance for all meals.			
			5. Does not feed self at all and resists efforts of others to feed him.			
			C. Dressing			
			1. Dresses, undresses, and selects clothes from own wardrobe.	+	78	3
			2. Dresses and undresses self, with minor assistance.			
+	78	0	3. Needs moderate assistance in dressing or selection of clothes.			
			4. Needs major assistance in dressing, but cooperates with efforts of others to help.			
			5. Completely unable to dress self and resists efforts of others to help.			

TABLE 1: Physical self-maintenance (continued)

Mentally impaired				Applicants to home		
Score	%+	% error		Score	%+	% error
			D. Grooming (neatness, hair, nails, hands, face, clothing.)			
			1. Always neatly dressed, well-groomed, without assistance.	+	75	8
+	37	8	2. Grooms self adequately with occasional minor assistance, e.g., shaving.			
			3. Needs moderate and regular assistance or supervision in grooming.			
			4. Needs total grooming care, but can remain well-groomed after help from others.			
			5. Actively negates all efforts of others to maintain grooming.			
			E. Physical Ambulation	+	42	3
			1. Goes about grounds or city.			
			2. Ambulates within residence or about one block distant.			
does not scale			3. Ambulates with assistance of (check one) a ( ) another person; b ( ) railing; c ( ) cane; d ( ) walker; e ( ) wheel chair			
			1 ( ) gets in and out without help.			
			2 ( ) needs help in getting in and out.			
			4. Sits unsupported in chair or wheelchair, but cannot propel self without help.			
			5. Bedridden more than half the time.			
			F. Bathing	+	53	6
			1. Bathes self (tub, shower, sponge bath) without help.			
+	29	10	2. Bathes self with help in getting in and out of tub.			
			3. Washes face and hands only, but cannot bathe rest of body.			
			4. Cannot___Will not _____wash self, but is cooperative with those who bathe him.			

5. Cannot___ Will not___try to
    wash self, and resists efforts to
    keep him clean.

Rep. = .93   Rep. = .93
n = 39   n = 36

*Adapted by M. P. Lawton and Elaine Brody from the Langley-Porter scale in M.
Lowenthal, *Lives in Distress*, 1964).

discriminate among mentally-impaired aged (left-hand column) as
compared with the healthier applicants to a home for aged (right-hand
column).

5. Instrumental self-maintenance

"Instrumental activities of daily living" are what Brody and Lawton
(unpublished) have termed a group of behaviors that are more complex
and less directly body-oriented than physical self-maintenance: using
the telephone, using public transportation, cooking, doing laundry,
cleaning the house, taking medicine, handling money, and shopping. A
preliminary version of the scale, designed for observer rating, is shown
in Table 2. For thirty-five female applicants to a home for aged and

TABLE 2:   Instrumental activities of daily living

Score	%+	% error	
			A. Ability to use telephone
			1. Operates telephone on own initiative—looks up and dials numbers, etc.
+	75	2	2. Dials a few memorized numbers.
			3. Answers telephone but does not dial
			4. Does not use telephone at all.
			B. Shopping
			1. Shops alone and returns home independently
+	44	15	with purchases.
			2. Needs to be accompanied on shopping trip.
			3. Completely unable to shop.
			C. Food preparation
			1. Plans, prepares, and serves adequate meals
+	35	2	independently.
			2. Prepares adequate meals if supplied with ingredients.

TABLE 2:   Instrumental activities of daily living (continued)

Score	%+	% error
			3. Heats and serves prepared meals, or prepares meals but does not maintain adequate diet. 4. Needs to have meals prepared and served.

D. Housekeeping
1. Maintains house alone or with occasional assistance (*e.g.*, "heavy work—domestic help").

Score	%+	% error
+	31	2

2. Performs light daily tasks such as dish-washing, bed-making.
3. Performs light daily tasks but cannot maintain acceptable level of cleanliness.
4. Needs help with all home maintenance tasks.
5. Does not participate in any housekeeping tasks.

E. Laundry
1. Does personal laundry completely.
2. Launders small items—rinses socks, stockings, etc.

Score	%+	% error
+	56	11

3. All laundry done by others.

F. Public transportation
1. Travels independently on public transportation.
2. Travels on public transportation on certain routes only.

Score	%+	% error
+	19	6

3. Use of public transportation limited to taxi cabs.
4. Travels only when accompanied by another.
5. Cannot travel on public transportation.

G. Responsibility for own medications
1. Is responsible for taking medication in correct dosage at correct time.

Score	%+	% error
+	54	8

2. Takes responsibility if medication is prepared in advance in separate dosages.
3. Is not capable of dispensing own medication.

H. Ability to handle finances
1. Manages financial matters independently (budgets, writes checks, pays rent, bills, goes to bank), collects and keeps track of income.

Score	%+	% error
+	77	8

2. Manages day-to-day purchases, but needs help with banking, major purchases, etc.
3. Incapable of handling money.

Rep = .94; n = 48

thirteen aged female clients of a family agency, criteria for Guttman scaling are met as shown in the left-hand column. A comparable instrument for the assessment of instrumental competence from self-report information gained from eighty-five female tenants of an apartment building for the elderly is shown in Table 3. These scales just

TABLE 3:   Philadelphia Geriatric Center instrumental role
            maintenance scale

	Score	%+	% error
A. How often do you cook a meal other than breakfast? (Lunch and dinner served in congregate dining room) 1. Twice a week or more 2. Once a week 3. Two or three times a month 4. Once a month 5. Less than once a month	+	12	5
6. Not at all			
B. How often do you go to a store to shop? 1. Five times a week or more 2. Two to four times a week	+	28	2
3. Once a week 4. Two or three times a month 5. Once a month 6. Less than once a month			
C. Where have you shopped in the last two months 0. Not at all 1. York House Store	+	64	1
2. Local neighborhood 4. Downtown, center city 8. Elsewhere (out of local area)			
D. How do you do most of your laundry? 1. Wash by hand, self 2. Wash in washer, self	+	72	10
3. Send it out 4. Done by other than subject			

Reproducibility = .94; n = 72

begin the process of conceptual differentiation and operational definition of the instrumental behavior of older people. A glaring omission is
the evaluation of competence in paid employment, and the determina-
tion of whether it belongs on the same continuum as other nonoccupa-
tional instrumental behaviors. The instrumental self-maintenance behaviors shown in Tables 2 and 3 are clearly feminine; sex-appropriate
instrumental role behavior for men is much more difficult to
specify.

6. Effectance

"Effectance" was defined by White (1959) as "what the neuromuscu-
lar system wants to do when otherwise unoccupied or gently stimulated
by the environment." Effectance is the motivation behind human needs
to create tension, to explore, to vary the psychoenvironmental field.
The richness of this concept has been demonstrated in the works of
Berlyne (1960) and Fiske and Maddi (1961). In accordance with our
focus on the behavioral definition of competence, effectance will be
used in this discussion to refer to *behavior* directed toward the creation
of tension, rather than in White's original motivational sense. The
behaviors classed under the term effectance are those requiring the
expenditure of some energy beyond physical and instrumental self-
maintenance and gainful employment, but not including behavior
whose primary function is social. Hobbies and recreational activities are
easy to count, as in the Activity section of "Your Activities and
Attitudes" of Cavan, *et al.,* (1949), and some sections of the Role
Activity ratings of Havighurst and Albrecht (1953). However, these
listings of memberships, group activity, and hobbies are an index of
effectance only for small segments of the total aged society. The
incorporation of a measure of the richness of the environmental

opportunities into the measurement of competence in this area would be one way of making such a measure less culture-bound. The upper reaches of the effectance sublevel are very apparent in the achievements of the sixteenth-century explorer, the astronaut, and the composer of Falstaff, but so far they have defied scaling. In any case, further development of measures of effectance is needed.

7. Social role

Social role competence has received much attention. Amount of social interaction is relatively easy to measure, and ratings of adequacy of role performance have been reliably made by a number of workers. Havighurst and Albrecht (1953), for example, verbally defined levels of adequacy in roles such as those of spouse, grandparent, parent, kinship group, informal social group, etc., and found social competence so measured to be related to variables such as happiness. The full range of social-role competence has not been covered, however, either at the upper or the lower end. At the low end, Main and Bennett (this book, Chapter 13) addressed themselves to the task of measuring "greeting behavior"—that is, the extent and appropriateness of a very few responses to the interviewer given by an applicant to the home for the

TABLE 4: Philadelphia Geriatric Center Minimal Social Behavior Scale

	Guttman scale*		
	Score	%+	% error
1. E goes to S and introduces himself: "I am _____ , Mr. _____ . I'm glad to meet you," extending hand.			
1) Score + if any noticeable response to greeting.			
2) Score + if response is verbal and appropriate.			
* 3) Score + if S offers hand to E.	+	84	8

TABLE 4:   Philadelphia Geriatric Center minimal social behavior scale (continued)

	Guttman scale*		
	Score	% +	% error

2 4. E says either (a) "Won't you have a seat?" or (b) "May I sit with you for a while?" depending on whether S is brought to E or E comes to S.
    4) Score + if (a) S sits without urging or (b) S assents or acknowledges E's comment.

3 5. E says "How are you today?"
    5) Score + if any noticeable response to question.
  * 6) Score + if response is verbal and appropriate.   +   70   8

4 7. E drops pencil by pushing it off desk, ostensibly by accident. If S does not pick up pencil spontaneously, E says "Would you pick up the pencil for me?"
    7) Score + if S picks up pencil at all.
    8) Score + if S picks up pencil spontaneously.

  9. E says, "I have something I want to show you." E holds in front of S Figure A of the Bender-Gestalt.
    9) Score + if S looks at Bender Card.

  10. "Here is a pencil." E offers it to S, puts paper in front of S and says, "I would like you to copy this drawing on this paper."
    10) Score + if S accepts pencil without further urging.
  * 11) Score + if S makes any mark on paper.   +   80   6
  * 12) Score + if S draws 1 approximate circle and 4-sided figures   +   58   6

  13. E says "How are you getting along?"
    13) Score + for any noticeable response to the question.
  * 14) Score + if the response is verbal and appropriate.   +   70   4

  15. E crumples scrap of paper, tosses it at the wastebasket or ash tray, purposely missing.
    15) Score + if S spontaneously picks up paper and deposits it in wastebasket.

*16. E says "I have a few questions I would like to ask you." (E administers questions 1-16 of Kahn-Goldfarb Mental Status Questionnaire).
    16) Score + if S makes any verbal response, irrespective of content, to all nine of questions 1-9.   +   64   4

*17. *E* places a magazine in front of *S*, busies himself
    with writing on pad while saying, "I'll be busy a
    minute."
    17) Score + if *S* turns at least one page of
        magazine.   +   30   8
18. *E* rises and extends hand saying, "Thank you very
    much, Mr(s). _____ ."
    18) Score + if *S* acknowledges *E*'s departure either
        verbally or with a gesture.

The remainder of the items are based on *E*'s judgment
of the behavior of the patient throughout the
interview:

    19) Score + unless inappropriate grimaces or
        mannerisms are readily apparent.
    20) Score + if the patient at any time looks *E* in
        the eye.
    21) Score + unless *S* obviously appears to avoid *E*'s
        gaze at all times, or stares at *E* fixedly.
    22) Score + unless *S* sits in a bizarre position or is
        in constant motion or is nearly motionless.
    23) Score + unless *S*'s clothes are obviously
        disarranged, unbuttoned, or misbuttoned.
   *24) Score + unless *S* is drooling or nasal mucus is
        visible or food deposits are conspicuous on
        clothes or face.   +   44   6
    25) Score + unless *S* attempts to move away from
        E before termination of interview without
        explanation.

Reproducibility = .94; n = 52

---

*Starred items are those that form an 8-item Guttman Scale.
Adapted by Lawton from A. Farina, D. Arenberg and S. Guskin. A scale for
measuring minimal social behavior. *Journal of Consulting Psychology*. 1957, *21*.

aged. This simple index has shown promise in predicting some aspects
of social adjustment to the institution. Farina, Arenberg, and Guskin
(1957) constructed a similar but somewhat more formalized scale for
measuring "minimal social behavior" among chronic psychotics. The
author adapted this scale for use with an elderly population, as in Table
4 (Lawton, 1966). The starred items, scored as indicated in the

right-hand column, formed a Guttman scale of minimal social behavior for fifty-two schizophrenics. The scale could probably be extended somewhat further downward to differentiate social behavior at the most vegetative level.

Some Practical Considerations in the Assessment of Competence

1. The behavior to be measured may be scrutinized in a variety of ways. The process of dressing, for example, may be directly observed by a psychologist, attendant, or a family member. It may also be reported by the subject himself; thus, questions like, "Did anyone help you to dress this morning?" or "Which of these (dressing operations) has anyone helped you with this week?" serve to operationalize the basis for the subject's self-rating of this aspect of daily living, though they risk the usual distortion of self-report.

The behavior may occur more than one step away from the ultimate consumer of the data, as in the case of archival records such as spontaneous nurse's notes commenting on the subject's dressing behavior. Further, physical "traces" of behavior (Webb, Campbell, Schwartz, & Sechrest, 1966) may be available long after the behavior has taken place, as in the instance where competence in eating is rated on the basis of the amount of food observed to have been spilled on clothes when they are collected at the end of the day.

2. The behavior to be measured may be natural, contrived, or some combination of the two. Naturalistic observation is traditionally contrasted with the preferred standardized psychological test situation which reduces the error of measurement somewhat. However, quasi-naturalistic methods are possible in which the behavior to be judged is functional and imbedded into an apparently unstructured situation, as in Main and Bennett's greeting behavior scale or the Minimal Social Behavior Scale.

3. The behavior to be measured should be relevant to the subject's

behavioral milieu. A recurrent problem in gerontological research is the use of instruments standardized on groups in environments other than those in which the geriatric population is likely to be found. The nonoccurrence of a behavior may be irrelevant to the older subject's competence in other areas because of constraints placed by the environment on that behavior. For example, in some institutional settings, dressing or feeding is routinely done by personnel because it is deemed easier than allowing the subject to do it himself. Competence in dressing oneself could not be appropriately measured in that setting unless a performance test of dressing could be contrived. Even in that event, a given degree of achievement in dressing would represent the overcoming of greater environmental inertia than the same achievement would in a person whose environment facilitated daily practice in dressing.

4. The range of behavior measured should be relevant to the subject population's range of capacities. When a measure devised for one population is used on an aged population, or one devised for one particular aged group is used on another, any of several negative effects on measurement may occur. First, if it is a contrived, testlike stimulus situation, the content of the stimulus may be so totally out of the range of experience of the individual that effective measurement is impossible: "Kinderspiel," said the aged clothing-cutter as he pushed away the pieces of the manikin object assembly test. Or, the behavior to be measured may be so culture-bound that it occurs only in certain subpopulations. Finally, the behavior manifested may be out of the quantitative range of the measuring instrument. Old people who are functioning at so high a level as to be able to maintain themselves in paid employment are not likely to be differentiated by a scale which measures adequacy of physical self-maintenance.

The need to tailor the measuring instrument so closely to both environmental opportunities and to the range of capacity of the older person has resulted in a tendency for each investigator to construct an instrument specific to his purpose. Thus, at the author's institution we have a scale of "Reaction to the Friday Kiddush Cart," devised with full knowledge of the ridiculousness of the idea of inferring anything at all about most people with this information. Yet, with the severely mentally-impaired aged Jewish residents of that ward this behavior is one of the few whose range of variation is wide enough to give some differentiation in terms of social competence. This failure to devise instruments of wide applicability may be a necessary early stage in the development of measurement in behavioral gerontology. It also may reflect some difficulty in achieving consensus on what tasks are relevant to the competence of old people. The fact is, however, that diveristy seems to be the order of the day, and at present the investigator would seem to be better employed evaluating his own subjects relevantly and accurately than in using better standardized instruments which may be less relevant and discriminating. Behavioral taxonomy is a laborious process, but it must precede genotypic measurement.

In summary, this paper has suggested that competence may be assessed at a variety of levels of human functioning, the levels being roughly differentiated from one another on the basis of the complexity of the demands made by behavior at each level on neurobehavioral integrating mechanisms. Advantages are seen in developing measures which will discriminate among all degress of competence, which will include environmental as well as individual factors, and which will measure competence at a single level independently of competence at other levels. While complexity is thus a major criterion for competence, a normative criterion is also necessary to set the limits of competence.

REFERENCES

Berlyne, D. E. Conflict, arousal and curiosity. New York: McGraw-Hill, 1960.

Birren, J. E. (Ed.) Handbook of aging and the individual. Chicago: University of Chicago Press, 1959.

Botwinick, J. Cognitive processes in maturity and old age. New York: Springer, 1967.

Cavan, R., Burgess, E. W., Havighurst, R. W., & Goldhamer, H. Personal adjustment in old age. Chicago: Science Research Associates, 1949.

Farina, A., Arenberg, D., & Guskin, S. A scale for measuring minimal social behavior. *Journal of Consulting Psychology,* 1957, *21,* 265-268.

Fiske, D. W., & Maddi, S. (Eds.) *The functions of varied experience.* Homewood, Ill.: Dorsey, 1961.

Gerard, R. Aging and levels of organization. In J. Birren (Ed.), *Handbook of aging and the individual.* Chicago: University of Chicago Press, 1959.

Havighurst, S., & Albrecht, R. *Older people.* New York: Longmans, Green, 1953.

Jahoda, M. *Current concepts of positive mental health.* New York: Basic Books, 1958.

Kahn, R., Pollack, M., & Goldfarb, A. Factors related to individual differences in mental status of institutionalized aged. In P. Hoch, & J. Zubin (Eds.), *Psychopathology of aging.* New York: Grune and Stratton, 1961.

Kaplan, O. J., Rumbaugh, D. M., Mitchell, D., & Thomas, E. D. Effects of level of surviving abilities, time of day, and test-retest upon psychological performance in seniles. *Journal of Gerontology,* 1963, *18,* 55-59.

Kastenbaum, R. *Gerontology: A psychosocial approach.* New York: Free Press, in press.

Katz, S., Ford, A. B., Moskowitz, R. W., Jackson, B., & Jaffe, M. Studies of illness in the aged—the index of ADL. *Journal of the American Medical Association,* 1963, *185,* (12), 94-99.

Krauss, T. C. Use of a comprehensive rating scale system in the institutional care of geriatric patients. *Journal of the American Geriatric Society, 1963, 10,* 95-103.

Lawton, M. P. Schizophrenia forty-five years later. Paper presented at the meeting of the American Psychological Association, New York, September 1966.

Lawton, M. P., Ward, M. W., & Yaffe, S. Indices of health in an aging population. *Journal of Gerontology,* 1967, *22,* 334-342.

Lowenthal, M. F. *Lives in distress.* New York: Basic Books, 1964.

Rosow, I. A Guttman health scale for the aged. *Journal of Gerontology,* 1966, *21,* 556-559.

Waldman, A., & Fryman, E. Classification of residents. In M. Leeds, & H. Shore (Eds.), *Geriatric institutional management.* New York: Putnam, 1964.

Webb, E. J., Campbell, D. T., Schwartz, R. D., & Sechrest, L. *Unobstrusive measures: Non-reactive research in the social sciences.* Chicago: Rand McNally, 1966.

White, R. W. Motivation reconsidered: The concept of competence. *Psychological Review,* 1959, *66,* 297-333.

Zeman, F. D. The functional capacity of the aged: Its estimation and practical importance. *Journal of the Mount Sinai Hospital,* 1946, *14,* 721-729.

11:: THE DIMENSIONS OF MORALE

M. POWELL LAWTON

A number of attempts have been made in gerontoiogical literature to define adjustment and morale in the aged person. Havighurst (1963), Cumming & Henry (1961) and Rosow (1963), among others, have reviewed morale's varied aspects preparatory to defining it in their own terms. This article will not attempt to cover this literature exhaustively. Rather, it will report on an attempt to measure morale in very old institutional residents, and in closing it will shed further light on definition of the term.

Some measures of morale assume unidimensionality (Kutner, Fanshel, Togo, & Langner, 1956). The present study was begun with the notion that morale is a multidimensional concept which should be measured accordingly. Factor analytic methods were judged most appropriate to this aim.

Some of the qualities which other workers have linked to morale are:

a. Absence of psychiatric symptoms; b. Optimistic ideology (Srole,

Part of this article was presented to the annual meeting of the Gerontological Society in New York, November 4, 1966. This study was partially supported by Grants MH-11053 and MHO2329 from the National Institute of Mental Health. Thanks are due Dr. Walter Harrison, Superintendent, and the staff members of the Lutheran Home for their invaluable assistance in providing subjects and criterion judgments. Staff members of the Philadelphia Geriatric Center also gave freely of their time for this project: Maurice Greenbaum, Silvia Yaffe, Hilda Salomon and Mark Shapiro. Finally, staff members of the Philadelphia Center for Older People and its director, Jean Hanson Fisher, were most helpful in providing subjects for the reliability study.

1956; Kutner et al., 1956; Cumming & Henry, 1961); c. Acceptance of status quo (Cumming & Henry, 1961); d. Lack of self-perceived negative change (Rosow, 1963; Perlin & Butler, 1963); e. Rejection of stereotypes about the aged (Oberleder, 1962); and f. Positive evaluation of the environment (Bennett & Nahemow, 1965; Dick & Friedsam, 1964; Taietz, 1953).

In addition to any attempt to sort out the components of morale, this study sought to construct a scale which would be an appropriate measure of morale among the very old. Most attempts to scale morale in the aged have used as subjects people with mean ages in the sixties (Kutner, et al., 1956; Cumming & Henry, 1961). Our own clinical experience indicated that the structure of test items written for the general adult population was frequently unsuited to people in the 70-90 age range. Experimental evidence suggests that the rate of information processing declines greatly with age. Indeed, the suggestion was made (Lindsley, 1964) that social inattention in very old people may be due to their difficulty in keeping up with the rate of information input of normal conversation. At any rate, verbally-presented questions of the usual type with multiple clauses, several response alternatives, and sometimes difficult vocabulary were often so complex as to preclude adequate response reliability. Tests which may be administered only in written form may have some of these same drawbacks, as well as offering difficulty to people with visual and language defects.

Therefore, it became obvious that many changes were required in the phrasing of questions from previously used scales, and in their response format, in order to make the questions comprehensible to the very old subjects. Precision achieved in testing younger groups through the use of sophisticated questions and multiple response alternatives had to be sacrificed in favor of the reliability gained in the very old group by making their task simpler.

The ideal length of scales is not only a function of the psychometric characteristics which are desired but also is a function of the subject group for whom the scale is designed. Scales such as the MMPI seem inappropriately long for an aged subject. On the other hand, the inherently low reliability of very short scales makes a substitute for some of the most frequently used morale scales seem desirable.

Thus, reasons for seeking another measure of morale are:

1) The need for a multidimensional definition of morale; 2) The need for a scale appropriate for the very old; and 3) The need for a scale of such length as to afford reasonable reliability while at the same time not causing undue fatigue or inattention.

Method

Choice of items

In early versions of the questionnaire, fifty items were written or taken from existing scales to represent the content areas which, on an *a priori* basis, were thought to be related to morale. Frequent rewording and changes in response format were made. After two item analyses of early versions, the form of the questionnaire which was finally used in the scale construction consisted of forty-one items, all but three having a simple dichotomous response alternative.

Subjects

Two groups of *S*s were used in the standardization sample:

a. York House sample. York House is an apartment dwelling for the relatively independent aged person, one of the constituents of the Philadelphia Geriatric Center. Of the 250 tenants, 208 were able to be found during the daytime and were willing to take the test. The mean age of this group was 77.9, and consisted of 70 men and 138 women; all were Jewish.

b. Lutheran Home sample. The name of every second aged resident of the Lutheran Home for Orphans and Aged, excluding those who were too ill physically, was chosen, and these people were asked to be present for the testing. Of the 110 so chosen, 92 took the test, 10 of them being male and 82 female. Their mean age was 78.8.

Test conditions

The items were phrased so that they could be responded to relatively easily whether the test was administered in written or in oral form. For the most part, testing was done in small groups of ten to fifteen subjects, though even under this condition, items frequently had to be read or explained by proctors. All other tests were administered orally and individually by psychologists. A Yiddish translation was used in the few instances where the subject preferred this language. The comparability of the two forms was not tested.

Criterion development

Since two populations were to be used, the Q-sort form was chosen in which to express criterion judgments, inasmuch as analysis of preliminary form scores indicated no difference in mean score between the two populations. However, the same sources of criterion judgments were not available in the two institutions.

In York House, 107 of the Ss were known to a staff member who was conducting another project on health maintenance. While this staff member is a psychologist, her contact with the tenants consisted mainly of informal observations and friendly conversations during the course of her work in arranging medical examinations and taking of histories. Thus, the basis for her judgments was not an "inner," but largely an "outer" standard, in Havighurst's (1963) terms. The only possible check in inter-rater reliability for this group was the judgment of a York House nurse who knew the tenants as a part of her work in the doctor's office and the health maintenance project. The difference in professional outlook between the two judges constituted a problem which was compensated for by giving to the judge the following discussion of morale:

Since morale is not easily defined, it may be useful to consider some of the things that morale *is* and some of the things that are less central to the idea of morale.

1. High morale means, first, a basic sense of satisfaction with oneself. The person of high morale has a feeling of having attained something in his life, of being useful now, and thinks of himself as an adequate person. There may be some who appear to have an inflated view of themselves—if this is a genuine feeling it would count in the direction of high morale. It if is a cover for more negative feelings about the self, it is not considered evidence of high morale.

2. High morale also means a feeling that there is a place in the environment for oneself—that the people and things in one's life offer some satisfaction to the individual—a fit between personal needs and what the environment offers. Thus, a person who does whatever he does with zest shows that he is responding in some way to what is outside himself. A person who struggles for mastery, whether successfully or not, feels that the setting within which he lives is worth struggling with. A person who enjoys solitude finds something in the environment to meet his needs.

3. High morale also means a certain acceptance of what cannot be changed. Some people like being old, and others do not, but those of high morale see old age in both its positive and negative aspects, and deal with it with zest and fortitude, but not in an unrealistic manner.

Many people who are of high morale are also: content with the institution, active, sociable, conforming in group living, and optimistic in outlook.

However, the above are not necessary components of high morale. One can imagine people who are inactive, solitary, nonconforming, or pessimistic in philosophy of life still having a basic positive self-regard, maintaining the struggle for mastery, and accepting reality. Also, while complaining is a frequent sign of low morale, it should not be viewed as necessarily so.

Psychiatric symptoms, such as depression, fear, paranoid suspiciousness, or childish temper are usually considered signs of low morale. However, signs of organic impairment such as loss of memory, poor orientation, or poor judgment should not be considered as indicating low morale unless they are accompanied by the other signs of low morale discussed above.

These observers were asked to arrange the 107 Ss in an eight-step Q-sort array according to their judgments of their morale.

The product-moment r between the psychologist's and the nurse's independent Q-sort judgments was .45, which was raised to .68 following consultation. Finally, the psychologist's revised judgments were used as the criterion for the York House group.

For the Lutheran Home group, criterion judgments using the same definition of morale were sought from the superintendent, chaplain, two social workers, two nurses and three matrons. Ratings were made initially on a five-point rating scale, with each judge rating only those residents whom he knew well. A meeting of judges was then held in which disagreements in ratings were discussed for each individual resident. Following this meeting, each judge performed an eight-point Q-sort of the residents with whom he was familiar. The Q-sort ratings of the judge with the highest average inter-judge correlation (.52) were then used as the criterion. This judge knew and ranked all 93 Ss.

Various attempts to increase the inter-judge reliability of both samples by redefinition of morale and by changing the mechanics of making the ratings were unsuccessful. Short of changing the basis for judgment from an exterior to an interior one by having psychologists make ratings following depth interviews, it would seem that the limit of inter-judge reliability was reached by this method. While these reliability estimates are low by usual standards, they are comparable to results obtained by others, such as Carp (1967), who have obtained ratings on adjustment from people of different occupations observing older people in a group living situation.

Since there was no mean difference in total morale score between the two subject groups, the two separately-done Q sorts were combined into a criterion population of 199 Ss with morale ranks ranging from one through eight in a forced normal distribution.

Results

The first forty-one item version of the morale scale correlated .47 with the criterion rankings. An item analysis rejected fourteen of the items whose relationship to the criterion (χ^2) was not significant at the .10 level. The intercorrelation matrix (ϕ coefficients) of the twenty-seven remaining items for the entire sample of three hundred Ss was factored by the centroid method and five more items whose communalities were less than .20 were removed. The remaining twenty-two items then formed the final version of the morale scale.

Reliability

The reliability of the scale was estimated in terms of internal consistency and test-retest correlation. The items were divided into two subsets by an *a priori* process of matching content. This procedure was deemed desirable because of the deliberate intent in choice of items to represent separate content domains; therefore, rough content matching was preferred to the odd-even technique. The Pearsonian *r* between test halves divided in this manner was .74, corrected to .79 by the Spearman-Brown formula (N = 300). The coefficient of internal consistency (Kuder-Richardson formula 21) was .81.

Test-retest reliability, being a function of the type of subject used, was tested on several groups. Twenty-five Ss from the York House group were retested three months following the initial administration of the scale. The Pearsonian *r* between scores on these two occasions was .75. Another group of fourteen Lutheran Home residents completed the scale again five weeks following the first administration. The *r* between testing occasions for this group was .91. Finally, twenty-five subjects from an adult education class in a day center for older people were given the morale scale on two occasions, approximately one week apart, resulting in a correlation of .80 between total scores on the two occasions.

Validity

Removal of the items which did not contribute to the validity of the scale did not change the correlation with the criterion appreciably, the twenty-two-item scale still having a correlation of .47 with the criterion (N = 199).

The validity coefficient for the York House group (r = .43), was significantly lower than that for the Lutheran Home group (r = .53). The mean morale scale score of the one hundred Ss from both samples judged to be above average in morale was 16.54 (S.D. = 4.02). The ninety-nine Ss from both samples who were judged to be below average in morale obtained a mean morale score of 12.75 (S.D. = 4.64). The difference between these two means is associated with a critical ratio of 6.12 (p < .001.

Cross-validation

The Morale Scale was administered to a group of York House South tenants three months following occupancy. Each of these tenants was interviewed for one-half to one hour in order to learn more about his past interests, activities, social contacts, and his present evaluations of York House South. On the basis of these interviews, the psychologist rated each S on the Life Satisfaction Rating Scale (LSR) (Neugarten, Havighurst, & Tobin, 1961) without knowledge of the S's responses to the Morale Scale or to similar questions. In addition, using the definition of morale given above, the administrator of York House South judged these Ss. Using the forty Ss on whom the psychologist and the administrator agreed in making their morale ratings, the correlation between Morale Scale scores and LSR ratings done by the psychologist was .57. Thus, rather than finding shrinkage in the process of cross-validation, the validity apparently increased. This finding may possibly be explained by the more stringent criterion measure used in the cross-validation, that is, the demand that only those cases in which inter-judge agreement is high be used in calculating the validity coefficient. If this be true, then it follows that the validity of the items in the original group may have been underestimated. This would have resulted in the discarding of some items with significant discriminating value, but also would suggest that the items having a significant criterion correlation may be better discriminators than the item analysis indicated.

Factor structure

Having gained knowledge of some of the psychometric characteristics of the scale, information was sought on the factorial structure of the items of best discriminative value.

A principal components analysis was performed on the twenty-two items of the scale using ϕ coefficients in the intercorrelation matrix. The unrotated solution indicated a general factor accounting for 22.3% of the variance, and five other factors with latent roots greater than one, the six factors accounting for 52.8% of the total variance. Inasmuch as interest was in the components of morale, orthogonal rotation was performed with the Varimax program, resulting in the factors indicated in Table 1. The relatively low communalities are one more reflection of the large amount of error variance which was seen earlier in the relatively low reliabilities and validity coefficients. The sources of this error will be discussed below.

TABLE 1: Rotated principal components analysis of Philadelphia Geriatric Center morale scale items

Item	Correct Response	I	II	III	IV	V	VI	h²
	Component I							
10. I sometimes feel that life isn't worth living.	No	40	33	35	16	22	00	46
12. Most days I have plenty to do.	No.	53	12	33	22	20	24	55

13. I have a lot to be sad about.	No	55	07	08	35	04	24	50
15. I am afraid of a lot of things.	No	73	03	08	28	06	12	64
Component II								
1. Things keep getting worse as I get older	No	-02	65	14	14	15	00	49
2. I have as much pep as I did last year	Yes	-07	70	01	-11	11	09	53
6. As you get older you are less useful	No	05	74	00	14	01	-05	57
9. As I get older, things are (better, worse, same) than/as I thought they would be	Better	33	49	30	-14	17	15	51
16. My health is (good, not so good).	Good	10	64	-01	13	07	13	46
Component III								
7. If you could live where you wanted, where would you live?	Here	-01	06	54	-14	18	40	51
14. People had it better in the old days.	No	04	-07	81	14	-13	-03	70
Component IV								
4. Little things bother me more this year.	No	15	36	19	54	06	10	49
8. I sometimes worry so much that I can't sleep.	No	31	20	00	55	13	13	47
17. I get mad more than I used to.	No	07	20	19	57	10	-11	43
20. I take things hard.	No	10	15	-06	71	10	18	59
23. I get upset easily.	No	02	-04	-03	71	-09	08	52
Component V								
11. I am happy now as I was when I was younger.	Yes	00	33	04	12	53	31	50
18. Life is hard for me most of the time.	No	33	29	12	33	39	08	46
21. A person has to live for today and not worry about tomorrow.	Yes	03	-08	-02	01	85	-05	74
Component VI								
3. How much do you feel lonely? (not much, a lot).	Not much	04	09	13	27	01	65	52
5. I see enough of my friends and relatives.	Yes	04	09	-07	-02	-02	72	54
19. How satisfied are you with your life today? (not satisfied, satisfied).	Satisfied	24	-06	28	20	17	46	42
Percent of covariance account for by component		7.7	12.2	6.7	11.7	6.5	7.6	

Interpretation of the Factors

In order to be able to use factor scales which do not overlap in item content, factors were grouped as in Table 1 so that each item appears on only one factor. However, in the interpretation of the content of the factors, loadings of .30 and over are utilized, resulting in the same item sometimes appearing two or three times.

Component I, Surgency: Items on this scale describe an individual with optimistic ideology, freedom from anxiety and depression, and, in addition, a feeling of readiness to remain active or engaged, as indicated by the opposite-sign loading on item 12. Later work has suggested that item 12 (Most days I have plenty to do) correlates in the opposite direction with other measures of morale. That is, a "Yes" response is associated with high morale among people somewhat more independent than the standardization group. The obverse of this component suggests an anxious, pessimistic individual who may or may not be engaged, but who feels that his present level of activity is quite enough, with the possible implication that any attempt to increase this level would appreciably raise his general level of dysphoria. The high-scoring individual, by contrast, shows a general satisfaction except in the area of activity, where he aspires to a greater filling of time than he now finds possible.

Component II, Attitude toward own aging: This component is rather clearly marked as being related to self-perceived change or lack of change as one ages, evaluation of the quality of change, and to some extent, stereotypic attitudes. For the most part, the content of these items is highly personalized, rather than stereotyped, however. This is the strongest of the rotated components, accounting for 12.28% of the variance (Table 1).

Component III, Acceptance of status quo: Inasmuch as only two items have principal loadings on this component, inclusion of items 9, 10, and 19 is necessary to understand the content of this dimension. The high scorer would be generally satisfied with the way things are, whether this be in the area of dwelling place, level of activity, generalized evaluation of present life, or comparison with the past. The only area not occuring in this satisfaction component is the interpersonal, which appears instead in Component VI.

Component IV, Agitation: Almost all the symptoms of anxiety which were included in the scale load on this component, as well as dysphoric mood elements. However, there is a driving, restless, agitated quality to the dysphoric mood, as suggested by the short temper (item 17) and insomnia (item 8) in the content of the items. This component, accounting for 11.76% of the variance, is one of the strongest.

Component V, Easygoing optimism: This weakest of the components contains only three items with any measurable loading. It seems to have both affective and ideological aspects. In negative form, depression is implied, while its positive pole connotes a capacity for the enjoyment of immediate pleasures.

Component VI, Lonely dissatisfaction: This component has been named for its obverse, since meaning seemed easier to express in this manner. While the content of the items loading on this component also seems to suggest acceptance or dissatisfaction with things as they now are, there is very little statistical overlap with Component III (Acceptance of status quo), as seen in the fact that only one item shows any notable loading on both scales, and as will be seen later, the correlation between the components of factor scores, derived from the components analysis, is low. The occurrence of strong loadings on two interpersonal items marks this component as having a relevance to social relationships which Component III does not have. The positive direction of this component could be consistent with satisfied engagement or disengagement, depending on the actual degree of social interaction.

Factor scores

Factor scores were calculated based on the components analysis, assigning unit weight to each item, and utilizing each item only once, as indicated by the grouping in Table 1. This procedure resulted in the use of only items with loadings of .39 or higher.

Scoring of the three hundred Ss according to this scheme resulted in factor scores whose intercorrelations are shown in Table 2. These values indicate that there are, in practice, moderate interrelationships among the factors as measured by these items.

TABLE 2:   Intercorrelations among factor scores

	I	II	III	IV	V
II	37				
III	29	22			
IV	52	39	16		
V	43	36	19	36	
VI	40	21	28	34	30
Total score	75	72	44	77	58

The test-retest reliabilities of the factor scores were determined on the twenty-five York House North Ss and the Ss from the adult education class. Table 3 shows these values. It is plain that the reliabilities of individual factor scores leave much to be desired.

TABLE 3:   Test-retest reliabilities of factor scores

Group	Factors						Total score
	I	II	III	IV	V	VI	
York House	.22	.81	.32	.67	.58	.38	.75
Day Center	.81	.89	.66	.84	.44	.84	.80
Number of items	4	5	2	5	3	3	22

Relationship of Morale Scores to Other Variables

a. York House vs. Lutheran Home. Critical ratios revealed no difference in total score between the two groups ($z = 1.34$, $p > .05$). The Lutheran Home group obtained a significantly lower score on

Component V, Lonely dissatisfaction. Because of the reversal of sign in naming Component V, directions of obtained scores on Component V are reversed in discussion. Thus a low score would mean least dissatisfaction. There were no other significant differences between the two groups.

b. Male vs. female. There were no significant sex differences for either total score or factor scores.

c. Older vs. younger groups. With Ss divided into younger (75 and younger, n = 120) and older (76 and above, n = 180) ages, no significant differences were found for either total score or factor scores.

d. High vs. low criterion scores. The 199 Ss for whom criterion Q-sort rankings were done were divided into high (Q = 1-4, n = 101) and low (Q = 5-8, n = 98) groups. Comparison of the means indicated that in each case, total and factor scores of the high group are greater than those of the low group.

e. Alien sample. The PGC Morale Scale has been employed in a more recent study of housing for the elderly. Among 380 older people about to move into planned low-income or lower middle-income congregate housing, total score was not related to age, sex, or marital status. High morale was seen to be significantly correlated with the following:
- Positive expectations for the new environment
- Anticipation of new neighbors being similar to themselves
- Satisfaction with preoccupancy level of social interaction
- Perception of self as more active than age peers
- Current paid employment
- Possession of phone, TV, radio
- Engagement in activities (dining out, movies, card playing, taking rides, reading)
- Mobility with respect to building and neighborhood
- Few daytime naps
- Physical health
- Interviewer ratings of vigor, comfort, energy level

Discussion

The discussion will be focused around two topics. 1) The Philadelphia Geriatric Center (PGC) Morale Scale as a measurement device and 2) the nature of morale as a construct.

The PGC Morale Scale as a Measuring Device

The success of the PGC scale in serving the purposes for which it was designed is mixed. In general, it has been infinitely easier for the very old and foreign-born to comprehend than many existing scales. Its final length has also proved to be most suitable: it does not tire subjects, it may be read to the *S* by the *E* without fatigue to either, and it has the advantage over shorter scales of greater reliability.

The validity coefficient between the scale and the criterion is only moderate. In order to put these validity estimates in proper perspective, however, it is worthwhile to review the reported validity of other instruments in use. Some instruments (e.g., the Kutner Morale Scale, Kutner, et al, 1956) were scaled on internal criteria and later demonstrated to have concurrent validity through correlations with such attributes as physical health, self-image, etc.

In a validity study of the Chicago Attitude Inventory, very high correlations of .74 and .64 were reported between judges' ratings and scores on the Inventory (Havighurst, 1951). The Inventory itself, however, consists of both "inner" and "outer" indicators of adjustment (Havighurst, 1963). Inasmuch as judges had available to them information on the *S*'s social behavior and activity patterns, the validity was probably increased over what it might have been had judges' ratings been correlated only with the *S*'s responses to "inner" questionnaire items. Nevertheless, these are impressively high validity coefficients, obtained from a well-functioning group of community residents. Britton (1963) obtained correlations of the order of .62 between the Chicago Attitude Inventory and the Cavan Adjustment Scale in a group of community-resident people of mean age seventy-two, again a relatively high value.

In an attempt to work solely with an "inner" definition of morale, Neugarten, Havighurst, & Tobin (1961) developed the Life Satisfaction Rating (LSR) as a criterion and the Life Satisfaction Indices A and B (LSIA and LSIB) as self-report instruments. While their criterion, the LSR, was highly developed and stable, the validity coefficients of .55 and .58 reported for LSIA and LSIB, respectively, reflect the fact that responses to some of these items from previous interviews were available to the judges in the material which they used in making criterion ratings. Therefore, the validity coefficients of .39 for LSIA and .47 for LSIB which were obtained between the LSIA and the LSIB scores, respectively, and the LSR ratings of a clinician interviewing fifty-two Ss more accurately reflect truly independent criterion-test correlations.

These latter estimates of validity are of the same order as the validity coefficients of the present study. Plainly, there are gross errors of criterion and measurement, whose sources will be discussed.

The criterion problem is ever-present, beginning with the difficulty of defining for judges high and low morale, and including adequate opportunity by which to observe and judge relevant behavior and the inner processes of the individual whose morale is being judged. The criterion development of Neugarten et al. (1961) appears to be the most nearly ideal of any yet reported. Concepts of morale were established by a long process of study, mutual discussion, and work with case materials. In making the judgments, much case material was available, including longitudinal data for the standardization group and depth interviews by an experienced clinician for the independent sample. In the present study, the criterion was necessarily limited to more casual observations gained from people whose primary activity in relation to Ss was other than that of rating their morale. The criterion was improved somewhat by the use of multiple judges and averaged rankings, and in the cross-validation by use of judge agreements only.

As a general axiom, there probably is some truth in the idea that any limitation on capacity probably adds error of measurement to psychometric instruments. Thus, the fact that the standardization subjects were very old, many of them foreign-born, physically ill, and perhaps limited in capacity for abstract thought, attention, and motivation, undoubtedly increased the total amount of error variance. The generally naive phraseology of the items, and the dichotomous response format, in an attempt to correct for other sources of error, may have introduced new error by not allowing for a sufficiently wide range of response.

Finally, many authors have commented on the frequent use of denial by old people. Unpublished data of the author from a home for the aged population indicates that denial is by far the most frequently observed mental mechanism as rated from psychiatric examination. As is the case with most defense mechanisms, some people are able to make denial into a positive adjustive style, while other fail to achieve satisfactory ego integration through its use. Attempts to predict Morale Scale scores from criterion ratings with the addition of a crude classification of Ss as "deniers" and "non-deniers" failed. A more meaningful cross-classification would probably be a dimension of integrated vs. unintegrated denial.

In light of the sources of error we may now legitimately ask whether there is, in fact, any purpose served by continuing to use self-report instruments such as the PGC Morale Scale. This same question has been asked repeatedly in the history of psychological testing, yet self-report instruments have, if anything, proliferated beyond all bounds. The following considerations lead one to feel that there is need for such an instrument in spite of its disadvantages:

1. Self-report is a form of behavior, and it has correlates on overt behavioral and attitudinal levels, even though their size may be lower than one wishes.

2. Overt behavioral indices of adjustment and morale are sometimes difficult to obtain, and observers' ratings frequently have as many sources of error as do self-reports.

3. On a group basis some predictability is gained for research purposes, even though use on an individual level may not be warranted.

Accordingly, the total score of the PGC Morale Scale is seen as a predictor which has moderately satisfactory reliability, high internal consistency, and modest validity which is about equal to that shown by many frequently used instruments. It also may be used with some people who are not able to respond to the usual complex questionnaire.

Use of the factor subscales as individual scores is less easily recommended. Some of the subscales have possibly acceptable reliabilities, and do individually discriminate high and lower criterion groups. The fact remains, however, that they are short scales and not as yet demonstrably superior to other short scales in common use, such as the Kutner, the Srole, or the Cumming & Henry morale items. Further work is needed to lengthen the scales and to demonstrate factorial stability in other populations before they can be used as subscales.

THE NATURE OF MORALE

The major purpose of the study was to clarify the meaning of "adjustment" in older persons. We have called the construct "morale," following common parlance, while realizing that historical use of this term in industry and other formal organizations may be somewhat different from our use. In the definition used by the judges, the components which have been stressed are freedom from distressing symptoms, satisfaction with self, feeling of syntony between self and environment, and ability to strive appropriately while still accepting the inevitable. An effort was also made to anchor within the definition some of the characteristics which have been considered less central to morale, such as conformity, activity, or social interaction. Items representing these aspects of morale were those chosen for inclusion in the original scale.

It is of interest to note, in passing, the content of the dropped items which showed no relationship to the criterion. Five attitudinal items, phrased in the third person, whose content was related to age, showed no correlation with judged morale. While three such items did correlate with judged morale, in general one fails to find support for Oberleder's (1962) findings of a relatively high acceptance of attitudinal and "factual" stereotypes about the aged among poorly adjusted institutional residents. This finding is also in line with Lowenthal's (1965) "morale" and "attitude" items which clustered separately and with a low correlation between the two domains.

Contrary to expectation, items expressing acceptance of specific aspects of the environment (e.g., food, neighbors, current economic level) were not related to morale, with the exception of one item—the wish to live elsewhere. Finally, while experience of change in physical health and emotional state were related to judged morale, perception of decreased appetite, poorer memory, and increased tendency to lose things were not. Apparently people can be to some extent aware of mental deterioration without becoming distressed over it.

One might wish for better representation of items relating to self-perceived discontinuity of personality and for a more subtly phrased group of items evaluating the environment. However, these are the only obvious gaps in content among the items originally chosen. The results of the validity study and the factor analysis do show that there are, in fact, internally consistent and externally validated groups of self-reported responses which show separate and combined relationships to externally judged morale.

Most of the factors which resulted make good sense psychologically, and tend to support the suggestions of earlier workers about the nature of morale. Thus Components I and V appear related to the usual definitions of morale in terms of optimism, positive thinking, and a carefree attitude toward life.

Component II is most closely related to Rosow's conception of adjustment (1963): to score highly on this factor, one would have to have a high sense of continuity of the self, in physical and emotional terms. On the other hand, notable for their absence in this factor are most items expressing attitudes toward aging in general; perception of continuity, insofar as it relates to morale, is a most personal thing.

As Cumming & Henry suggest (1961), the capacity to be satisfied with the way things are seems to be related to morale, as seen in Component III, and to some extent, in Component VI. However, these components express satisfaction with the staus quo in quite general terms (Component III) or in close interpersonal terms (Component VI). The kinds of evaluations of concrete aspects of the environmental setting which for Taietz (1953), Dick & Friedsam (1964), and Bennett & Nahemow (1965) were related to various indices of adjustment, did not correlate with our criterion. The definition of morale provided for the judges may possibly have caused them to overreact against the inclusion of indicators of conformity and high satisfaction with their institutions in their ratings. Possibly, the two subject groups may have been willing to express only a very narrow range of such evaluations. In any case, in view of the repeated findings by others that the capacity to view the concrete details of one's daily life as pleasant is related to, though not necessarily the same as, good adjustment, leads one to feel that it is worthwhile attempting to improve measures of this dimension.

Finally, Component IV, instead of being called "Agitation" might well be called an "old folks' manifest anxiety scale," with its combination of dysphoric ideology and symptoms of anxiety. In many ways these items are reminiscent of the kind of item found to be most useful in the Midtown study (Srole, et al., 1962), and are not at all age-linked.

Further work needs to be done to determine the degree of overlap among these dimensions, and their stability in other populations. Certainly, the roughly approximated factor scores do not provide an adequate estimate of degree of content in common. In the unrotated factor solution, the first general factor showed loadings greater than .30 on all but four of the items. One could, if he wished, thus look upon morale as being a generalized feeling of well-being with diverse specific indicators. For many research purposes, this is sufficient, and use of the total score is indicated. On the other hand, for conceptual purposes it is clear that neurotic symptomatology is not synonomous with poor morale, and that pessimistic ideology may or may not accompany an ability to accept the status quo. Further, attitudes toward one's own aging appear to be the most independent of the dimensions (judging by its low inter-correlations with other factors plus its high reliability). Apparently, while the feeling of continued physical and personal competence as one ages is related to general morale, it is not necessarily an accompaniment to other aspects of morale.

The relationship of morale, or of any of the dimensions of morale, to overt behavior is certainly moderate at best in the same way that classical psychometric instruments which measure attitudes, ideology, or self-sentiments fail in being excellent predictors of behavior. The gerontological literature has yielded many correlations between morale and other behavior or internal states. Improvement of the present subscales should lead to the means by which better predictors of behavior could be determined, and ultimately lead to identifying some of the processes which intervene between inner state and behavior.

REFERENCES

Bennett, R., & Nahemow, L. The relations between social isolation, socialization and adjustment in residents of a home for the aged. In M. P. Lawton & F. Lawton (Eds.), *Mental impairment in the aged.* Philadelphia: Philadelphia Geriatric Center, 1965.

Britton, J. G. Dimensions of adjustment of older adults. *Journal of Gerontology,* 1963, *18,* 60-66.

Carp, F. *A future for the aged.* Austin: University of Texas Press, 1966.

Cumming, E., & Henry, W. E. *Growing old: The process of disengagement.* New York: Basic Books, 1961.

Dick, H. R., & Friedsam, H. J. The adjustment of residents in two homes for the aged. *Social Problems,* 1964, *11,* 282-290.

Havighurst, R. J. Validity of the Chicago attitude inventory as a measure of personal adjustment in old age. *Journal of Abnormal Psychology* 1951, *46,* 24-29.

Havighurst, R. J. Successful aging. In R. H. Williams, C. Tibbitts, & W. Donahue (Eds.), *Processes of aging.* New York: Atherton Press, 1963.

Kutner, B., Fanshel, D., Togo, A. & Langner, T. S. *Five hundred over sixty.* New York: Russell Sage Foundation, 1956.

Lindsley, O. R. Geriatric behavioral prosthetics. In R. Kastenbaum (Ed.), *New thoughts on old age.* New York: Springer, 1964.

Lowenthal, M. F., & Boler, D. Voluntary vs. involuntary social withdrawal. *Journal of Gerontology,* 1965, *3,* 363-371.

Neugarten, B., Havighurst, R. J., & Tobin, S. S. The measurement of life satisfaction. *Journal of Gerontology,* 1961, *16,* 134-143.

Oberleder, M. An attitude scale to determine adjustment in institutions for the aged. *Journal of Chronic Disease,* 1962, *15,* 915-923.

Perlin, S., & Butler, R. N. Psychiatric aspects of adaptation to the aging experience. In J. E. Birren, R. N. Butler, S. W. Greenhouse, L. Sokoloff, & M. Yarrow (Eds.), *Human aging.* (Public Health Service Publication No. 986) Bethesda, Md.: U.S. Public Health Service, 1963.

Rosow, I. Adjustment of the normal aged. In R. H. Williams, C. Tibbitts, & W. Donahue (Eds.), *Processes of aging.* Vol. II. New York: Atherton Press, 1963.

Srole, L. Social integration and certain corollaries. *American Sociological Review,* 1956, *21,* 709-716.

Srole, L., Langner, T. S., Michael, S. T., Opler, M. K., & Rennie, T. *Mental health in the metropolis.* New York: McGraw-Hill, 1962.

Taietz, P. Administrative practices and personal adjustment in homes for the aged. Cornell University Agricultural Bulletin No. 899, July 1953.

12:: VIRO: A SCALE FOR ASSESSING THE INTERVIEW BEHAVIOR OF ELDERLY PEOPLE

ROBERT KASTENBAUM and SYLVIA SHERWOOD

As a source of data, gerontology leans heavily upon the interview situation. Although this statement has its major application to psychosocial research, on many occasions health and medical data also are obtained via the interview. Yet it is not very often that we concern ourselves primarily with the transaction between interviewer and interviewee. The transaction is more or less taken for granted. Is it possible that we are losing something valuable by neglecting the transaction? Does the interview itself constitute a type of relevant data? Is it possible that an elusive but indispensable substance is being allowed to evaporate without leaving a clear impression in our experimental records?

In this paper we are arguing for the desirability of capturing and preserving the essence of the interpersonal transactions in *every* data-gathering situation—not merely those few studies that focus upon the transactions *per se*. The specific procedure that will be described here is a sort of uneasy compromise among various conceptual, methodologic, and economic demands. Both its advantages and drawbacks might be instructive. Let us begin with a brief consideration of those factors which led us to believe that a procedure such as the VIRO should be developed.

This paper is expanded from a presentation made at the 1967 annual meetings of The Gerontological Society, Inc. (St. Petersburg, Fla.) The research reported here was supported in part by Department of Health, Education & Welfare grants MH-14889, MH-1520, CH23-26 and HS00470 (formerly CH00436).

The Need to Assess Interview Behavior in Gerontological Research

There are a number of reasons why it makes sense to devote attention to the assessment of interview behavior in gerontological research.

(1) No matter what age levels are involved, the relationship between interviewer and interviewee cannot be taken for granted. Problems of interviewer effect and the dynamics of the interview relationship are well recognized in the psychological and sociological literature. Rosenthal (1963) and other psychologists have made it evident that interviewer or examiner variables can exert a strong influence on the relationship and the data obtained. Schafer (1950) has helped several generations of clinical psychologists by his analysis of pertinent factors in the psychodiagnostic situation, and Sullivan (1954), Haley (1963), and others have done much to illuminate the dynamics of the interview relationship. Sociologists and social psychologists have studied differential effects on the interview of disparities in group membership and other characteristics between the interviewer and interviewee. Benny, Riesman, and Star (1957), for example, found from an examination of survey and other quantitative research studies that disparity in age and sex between the interviewer and respondent differentially affect the response. Katz (1942), examining class differences and response in a lower socio-economic area of Pittsburgh, found that opinions expressed to working-class interviewers especially hired and trained for the experiment were consistently more radical than those expressed to a similarly hired and trained group of middle-class interviewers. Robinson and Rohde (1946), in a controlled study of anti-Semitism in New York City, found, as might be expected, that differential anti-Semitic response was expressed depending upon the degree to which the interviewer was seemingly Jewish or non-Jewish. Hyman, Cobb, Feldman, Hart, & Stember (1954, pp. 158-170), summarizing the results of a number of NORC studies as well as others concerning disparities in sex, residence, ethnicity, and race between interviewer and interviewee, feel that both the consistency of the results and the fact that the findings support what might be logically hypothesized, tend to

support the "belief that the data . . . . represent effects arising primarily from processes within the respondent rather than within the interviewer (p. 158)."

Discussing the role of the participant observer, the respondents' images of him and how they are reflected in the data, social scientists (Vidich, 1955; Rice, 1930; Dexter, 1957; Kincaid & Bright, 1958; Lenski & Leggett, 1960) have indicated the importance of the personal equation of the interviewer. Caplow (1957) has pointed to the relationship between information and therapeutic interviewing, indicating that the influence of the interviewer is never fully neutral.

Many of the points made by these writers have direct application to gerontological research, simply because both elders and their interviewers are people. However, there are additional problems of special relevance to gerontology: (a) fluctuating level of responsiveness; (b) membership in an "untest-wise" generation; (c) sensory deficits; (d) motor deficits; (e) cognitive deficits; (f) limitations in available energy; (g) "socially desirable response" strictures; and very often the (h) generation gap between interviewer and interviewee (Donahue, 1965).

These complications are familiar enough to most gerontologists. We mention them here as a reminder that separately, and in various combinations, these factors are likely to influence the quality of the interview relationship—often adversely. Not only must the experimenter be mindful of the appropriate statistical techniques for analyzing his data, but also he must consider the relationship context from which the data are obtained. And it is difficult to imagine how the relationship can be taken into account without some effort at assessment.

There are times when the research effort is directed specifically toward one or more of the problems listed above. But if the study is *not* concerned with fluctuating level of responsiveness, cognitive deficit, etc., then it is likely to be influenced by these variables without any way of determining the nature or extent of the influence. We are by no means suggesting that these factors can be studied adequately merely by adding an interview assessment measure. However, it should be possible to assess some of the more salient aspects of the interpersonal transaction and, by so doing, to take into account the momentary state of the individual as it is a function (in part) of all the variables that have been mentioned.

(2) Interview behavior is behavior. Some elderly individuals manifest relatively low "behavior output." Therefore, often we cannot afford to waste any behavior that is available to our observation. Furthermore, important insights for understanding differential developmental processes in aging may come to light when we examine behavior in the interview situation in relation to other aspects of behavior. For example, interesting findings were discovered with respect to the VIRO and other measurements in separate studies conducted by the authors. In a longitudinal study of elderly residents at Cushing Hospital in Framingham (MH14889), sex and ethnic group differences were found in VIRO measurements over time. Based on three measurements—the first at time of patient entry, the second somewhere in the middle and the third about a year after institutionalization—the New England Yankees were found to measure higher on social intactness than did the first-generation Italian or Irish elderly on admittance and tended to retain this trait to a large degree even when suffering from a decline in vigor and orientation. Females entering the hospital tended to be rated lower in Vigor than males and were more likely to deteriorate in relationship measurements after institutionalization.

In a study of applicants to the Hebrew Rehabilitation Center for the Aged (CH23-26; HS00470), statistically significant correlations were found among each of VIRO dimensions, but higher correlations were found between Vigor measurements and Relationship (.456) and Vigor and Intactness (.615) than between Vigor and Orientation (.366). Statistically significant correlations were also found between each of the VIRO dimensions and functional health status, life pattern, and psychological status ratings made by an interdisciplinary team of clinicians consisting of a physiatrist, psychiatrist, internist, social worker, and public health nurse. Findings such as these suggest both the importance of social background and group expectations in VIRO behavior as well as the interrelatedness of psychological, social, and biological development.

(3) There are even times when the interview transactions comprise *all* the behavior we have available to us for research purposes. If our research brings us into contact with greatly impaired subpopulations of the aged, we are likely to find ourselves forced to rely upon indirect sources of data—for example, biographical information that is limited in scope and of problematical veracity. We may rely also upon ratings or comments from other people who currently have some contact with our *S*s. Would it not be sensible to utilize fully whatever *direct* observations we are in a position to make?

We do not really know what our elderly *S* was like five years ago. We do not really know by what operations his daughter or the ward nurse have arrived at their ratings or descriptions. And we are just not going to obtain an adequate performance from him on the standard tests or tasks that other *S*s obediently do for us. We may increase the *S*'s misery, and our own, by confronting him with research procedures with which he cannot cope for one reason or another. Instead of having only an unscorable test protocol or incomplete perceptual-motor task performance to show as a souvenir of the encounter, we might also have an accurate assessment of those behaviors the *S* did exhibit during the session. When we cannot reasonably expect the *S* to do "our thing," in the way we would like him to do it, then we might as well be prepared to observe how he does "his own thing"—his response to the situation.

This lesson was learned the hard way by one of the writers (Robert Kastenbaum), during a series of psychotropic drug studies with geriatric patients. A wide variety of psychodiagnostic instruments yielded relatively little information concerning many of the patients. But information pertaining directly to the patient's behavior in the interview situation (apart from the tests and tasks) did prove dependable and useful. Did the patient ever reach out and touch the interviewer? How much did the interviewer's own mind wander from the matters at hand during the session? Answers to these questions were available, and contributed to a meaningful analysis of the experimental conditions (Slater & Kastenbaum, 1966).

(4) So far we have been emphasizing the usefulness of interview behavior information either to help make the best of difficult research situations or as such information correlates with other variables. However, there are also perspectives from which this kind of data is first-choice, precisely what we want to know. If our aim is to predict the S's behavior in a subsequent two-person situation, then it is logical to determine how he now behaves in a two-person situation. This material is also of prime value when the behavior in the relationship is viewed as the "dependent" variable. For example, we may want to determine the relationship between background (demographic or life-history) variables and the S's present mode of functioning. To illustrate the latter approach, we might be interested in learning whether ethnic-associated patterns of interpersonal behavior become more or less distinct from each other with increasing adult age.

Certain theoretical approaches require data on the interviewer-interviewee transaction if they are to thrive. Some psychoanalytic systems assume the availability of process as well as content data. Field theory approaches deal with immediate processes. Those developmental theories that are sensitive to the dynamics of the immediate situation also require transactional data. For example, in developmental-field theory the assessment of the individual's developmental level is held to be dependent upon the assessment of his immediate environment as well as so-called "intraindividual" variables (Kastenbaum 1964, 1966, and this volume, Part I, Part III). How the interviewer and interviewee greet or take leave of each other can provide data (see Main & Bennett, this volume, Part II, Chapter 13) as important as any test-bound responses.

Criteria for a technique

There are numerous constraints upon us when we attempt to develop a technique that will serve the purposes sketched above:

(1) It should be suitable for use by interviewers with varying types of

experience. There is not much point in developing an instrument that would require the special talents of an existential psychoanalyst or a raw-empiricist bred sociologist. The requirement demands a technique that can be used effectively by people who have certain basic skills and personal maturity, but who otherwise may differ greatly from each other. The procedure would be developed with the intent of utilizing what is held in common and shared by all competent interviewers. The research director would then be able to assign interviews to available staff or to recruit from a broad spectrum of disciplines (giving him greater flexibility with regard to available manpower and funds).

(2) The technique should not add much time to the interview or research session.

(3) The ratings should be fairly easy to make, once the interviewer has become familiar with the procedure and gained some experience.

(4) The technique should lend itself to consistent (reliable) ratings. Although not the place to pursue the subject in detail, it should be pointed out that there is more agreement on the necessity for "reliable" ratings than agreement on operational procedures, or, for that matter, actual attempts to determine reliability. Although many researchers use correlation techniques for computing reliability, Robinson (1957) believes that measures of "agreement" rather than correlation are more appropriate. In any event, problems of reliability are being studied and a number of potentially useful techniques based on different (although not necessarily opposing) assumptions have been developed both by social scientists and medical researchers (Robinson, 1957, 1959; Fletcher & Oldman, 1964; Hunt & Schwartz, 1965; Armitage, Blendis & Smyllie, 1966; Buehler, 1966; Spitzer, Cohen, Fleiss, & Endicott, 1967).

(5) It is important that the technique be capable of almost limitless replication. There are few existing techniques that can be applied again and again to the same S. A single alternative form is available for some psychodiagnostic devices—but what do you do the third time . . . or the fifteenth? Alternative form or not, how often can we ask a S to perform the same task? Motivation, practice effects, and who-knows-what-else may operate to influence subsequent performances. In some

studies, of course, a single contact with the S is deemed sufficient. But sometimes research purposes can better be served by contacting Ss on a daily or weekly basis over a protracted period of time (as, for example, in carefully monitored treatment-effect studies). Longitudinal research may also require many contacts, even though these are spread over longer intervals of time. It would be very helpful to have available at least one procedure which could be used at every contact without "wearing out" or exercising a differential influence upon S at various points in time.

(6) The variables or dimensions that are yielded by the procedure should be relevant to many theories without being a "house prisoner" of any particular theory.

(7) Some kind of balance should be achieved between atomistic and molar variables. It might be useful to know how many times S scratched his left ear with his right hand, but information on a somewhat more general level of observation may prove more useful. On the other hand, instead of receiving only the general impression that the S is a "passive-aggressive personality," we might be more enlightened to learn whether he snarled or smiled at the interviewer. There is a need, in other words, to seek the most fruitful *level* for observation and report, and to seek, of all possible dimensions, those which are most likely to be salient and representative.

Variables that reflect idiosyncratic behavior in an unknown context will not prove informative. While all behavior may have meaning, we frequently lack the knowledge to make this generalization satisfactorily useful. Any role must have meaning and value in the defined context.

(8) Research interviews have been emphasized here. These can be divided into contacts in which the interview method itself carries the burden of data-gathering, and those in which the relationship developed between the interviewer and respondent provides the framework within which the "pay-off" tasks are introduced. Those studies which make strong use of the interview may be able to afford (in time, energy, and money) the development and use of detailed interaction assessment procedures that will meet their special needs. Often, however, even interview-type studies do not include any measure of the process, or the

S's general behavior in the situation. For both types of research interviews there is need for an assessment instrument. The need is just a little less obvious in the latter case.

But there are also many contacts with elderly people in which research is not the primary purpose. Social workers, public health nurses, and numerous other professionals have a variety of non-research contacts. The interview may be intended to provide information to the elder, or to offer emotional support and guidance. It may be an information-gathering interview, but with practical decisions, not general contributions to knowledge, as the goal. It may be a "social visit" type of interview, in which other purposes are allowed to emerge if appropriate.

In many of these situations it would be useful if the research dimension could be added without imposing a substantial burden upon busy personnel. Do male and female patients differ in the rapidity with which they adjust to an institutional placement? How useful are regular "social visits" in maintaining the morale of elders? What can be learned from examining this particular agency's experiences with its particular population of elders that would be helpful in recruiting and training future personnel? Is there some way of utilizing the agency-client transactions as a basis for planning future programs? For supporting budget requests? These are a few of the questions that might occur to people who are engaged in some kind of service contact with elders. There may be times when it is not practical to introduce a major research effort; but it would only be of benefit if a research dimension based upon actual direct observations could become a continuing part of the interview program and not itself make excessive demands on the agency. Furthermore, such research efforts can contribute to the action goals. For example, in a study by Bales and Hare (1965), a procedure was devised so that by comparing it with a "reference group" population, it was possible to make diagnostic use of the interaction profile.

In other words, the type of procedure for which we are questing would be amenable to use in a great variety of interviews, including many that are conducted for purposes other than research.

The VIRO technique

The technique to be described here was developed in an attempt to meet many of the needs and requirements that have been mentioned. The most immediate concern was to come up with a procedure that could be incorporated into an ongoing clinical psychology service, and into research projects that were already in progress in two different geriatric settings. As background, we had available to us a variety of scales and rating procedures that had been developed and applied in previous geriatric studies at Cushing Hospital (an all-geriatric facility operated by the Commonwealth of Massachusetts). We also had five years of clinical experience with aged patients at Cushing Hospital to draw upon. Many of the decisions centered upon the process of eliminating possible items and dimensions. The available pool of potentially relevant and useful elements was much larger than those which could be included in a compact scale. The VIRO has turned out to consist mostly of items found useful in previous research plus a few new additions. But the format—how the observations were to be made and treated—proved to be somewhat different from what had gone before.

We are aware that the VIRO offers far from an adequate solution to the problems and challenges that were touched upon in the first section of this paper. Compromises have been made between what might be considered ideal and the demands of an easily used instrument. Yet an effort has been made to come to terms with each of these problems; we hope this effort proves of some value to the field.

Chart I indicates the procedure for scoring VIRO scales. Chart I, Part I specifies the VIRO items set up in pre-coded IBM card format, thereby facilitating computer analysis. (VIRO ratings in the CH23-26 and HS00470 projects (S. Sherwood, Principal Investigator) are key punched according to the card format presented in Chart I, Part 1. Some computer "runs" have been made using the facilities of the Harvard Computation Center. Data-text programming in connection with the above card format can be made available for scoring VIRO ratings: i.e., scorings for Vigor, Social Intactness, Relationship, Orienta-

CHART I—Part 1: Viro Dimensions

ID No.						Proj.			Deck		Card	
(1)	(2)	(3)	(4)	(5)	(6)	(7)	(8)	(9)	(10)	(11)	(12)	(13)

Date of interview　　　　　　　　　　　Type of interview

　　　　(14) (15) (16) (17) (18) (19)　　　　　　(20)

Viro in Precoded IBM Card Format

For each of the variables listed below, the interviewer is to rate the applicant in the ways specified and place the appropriate scores in the columns designated:

1. First Impression (snapshot opinion) and Changes During Interview
   DIRECTIONS FOR SCORING FIRST IMPRESSION AND CHANGE SCO
   FOR EACH OF THE THREE VARIABLES (A, B, and C) LISTED IN
   TION 1: Rate from 0 to 3 (four-point scale) your *first* impression and p
   the appropriate score in the column designated.
   Indicate in the columns designated (two columns provided for this pu
   for each variable) whether change in this impression occurred durir
   interview:
   Code 00 if there was no apparent change.
   If a change occurred during the interview, code the *direction* (+ or -
   first column provided and the *magnitude* (the greatest scale change c
   at any time during the interview) in the *second column* provided. Sin
   starting out with a four-point scale, this change may vary fron
   maximum amount of positive change) to -3 (the maximum amoun.. .. ..--
   tive change).
   Thus, +1, +2, +3 indicate the various degrees of possible positive change; -1,
   -2, -3 indicate the various degrees of possible negative change.
   Note: If change in both directions occurred during the interview, code only
   the *positive* change.

	First Impression	Change	Score
A. (3) Vigorous . . . . (0) Feeble	cols. 21 ——	—— (22)	—— (23)
B. (3) Receptive . . . . (0) Closed	24 —	—— (25)	—— (26)
C. (3) Comfortable . . . . (0) In distress	27 —	—— (28)	—— (29)

(Interviewer need not fill out the rest of this page)

PRESENTATION SCORE (Sum of cols. 21-29)　　　　—— (30)　—— (31)

2. Behavior and Attitudes Manifested During Interview
   DIRECTIONS: Rate from 0 to 3 (four-point scale) each of the variables listed
   in Section 2 and place the appropriate score in the column designated.
   (For the first six variables in this section—A, B, C, D, E, and F—rate by
   averaging over the interview session.)

(continued)

CHART I—Part 1: Viro Dimensions (continued)

ID No.	Proj.	Deck	Card

		Column
col. 32	A. (3) Quite Trustful . . . . (0) Quite Suspicious	32 ___
col. 33	B. (3) High Energy Level . . . . (0) Low Energy Level	33 ___
col. 34	C. (3) Fluent Speech . . . . (0) Minimal Speech	34 ___
col. 35	D. (3) Keen Attention . . . . (0) Poor Attention	35 ___
col. 36	E. (3) Controlled Thought . . . . (0) Tangential, Fragmented	36 ___
col. 37	F. (3) Eager Participation . . . . (0) Reluctant Participation	37 ___

(For the next three variables in this section—G, H, and I—rate according to their peak occurrence.)

col. 38	G. (3) Keen Self-Perspective . . . . (0) No Self-Perspective	38 ___
col. 39	H. (3) Engrossment in Own Ideas/Feelings . . . . (0) No Self-Engrossment	39 ___
col. 40	I. (3) Engrossed in Relationship . . . . (0) No Shared Engrossment	40 ___

(For the last variable in this section—J—rate according to the termination phase of the interview.)

col. 41	J. (3) Eager to Continue Session or see Interviewer again . . . . (0) Eager to End Session	41 ___
cols. 42-43	INTERACTION SCORE (Sum of cols. 32-41) (Interviewer need not fill out)	cols. ___ ___ (42) (43)

KEYING COLUMNS. DIRECTIONS: At times *one* of the variables in Sections 1 and 2 appears to be most crucial in the interview. If *one* of these variables is clearly salient, the variable is to be coded on cols. 44-45 by recording the number of the column representing the variable in question. For section 1, record the column representing the first impression (col. 21 for variable A, col. 24 for B, col. 27 for C).
Code 00 if there is no salient variable.

cols. 44-45   Keying columns (to be filled in by interviewer)

___   ___
(44)   (45)

3. Mental Status Questions
   DIRECTIONS: For each of the items listed in Section 3 (A, B, C, D, E, F, G, and H), place the appropriate score in the column provided.

Column

col. 46   A. Knows Own Age (If other than Score 3, check direction)
   SCORE: (3) Precisely; (2) Within 2 years; (1) Within 10 years;
             (0) Beyond 10   46 ___
                  Underestimation;   Overestimation

(continued)

CHART I—Part 1: Viro Dimensions

ID No.	Proj.	Deck	Card

Column

col. 47   B. Knows day of week   47 __
    SCORE: (3) yes; (0) no
col. 48   C. Knows month   48 __
    SCORE: (3) yes; (0) no
col. 49   D. Knows year (If other than Score 3, check direction)   49 __
    SCORE: (3) Precisely; (2) Within 2 years; (1) Within 10 years;
        (0) Beyond 10
              Underestimation;   Overestimation
col. 50   E. Knows Community   50 __
    SCORE: (3) yes; (0) no
col. 51   F. Knows Street   51 __
    SCORE: (3) yes; (0) no
col. 52   G. Remembers Examiner's name   52 __
    SCORE: (3) yes; (2) partially; (0) no
col. 53   H. Estimate of Duration of Interview (If other than Score
    3, check direction)   53 __
    SCORE: (3) Within 5 min.; (2) Within 10 min.; (1) Within 20
      min; (0) more than 20 min.
           Underestimation   Overestimation

    (Interviewer need not fill out cols. 54-58)

cols. 54-55 ORIENTATION SCALE (Sum of cols. 46-53)   __ __
                                    (54)   (55)

col. 56   Direction of error of A
    (1) underestimation; (2) overestimation; (0) no error   56 __
col. 57   Direction of error of D
    (1) Underestimation; (2) overestimation; (0) no error   57 __
col. 58   Direction of error of H
    (1) underestimation; (2) overestimation; (0) within 5 min.
                               58 __

CHART I—Part 2: Guide to Rating of Viro Scales

Ratings are based on expectations of normal behavior but the highest score (3) is used to indicate normal or supernormal reactions. Score of 0 indicates extremely negative or totally absent response.

SECTION I—PRESENTATION

    Ratings are made on basis of first impression (less than one minute from time of initial contact).

A. Cols. 21-23 (3) Vigorous   (0) Feeble
    Vitality scale—hearty handshake, impression of capacity for effective, decisive movement vs. flaccid tonus, impression of weak, slow, ineffective movement.
                                                (continued)

CHART I–Part 2: Guide to Rating of Viro Scales (continued)

B. Cols. 24-26 (3) Receptive   (0) Closed
Welcoming gestures, facial expression that lights up at E's approach, implicit movements toward interviewer, impression of extending self and shortening distance between self and interviewer vs. no gestures or expressions that acknowledge presence of interviewer, or implicit, aversive, shrinking-away movements, impression of withdrawing self and lengthening distance between self and interviewer.

C. Cols. 27-29 (3) Comfortable   (0) In Distress
Pained expression, moaning, writhing, awkward position or posture suggesting bodily discomfort vs. absence of these behaviors and general impression of being at ease, not preoccupied with body condition.

SECTION II–CONFRONTATION (INTERACTION)

A. Col. 32 (3) Quite Trustful   (0) Quite Suspicious
Repeated questioning such as, "Why are you asking me these questions?" "What is this all about?" Repeated failure to answer questions adequately when there is no indication of mental incapacity or knowledge. Eyeing E as though E were on a mission of mischief vs. none of these behaviors.

B. Col. 33 (3) High Energy Level (0) Low Energy Level
Both verbal and nonverbal behavior have a convincing intensity or power, intensity "output" is normal vs. mumbling, weakly-uttered speech, minimal intensity and output of behavior.

C. Col. 34 (3) Normal Fluent Speech   (0) Minimal Speech
Normal flow in which words are integrated into statements and statements into larger contextual units vs. "yes", "no", "don't know" responses, sentence fragments, lack of elaboration or stumbling bits of speech. (Distinguish this item from energy level.)

D. Col. 35 (3) Keen Attention (0) Poor Attention
  (a) Applies to subjects at least moderately well-oriented.
      Loses track of conversation, responds as though previous conversation had not taken place, seems to take no notice of changes in E's topic, intensity, personal behavior vs. seems to anticipate the next question, response indicates that previous conversation has registered, notices changes in E's speech or behavior.
  (b) Applies to subjects who are disoriented and who may not be able to answer appropriately.
      Listens attentively, watches interviewer when being questioned, tries to answer appropriately vs. wandering attention, seems not to be trying to answer, looks away from interviewer.

E. Col. 36 (3) Controlled Thought   (0) Tangential Thought
Maintains a frame of reference with fairly clear boundaries, context of statements is clear or becomes clear readily, thoughts follow in logical or reasonable sequence vs. conversations peppered with irrelevant statements and expressions, context of remarks not clear, takes off from mutual topic in idiosyncratic ways, "train of thought derailed."

(continued)

CHART I–Part 2: Guide to Rating of Viro Scales (continued)

F. Col. 37 (3) Eager Participation   (0) Reluctant Participation

Responsive to all questions and comments, spontaneous vs. choreful reaction to E's questions, volunteers nothing, complains about effort of responding. E must expend considerable energy of his own to extract responses from subject. (Distinguish from trustful-suspicious dimension and energy level.)

G. Col. 38 (3) Keen Self-Perspective   (0) No Self-Perspective

Comments about his own role in the interview situation, expresses awareness of how he might look to others, wonders "How am I doing?" or expresses an opinion on that, divides his own experience into favorable and unfavorable, strong and weak, and other categories, vs. no awareness that he is being interviewed, absence of all the other characteristics mentioned above, labels his experiences or functioning as all good or all bad.

H. Col. 39 (3) Engrossed in Own Ideas/Feelings   (0) No Self-Engrossment

Animated, "alive" when talking about his life or opinions, as shown in sparkling or intense eyes, appropriate gestures, body posture, speech patterning—may also be shown by deeply reflective, inward-turning behavior, "lost in own thoughts and feelings" to such an extent that E's presence seems momentarily ignored. These are two different patterns of self-engrossment vs. flat, neutral, transient, "uncommitted" behavioral and expressive "commentary" when talking about his life or opinions, not "caught up" in his internal life. Talks about himself in same, rather uninvolved way he talks about most everything else.

I. Col. 40 (3) Engrossed in Relationship   (0) No Shared Engrossment

Direct eye contact, S and E meet on common ground, or in same universe of discourse, interested in E as a person, may affectionately touch E vs. absence of these characteristics, perhaps related to a type of self-engrossment that shuts off the relationship, gross disorientation, or impression of deciding to keep E at a distance.

J. Col. 41 (3) Eager to See Interviewer Again   (0) Eager to Discontinue Session

Verbal expression of wishing interview to continue, or another contact to be made (with appropriate nonverbal commentary) vs. inquiring how much longer this is going to last, "Is this the final question?", "I hope I don't have to go through something like this again.

	Column	
Col. 59 VIGOR: Add the scores in the following cols.:	—	
col. 21 + col. 33 = (SUM = VIGOR RAW SCORE)	(59)	
Cols. 60-61 RELATIONSHIP: Add the scores in the following cols.	—	—
col. 24 + col. 32 + col. 37 + col. 40 + col. 41 =	(60)	(61)
(SUM = RELATIONSHIP RAW SCORE)		
Cols. 62-63 INTACTNESS: Add the scores in the following cols.:	—	—
col. 34 + col. 35 + col. 36 + col. 38 + col. 39 =	(62)	(63)
(SUM = INTACTNESS RAW SCORE)		

tion, Presentation, and Interaction.) Part 2 of Chart I presents specifications for rating VIRO items.

(1) *Dimensions.* Use of VIRO yields scores on four dimensions: Vigor, Intactness, Relationship, and Orientation. Each VIRO item contributes to one and only one of these dimensions. As the term implies, Vigor refers to the energy level manifested by *S* during the course of the interview. (This statement will be expanded upon later.) Intactness refers to *S*'s cognitive functioning with respect to socially appropriate behavior during the interview proper. Relationship pertains to his level and style of interacting with the interviewer. Orientation is a measure of *S*'s cognitive functioning as assessed by direct questioning concerning time, place, and interview content. It requires a simple mental status examination. Intactness, then, represents cognitive aspects of *S*'s interview behavior in terms of maintaining a conversation within a social context, while Orientation represents his response to specific questions, tapping short-term memory and learning ability. Except that the Orientation scale used in the VIRO does not ask "Who is the President of the United States?" and "Who is the past President?", it is very similar to the Mental Status Quotient (the MSQ) described by Goldfarb (1964).

The VIRO dimensions can be assessed indefinitely, in interview after interview. They require no special operations being performed on or by *S*. A mental status examination can be repeated a number of times, but not indefinitely. The O in VIRO can be included in many types of study, but may have to be phased in and out in those that require many interviews closely massed in time. In a few contexts it may be considered necessary to omit Orientation altogether, as when it is feared that a period of direct questioning might interfere with other purposes of the interview. It is possible that a mental status "judgment" scale for rating the *S*'s orientation for time, place, etc. can be developed that will reliably correlate very highly with the direct questioning approach to measuring Orientation. Under such circumstances the "judgment" scale can be used to give at least some measure of

Orientation when considered necessary to eliminate the "direct-questioning" Orientation scale being used here.

(2) *Other characteristics of VIRO.* As can be seen from Chart I and the discussion below, VIRO scores are also classified in terms of their source. Items that come from two different sources may both contribute to the same score (e.g., Vigor is comprised of Presentation Item A, and Interaction Item B). We are thus in position to examine either the S's general level on a particular dimension, or how he impressed us when we looked at him from a particular vantage point, without dividing this impression into specific subvariables. This distinction will become clearer as we continue with a description of VIRO.

It is intended that each item rating be independent of all others. Ideally, no theoretical or personal bias should interfere with independent ratings (insofar as it is really possible to eliminate or reduce these biases). An interviewer may have arrived at his own private (and never explicit) conclusion that a person who shows keen attention also has adequate control over his thoughts, and vice versa. In VIRO ratings, however, high or low ratings on either of these items have no necessary implications for the rating that is to be made on the other item. VIRO is intended to maximize the possible combinations of item scores—and, in this way, approximate more closely actual intra- and interindividual differences.

Another requirement made of the VIRO rater is that he limit his entries to what he has actually observed. This requires a clear appreciation of the distinction between an observed behavior and its likely or possible explanation. It is a difficult distinction to keep in mind. Many of us have been trained in such a way that we no longer see behaviors—we see theoretical constructs instead. Much of the training period for VIRO raters is concerned with alerting the interviewer to convey what he observed, rather than why he believes it was there to be observed. (This, of course, is not intended as a criticism of explanatory efforts—it is simply an effort to make the basic observations available as a separate unit for possible explanations by anybody who cares to make them, including, but not limited to, the interviewer.)

Other characteristics of VIRO rating and scoring will be mentioned as we move along.

(3) *Presentation.* The first ratings to be made during an interview contact consist of three items. These represent the bipolar variables of Vigorous-Feeble, Receptive-Closed, and Comfortable-In Distress. Of special importance here is the requirement that all these ratings be made within the first minute of contact, that is, within sixty seconds of the interviewer's entry into S's physical and social space (or vice versa). Experienced raters are expected to perform this task in even less time, about thirty seconds.

What is the purpose of this procedure? It is intended to capitalize upon our tendency to form quick "first impressions" and their relationship to subsequent impressions. From our present viewpoint, however, we are concerned chiefly with the possibility of utilizing the first impression to improve our overall assessment of S.

The usual fate of the interviewer's first impression is mysterious indeed. Does he deliberately reject it because it is based upon insufficient observation? Does he, at another extreme, inadvertently pattern the rest of his observations upon the first impression? Or does he himself later not have much idea about what his first impression was and how it might fit in with his other observations? An attempt has been made to take some of the mystery out of this. Having a first impression is legitimized and given an explicit place. The interviewer and the S confront each other. The interviewer guides his global first impression into the three items by which we attempt to differentiate it. He is then free to proceed with the session proper, having had his first impression and having had done with it. The Presentation score (summation of the three component items) may be predictive or nonpredictive of the observations made later. But it remains as a separate unit for potential analysis.

We might point out that there is a special value in this evanescent Presentation phase since conventional greeting behavior produces many similarities in the initial phase of interviews conducted for a variety of different purposes. It is true enough that there might be subtle differences between the way an interviewer approaches an S he is going to test and one to whom he is prepared to pay a social visit. But these differences would seem to be relatively minor in comparison with the larger differences that will emerge as the specific purpose of the session is worked out. Thus, the Presentation score provides information that is comparable across types of interview. It is also worth noting that the very limited time period involved gives us a sharp focus on the scope of observations. Reporting what one has observed in a minute or less of preliminary interview time is a great deal more specific than, for example, reporting that the *S* has been "depressed for quite a while."

(4) *Interaction.* Most of the remaining items in VIRO are rated on the basis of what transpires during the total session. The items which comprise the Orientation subscale are an exception; these are based upon mental status questions which, as previously noted, can be excluded if necessary.

The first six Interaction items (Chart I, Part 1, Section 1, A through F) are rated according to *S*'s typical behavior throughout the length of the session. If the action were randomly frozen at one or more points during the interview, the *S*'s behavior at those points would most likely be represented by his item score. These are averaged scores.

The next three items (G through I) are rated on a different basis. Here the interviewer assigns the *highest or peak score* that is justified by *S*'s behavior. For example, at that point in time when *S* displays the greatest self-perspective (Item H), just how much perspective does he display?

The final Interaction item (J) is rated on the basis of *S*'s behavior as the session draws to a close. This is the "endgame" item. With this item we acknowledge the significance of endings as, with the Presentation section, we acknowledged the significance of beginnings.

This rating procedure probably requires some comment. *If* we were designing an assessment instrument that was to be used only for intensive research projects, then it would have been possible to handle the ratings differently. We could have required a *series* of periodic ratings for all (or almost all) the items. This would have provided us with a valuable behavior-over-time pattern from which special measures such as peaks could be derived. We think this more intensive procedure should be explored when an opportunity presents itself; however, it makes too many demands on the interviewer to be practical for the broad uses VIRO is intended to serve.

Those items selected for peak rating might be regarded as theoretical luxuries. The concepts of engrossment and perspective are of particular importance in developmental-field theory (Kastenbaum, 1965) and, we believe, also of potential value to those employing a variety of other theoretical approaches. Among other uses of these three items is determining the ability of elderly Ss to retain both engrossment and perspectivistic footings. Is he still able to "go all out," "lose himself," "get carried away?" Is he still able to "stand back and look at himself?" Is he able to see how events relate to each other apart from his own momentary concerns?

(5) *Orientation.* This mental status scale consists of eight items. It is similar in many ways to most other mental status examinations which in some cases may be preferable (cf. Goldfarb). The interviewer must remember to give his own name clearly to S, repeating if necessary to give the S every opportunity to recall the name when it is requested later in the session. Allowance should be made for the difficulty of the name considering ethnic background and length of name.

(6) *Presentation Follow-Up.* When the session has ended, the interviewer is asked to make new ratings on the three Presentation items. These ratings are based upon the trend of the S's behavior with respect to these dimensions as the session continued. Did S for example, turn out to look as Closed and In Distress as he appeared to be at first? Did his Vigor remain about the same, decrease, or increase? The ratings themselves are not comparative; they are scored again. Comparisons are made later for analytic purposes.

(7) *Keying Variable.* Another effort has been made to permit the interviewer to convey a reasonable impression of how this particular S behaved during this particular session (within all the limitations that

have already been acknowledged). Ordinarily, each item or dimension on a behavior assessment scale is treated as though it is "equal" to all others. Often, in fact, development of the scale calls forth special efforts to insure a homogeneous level. Nevertheless, people in "real life" do not invariably follow this homogeneous pattern. On one day an individual may be so lacking in Vigor that this dimension is quite salient; it should be taken into account in interpreting his behavior along other dimensions. On another day the individual's Vigor was within its accustomed bounds, but he was so engrossed in his own thoughts and feelings that this strongly influenced everything else that transpired. On yet another day he will not be that far out on any dimension. The keying variable would be used in completing a VIRO report in the first two examples, but not in the third. In other words, the keying variable is invoked when something so special is in evidence that *not* to call attention to it would result in an implicit falsification of the record.

Any of the VIRO items could be selected as the keying variable for a particular session. The most important point is to note that there was some exceptionally influential or salient factor at work. Accurate designation of this factor is difficult in some instances. If the S utters scarcely a word during the entire session, the Minimal Speech obviously suggests itself as the keying variable. (This is quite apart from possible *explanations* of the inadequate speech: aphasia, poor command of English, fright, resentment, etc.) But in other instances the rater must content himself with approximating the keying factor. If S spent most of his time "looking funny" at the interviewer, and evading his remarks, then Quite Suspicious might be used as the keying variable—but Reluctant Participant would also be a plausible entry.

In practice at Cushing Hospital it was found that keying variables seem to be appropriate about 10% of the time. This percentage is likely to vary according to the population of Ss with whom one is working and, possibly, the nature of the interview format.

It is possible that a mental status "judgment" scale for rating the S's Orientation for time, place, etc. can be developed that will correlate highly with the objective "test" questions. Under such circumstances the Orientation "judgment" scale can be used to give at least some measure of Orientation when considered necessary to eliminate the Orientation direct-questioning.

(8) *Scoring the items.* VIRO items are scored on a four-point scale. The high-number side of the bipolar dimension represents the socially-valued end of the variable (e.g., Receptive, Not Closed; Keen, not Poor Attention).

The highest possible score on a VIRO item means that S is somewhere within the normal adult range. His behavior is competent enough along this dimension so that we do not find ourselves making special allowances for his age, his medical condition, etc. VIRO is not designed to differentiate among those elders who function exceptionally well. Ss in this latter category are fairly amenable to a variety of psychological procedures. It is the more or less troubled or impaired elder for whom an assessment procedure such as VIRO is particularly useful. An extremely low item score, then, means that a valued kind of behavior was completely or almost completely absent during the interview (e.g., showed no Self-Perspective), or the negative side of a behavioral dimension was predominantly in evidence (e.g., Tangential, not Controlled Thought). But a high score means only that S has at least crossed the threshold to the level of behavior we expect of more or less "normal" adults. The top score for Fluent Speech, for example, does not distinguish between normally fluent speech and eloquent speech.

(9) *Obtaining scale scores.* More sophisticated statistical analysis may be attempted as the usefulness of the scale is more fully explored; but at the present time the scale score for each of the VIRO dimensions (Vigor, Intactness, Relationship, Orientation) is simply an addition of raw scores or weights recorded by the interviewer for the relevant items. As conceptualized, each item contributes to only one dimension.

The items comprising the Orientation dimension are listed as a unit in Chart I under the label *Mental Status Questions* (see columns 46-53). However, the items comprising the "judgment" subscales (VIR) are not listed as separate units. While the item content for each "judgment" subscale can also be gleaned from Chart I (see columns 59-63), the items, the section and the place within the section for the VIR subscales are summarized in Chart 2.

(10) *Profile Analysis.* A visual picture of the VIRO profile can be useful, particularly in the clinical situation. Since the dimension scores consist of varying numbers of items, a simple profile analysis form has been devised that translates the scores into the same numerical scale. A thirty-point scale is used. In this profile the raw score from each of the scales is multiplied by an appropriate constant in order to obtain comparable numerical score values for each dimension. The raw score values of the Vigor scale vary from 0 to 6; the Intactness and Relationship scales vary from 0 to 15, and the Orientation scale varies from 0 to 24. Therefore, in order to place raw scores of each dimension on visually comparable numerical locations on the profile form: the Vigor subscale value is multiplied by 5; the Intactness and Relationship scales are multiplied by 2; and the Orientation scale is multiplied by 1.25. By connecting the dimension scores as located in the profile form, a simplified visual profile of an S's interview behavior is provided.

Figure 1 presents a sample profile. The same S has been interviewed

CHART 2:   Subscale item content

Subscale	Item	Location of Item*
VIGOR	Vigorous-Feeble	Presentation A
	High–Low Energy Level	Interaction B
INTACTNESS	Fluent–Minimal Speech	Interaction C
	Keen–Poor Attention	Interaction D
	Controlled-Tangential Thought	Interaction E
	Keen–No Self-Perspective	Interaction G
	Self-Engrossment–No Self-Engrossment	Interaction H
RELATIONSHIP	Receptive–Closed	Presentation I
	Trustful–Suspicious	Interaction A
	Eager–Reluctant Participant	Interaction F
	Engrossed–No Shared Engrossment	Interaction I
	Eager to Continue–Discontinue Session	Interaction J

*Refers to section of the scale and place within the section.

on two occasions. During the first interview (solid line), his behavior was rated at the top along three of the four dimensions. (Raw scores of 15, 15, and 24, respectively, convert to the top "profile" score of 30 for the IRO dimensions). His Vigor score (raw:4/profile:20) was somewhat lower. During the second interview (broken line), his IRO behavior remained at the top, but the relatively lower Vigor rating

FIGURE 1: Sample clinical configurations

Scale Score on a 30-point basis	Raw Scores VIGOR	VIRO profile Raw Scores Intactness	Relationship	Orientation
30	6	15	15	24
29				23
28		14	14	22
27				
26		13	13	21
25	5			20
24		12	12	19
23				18
22		11	11	
21				17
20	4	10	10	16
19				15
18		9	9	14
17				
16		8	8	13
15	3			12
14		7	7	11
13				10
12		6	6	
11				
10	2	5	5	9
9				8
8		4	4	7
7				6
6		3	3	
5	1			5
4		2	2	4
3				3
2		1	1	2
1				
0	0	0	0	1 0

declined even further. Clinical experience with geriatric patients at Cushing Hospital has suggested that this particular pattern of change may forecast impending danger. Some patients from whom such a profile was obtained soon were struggling for their lives in a medical crisis, or had deteriorated so much that they did not seem to be the same people. Clinically in the Cushing Hospital samples there have been false positives and false negatives; but enough incidents have been found to cause alarm when this kind of profile is discovered.

Obtaining VIRO profiles for a series of contacts with the same patient not only permits us, at least on a superficial level, to relate these to circumstances of possible clinical significance, but also to initiate more systematic research to test and refine the initial observations. For the pattern that has been mentioned, for example, further analysis suggested that the decline in Vigor was somewhat more likely to be followed by serious disturbances in men than in women. Yet the sex difference itself cannot be interpreted adequately without taking a number of other variables into account. It may be, for example, that in contrast with men, a drop in Vigor is more likely to signal lowered morale or depression in women rather than negative change in medical status. This hypothesis is in line with findings from a recent study of applicants to the Hebrew Rehabilitation Center for Aged, an extended care facility combining permanent residence and hospital functions. The data indicated that male applicants tended to be in better functional health than the female applicants. But it was also noted that a larger proportion of females were judged to be limiting their physical activities more than their physical condition would require. Furthermore, females tended to score lower than male applicants on the Lawton Morale scale (described in Chapter 11) (Sherwood, 1969, pp. 223-224). Following the same hypothesis presented in the study of applicants to an extended care facility, institutionalization may represent a greater role loss for women than for men, resulting in lowered morale and increased states of depression and apathy which are reflected in the Vigor scores.

From the above it can be seen that VIRO profile analysis can be a useful tool in an ongoing attempt to relate ethnic background, personality, and initial health status to each other and to the geriatric patient's hospital career. Profile analysis suggests hypotheses. With the use of appropriate research designs, profile analysis can also be used to test hypotheses.

Of course, a more sophisticated analysis—certainly important in the testing of hypotheses—requires that scores be converted to what are usually referred to in statistical analysis as standard scores or z scores in order to make the scores for each of the dimensions comparable. (The difficulty with standard scores is that they have to be recomputed each time the sample changes since the z score is based on the score's distances from the mean and the standard deviation of the distribution of scores of which it is a part. Perhaps sometime in the future it will be possible to standardize the VIRO on a random (representative) sample of the population to whom it is to be applied.) (Cf. Spiegel, 1961, p. 73; Runyon & Haber, 1968, pp. 70-76; Parl, 1967, p. 99). Since the z score is based on the score's distance from the mean and the standard deviation of the distribution of scores of which it is a part, what may be numerically comparable scores for each of the dimensions on the simple profile analysis form presented above may not necessarily represent the same thing for each of the scales. Thus a "20" on one dimension on the simple profile analysis form may be above the mean, but on another dimension it may be below the mean. Or even if they are in the same direction from the mean, a "20" on one of the dimensions may represent a distance much further from the mean than a "20" on another dimension. For example, in an analysis of VIRO scores of some three hundred applicants to the Hebrew Rehabilitation Center for Aged, a "20" simple profile analysis rating for the Vigor scale was 1.025 below the mean of the group, resulting in a $-.1454$ z score; a "20" simple profile analysis rating for the Intactness score was 4.454 below the mean of the group, resulting in a $-.6968$ z score; a "20" Relationship score was 2.920 below the mean, resulting in a $-.4905$ score; and a "20" Orientation score was 1.0763 below the mean, resulting in a $-.1374$ z score. (This study was supported by Public Health Service Grant HS 00470.)

In examining VIRO profiles (for either clinical or research purposes), it is worth paying attention both to the general level of the ratings (high or low scores) and to relative scores within the pattern. (The more sophisticated analysis in which standard scores are used can be particularly valuable here.) A low Vigor score, for example, does not necessarily have the same implications if it is within the context of a generally low profile as it does when it is conspicuously lower than the other scores.

Two elders may be quite low on the Orientation scale. But one of these people may have a high score for Intactness. This is not a contradiction. It suggests that while both Ss have difficulty in answering direct questions about their environments, one nevertheless retains his ability to function on a successful cognitive social level within an interpersonal relationship. We do not have to choose between Orientation and Interaction scores as indices of S's cognitive functioning—we use both measures. If, for example, the low-Orientation/high-Interaction elder also has a high Relationship score, we are even more likely to conclude that his deficits do not massively interfere with his ability to participate in the give-and-take of human relationships. We have, in fact, interviewed geriatric patients who were able to form rather good relationships and keep up their parts despite evidence (Orientation scale and other mental tests) that they were suffering from appreciable cognitive impairment.

We have given just a few examples of how profile analysis can be used to compare the individual with himself over time and with other individuals. The resourceful clinician and researcher can undoubtedly discover many other uses and patterns.

Training and reliability

The first research uses of VIRO were made at Cushing Hospital and at The Hebrew Rehabilitation Center for the Aged (Boston). Both sets of studies had something in common (all Ss were elderly, emphasis was upon psychosocial variables, etc.), and something distinct (hospitalized vs. nonhospitalized aged, psychologically-oriented vs. social work-oriented interviewers, etc.). It was our intention that both interviewing staffs attain the same level of competence in scoring VIRO and learn to use the instrument in the same way. A small cadre of clinical researchers from Cushing Hospital aided considerably in this venture.[1] Written specifications were prepared as guidelines for rating VIRO dimensions. During the first year, in particular, much of the interviewer training was conducted in joint sessions. Explanations and discussions of the procedure were followed usually by simulated interviews in which staff members enacted the role of patients. On several occasions it was possible for the interviewing staff of both research projects to meet at Cushing Hospital for group training based on interviews with elderly patients there. One social worker interviewer was employed by both projects.[2] On each of these occasions he took the role of the active interviewer, while the other staff members observed interview sessions behind a one-way mirror. After each of the interviews (simulated or otherwise) each staff member would make independent VIRO ratings. We would then discuss the interview and all of the ratings in considerable detail. In this way it was possible to establish better guidelines for rating than had been put into printed words; the interviewers could see for themselves the difference between a medium-low and a medium-high score performance along a particular dimension. Reliability in the training sessions was considered adequate when ratings were consistently within .5 of the mean of the group.

Based on the experience in training sessions, the specifications have been reworded from time to time, hopefully so that the instructions for rating of the items have become clearer.

Since that time new raters have been added both to these projects and to new projects undertaken by the authors. From time to time demonstration VIRO training sessions have taken place using the simulated interview technique described above. More usually, or at least in addition to such demonstrations, the rater-in-training is given the opportunity to co-interview elders in private sessions with a more

[1] Our grateful appreciation is extended in particular to Paul T. Costa, Jr. and Neil McLaughlin.

[2] Our grateful appreciation is extended to Gerald Robbins, M.S.W., the research social worker on both projects.

experienced interviewer. Only one of the staff members actually conducts the interview but both staff members fill out the VIRO rating forms. The ratings are compared immediately after the interview, at which time the rater-in-training has the benefit of discussing any differences with the more experienced interviewer.

Our experiences in training raters to date have been encouraging. Within three such interview sessions interjudgment agreement has tended to be close enough to persuade us that the VIRO has the potential to yield fairly reliable results. From our experience the items that appear to have the most difficulty are those dealing with engrossment—engrossment in own feelings and ideas as well as engrossment in the relationship. As might be expected, we have found that it is relatively easy to obtain almost perfect agreement at the extremes—that is, for those Ss who have either markedly reduced or markedly good ability to behave within the interview situation.

It is likely that item reliability in general could be increased by adding more choice points to the present four-point rating scale. This would also have the added advantage of allowing measurement of a greater variability of behaviors. It might also be worthwhile to add a few more items. These additional items, if well chosen, might reduce some of the ambiguity and uncertainty encountered in attempting to represent complex behaviors along a relatively few dimensions.

Although our experience has led us to believe that it is not difficult to train interviewers to rate reliably on the VIRO dimensions, not enough data have been systematically collected and statistically analyzed to allow us to draw formal conclusions concerning the difficulty of obtaining reliability of VIRO ratings. However, as part of a larger reliability study of social worker judgments and other data being collected at projects in which the Department of Social Gerontological Research is involved, reliability data concerning the VIRO are currently being collected on a systematic basis. Although two staff members are present during an interview situation, as in the training sessions, only one of the staff members actually conducts the interview. Both staff members fill out the interview form, including VIRO ratings. It should be pointed out that some of the ratings are being made by staff members who have had only a minimal training in making VIRO judgments. The results of these extensive tests will be reported at some future time.

Suggested VIRO uses

Several possible uses of the VIRO were mentioned earlier. Here we will list and describe briefly some of the purposes to which VIRO either has been, or could be, put to fruitful application.

(1) *Screening.* There are times when decisions must be made regarding the disposition of large numbers of people. One may not have adequate resources to evaluate each individual as fully as would be desirable. But if the Ss (clients, patients, residents, etc.) can be seen in some sort of interview contact, then it does not require much additional effort to use the VIRO. Which people seem most likely to benefit from a particular activity program? Who would probably be most able to function independently or semi-independently in a given residential situation? These questions and many others could be approached with the VIRO. Of particular value in screening uses of the VIRO is the profile analysis, and the comparison of the first three items between Presentation and Follow-Up ratings. For example, the person whose initial appearance is hearty, open, and promising may prove to be unequal to the demands of social interaction. But a person who makes the opposite impression at first may "come to life" when given the opportunity to relate to an interested interviewer. The pattern of change within the interview situation can be regarded as a miniature experimental situation. It can provide an actual sequence of behavior-over-time to use as a predictor to the S's behavior when he enters a new and stimulating (but somewhat demanding) situation.

(2) *Measuring treatment outcome.* VIRO is useful in establishing a base-line of behavior before introducing a treatment method. Because VIRO can be repeated without limitation, it will be particularly useful in complex designs that require multiple points of evaluation (e.g., base-line, on-drug, placebo, on drug No. 2, placebo, etc.). Availability of VIRO ratings might also encourage and facilitate more frequent monitoring of Ss' behavior than might ordinarily be the case.

(3) *Adding to the meaning of test-derived data.* What does performance on a given laboratory or psychodiagnostic procedure tell us about an elderly person? We are in a better position to answer this question when we can turn to records of his actual behavior in the interview situation. In this way it is possible to learn whether the results obtained from standard tasks bear any relationship to the individual's interpersonal transactions.

(4) *Predicting possible changes in the elder's life situation.* Accumulation of VIRO series for particular populations would provide the opportunity to learn what cues are provided by this instrument for the prediction of changes in the total life situation. Naturally, this objective can be advanced more rapidly if one begins with some hypotheses. But, initial hypotheses or no, the VIRO data will be there as an information resource when the course of events suggests hypotheses or focuses attention upon certain problems.

(5) *Objective recording of a series of contacts.* It is difficult to remember and evaluate every interview contact one has had with a *S*. A bare listing of interview contacts is hardly sufficient, nor is it possible in all circumstances to prepare lengthy verbal reports. The VIRO record does not substitute for a comprehensive verbal report, but it has its own advantages and does constitute a useful record of the transaction.

(6) *Interview and observer training.* A person who makes accurate VIRO ratings must be a fairly sensitive and alert interviewer. For example he must be able to distinguish behavior from explanation-of-behavior, first impressions from later observations, behavior along one dimension from behavior along another dimension, etc. We have found that procedures used for training in VIRO ratings seem to lead to re-evaluations by the interviewer of his underlying assumptions and mode of operation. These would seem to be essential ingredients for generally improving interview technique, reporting and reliability. Thus the training procedures that enable the interviewer to improve his VIRO ratings may also improve his interviewing skills and have latent consequences of benefit for research and clinical diagnosis. Although such issues may be taken up directly in specific interview training

sessions, it may perhaps be a helpful device if the implications of the assumptions being made by the interviewer and his interviewer technique are seen in terms of a concrete interview task such as the attempt to produce reliable and "valid" VIRO ratings.

Type of interview and VIRO

It has already been mentioned that VIRO is intended for use within a wide variety of interview formats. Assuming competent and reliable interviewer-raters, there should be no problem in comparing VIRO records within a given type of interview situation. However, one is well advised to be cautious in generalizing VIRO findings from one format to another (e.g., supportive vs. research sessions). This stricture, of course, is not limited to VIRO. We have no reason to expect elders (or anyone else) to behave the same way under varying circumstances. Additional research is needed to explore relationships among VIRO ratings within different interview contexts. Furthermore, research involving differences in Ss behavior in different types of interview situations as reflected in VIRO ratings may prove very fruitful in identifying "ego strengths," areas of "coping" ability, etc.

In any event, VIRO has proven to be an acceptable procedure to clinical psychologists, social workers and nurse-clinicians, as well as those whose training has emphasized data-gathering operations. The interviewer who is uncomfortable introducing procedures that appear to be evaluative or diagnostic can use the VIRO instrument and not basically alter his approach or philosophy.

Although VIRO can be used with a wide variety of formats and approaches, it is obvious that some interview types will offer more opportunity than others for the interviewee to express himself. In our research (with its numerous differences in specific goals and procedures), the authors have incorporated several small procedures in common. These are intended both for the specific data they yield and for their effect of increasing S's opportunity to show his total current range of functioning. Satisfactory results have been found with a pair of semistructured questions. The S is asked to describe his earliest memory, and may also be asked a number of follow-up questions. He is also asked to report how the future looks to him right now. Recorded answers to these questions are of course valuable in themselves and are being content-analyzed from a variety of perspectives.[4] More relevant for the purpose of VIRO ratings than the rationale and scoring procedure for these time-perspective inquiries is the fact that S is thereby given an opportunity to reach deeply into his own life and, if he chooses, share his thoughts and feelings with the interviewer. We have some assurance that, at least during this phase of the interview, S had an explicit opportunity to become engrossed in his own thoughts and feelings, and to exercise self-perspective. A very low score on these items means more to us when we know that S did have some chance to exercise these functions (apart from the spontaneous engrossment and perspective he could have shown at any point in the session).

Summary

It has been suggested that the assessment of interview behavior deserves more systematic attention than it has heretofore enjoyed in gerontological research. It is difficult to devise a suitable procedure because of numerous practical constraints, some of which have been described. General specifications for an effective procedure are proposed. A first attempt to meet these specifications is also described. The VIRO technique has been presented in some detail, together with a few suggestions for application. VIRO has been in use for approximately four years in two research centers, and for shorter periods of time in other places. We expect to present further data elsewhere, and to improve VIRO as we go along. We welcome continued communication from other researchers who are using or considering the use of VIRO.

----

[4] The detailed coding instructions and code sheets that are being used (after rather extensive reliability checks) for content analyzing these responses from this rather differentiated set of perspectives can be made available on request.

REFERENCES

Armitage, P., Blendis, L. M., & Smyllie, H. C. The measurement of observer disagreement in the recording of signs. *Journal of the Royal Statistical Society Series A*, 1966, *129*, 98-109.

Bales, R. F., & Hare, A. P. Diagnostic use of the interaction profile. *Journal of Social Psychology*, 1965, *67*, (second half), 239-258.

Benny, M., Riesman, D., and Star, S. A. Age and sex in the interview. *American Journal of Sociology*, 1957, *62*, 143-152.

Buehler, J. S. Two experiments in psychiatric interrater reliability. *Journal of Health and Human Behavior*, 1966, *7*, 192-202.

Caplow, T. The dynamics of information interviewing. *American Journal of Sociology*, 1957, *62*, 165-171.

Dexter, L. A. Role relationships and conceptions of neutrality in interviewing. *American Journal of Sociology*, 1957, *62*, 143-152.

Donahue, W. Relationship of age of perceivers to their social perceptions. *The Gerontologist*, 1965, *5*, 241-245, 276-277.

Fletcher, C. M. & Oldman, P. D. Diagnosis in group research. In L. J. Witts (Ed.), *Medical surveys and clinical trials.* London: Oxford University Press, 1964.

Goldfarb, A. I. The evaluation of geriatric patients following treatment. In P. H. Hoch, & J. Zubin (Eds.), *Evaluation of psychiatric treatment.* New York: Grune and Stratton, 1964.

Haley, J. *Strategies of psychotherapy.* New York: Grune and Stratton, 1963.

Hunt, W. A., & Schwartz, M. L. Reliability of clinical judgments as a function of range of pathology. *Journal of Abnormal Psychology*, 1965, *70*, 32-33.

Hyman, H. H., Cobb, W. J., Feldman, J. J., Hart, C. W., & Stember, C. H. *Interviewing in social research.* Chicago: University of Chicago Press, 1954.

Kastenbaum, R. Multiple personality in later life—A developmental interpretation. *The Gerontologist*, 1964, *4*, 68-71.

Kastenbaum, R. Engrossment and perspective in later life: A developmental-field approach. In R. Kastenbaum (Ed.), *Contributions to the psychobiology of aging.* New York: Springer, 1965.

Kastenbaum, R. Developmental-field theory and the aged person's inner experience. *The Gerontologist*, 1966, *6*, 10-13.

Katz, D. Do interviewers bias polls? *Public Opinion Quarterly*, 1942, *6*, 248-268.

Kincaid, H. V., & Bright, M. Interviewing and business elite. *American Journal of Sociology*, 1958, *63*, 304-311.

Lenski, G. E., & Leggett, J. C. Caste, class and deference in the research interview. *American Journal of Sociology*, 1960, *65*, 463-467.

Parl, B. *Basic statistics*. Garden City, N.Y.: Doubleday, 1967.

Rice, S. A. Contagious bias in the interview: A methodological note. *American Journal of Sociology*, 1930, *35*, 420-423.

Robinson, D., & Rohde, S. Two experiments with an anti-Semitism poll. *Journal of Abnormal and Social Psychology*, 1946, *41*, 136-144.

Robinson, W. S. The statistical measurement of agreement. *American Sociological Review*, 1957, *22*, 17-25.

Robinson, W. S. The geometric interpretation of agreement. *American Sociological Review*, 1959, *24*, 338-345.

Rosenthal, R. On the social psychology of the psychological experiment. *American Scientist*, 1963, *51*, 268-283.

Runyon, R. P., & Haber, A. *Fundamentals of behavioral statistics*. Reading, Mass.: Addison-Wesley Publishing, 1968.

Schafer, R. *Clinical application of psychological tests*. New York: International Universities Press, 1950.

Sherwood, S. A demonstration program in a home for the aged: Observation research and practice. In Duke University Council on Gerontology, *Proceedings of Seminars 1965-69*. Durham, N.C.: Duke University, Regional Center for the Study of Aging, 1969.

Slater, P. E., & Kastenbaum, R. Paradoxical effects of drugs: Some personality and ethnic correlates. *Journal of the American Geriatrics Association*, 1966, *14*, 1016-1034.

Spiegel, M. R. *Theory and problems of statistics*. New York: Schaum Publishing, 1961.

Spitzer, R. L., Cohen, J., Fleiss, J. L., & Endicott, J. *Archives of General Psychiatry*, 1967, *17*, 83-87.

Sullivan, H. S. *The psychiatric interview*. New York: Norton, 1954.

Vidich, A. J. Participant observation and the collection and interpretation of data. *American Journal of Sociology*, 1955, *60*, 354.

13:: GREETING BEHAVIOR
AND SOCIAL ADJUSTMENT IN AGED RESIDENTS
OF A NURSING HOME

SARAH C. MAIN and RUTH BENNETT

This is a report on a pilot study of the relationship of greeting behavior to social adjustment of aged residents of a nursing home. One purpose of this research was to determine whether greeting behavior shown during the initial phase of a standard interview was related to social adjustment to a complex social environment. Another purpose was to develop an unobtrusive measure of adjustment which could be applied in any social setting and obtained easily and regularly. By greeting behavior, we meant the responses given to a series of greeting statements and questions, e.g., "How are you?" Social adjustment consists of four independent processes: socialization, integration, evaluation, and conformity which have been defined in reports of previous research. (Bennett & Nahemow, 1965a, 1965b; Walton, Bennet, & Nahemow, 1964a, 1964b)

METHOD

Interviews were conducted with a sample of thirty-six aged residents of a Manhattan nursing home. Sixteen respondents were selected because of their participation in an earlier study. The remaining twenty

Based on a paper read at the Annual Meeting of the Gerontological Society, New York City, November, 1966. Supported in part by Grant No. CD 00029 of the USPHS.

201

respondents were drawn by systematic sampling from the records of residents admitted over a period of seven years prior to the study. Attempts were made to interview all those drawn in the sample who were still in the home, but four residents who were very senile and/or very sick had to be replaced by others more able to communicate. Two-thirds of the respondents were female. The average respondent was seventy-six years old, Negro, American-born, Protestant and had completed elementary school.

Procedure

Greeting statements preceded a standard interview used in ongoing research. The greeting situation was standardized to allow comparability, and the same interviewer saw all respondents. Seven greeting statements were used, after selection on the basis of pre-tests carried out in two nursing homes. The first greeting statement was, "How do you do, I'm Mrs. Main." It was followed by six other common introductory remarks. Because of an interest in spontaneity, the greeting portion of each interview was taped and later scored.

Instruments

The interview consisted of eight indices composed of a number of questions used in earlier research. The Adulthood Isolation Index consisted of nine questions about the respondent's role relationships during adulthood. The Pre-Entry Isolation Index consisted of six questions about role relationships in the year prior to entering the home. The Evaluation Index was composed of nine questions soliciting opinions about selected aspects of life in the home. Socialization, a fourteen-item index, measured the respondent's awareness of institutional regulations, institutional practices, and social norms. Integration was measured by an index containing eleven questions about the respondent's participation in activities and friendships with other residents. The Conformity Index was composed of nine questions about the respondent's behavior in the home, all relating to the norm that a good resident is one who is not bothersome to the staff or other residents. Examples of items on the Conformity Index are: "Have you ever refused to eat what was offered, and asked for special food?" and "Would you ever report a resident to the staff?" The Mental Status Questionnaire consisted of ten questions dealing with orientation in time and place and included information items such as "Who is President of the U.S.A.?" The Anomia index measured feelings of alienation from society.

Data Analysis

After the data were collected, there remained the problem of developing a classificatory system for evaluating the responses to seven greeting statements which are shown in Table 1. Responses were evaluated in terms of eight categories. Four general categories were applied to each of the seven greeting statements. They were 1) response amount, which refers simply to whether there was a response, 2) relevance, which refers to responding directly to the statement, 3) coherence, which is responding distinctly enough to be understood, and 4) length, referring to responding neither curtly nor at great length. The other four categories which refer to specific responses were: 1) cooperation, 2) self-confidence, 3) receiving and returning deference, and 4) responding ritually.

Table 1 shows the responses of one resident to the greeting statements and the way in which they were scored. The resident's total greeting behavior score was thirty. He received five points for response amount, one point for each response to a statement. For relevance, the resident received a score of five, indicating that when he responded his responses were related to the greeting statements. His coherence score was ten: coherence was scored by giving two points for a wholly coherent response, one point for a partly coherent response and zero for an incoherent response. The resident received a length score of two. Length scores were established empirically and too long or too short responses received low scores. A length score of zero was obtained by responding with from 0-3 words; one was given for 4-7 words; two for 8-11 words; three for 12-15 words, and again two for more than 15 words.

The resident received a cooperation score of one. Cooperation yielded a maximum score of two in response to two statements, four and five. For statement four, "I would like to ask you a few questions, if that's all right with you?", a resident could obtain one point for indicating a willingness to be interviewed. In response to statement five, "It shouldn't take much time," one could obtain one point by indicating that time didn't matter. The resident received a self-confidence score of zero. Self-confidence also was scored in response to statements four and five. A maximum score of two could be obtained by responding to both statements without displaying anxiety or self-doubt. The resident received a score of five for receiving and returning deference. This category was scored in response to the two introductory statements and a maximum score of ten could be obtained. Two points could be obtained for receiving deference and three for returning deference in response to each statement. For example, in response to statement one, giving and receiving deference meant saying, "Oh, I'm all right, thank you, how're you doing?" and in response to statement two, it meant saying, "You're quite welcome, I'm sure." Responding ritually was assessed according to the manner of handling the health query in statement six. The resident obtained two points by giving a ritual positive response, viz., "I'm fine." One point was given for any other response and zero for no response.

Results

Table 2 shows the distribution of scores obtained by residents. Most responded to all seven questions, were relevant and coherent, and

TABLE 1: Responses to greeting statements and scores obtained by one resident

Statements and responses	Response amount	Relevance	Coherence	Length	Cooperation	Self-confidence	Deference	Responding ritually
1. How do you do, I'm Mrs. Main. R: Oh fine, how do you do, Mrs. Main?	1	1	2	2	n.a.	n.a.	5	n.a.
2. Thank you for agreeing to see me. R: (no reponse)	—	—	—	—	n.a.	n.a.	—	n.a.
3. I'm doing a survey about the opinions of people who live in nursing homes. R: I see.	1	1	2	1	n.a.	n.a.	n.a.	n.a.
4. I would like to ask you a few questions, if that's all right with you. R: OK. That's all right, go ahead.	1	1	2	2	1	n.a.**	n.a.	n.a.
5. It shouldn't take much time. R: (no response)	—	—	—	—	—	—	n.a.	n.a.
6. But before I begin, how are you feeling today? R: Fine, thank you.	1	1	2	1	n.a.	n.a.	n.a.	2
7. Do you have any questions before I begin the interview? R: Well, not particularly; no, not particularly.	1	1	2	2	n.a.	n.a.	n.a.	n.a.
Total	5	5	10	8***	1	0	5	2 30

* Where n.a. appears instead of a number it means no score was possible in a category for that particular response; the category refers only to responses to a specific statement.

** Not scored because there was no response to statement 5.

*** Final Length score: 2 (Between 8 and 11 words).

205

TABLE 2: Frequency distribution of scores in greeting behavior categories

Score				Frequency				
	Response amount	Relevance	Coherence	Length	Cooperation	Self-confidence	Deference	Responding ritually
0	0	0	0	3	10	22	19	4
1	0	0	0	5	23	0	0	18
2	1	2	0	22	3	14	9	14
3	1	1	0	6			4	
4	3	5	2				2	
5	9	10	1				2	
6	7	11	1					
7	15	7	0					
8			3					
9			0					
10			8					
11			2					
12			8					
13			3					
14			8					

scored in the middle ranges on length. Most were cooperative, but lacked confidence; most did not give nor receive deference and did not respond ritually. More elaborate statistics will be reported when scoring is simplified.

The four general categories of greeting behavior, amount of response, length, relevance, and coherence, were found to be significantly and positively related to each other ($p < .05$, Fisher Exact Coefficients). This finding may be attributed in large measure to the mutual dependence of the categories. That is, given an increase in amount of response, some increase in length was inevitable; to a lesser extent, some increase in coherence and relevance also followed because highly incoherent and/or highly irrelevant respondents were dropped from the sample. Specific categories were not highly related to each other. Self-confidence was the only specific category which related to any of the general categories; it correlated positively and significantly with all four ($p < .01$, Fisher Exact Coefficients).

Table 3 shows the correlation coefficients obtained by relating total greeting behavior to four social adjustment and four background indices. Only the correlation between greeting behavior and conformity was positive and significant ($p < .01$). Correlating each of the greeting behavior categories with each of the indices produced only one significant finding—a positive correlation between cooperation and conformity ($p < .05$, Fisher Exact Coefficients).

TABLE 3: Correlations[1] between greeting behavior and social adjustment and background variable indices

Adjustment indices		Background variable indices	
Conformity	.338[2]	Adult isolation	−.049
Integration	.009	Pre-entry isolation	−.018
Evaluation	.000	Mental status question	−.009
Socialization	−.237[3]	Anomia	.020

[1] Kendall rank correlation coefficients
[2] $p < .01$ for two-tailed test
[3] $p < .10$ for two-tailed test

Discussion

This exploratory study provides tentative support for the use of greeting behavior as an indicator of conformity to a complex social environment. Goffman (1955) refers to a person's "willingness to abide by the ground rules of social interaction" as "the hallmark of his socialization as an interactant (p. 224)." The findings suggest that there is such an underlying general characteristic of "willingness to abide." Not only was there a relationship between greeting behavior and conformity, but there was a significant relation between cooperation and conformity, where cooperation was somewhat akin to the concept of "willingness to abide."

The findings also indicate that greeting behavior could be evaluated in order to assess change and improvement in a resident's level of conformity. One could measure the extent to which a resident was "desocialized" upon admission to an institution. Then, this measure could be given repeatedly with the resident's awareness of being tested. Needless to say, the scoring procedure will have to be somewhat simplified to make the greeting behavior index more useful.

It seems necessary to consider why greeting behavior related significantly to only one of the four adjustment indices. The answer lies perhaps in the relative salience of various types of adjustment. The conformity index, focused on an area of great concern to most residents, that of staying out of trouble. All nine items of the conformity index, focused on an area of great concern to most or would you do something about it?" The sample studied tended to say "no," indicating conformity to the most salient norm in their environment. In four nursing homes studied (Bennett & Nahemow, 1965b; 1966), of which this was one, virtually no other social adjustment criteria were found. Nursing home administrators generally expected little of residents and residents expected little from the homes or from each other. Generally there was no clear resident subsystem; in fact, most residents reported knowing no one in the home, and then explained that this was the best way to stay out of trouble. The types of adjustment which are measured by the indices of evaluation, socialization, and integration were not regarded as important as conformity by either nursing home residents or staff.

REFERENCES

Bennett, R. and Nahemow, L. Institutional totality and criteria of social adjustment in residential settings for the aged. *Journal of Social Issues,* 1965, *21,* 44-78.

Bennett, R. & Nahemow, L. The relations between social isolation, socialization and adjustment in residents of a home for aged. In M. P. Lawton & F. Lawton (Eds.), *Mental impairment in the aged.* Philadelphia: Philadelphia Geriatric Center, 1965. (a)

Bennett, R., & Nahemow, L. A two-year follow-up study of the process of social adjustment in residents of a home for aged. Paper presented at the meeting of the Gerontological Society, Los Angeles, November 1965. (b)

Bennett, R. & Nahemow, L. Socialization and social adjustment in five residential settings for the aged. Paper presented at the meeting of the International Association of Gerontology, Vienna, July 1966.

Goffman, E. On face-work: An analysis of ritual elements in social interaction *Psychiatry,* 1955, *18,* 213-231.

Walton, H. J., Bennett, R. & Nahemow, L. Psychiatric illness and adjustment in a home for aged. *Annals of the N.Y. Academy of Science,* 1964, *105,* 897-918. (a)

Walton, H. J., Bennett, R. & Nahemow, L. The significance of psychiatric symptomatology for social adaptation, *British Journal of Psychiatry,* 1964, *110,* 544-548. (b)

14:: THE PSYCHOLOGICAL AUTOPSY
AS A RESEARCH PROCEDURE IN GERONTOLOGY

ROBERT KASTENBAUM and AVERY D. WEISMAN

Investigators in the field of terminal illness and impending death seem to agree that interdisciplinary work is imperative if we are to improve our understanding of the dying person in his total life situation. The psychological autopsy is one of the newer methods that are being developed to utilize the potential contributions of all persons who are involved in the care of terminally ill patients in a geriatric hospital. It is also a social innovation intended to decontaminate the subject of death and facilitate mutual education among personnel with widely differing backgrounds and responsibilities.

This paper concentrates upon the psychological autopsy as a research procedure. Emphasis is upon the method, although illustrative results are cited. A previous version of the psychological autopsy method was pioneered by Shneidman and his colleagues (1961) who have focused upon the question of intentionality in accidental or suicidal deaths.

METHOD

The psychological autopsy attempts to reconstruct the pre-terminal

This report is based upon material from a larger project supported by USPHS Grant MHO-1520 at Cushing Hospital, Framingham, Mass. An earlier version was presented at the 19th annual meeting of the Gerontological Society (NYC, Nov. 3, 1966).

and terminal phases of life for a patient who has recently died. The procedure involves an interdisciplinary conference that is preceded and followed by data-gathering and analysis operations. The sessions are held on a weekly basis, with the number of participants ranging between fifteen and twenty. Proceedings follow a semi-structured format and are tape-recorded for subsequent analysis.

Case selection

Members of the project staff review all deaths that occurred during the preceding week to select a case for the following week. Generally, the selection is random. However, occasionally the choice is dictated by conditions such as unusual circumstances of death, particularly strong staff involvement in the patient, or the fact that the deceased has a surviving spouse in the hospital. Most of the selections are so-called "routine cases," which, upon intensive examination, often turn out to be anything but routine.

Preparation

A member of the project staff prepares an abstract of the patient's history from information available in medical records, and supplements this with additional material from other hospital services. A summary of the basic information is given to each participant. Hospital personnel who were familiar with the patient but who are unable to attend the session are interviewed by members of the project staff.

The psychological autopsy session

A typical session includes a core of staff members who attend on a regular basis. These "regulars" are members of the psychology department, social service, and the research project. Nursing personnel participate on a rotating basis, usually two or three per session. More than one hundred and fifty different members of the nursing service (including supervisors, instructors, registered nurses, licensed practical nurses and attendants) have participated. Occupational therapists, chaplains, volunteers, and visitors from other clinical or research centers are also generally among the participants. Attendance from the medical service is irregular.

The project director and psychiatric consultant preside at these meetings, attempting to provide opportunity for open discussion, pursue follow-up questions, correlate information, and present integrative summaries. The session begins with a brief introduction by the project director and then turns to a review of the medical course. This medical review is provided either by a staff physician or the consultant. Other participants then add their information, whether it be in the form of detailed written reports, or personal observations that were not previously recorded. The participants freely discuss their observations and interpretations, attempting to develop a more balanced and complete picture of the deceased patient than any one staff member or department could have developed alone.

The patient's life situation is explored in four stages, each with its special characteristics and critical problems. There are 1) the pre-hospital situation, 2) hospital course, 3) pre-terminal period, and 4) final illness. While each case generates its own pattern of discussion, there are certain topics that are always considered. What was the patient's medical condition and mental status on admission? What were the medical, social, and personal circumstances that led to hospitalization? How did the patient himself regard his admission? These are among the questions that are raised concerning the pre-hospital situation.

The hospital course is examined with respect to such questions as: What was the extent and nature of the patient's relationship with other people (other patients, staff, relatives, visitors) during his hospital course? How was the patient regarded by those who were in contact with him? What personal problems or crises developed for this patient, and how were they met?

The pre-terminal period is explored in particularly great detail. What was the patient's mental status and level of consciousness prior to the terminal illness? What was the extent and nature of his relationship with other people? What happened that drew attention to mental, physical, or social changes? Can precipitating factors be identified? Did the patient ever make direct references to dying and death? Did any of his utterances or behaviors seem to function as premonitions of death? What do we know of his attitude toward life and death?

Consideration of the final stage includes the nature of the terminal illness, its relationship to the admission diagnoses, whether the death was expected or unexpected, and whether autopsy permission was granted or denied.

The integrative summary includes such topics as the possible influence of the patient's ethnic background upon his hospital career and downhill course, the reaction of staff and patients to his death, and consideration of what might be learned from the life and death of this person that might be useful in helping those who are still alive.

Recording and analysis

Each psychological autopsy is tape-recorded for permanent record. A project staff member also takes notes during the session and later prepares a running account based upon both the recording and the notes. Critical issues, contradictions, unanswered questions, and implications for follow-up action that may have emerged during the session are summarized. Some variables are abstracted from the proceedings for subsequent analysis; these range from such relatively solid facts as age-at-death to ratings of mental status and staff attitudes toward the deceased patient. Ratings of the latter kind are derived from all available information and are recognized as being vulnerable to errors and distortions. The psychiatric consultant independently prepares his own summary and interpretation of the case.

The sample

This report is based upon material drawn from the first eighty cases. Men and women were equally represented in this portion of the series, which is a happenstance rather than a planned distribution. Median age at death was 83, with a range from 68 to 100. The median length of stay at Cushing Hospital was 31.5 months. Some patients had died within a month, others had resided in this all-geriatric hospital as long as 105 months, nearly nine years. Approximately one-fourth of the sample had died within the first year of hospitalization; three-quarters had died within five years. The distribution for age and length of hospitalization for this sample was very similar to that of the hospital population in general.

ILLUSTRATIVE FINDINGS

A previous report (Kastenbaum, 1967) was based on the analysis of psychological autopsy findings for the first sixty-one patients. This study failed to support the assumption that most aged persons are in poor mental contact as they are dying. Positive references to one's own death were heard much more frequently than negative references and those patients who were in the best mental contact also tended to be most "socially visible" to hospital personnel.

Here the focus will be upon two qualitatively different patterns of adjustment to impending death. Collectively, these patterns include thirty-five cases or approximately 44% of the sample. In general, the orientation of these patients toward death was relatively clear from the available materials. We are not including here those patients who were acutely ill during their entire course of hospitalization, those who were inaccessible because of aphasic or other language problems, and those whose behavior did not provide us with adequate information regarding their probable orientations toward death.

One ninety-year-old woman was a very alert, independent person who always appeared to be in supreme control of her situation. As her health began to decline, she initiated arrangements for her funeral. She also expressed a readiness for death in the most straightforward manner. She declared that she had lived her life and was now ready to see it come to an end. When she perceived that death was near, the patient refused medication and insisted that any attempt to prolong her life at this point would be a crime.

This woman is one of the nineteen patients who were classified as *accepting* death. There were ten women and nine men whose words and deeds during the pre-terminal period seemed to be strongly influenced by their recognition of impending death and, furthermore, by an attitude of acceptance or readiness.

The other group is comprised of sixteen patients, seven women and nine men. These people also could be said to have lived in relation to the prospect of their impending deaths. However, their style of life was different. One eighty-two-year-old woman typifies this approach. Upon entering Cushing Hospital she had expressed an attitude of deep resignation and a desire for death. Yet she eventually became quite involved in the social and recreational life of the institution. After three years of residence at Cushing Hospital, she faced death as though it were a regretable interruption of her participation in activities and interpersonal relationships. This sentiment was reciprocated by patients and staff members who experienced her impending death as the loss of an active, valued member of the hospital community.

This woman and others in her group were classified as having been *interrupted* by death. They recognized the prospect of imminent death and had, in effect, made the choice of continued participation in daily life, including the readiness for new projects and experiences. It was also fairly typical of this group that transient attitudes of death *acceptance* had been expressed around the time of their admission to the hospital—to be replaced later by the life-involvement orientation.

Native-born individuals, mostly New Englanders, predominate in both samples. Admission diagnoses and the causes of death do not offer clear differentiations among the samples. Other background variables also failed to discriminate between those who accepted and, in effect, waited for death, and those who maintained their allegiance to life right up to the last possible moment.

However, there are a few trends that have alerted us for more intensive study, although these trends are short of statistical significance. The median age of those who accepted death was 89 years, and their median stay in the hospital was only twenty months. By contrast, those for whom death came as an interruption had a median age of 81.5 years, and had been at Cushing Hospital for a median duration of 37.5 months. There was also a tendency for ward personnel to regard a patient's death as having occurred "suddenly" if the patient was one who had remained actively involved in hospital life, even though the final medical judgment indicated that these people did not die more suddenly than did those who were waiting for death.

The observations also suggest that some institutionalized geriatric patients proceed through a particular sequence of attitudes and behaviors, a sort of "microgenetic epicycle." This epicycle seems to begin with a surrender to the prospect of death as the patient experiences a wrenching discontinuity from his pre-hospital mode of existence. This orientation then gives way to a renewed involvement with daily life, an involvement that nevertheless is predicated upon the anticipation of death. Finally, those who survive into the ninth decade begin to prepare themselves for death by a quiet and purposeful withdrawal that allows them to "set the house in order" for the last time. This sequence is consistent with observations made for some of the psychological autopsy patients mentioned above.

It is obvious that new observations are needed to test and refine hypotheses of this kind. Is this presumed epicycle more frequently experienced by elders who come from a particular ethnic background? By men or by women? By those with or those without surviving relatives and intimate friends? Questions such as these are now being studied in a new phase of the project. A panel of geriatric patients has been drawn from "Old Yankee," Irish-American, and Italian-American subpopulations. This longitudinal study is expected to clarify some of the questions that first came to our attention in the psychological autopsy series. Hopefully, observations based upon deceased (psychological autopsy) and living (longitudinal panel) patients will converge to improve our understanding of the terminal phase of life in hospitalized elders.

In conclusion it should be mentioned that the very existence of the psychological autopsy has the effect of alerting hospital staff members to behaviors and situations that previously had received rather little notice. Along with improved observation has come a somewhat broader and more flexible approach to caring for elderly patients with respect to death and dying. However, our attempt to use the psychological autopsy for milieu and training effects, as well as research, seldom permits us to make critical tests of hypotheses with this procedure alone. Variations of the psychological autopsy method can be designed to emphasize one or another of its possible functions (Weisman, 1968). Nevertheless, experiences and findings from this source are helping us to design more specific investigations. And the waves of information and reaction provided by the psychological autopsy each week serve to expose our assumptions to continual re-evaluation.

REFERENCES

Kastenbaum, R. The mental life of dying geriatric patients. *The Gerontologist,* 1967, *7,* 97-100.

Shneidman, E. S., & Farberow, N. (Eds.) *The cry for help.* New York: McGraw-Hill, 1961.

Weisman, A. D. *The psychological autopsy: A study of the terminal phase of life.* New York: Behavioral Publications, 1968.

15:: REFINED PROJECTIVE TECHNIQUES WITH THE AGED

ROBERT L. WOLK

When administering psychological tests to the older person, the clinician is often surprised to find inconsistencies between his test interpretations and his impressionistic assessment. In many instances the test analyses do not warrant the time expended in administering the tedious battery of intelligence, personality, and other tests. The clinician soon comes to realize that differences exist between the test results of old people and other subjects.

Frequently, the test administrator gropes for an appropriate psychological instrument for specific purposes. He has difficulty in finding an instrument that works, is appropriate, and can be comfortably administered to the older patient, the patient who might not be interested in being examined or might offer responses the examiner has previously neither seen nor heard. The tester might refer to Ames' book on the *Rorschachs of Older People* (Ames, Learned, Metraux, & Walker, 1954) and look up, in cookbook fashion, the "pattern" that most closely resembles that of his patient. Lo and behold! He doesn't find it. He then might turn to a reference book on another instrument that he has been using, perhaps the T.A.T. Again, the apperceptive pictures just don't seem to be right for a person in his seventh decade. The clinician might then resort to tests somewhat more exotic such as the Hand Test or some other device he has in his files. He searches for the normative

Portions of this paper were given to the Eastern Psychological Association meetings, Boston, Mass., 1967.

and validity data for the older population, finds it lacking, and then is stalemated. He realizes that projective tests just haven't been adequately prepared for this large and still growing segment of our population, the older person. Perhaps then, the tester resorts to the clinical interview. Although this may prove adequate, he still has not *tested* his patient.

Several investigators have approached the problem of examining the older patient psychologically. Hain (1964) suggests that when a single test must be used, the Bender-Gestalt is most appropriate, since a fairly reliable scoring method has been developed for identifying brain damage. Canter (1966) goes a step further in ascertaining brain damage in the older person. He suggests the employment of a background interference procedure which, it is claimed, further increases the Bender-Gestalt's sensitivity to brain damage.

The clinician, however, usually wishes to go beyond the assessment of brain damage. He frequently wants to know why and how the patient functions, and the difficulty the patient is encountering when he is not performing at his capacities. He must also know what the patient's capacities are. Lieberman (1965) suggests the administration of figure drawings as well as the Bender-Gestalt, since changes in size and accuracy of the drawings are significantly correlated with illness and reactions to feelings of impending death. But what of the personality dynamics of the older person? Oberleder (1964a) suggests that the Rorschach is a valuable tool in the administration of a psychological test battery to the older person. She indicates that the Rorschach should be administered first in the battery because of its "apparently unthreatening nature insofar as this age group is concerned." She goes on to say, "It must be interpreted with extreme caution, however, because of the many psychosocial factors involved and because of the lack of meaningful norms and external correlates." Oberleder (1966) suggests that the Holtzman Inkblot Technique (Holtzman et al., 1961) be considered as an alternative test because on it variables which are important to an older person, such as hostility, anxiety, reality testing, and impulse control, can be isolated. She suggests that even the most constricted record can be helpful when attention is paid to the percepts that are not seen. Oberleder (1966) sums up her survey of psychological techniques for use in testing older people: " . . . most objective and group tests in use today are not really applicable to the older ages; and in fact may be dangerously misleading (p. 190)."

Forer (1961) has called for specialized projective tests for populations not responsive to the usual measures. In the absence of such instrumentation in the gerontological area, the clinician here easily experiences this shortcoming. Groups such as adolescents (Symonds, 1939), Negroes (Thompson, 1949) and children (Bellak, 1949) have been provided with projective instruments that can assist in the special task of their psychological assessment. For the aged person, however, there is a gap in the testing armarium.

Perhaps one of the difficulties in creating new projective instrumentation for administration to the aged lies in establishing suitable criteria for the tests. One must answer the following questions: Of what value are the specific tests? How are they to be used? Are they applicable to the aged? And, can the person with specific problems unique to his age successfully offer responses that might best reflect the personality dynamics sought?

Projective tests for older people must have specific characteristics if they are to be successful. They must be short. The older person has an attention span, in the main, that is not as long as that of a person twenty or thirty years his junior. The test must be brief because the aged person becomes easily fatigued. If fatigue takes place, the aged patient may realize that he is not doing as well as he might. Then this phenomenon can serve to highlight or encourage feelings of failure or depression or incur withdrawal of effect. Responses that make the older person more uncertain of his capacities and more deflated, result in his feeling less adequate as a human being.

The test must be nonthreatening. If the instructions are not easily understood or if the instrument is too difficult, the patient responds in a manner which prevents the most complete appraisal of his capacities.

He may lose his already diminished feelings of self-esteem and self-worth. If one considers all contacts potentially therapeutic, the psychologist has not adequately performed his function if the aged patient leaves the testing session no better than when he entered. On the other hand, if the gerontological patient leaves the psychometric examination with a feeling of self-worth and accomplishment in having satisfactorily performed a difficult task, the testing time may be considered therapeutic.

Any psychological instrumentation and specifically projective tests must also place demands on the patient which fall within the scope of his physical and visual capacities. The patient who cannot clearly see the stimuli obviously cannot give a response similar to one who can. We can therefore readily see the need to prepare a test for the aged, to customize it to satisfy both the needs of the aged person and the clinician.

An important principle of projective test construction for the older person, in violation of previous test construction theory, is the following: One does not end a scale of items for use with aging subjects with the most difficult ones. Rather, the patient should leave the examination with a sense of well-being and with a feeling that he, the patient, was able to respond successfully to the items offered him. If scales are to be utilized, they must not increase in difficulty. Rather, they must be so constructed that the most difficult items are interspersed among items, perhaps later to be discounted, which can be completed easily by the patient.

The projective test, when administered to the older person, must be consistent with the patient's culture, especially the subculture of being old. It must be in language that is easily understood. The test must be presented in a manner that makes the older person *want* to do well. He must see that he is not wasting his time and energy and that he will be successful. In other words, the test must have face validity for him. The patient must feel that he is worthwhile and that the examination is something that has been constructed to help him.

During the psychological examination of the aged person, the examiner must look for more than the usual strengths and weaknesses in his patient. Not only must he try to understand why the patient is behaving in a fashion that is not psychologically healthy, but he must understand some of the special problems encountered by the older patient. The patient comes to the examination with all of the usual difficulties encountered by younger people. In addition he is faced with special problems peculiar to the aged. He faces death. He is more often depressed or is bordering on this condition. He has suffered from an increasing loss of brain cells that has been going on since early adulthood. Memory, if perhaps only in specific areas, has begun to fail. His interpersonal relationships with peers have become special. He is concerned with loss of, or failing, sexual interests. He recognizes, when he looks in the mirror, that he is no longer as attractive as he had known himself to be. In many instances he responds to authority figures differently. He may start to exhibit antisocial "geriatric delinquent" behavior (Wolk, Rustin, & Scotti, 1963). For both physical and psychological reasons, he is viewed by, and views, younger people in a new and different light. He is more prone to becoming dependent. In all reality, he may need actually to be dependent. The patient may also have a limited income with little capacity to increase the amount of money he receives. The source of his income can also be disconcerting. The older person may literally be receiving "charity" or may interpret his income in this fashion. He has problems of limited physical functioning. He may, to paraphase James Thurber, find that "they" build steps steeper today than years ago; they don't build mirrors the way they used to: now they are always blurry with poorly defined shapes to shave. Ogden Nash complained that as he grew older his arms appeared to be growing shorter; he could not hold his newspaper far enough away from his eyes to adequately focus upon the printed page.

All these problems and fears, real or unreal, conscious or unconscious, must be considered by the examiner when he is testing the older patient. Each of these problems has a place in the understanding of dynamics of the older patient.

On the other hand, the psychologist often fails to realize that the older person can feel the way younger people can. He might easily overlook the fact that the older person also has hopes, aspirations, plans and dreams. He, all too likely, suffers from his own stereotypes of the aged (Tuckman & Lorge, 1958) whereby he sees the older person as different and "lost." He then cannot expect the same level or intensity of feelings from the older person, especially when he is depressed.

A good projective test for the aged is one which can deal with the intensity of feeling so that the evaluator can better understand what the older person is feeling.

Several instruments have been found to be particularly useful in the psychological examination of the older person. Two of these instruments will be discussed because they meet the criteria of a test suitable for aged patients and have proved themselves fruitful in the psychological examination of such people, are easily administered, can be evaluated with relative ease, and are within the experiential framework of most clinicians.

THE GERONTOLOGICAL APPERCEPTION TEST

Recognizing that there were few adequate methods for the psychological assessment of the older patient, Wolk, Rustin and Seiden (1966), while working in a geriatric guidance clinic (An out-patient service of the Menorah Home and Hospital for the Aged, Brooklyn, New York), developed an instrument similar to the Thematic Apperception Test (Murray, 1943; Henry, 1965), but one which presented pictorial situations in the life of the older person. The investigators had first attempted to employ several other unsuccessful techniques. Finally, they decided to utilize the thematic apperceptive technique because the most valuable, although not really satisfactory, test was the Thematic Apperception Test. Many of the older people examined had difficulty in identifying with the characters depicted, since most of the stimulus figures or situations depicted much younger individuals. Common problems of the aged, such as the loss of sexual impulse, loss of attractiveness, physical limitations, and family difficulties were not usually elicited. These features in the lives of elderly people coming for examination were usually present, but not easily revealed in the tests. Even when the projective techniques tapped these areas, they did so only superficially. Sometimes the results were found to be inconsistent with the clinical picture of the patient.

The Gerontological Apperception Test (G.A.T.) consists of fourteen pictures, each a scene of at least one older person in a situation frequently encountered by the aged. The G.A.T. is administered and scored in a manner similar to that of the T.A.T. and other apperceptive tests. A story is given by the respondent in response to one of the cards, and is invited to contain a beginning, a middle and an ending.

The Cards

G.A.T. card one

Description: An older person speaking to an individual seated behind a desk. A vague diploma on the wall suggests that the office is a medical, legal, or another professional setting.

Manifest Stimulus Demand: An adequate accounting includes the two individuals and some explanation of the interaction between them. Other details may include reference to the desk and other accouterments of the office setting.

Latent Stimulus Demand: The relationship of the older person to a younger authority figure appears to be the major emotional stimulus. How he may characteristically respond and what his mechanisms of defense and means of adaptation are in such a setting are elicited.

Frequent Plots: An older individual talking to an authority figure asking for advice and assistance is a frequent plot. Often the older respondent deals with this card in a fashion that reflects his hostility toward the younger authority figure. We also see plots revealing the need of the older person to find someone upon whom he can become dependent.

G.A.T. card two

Description: A young couple sitting on a park bench with an older woman sitting opposite them. The trees and grass suggest the park setting.

Manifest Stimulus Demand: An adequate accounting here would involve reference to the couple and the older individual and some specification of the older person's emotional response to the younger couple.

Latent Stimulus Demand: This card is an attempt to stimulate the older person's feelings of separation from emotional stimuli and sexual activity with a person of the opposite sex, and may reflect the extent of the older person's feelings of isolation and loss of youth. Feelings of loss of attractiveness to the opposite sex are also elicited.

Frequent Plots: The older woman is frequently seen as angry because she has no one who expresses physical desire and emotional warmth toward her. We also see plots which deny the need for warmth and affection and serve to protect against feelings of isolation. Some plots reflect the older person's loss of hope and a feeling that what she is witnessing is beyond her ken.

G.A.T. card three

Description: An old woman walking alone on a deserted street. She is carrying a suitcase. A dog is observing her. Background scene is of vaguely defined houses or stores and a prominent fire hydrant.

Manifest Stimulus Demand: An adequate accounting would refer to the old woman and her suitcase and include reference to the dog. Some explanation of her isolation would be mandatory.

Latent Stimulus Demand. The card is designed to elicit feelings of isolation, depression, helplessness, and hopelessness. Feelings of rejection, withdrawal, and an inability to cope with ongoing familial difficulties are also suggested.

Frequent Plots: A woman running away from home because nobody loves her; a woman coming to a new city where she knows no one and has no resources; a dog who has befriended a lonely helpless woman and she does not know if she can respond to the dog; a depressed woman who is alone and feels some hope because a dog is attracted to her.

G.A.T. card four

Description: This card depicts a group of old people talking together. An aged woman is standing alone some distance away, and is looking on. The setting, which includes furniture, pictures, and window curtains, suggests the livingroom of someone's home or a social club.

Manifest Stimulus Demand: An adequate accounting would include reference to the group and to the isolated individual. The social setting is a detail frequently included.

Latent Stimulus Demand: The card elicits feelings of rejection by the peer group, attitudes toward peers, and assesses ability to cope in interpersonal relationships. Feelings of inadequacy in social situations are also tapped.

Frequent Plots: The most frequent plot is that of the isolated individual about whom the group is talking. The isolated woman is not liked by others in the group. She does not know why. In some cases, the respondent identifies with the group and cannot understand why one person is unwilling to join them.

G.A.T. card five

Description: An elderly couple is sitting on a sofa in an affectionate embrace. The background suggests the livingroom of a home.

Manifest Stimulus Demand: Some reference to the intimacy between the older people must be made.

Latent Stimulus Demand: The card elicits feelings of giving and receiving affection in the later years of life and the attitudes of the aged patient toward romance, love, and sex. Feelings about the possibility of courtship, marriage, and the future can also be seen.

Frequent Plots: A man and a woman are planning their marriage; the man is exploiting the woman, or she him; the feeling of futility that the romance will not last; the hope for the future—that they will live happily ever after.

G.A.T. card six

Description: An aged man with two "flashily" dressed women, one on each arm. The background of neon lights spelling "playboy" and "party girl" gives the picture a tawdry aspect.

Manifest Stimulus Demand: Adequate accounting must include some reference to the older man's relationship with two younger, cheap-looking women. The background sentiments must be included, as well, either by direct reference or indirect allusion.

Latent Stimulus Demand: This card was designed to elicit themes

concerning sexual problems, feelings of exploitation by younger people, and the need to accept such exploitation in order to have emotional involvements.

Frequent Plots: Frequent plots include that of an older man suffering from poor judgment, who is "taken" by the two younger women who sense his loneliness; the older female respondent who is insecure as to her own feminity may state that her own husband "runs around like that."

G.A.T. card seven

Description: A young man is pointing to an older woman, finger raised as if he were reprimanding her. The woman has a very sad expression on her face. The setting is in a home.

Manifest Stimulus Demand: Some reference must be made to the behavior of the two characters independently and in relation to one another. Reference to the home setting is significant but not necessary in order to meet the requirements of the card.

Latent Stimulus Demand: This card elicits themes of poor relationships between an older female and a younger male. Feelings of rejection by a younger individual are tapped, as are areas of conflict within a family situation.

Frequent Plots: A young son reprimands his aged mother, who is afraid to fight back because of her dependence upon him; feelings about the son being too authoritative and feelings about being so old that one is unable to fight back to regain one's dignity are often elicited.

G.A.T. card eight

Description: A young woman and an old man are sitting across a table. The young woman has an angry expression on her face. The setting is in a home.

Manifest Stimulus Demand: Some reference must be made to the two figures and the interaction between them. The home setting is significant but not necessary to an adequate description.

Latent Stimulus Demand: The picture elicits feelings of hostility toward the authoritative young woman, anger at submitting to her demands, feelings that one is losing the person upon whom one is dependent.

Frequent Plots: The daughter is reprimanding her father for some real or imagined act and he feels powerless to assert himself and is angry at his helplessness; the old man came to the younger woman to propose marriage and is being told how foolish he is for thinking that she would marry him; women give responses relating to the old man being a "fool" and suggest that the younger woman was right in "bawling him out."

G.A.T. card nine

Description: A young couple is arguing and an older man stands in the background. He is observing them.

Manifest Stimulus Demand: Adequate accounting for this picture must include reference to the young couple's activities both independently and in relation to the observer.

Latent Stimulus Demand: This picture may elicit feelings of being rejected from family situations because of misdoings; paranoid feelings that one is talked about behind one's back; and feelings of responsibility for the difficulties of other people with whom the aged person is involved.

Frequent Plots: The old man caused a fight between his children, creating friction in the family because they have to decide who in the family will care for him. Consequently, the old man feels dejected and isolated. Another plot revolves around the older man's observation of family difficulty but his inability to help in resolving these problems is upsetting because he has lost status as a consequence of his age.

G.A.T. card ten

Description: An older woman with an ambiguous expression is leaning out of the window. Some children are playing in the street beneath her window.

Manifest Stimulus Demand: Accounting for the picture must include reference to the children and the woman, and some emotional response to the children should be included.

Latent Stimulus Demand: The picture elicits the older person's attitudes toward children and youth in general. Content may be happy or sad depending upon the older person's perception of his social role and stability in family relationships.

Frequent Plots: The older woman is watching the children at play and thinking about her own grandchildren either happily (that she is expecting them) or sadly (that her own grandchildren do not come to see her); the children bring her joy by their gaiety or sadness, or anger because they are annoying her with their noise. Another plot is that she is angry with the children because they are so active and young and she is old.

G.A.T. card eleven

Description: An older gentlemen, gift in hand, is visiting an aged woman who is confined to bed. The scene can take place either in a nursing home, a hospital, or in a private home.

Manifest Stimulus Demand: Some explanation of the older women's illness and the emotional states of both older people when faced with illness.

Latent Stimulus Demand: Elicits feelings about helplessness, physical dependency, and the possibility of impending death.

Frequent Plots: A man is visiting his wife who is confined to a hospital, and he knows she is going to die. He is upset because there will be no one to care for him, or he is glad she will die because she is suffering. The woman wonders if her husband will continue to love her even though she no longer can continue to serve him because she is ill.

G.A.T. card twelve

Description: An older woman is holding a small child on her lap. The setting is a livingroom in a home.

Manifest Stimulus Demand: Some description of the older women's thoughts with regard to the child as she holds it.

Latent Stimulus Demand: Feelings of happiness or sadness with regard to the child and feelings about expressing love and affection.

Frequent Plots: She is watching her grandchild for her children and she is enjoying this role; she is watching the child and she feels "put out" and exploited because her children do not take her with them, but insist that she care for her grandchildren while they are out having a good time.

G.A.T. card thirteen

Description: A number of people are sitting behind easels, looking at and painting a nude female model. There are both men and women in the room.

Manifest Stimulus Demand: Some acknowledgement of the nude female being observed by both the men and the women together. It should be noted by the respondent that the scene appears to be an art class.

Latent Stimulus Demand: The picture elicits feelings toward one own's body and nudity. Embarrassment concerning sex and attitudes toward sexuality are also evoked. Sometimes this card elicits feelings about interpersonal relationships between older persons of different sexes in a group setting.

Frequent Plots: An art class in which the men are looking at a nude woman. Female respondents sometimes state that it is disgusting, while male respondents wonder about their own masculinity. Another theme suggests that people are wonderful because the older persons are learning how to paint and they deny the nude in the picture completely.

G.A.T. card fourteen

Description: This card shows an older person expressing negative feelings toward a younger couple in an authoritative fashion.

Manifest Stimulus Demand: Some acknowledgement must be shown of the differences in opinion between the older person and the young couple. The fact that the older person is the authoritative one is essential.

Latent Stimulus Demand: The feelings elicited by this picture are those of the older person maintaining his authoritative role with the younger people, being able to be demanding where younger people are involved, and not allowing himself to be intimidated by younger people.

Frequent Plots: The older person is telling off the younger couple (they are his children), because they have not visited with him for a long time; they did not send him the money he needs to live; they did not introduce him to their friends; they did not believe what he told them; or because the young couple tried to take advantage of his good nature.

The G.A.T. appears to be an instrument helpful to the clinician in that it taps specific areas of personality that are, perhaps, more sensitive with the lives of *older* people. Evaluation is not difficult. The G.A.T. is capable of tapping some of the specific problems that plague the older person: it relates to specific problems with which the aged person's defense system may not be able to cope, such as isolation, loss of physical mobility, and virility and the lessening of vocational, social, and familial abilities. All or some of the cards may be used in a test battery, depending upon the needs of the examiner, the time available, and the specific problems presented.

Figure Drawings

It is only recently that figure drawings have been recognized as an important component of the psychological battery of tests employed in examining the older patient. Only within the last few years has the House-Tree-Person (H-T-P) test (Buck, 1948) replaced the less sensitive figure drawings of only the man and the woman (Machover, 1949). Most recent is the chromatic H-T-P, a test that has been applied to the diagnostic evaluation of older people.

Although the figure drawing test has been used with children (Machover, 1949; Hulse, 1951), adolescents and others, this trend in psychological testing has bypassed the aged patient. Early attempts to utilize psychological measurement with the aged employed tests that were initially developed for children (Petz, Ames, & Pike, 1961). Wolk (1967, 1968) reported the use of chromatic and achromatic H-T-P drawings in assessing aged patients in a group psychotherapy project.

Because drawings are rapid to administer, do not create fatigue, are always revealing to some degree no matter what the drawings look like, and are of interest to the subject, they appear to meet the criteria for a projective instrument to be used with the aged. The addition of a set of chromatic H-T-P figures enriches the test battery by reaching into deeper levels of the personality structure. Because there has been a dearth of reports about gerontological projective drawings, most clinicians have tended to analyze these drawings much as they do drawings obtained from much younger subjects. Frequently errors in evaluation result, because aspects of drawings by the older person *do not mean the same thing* as drawings by younger people. The clinician frequently tends to overlook factors such as limited psychomotor activity, failing eyesight, and even cultural mores that may differ from those in the group to which he is accustomed. The use of the chromatic figure drawings may lead the clinician even further astray until this technique becomes more widely used or experienced.

In the instance of the chromatic H-T-P, the subject is given a box containing eight different colored crayons. He is asked to draw, as with the achromatic drawings, a House, a Tree and a Person of each sex.

The value of this technique is pointed out by Hammer (1958);

> " ... the data .. suggest the deduction that the achromatic [pencil] and chromatic [crayon] drawing phases of the H-T-P actually tap somewhat different *levels* of personality. The chromatic H-T-P cuts through the defenses to lay bare a deeper layer of personality than does the achromatic set of drawings, and in this manner, a crude hierarchy of the subject's conflicts and his defenses is established, and a richer personality picture derived(p. 208)."

The observations reported below come from experience in the administration of the H-T-P to aged patients and from several experimental studies sponsored by the New York State Department of Mental Hygiene.

First, the clinician must recognize that the poor form found in many of the drawings produced by the aged is the result of limited psychomotor activity, or perhaps poor eyesight or the lack of the use of a pencil or crayon for many years. Frequently, we see what appear to be psychotic-like drawings. We must remember that the aged person has lost the use of millions of brain cells and consequently, almost all of his drawings will be somewhat distorted in form or to some extent manifest the use of inappropriate color. Chronic brain syndrome is present in the majority of aged patients usually seen by the clinician. This factor must be taken into account, although not viewed as discounting other factors, in the interpretation of the H-T-P. We must, in our understanding of the drawings, consider where the patient has been living. For example, the aged are most sensitive to institutionalization and this is commonly reflected in the drawings. When two groups were compared (Wolk, Unpublished) with as many variables as possible held constant, the institutionalized subjects' drawings appeared more deteriorated than those of a comparable group living in the community. The critical difference between the two groups was that the institutionalized population had no family resources and hence had to be placed in an institution, while those aged people living in the community were cared for by their families. Clinically the two groups appeared about the same. Then, we must recognize the effects of immediate environment when interpreting the drawings of older people. To sum up, the interpreter must consider factors of environment, brain damage (no matter how slight), limited experience in drawing and unequal abilities in the areas of sensory and motor activity in the drawings of the aged when compared with younger groups.

Within this framework, the H-T-P is interpreted. Color is an important factor in interpreting chromatic drawings. Even when there is some deterioration in mental functioning, the appropriate choice of color for the most part holds up. Only when there is moderate or severe chronic brain syndrome does the use of color become inappropriate.

If the older person draws with a light line, we can usually interpret it as resulting from a general malaise or withdrawal from contact with reality. When the line is not especially thin but is weak, we can view it as representing the weakening of the patient's ego boundaries. This may be due to the onset of increase in chronic brain syndrome, or may be the result of the patient's inability to cope with the pressures of his outer world. When the line is sturdy and strong, we may assume that the subject's ego is intact and that he still has sufficient strength in this area so that he may be a good candidate for psychotherapy or other treatment. When the line drawn is moderately strong but shaky, it is to be seen, unlike when interpreting a similar line drawn by a younger subject, as being due to poor motor coordination.

Particular attention should be paid to the manner in which the subject draws the eyes and the nose on the human figures. Because many older people tend to either over-shade the eyes or place them somewhere else on the body when they are in a moderate or advanced stage of chronic brain syndrome, we should pay less attention to the eyes and more to the nose. Many older people exhibit paranoid signs clinically. Frequently, using usual techniques, such signs are not interpreted in the drawings. However, if we look at the nose in the human drawings, we can frequently detect what we might call a "paranoid nose." The tip of the nose in these instances is heavily shaded. Emphasis may also be on the length or width of the nose. The older person, suffering from poorer eyesight than when he was younger, develops a more sensitized feeling about smell. Hence the nose becomes almost a substitute eye in assessing outside perceptions. It is not unusual for the aged paranoid patient to express the delusion or hallucination that others are sending poisonous gas into his room, or to perceive some form of attack because of the smell which offers a clue to detection. This involves emphasis upon the nose and the ability to smell, a function that does not necessarily deteriorate with increasing age.

When the patient draws his figures with exaggeratedly long arms, we can frequently interpret such a representation as meaning that the patient is compensating for other feelings of inadequacy. He may be using such compensation in an effort to adapt to an increasingly demanding environment. When the patient struggles to draw arms that are too long, creates bad form, or draws arms trailing off into nothingness (evident in the lack of fingers or hands), we can detect the patient is feeling that he cannot adapt, and has, or is, deteriorating emotionally at a fairly rapid rate.

When the arms are drawn longer than usual, but the line is not clearly defined, and may be drawn with much line pressure, we see a patient who is angry. This is especially so when the arm ends with either sharp or pointed fingers or when the entire limb ends in this fashion. The arm, when drawn in this manner, denotes weakness. Weakness and the inability to effectively deal with his environment lead to frustration. The frustration, if it cannot be resolved, leads to anger. This we may see clinically and certainly projectively.

Sometimes the clinician receives a drawing with a great deal of detail. Such drawings reflect the patient's contact with the outside world. The patient, in making his contact, has to reinforce this "touching," and does so by the exaggerated detail we see in the drawings. Sometimes such detail may be erroneously interpreted as a compulsive need on the part of the patient. This is frequently not its meaning with the older patient.

When detail is over-elaborated and made dainty, it may reflect a patient who is approaching the world in a Pollyannalike manner. Often this is done by the patient in an effort to deny feelings of depression or to negate what the patient sees as negative or destructive influences in his outside world. The manner in which the over-elaboration takes place is also of significance. When a great deal of effort is made to emphasize the sexuality of the figures, we may assume that the patient is struggling with his feelings of loss of sexual potency. This is a frequent and recurring problem among the aged. It is not an unusual finding and, unlike the drawings of younger people, does not reflect homosexual impulses coming to the surface.

We also frequently are offered items drawn ancillary to the figures. This is particularly true with the human figures. In this instance, interpretation is essentially similar to that of the drawings of younger people. Umbrellas, pipes, stove hats, and other such phallicized objects frequently appear in the drawings of older people. This too is frequently seen as the patient's attempt to maintain bodily contact with his outer world. If he can make contact with the ancillary objects, they serve as mediators between himself, his feelings, and those objects and feelings in the world beyond his own internal world and body.

The examiner can frequently better understand his patient's attitudes toward feelings about growing old. The patient can be asked how old he thinks the tree is that he just drew. Frequently, the nature of the response is " . . . The tree is three hundred years old," or "It is only a little baby tree," etc., offering a picture of feeling either almost at "the end of the road" or perhaps still possessing hope and promise.

Figure drawings, in many instances, can be interpreted by the examiner much as the H-T-P drawings done by younger people. In these instances, however, it must be remembered that the person who did the drawings is old, perceives his life somewhat differently than the younger person, and possesses different abilities. Perhaps the most important aspect of the drawings reflects his life, needs, values, and aspirations that are somewhat different than usually seen. Sex drives of the older patient are not the same as the sex drives of the younger person. For the elderly, it means striving to recapture what once was; for the younger individual, it relates to new and more aspiring heights. Seeking new relationships for the older person frequently means seeking a type of contact with another person, usually someone younger, because of a need to find someone whom he can view as a parental figure or perhaps even someone whom he can parentify. While there certainly is some overlapping with the needs of the younger person, the younger individual's needs are somewhat different in this area. He may also be looking for more equal, companion-types of relationships with fewer "hooks."

Depression is much more in evidence in older people than in the young. The clinician must look more carefully for such signs among his older patients. He may see these signs in the usual ways in the drawings, in shadings, in the use of a great deal of black in the chromatic drawings; or he may see the signs of depression in the rigid posture of the figures, the back views (which also can mean withdrawal from the real world), the sad expressions on the faces of the human figures, the encapsulated house, as well as the tree that is bare and lacks leaves.

The clinician is encouraged to use the two instruments described here, the Gerontological Apperception Test and the House-Tree-Person test, for the psychometric evaluation of the older patient. With only a little experience, such instrumentation will be found to be most useful and helpful in the evaluation of the gerontological patient.

REFERENCES

Ames, L. B., Learned, J., Metraux, R. W., & Walker, R. N. *Rorschach responses in old age.* New York: Hoeber-Harper, 1954.

Bellak, L. *The Children's Apperception Test.* New York: C.P.S. Co., 1949.

Buck, J. N. The H-T-P technique, a qualitive and quantative scoring method. *Journal of Clinical Psychology,* 1948, *5,* 1-120.

Canter, A. A background interference procedure to increase sensitivity of the Bender-Gestalt test to organic brain disorder. *Journal of Consulting Psychology,* 1966, *30,* 91-97.

Forer, B. Custom-built projective methods: A symposium introduction. *Journal of Projective Techniques,* 1961, *25,* 3-5.

Hain, J. D. The Bender-Gestalt test: A scoring method for identifying brain damage. *Journal of Consulting Psychology.* 1964, *28,* 34-40.

Hammer, E. F. The chromatic H-T-P, a deeper personality-tapping technique. In E. F. Hammer (Ed.), *The clinical application of projective drawings.* Springfield, Ill.: Charles C. Thomas, 1958.

Henry, W. E. *The analysis of fantasy.* New York: Wiley, 1965.

Holtzman, W. H., *et al. Inkblot perception and personality.* Austin: University of Texas Press, 1961.

Hulse, W. C. The emotionally disturbed child draws his family. *Quarterly Journal of Child Behavior,* 1951, *3,* 152-174.

Lieberman, M. A. Psychological correlates of impending death. *Journal of Gerontology,* 1965, *20,* 181-190.

Machover, K. *Personality projection in the drawing of a human figure.* Springfield, Ill.: Charles C. Thomas, 1949.

Murray, H. A. *Thematic Apperception Test manual.* Boston: Harvard University Press, 1943.

Oberleder, M. Aging: Its importance for clinical psychology. In L. E. Abt, & B. F. Reiss (Eds.), *Progress in clinical psychology.* New York: Grune and Stratton, 1964.

Oberleder, M. Effects of psycho-social factors on test results of the aging. *Psychological Reports,* 1964, *14,* 383-387. (a)

Oberleder, M. Adapting current psychological techniques for use in testing the aged. *The Gerontologist,* 1967, *7,* 188-191.

Petz, K. S., Ames, L. B., & Pike, F. Measurement of psychologic function in the geriatric patient. *Journal of the American Geriatric Society,* 1961, *9,* 740-754.

Symonds, P. M. Criteria for the selection of pictures for the investigation of adolescent phantasies. *Journal of Abnormal Social-Psychology,* 1939, *34,* 271-274.

Thompson, C. E. The Thompson modification of the Thematic Apperception Test. *Rorschach Research Exchange,* 1949, *13,* 469-478.

Tuckman, J., & Lorge, I. Attitudes toward aging individuals with experiences with the aged. *Journal of Genetic Psychology,* 1958, *92,* 199-204.

Wolk, R. L. Rustin, S., & Scotti, J. The geriatric delinquent. *Journal of American Geriatric Society,* 1963, *2* 653-661.

Wolk, R. L., Rustin, S., & Seiden, R. A custom made projective technique for the aged: The Gerontological Apperception Test. *Journal of the Long Island Consultation Center,* 1966, *4,* 7-17.

Wolk, R. L., & Goldfarb, A. I. The response to group psychotherapy of aged recent admissions compared with long-term mental hospital patients. *American Journal of Psychiatry,* 1967, *123,* 1251-1257.

Wolk, R. L. Projective drawings of aged people. In J. Buck, & E. F. Hammer (Eds.), *Advances in the H-T-P: Variations and applications.* Los Angeles: Western Psychological Services, 1968.

16:: THE SZONDI TEST AND GERONTOLOGY

CHARLES TAYLOR

The Szondi test was introduced to America in the late 1940's and had a considerable vogue for some years thereafter. After a decade and more of use the consensus was that the test was based on questionable assumptions about genetic characteristics, that the pictures used were not psychologically equivalent, and that the meaning and validity of the responses were difficult to ascertain (Borstelmann & Klopfer, 1953; Fiegenbaum, 1951). For these reasons, very little research at present reports the use of the Szondi.

It is interesting, however, that the field of social gerontology has taken no account of the large number of references to the aging process which can be found in the authoritative introduction to the test written by Deri (1949). Probably no more complex picture of the developmental aspects of personality change over the lifetime exists elsewhere. Indeed, none of the highly critical general reviews of the instrument considers the developmental aspect in any detail. Although Deri has herself required "good will" on the part of the reader in regard to the statistical analyses performed (a request certainly in order since practically no data is given), a careful reader must come to grips with this detailed analysis of personality trends through the lifetime.

The test itself utilizes forty-eight pictures of mental patients, each of which belongs in one of eight diagnostic categories. These are presented to the subject in six sets, presumably equivalent in stimulus value, from each of which he has been asked to pick the two he likes best and the two he likes least. The test is child's play to administer and to score, though admittedly difficult to interpret. The supposition of the test deisgners that tension in need systems determines the appeal of the various pictures has not been fruitfully supported. For all that, it seems quite clear from a variety of studies that various age groups do choose different pictures and combinations of pictures. These choices are similar to the original data given by Szondi (1952 with Hungarian subjects, with American samples (Fancher, 1956, 1962; Fancher & Weinstein, 1956), and with Israeli children (Schubert, 1954). The material in the Deri book regarding maturity and old age is much more plentiful even than that for the earliest years.

The picture of personality change given by Deri can be summarized in four major areas or vectors. The first, the sexual vector, is concerned with alternatives of passive yielding to people and things as opposed to active, aggressive, manipulation of people and objects. She attributes to older people, as compared to younger adults, more concrete behavior, more need for tenderness, and less willingness to manipulate other people and things to personal advantage.

The second vectorial category, the paroxysmal, opposes needs for aggressive outbursts and for expression of the tender emotions. Deri here attributes to the aging a lessening of strong ethical controls over behavior and an increasing tendency toward expressing emotions without reserve, accompanied by free-floating anxiety over the difficulty of expressing their feelings in socially acceptable ways.

The contact vector is concerned with opposing needs to cling to objects and to derive pleasure from them, as opposed to control over such objects and persons. Here is presented the conviction that older persons lean upon objects and persons while denying that they give pleasure, with anxiety over losing such objects.

The last vector, the ego vector, is concerned with the need to fuse with objects and persons in the environment and the contrasting need to keep the ego free from blending with the environment. Here older persons tend to structure their world to their own pattern of needs, do not question value judgments made by authoritative figures, and cathect poorly to objects and persons in the environment. It presumes in old age a period of relative calmness and emotional sterility. The kinds of statements used by Deri and the direction of change over time is shown as Appendix A. These statements, though rich in interpretive meaning, are not sufficiently operational to permit age comparisons.

The present research utilizes 200 adults between the ages of 40 and 80, with 25 males and females in each decade. Each subject was given at least six administrations of the test by graduate students in training in courses in projective techniques. The subjects came from a single college community and were all non-institutionalized persons, with no significant differences between groups in self-perceived health, educational levels, or socioeconomic status.

Although Deri does not give material in her standard text with which one could make statistical comparisons, the earlier work of Szondi in Hungary does have percentages of response for various ages. Because of the very minimal data given, it was not possible to make statistical comparisons between those data and the ones here presented.

Inspection of Table I shows that trends in picture selection follow the Szondi pattern. In none of the three most common signs in each vector is there a sharp divergence from the Szondi data.

TABLE 1: Percentage of subjects at various ages falling in most common vectorial categories

Ages	Sexual			Paroxysmal			Ego			Contact		
	h s + +	h s + -	h s + 0	e hy - -	e hy 0 -	e hy + -	k p - -	k p - -	k p 0 -	d m + +	d m + -	d m 0 +
21-30	23	16	17	10	16	27	28	13	4	10	13	21
31-40	23	10	18	8	15	23	29	6	11	8	14	17
41-60	29	13	21	7	17	18	40	6	7	11	13	14
41-50	*26*	*10*	*18*	*10*	*15*	*16*	*48*	*3*	*8*	*13*	*12*	*16*
51-60	*25*	*13*	*20*	*10*	*17*	*15*	*45*	*4*	*12*	*15*	*12*	*25*
61-70	24	24	12	13	19	6	43	5	9	15	15	23
61-70	*26*	*20*	*22*	*15*	*21*	*13*	*45*	*5*	*10*	*16*	*17*	*28*
71-80	38	11	34	21	27	7	54	4	16	10	6	33
71-80	*40*	*14*	*28*	*21*	*28*	*9*	*48*	*5*	*12*	*8*	*14*	*37*

Regular type figures-Data from Szondi's *Triebdiagnostik*; Italic figures—Data from this study.

This concordance, together with the fact that the pictures within the sets are not psychologically equivalent, requires some explanation. For example, in the homosexual category (here meaning passivity and desire for tender emotions), one picture was chosen by the subjects eight times more frequently than the least frequently chosen. Perceptual elements of the pictures have been frequently studied (Klopfer & Borstelmann, 1950; Lefford, 1954; Schubert, 1954; Hamilton, 1959). Such aspects as age, sex, grooming, dress, and other psychological and aesthetic elements play a part in the choosing of the pictures. Age trends in reacting to such features have seldom been shown.

To test whether there are differences in attributed perceptual characteristics of the stimulus pictures, the objective clusters, which had been arrived at by Davis and Raimy (1952) in a study of the stimulus value of the pictures, were employed. The pictures were given as a unified whole, and administered to four groups of subjects, aged 41-50, 51-60, 61-70 and 71-80, each group having five subjects of each sex; all had been previously included in the main sample. Sixteen adjective clusters were available, with each assigned one of the adjective clusters (such as "sad, hopeless, grieved and pained" or "pleased, amused, contented, happy and joyous"). Pictures most frequently chosen as liked in the main administration of the test over the six earlier administrations were more frequently seen by older subjects as passive, shy, loving, and weary, no matter what the diagnostic category. Cards disliked by older people were attributed domination, revenge, or anger. For persons in the younger of these age ranges, cards liked were more frequently described as pleased, amused, wise, or embarrassed; cards disliked were more often seen as doubtful, unpassive, or threatened. It will be seen that the clusters for liking in the older groups were more impassive or introverted than the more open affective tone of the younger; for disliked cards, the trend was reversed, with older persons using more open expressions and younger more guarded ones.

These exploratory findings lead to a conclusion that stimulus pictures of the present sort may, with more elaborated cognitive assumptions, give important insights into changing personality patterns with age. The Szondi pictures are probably no better than other pictures which could be chosen. The relative ease of administration of such a type of instrument, even in very large samples, with seemingly less emotional tension than many other projective tests, would seem to make worthwhile a new look at the Szondi approach as a useful tool to provide insights into the personality pattern over the adult life span.

REFERENCES

Borstelmann, L. J., & Klopfer, W. G. The Szondi test: A review and critical evaluation. *Psychology Bulletin,* 1953, *50,* 112-132.

Davis, E. N. & Raimy, V. C. Stimulus functions of the Szondi cards. *Journal of Clinical Psychology,* 1952, *8,* 155-160.

Deri, S. K. *Introduction to the Szondi test.* New York: Grune & Stratton, 1949.

Fancher, E. C. A comparative study of adolescents with the Szondi test. *Journal of Genetic Psychology,* 1956, *88,* 89-93.

Fancher, E. C. A comparative study of American and Hungarian developmental trends with the Szondi test. *Journal of Genetic Psychology,* 1962, *101,* 229-253.

Fancher, E., & Weinstein, M. Szondi study of developmental and cultural factors in personality: The seven-year-old. *Journal of Genetic Psychology,* 1956, *88,* 81-88.

Fiegenbaum, L. An investigation of some aspects of the Szondi test. Unpublished doctoral dissertation, University of Kentucky, 1951.

Hamilton J. T. A study of incidental stimulus values in the Szondi test. *Journal of Clinical Psychology,* 1959, *15,* 322-324.

Klopfer, W., & Borstelmann, S. The associative valences of the Szondi pictures. *Journal of Personality,* 1950, *19,* 172-188.

Lefford, A. An experimental study of the Szondi test stimuli. Unpublished doctoral dissertation, New York University, 1954.

Schubert, J. The stimulus value of the Szondi pictures: A theoretical and empirical study. *Journal of Projective Techniques,* 1954, *18* 95-106.

Szondi, L. *Experimental diagnosis of drives.* New York: Grune and Stratton, 1952.

APPENDIX A: Age trends in personality factor

CHILDHOOD	ADOLESCENCE	MIDDLE YEAR	OLD AGE

Sexual vector

Plus s—"Tendency for uninhibited aggressive manifestations."
high   decreasing   high
Plus h minus s—"Submissive, low need for physical activity."
low   relatively high   relatively high   most frequent
Minus h plus s—"Suppressed need for tenderness, with aggression."
high   low   decreasing

Paroxysmal vector

Plus e—"Strict control of aggressive feelings."
low   high   decreasing
Minus e"Likelihood of aggressive outbursts."
high   decreasing   decreasing   increasing
Plus-minus e—"Ambivalence in handling aggression."
high   low   high
Open e—"Emotions discharged readily."
                                                         high

Plus hy—"Need to exhibit emotions."
high   low   increasing
Open hy—"Need to live out the libido."
high   low   increasing
Plus e minus hy—"Strict control of the emotions without exhibitionism."
high   high   low
Minus e plus hy—"Seeking own egotistic advantage."
high   low   high
Minus e minus hy—"Control of violent emotions with free-floating anxiety."
high   decreasing   increasing
Plus e plus hy—"Interest in the expression of emotions."
low   high   low
Open e open hy—"Momentary lack of tension within series of sudden outbursts."
fairly even   fairly even   relatively high

Contact vector

Plus-minus d—"Ambivalence in looking for new cathexis and in clinging to old."
high   decreasing   increasing
Plus m—"Enjoying external objects and leaning on them for support."
                                                         high
Minus m—"Denial of need to lean on others."
high   decreasing   low
Plus-minus m—"Attempt to enjoy environment and denying possibility of
                    enjoyment."
high   high
Plus d minus m—"Attempt to master environment, without pleasure in activity."
high   decreasing   rare beyond 60

APPENDIX A: Age trends in personality factor (continued)

CHILDHOOD	ADOLESCENCE	MIDDLE YEAR	OLD AGE

Contact vector (continued)

Minus d minus m—"Cathexis with denial of need for it."

CHILDHOOD	ADOLESCENCE	MIDDLE YEAR	OLD AGE
high		high	low

Plus d plus m—"Conflict because of multiplicity of valued objects."

low			high

Open d plus m—"Clinging to objects for love and enjoyment."

	low	high	most frequent

Open d minus m—"Negativism."

high		decreasing	rare

Plus-minus d, plus-minus m—"Restless tension and moodiness."

low	low	high	high

Ego vector

Plus p—"Tendency to cathect outside objects."

rare	high	high	rare

Minus p—"Unconscious tendency to structure environment."

more frequent	high	high	more frequent

Open p—"Relative calm over personality-environment relationships."

fairly even	fairly even	fairly even	decreasing

Plus k—"Need for emotional independence."

high	decreasing	increasing	low

Minus k—"Unquestioning acceptance of value judgments made by others."

low			high

Plus-minus k—"Tension over repression of emotional needs."

rare	decreasing	lowest	increasing

Open k—"Primary narcissism."

high		decreasing	stable until 80

Open k minus p—"Action from 'intuitive feelings' without interest in rational processes."

relatively frequent	low	low	frequent

Plus-minus k minus p—"Rebellion against external laws, not daring to ignore."

high		decreasing	increasing

Minus k minus p—"Acceptance of the world at face value."

high	decreasing	decreasing	increasing

Minus k open p—"Compulsive control of id impulses."

high	high	decreasing	decreasing

Minus k plus p—"Conformity to expected social norms."

high	high	decreasing	rare

Plus-minus k plus p—"Strong control of need structure."

rare	rare	rare	least

Plus k plus p—"Intellectual intrajection of emotional life."

rare	rare	rare	rare

Open k plus p—"Seeking complete union with the environment."

rare		low	rare

17:: THE EARLIEST MEMORY AS DATA
FOR RESEARCH IN AGING

SHELDON S. TOBIN

The reconstruction of the earliest memory is useful data for research in aging not only for its insights into past life but also for its potential in revealing current concerns of the aged respondent. Current concerns can be assessed by measuring their expression in the reconstruction of the earliest memory to the extent that this reconstruction reflects the synthesis of a meaningful early event within the context of current environmental concerns. Since the recalled event is selectively chosen from among a storehouse of memories, its recall and expression at an advanced age may be congruent with contemporary adaptive concerns. This reconstructive synthesis of the early memory, it would appear, is a result of the active reorganization of past events that serves the present needs for adaptation.

Through reminiscence it may be possible to tap the covert affect that is associated with the current adaptation, as contrasted with the more overt level that is tapped by direct questions. For example, in reconstructing earliest memories, aged respondents seem unaware of how their reconstruction is actively influenced by the present concerns.

This research was supported in full by USPHS Grant No. HD-00364, Adaptation and Survival Under Stress in the Aged, from NICHD; Morton A. Lieberman, Principal Investigator; Sheldon S. Tobin, Project Director. I am deeply indebted to the Jewish Federation Homes of Chicago for their facilitation of this investigation. For assistance in gathering and making available to me earliest memory data, I am indebted to Dr. Paul Fine, Dr. Daniel Offer, and Mrs. Virginia Robinson.

This lack of awareness is manifested in data presented in this paper. Earliest memories gathered at a six month interval are perceived as identical by the aged respondent, but in reality are often quite different in affective content. Data gathered by direct questions or more conventional projective tests do not reveal the same intense quantity or quality of negative affectivity as are found within the earliest memory.

If the earliest memory can be useful for tapping the present covert affective level, it takes on added value because of the limitations of conventional projective-test data for assessment of the aged. The aged respondent is usually quite willing to talk about his past life. This stands in marked contrast with the resistance of the aged to standard projective tests. Indeed, the request to reminisce is usually perceived by the aged as an interest in their well-being and recognition of their wisdom. Standard verbal projective tasks, such as the Sentence Completion Test, are often perceived as a mixture of infantilism and threat. Visual projective tasks, such as the Rorschach Inkblot Test and the Thematic Apperception Test, have the added disadvantage of being contaminated by sensory deficits that limit the subject's ability to perceive and respond. The data gathered by verbal reports of the past are not likely to be limited by sensory deficit nor is the request to reconstruct the earliest memory perceived as an infantilizing or threatening test.

The Earliest Memory

The contemporary view is that the earliest memory reflects the synthesis of a meaningful early event within the context of current environmental transactions. As Schachtel (1947, p. 3) has succinctly stated: "Memory as a function of the living personality can be understood only as a capacity for the organization and reconstruction of past experiences and impressions in the service of present needs, fears and interests."

This process of organizing the earliest memory in the service of current adaptation is indeed a complex one which necessitates mechanisms for translating unconscious, or latent, content to a manifest level. In turn, therefore, in analyzing this complex process, the investigator has a choice of models. He can choose to focus, as did Freud, upon the concealing properties; or he can elect to focus, as Adler did, upon the revealing properties of the reconstruction. Thus the approaches of Freud and Adler, which at first appear to be conflicting, reflect the alternate models available in the study. For Freud (1938), earliest memories were like screen memories. He felt that they were unrevealing because of their banal and often meaningless content, where concealment has occurred through repression of persistent dynamic content. On the other hand, for Adler (1937) the manifest content of the earliest memory reflected the individual's persistent and characterological style of life, which Adler assumed to be the revealing properties of the earliest memory.

The two approaches, however, are not mutually exclusive; each suggests a different kind of investigation. The screen memory approach of Freud lends itself more to psychoanalytic studies where, through intensive psychotherapeutic techniques, latent conflicts become revealed; and in turn, the conflicts can be related to the patient's mechanisms for concealment that are represented in the earliest memory. Adler's "revealing" approach lends itself to the study of earlier memories where commonalities among the earliest memories of groups of people with similar characterological dispositions can be explored by more quantitative scoring procedures. The two approaches, therefore, focus on two different types of variability.

In intra-individual studies the earliest memories of the same person are compared at intervals over time to uncover latent content, as contrasted with inter-individual studies where different individuals or groups are compared to study characterological dispositions. Intra-individual variability has been the focus of those clinicians (Chess, 1951; Glover, 1929; Greenacre, 1949; Ivimey, 1950; Kahana, 1953;

Kris, 1956, Niederland, 1965; Reider, 1953; Saul, Snyder & Sheppard, 1956) who have explored the modification in the reportage of the earliest memory as a function of the lifting of repression consequent to psychotherapy. Inter-individual variability has been the focus of investigators (Brodsky, 1952; Burnell & Solomon, 1964; Friedman, 1950; Hanawalt & Gebhart, 1965; Holmes, 1965; Langs, Rotherberg & Fishman, 1960; Langs, 1965a; Langs, 1965b; Levy & Grigg, 1962; Lieberman, 1957; Mayman & Ferris, 1960; Mosak, 1958; Rieff & Scheerer, 1959; Stern, 1935; Wynne & Schaffzin, 1965) who have used the revealing approach to contrast the more manifest qualities of the earliest memories with varied levels of behavioral adaptation.

The series of investigations reported here differ from both of the classical approaches by an initial attempt to demonstrate how the present ecology, and/or the adaptive concerns of institutionalization, become incorporated into the earliest memory. By comparing the earliest memory for an institutionalized sample to both a matched sample on a waiting list for instutionalization and a matched community sample, it becomes possible to investigate how the current environmental transaction is reflected in the reconstruction of meaningful early events.

Following this initial exploration of institutional effects on the earliest memory by a cross-sectional analysis, further issues to be explored include: the comparison of the earliest memories of aged and younger samples; the role of childhood trauma in the reconstruction of the earliest memory of adults; the relationship between the earliest memory and the process of spontaneous reminiscence in the aged; and the perception of personal reminiscence by the aged, in which the focus is on the meaning of reminiscence as adaptive or maladaptive to the institutionalized aged respondent.

The initial exploration, that of assessing institutional effects on the reconstruction of the earliest memory, has necessitated the development of an index for the measurement of the affective experience of this severe, environmental stressor. The literature on the effect of institutionalization suggests the quality of the affective experience to be measured. From participation-observation studies of patients in state mental hospitals, Goffman (1961) has described an experience in total institutions as "self-mortification." A number of investigators (Aldrich & Mendkoff, 1963; Camargo & Preston, 1945; Kay, Norris & Post, 1956; Lieberman, 1961; Roth, 1965) have found institutionalization of the aged to be associated with heightened morbidity, high rates of mortality, and gross psychological disability. When institutionalized and community samples are compared, findings (Fink, 1957; Lakin, 1960; Laverty, 1950; Lieberman & Lakin, 1963; Mason, 1954; Schrutt, 1958) suggest that the impact of institutional relocation can be characterized by an increased feeling of narcissistic loss. Thus it appeared that focusing on such severe losses as personal illness or mutilation, as well as death of close family members, would be those narcissistic-loss thema that may show an increased expression in the earliest memories of institutionalized aged. The attempt, therefore, has been to develop an ordinal scale where higher levels relate to the greater manifestation of experienced loss.

Development of the Introduced Loss Scale

The earliest memory was gathered by asking the question: "What is the first thing you can remember—going back as far as you can?" This question was the lead item of a rather extensive, focused interview designed to gather life history data. These data were not gathered by clinicians, but rather by trained interviewers who were carefully selected. The interviewers shared characteristics of being women aged 30-45; they enjoyed relating to the very old and their main purpose in working was to be a professional worker within a research context. The earliest memory was operationally defined as the answer to the specific question which sometimes included more than one memory as well as the elaboration of the same recollection when given in response to the next question, "What other things can you remember about being very young?"

These earliest memory data were gathered from three samples of community (N = 40), waiting list (N = 100), and institutionalized (N = 100) aged. These three samples are comparable in age (mean age of 78), sex, socioeconomic class, education, level of organic impairment, ability, ability to care for their own physical needs, and ethnic background. The community sample was drawn from a population of aged who would be eligible to apply to one of three sectarian homes for the aged in which the institutionalization sample resides. Indeed, three of the forty aged in the community sample have since entered one of these homes. The waiting-list aged were interviewed after applying for admission to one of the three homes. While they are still residents in the community, these waiting-list aged have undergone the disruptive events that lead to application for institutionalization. Factors prompting application for admission include physical illness and adverse changes in their social environment.

To develop the loss scale, a pool of 120 earliest memories was analyzed for the dominant themes. This pool of 120 memories consisted of two repeat earliest memories that were collected from sixty respondents at a six-month interval; fifty-four memories gathered from aged respondents in the community sample while residing in the community at both times; and sixty-six memories gathered from the waiting-list sample who were first interviewed when on the waiting list, approximately four months pre-admission, and then interviewed again at two months post-institutionalization. This tactic of using sixty respondents with two repeat memories permits the comparison of a sample in the process of becoming institutionalized to a control sample who have remained in the community for a comparable period of time; a comparison that can be made after unblinding the sixty respondents for sample membership (community or "pre-post" institutional sample) and time of interview (especially pre- or post-institutional for the second sample).

The poll of 120 earliest memories were first analyzed for thematic content. Because many of these earliest memories had several manifest thema, it was apparent that the dominant theme was often different from the theme reflecting greatest loss. For example, a memory may have both a dominant theme of threat of interpersonal injury and a secondary theme of a greater expression of loss such as death of mother. When earliest memories were sorted separately for dominant thema and highest loss theme it became apparent that fifteen useful categories were employed in making judgments. These fourteen categories were then reduced to five categories to form a five-point ordinal scale where the low end (a score of one) represented the least expression of loss, and the high end (a score of five, the highest expression of loss.

After unblinding for sample membership and time of interview, it became evident that the scoring by the highest level of introduced loss revealed more change than the dominant theme. The dominant theme appeared to be more stable, but the nature of the change on the scale of the highest level of loss suggested the meaningfulness of this latter scale for assessing institutional effects. That is, on the scale of the highest level of introduced loss, thirty-three respondents (55%) in the pre-/post-institutional sample manifested increased loss over time as compared to only six of the twenty-seven respondents (or 22%) in the community sample.

The scale of the highest level of introduced loss then becomes the focus of this investigation. The earliest memory of each respondent was placed into one of five categories, where the categories are ranked from non-loss to most extreme introduced loss. The positive end of the ordinal scale contains non-loss themes, usually of family or peer interaction (Level 1), as well as themes of direct gratifications (Level 2). The next three levels include interpersonal losses or threat of injury (Level 3), personal illness and mutilation themes (Level 4), and deaths, usually of close family members (Level 5). The scale, of the most extreme loss introduced into the earliest memory, is reproduced below and includes two examples of each level.

Level 1. Non-loss themes

Scores of 1 may include guilt, anxiety, aggressiveness, and

themes may vary in level of primitiveness of impulse expression, but all such themes are to be scored 1 unless there is evidence for scoring 2, 3, 4, or 5. Usual themes are of family or going to school.

Examples: I used to have another fellow. We used to go out for good times. We used to go to a concert. Listen to music. We used to play ball. You know how kids are.

It's been so long ago. There were seven children and I was the only daughter. As soon as I could walk I helped my mother in the house. I'd wash the dishes. There was a houseful of children. My mother was always cooking. I was about ten years old.

Level 2. Non-loss: Loss-defended themes

No direct loss is expressed, but in the theme the respondent is the recipient of direct and primitive gratification. Receiving narcissistic support is the central issue but overt loss is not introduced. That is, the flagrant wish and seeking for gratification is interpreted as cloaking an underlying fear of deprivation and loss.

Examples: I remember as in a dream—my father being in the army and coming home on furlough. He was good-looking, tall and dark and handsome. He used to bring us presents when he came. I was about four or five.

I can remember I was eight years old. I sang in the synagogue. Everybody was admiring me. My family was very satisfied by me. I sang so good. Everybody was saying I had such a nice voice. When I was a year older they put me in for an alto soloist in the synagogue. I kept singing until I got my tenor voice. That was unusual, I never had to take a rest when my voice changed.

Level 3. Interpersonal loss themes

Losses at level 3 include: separation, loneliness, and threat of injury. For example, score a 3 for "mother went to the store and I cried because I was alone" or "I thought my teacher was going to hit me."

Examples: My mother and father going on a shopping trip for our place of business. Though we had supervision, I felt very lonely. (How old?) I wouldn't really know, but probably four or five or six.

Five or six years. Our house burned down. I heard, "Fire, fire, fire." Straw in the barn. Our maid came and picked all of us up and our house burned. A teacher picked all of us up and took us with him to stay awhile. We had a business inside with manufacturing materials and all that burned. My mother fainted. We kids—we was six kids then; I was the oldest.

Level 4. Injury (or mutilation) themes

Where respondent is physically hurt a score of 4 is given. Themes of illness, being sick, and physical impairment are typical of scores for Level 4.

Examples: I can remember being at my mother's breast. Maybe I remember my sister being at her breast. When I was two I had scarlet fever . . . I just remember that I had it, no details.

I was ten years old. Rabid dog bit me on the leg. Father took me to the doctor. Doctor not there . . . threw clothes in alley. Doctor came . . . gave father a prescription for some medicine. Two men came in and tried to burn it out . . . five marks of teeth. For six months doctor came and scraped off skin. Doctor and two men had to hold me. Very painful. Scars of it yet.

Level 5. Death themes

Themes of death, usually of close family members, are scored 5. Where respondent focuses on a family member where the interaction is not one of the other dying, but if in the elaboration there is the discussion of the death of the other, then a score of 5 is given. For example, if respondent talks of playing with a sibling and then adds "he died two years later," the score of 5 is given.

Examples: When my mother was sick in bed and she passed away and I cried. I was about five or six (cries). I try not to think about it.

Remember when I was about eight or ten years old. Went on a swing in my backyard. Went all by myself. It was nice. (Big smile). Remember my brother died of a very bad sickness when I was about eight years. He lived one week and that's all. Doctors didn't know what to do for him. I suppose I felt bad, but I don't remember so far back. He was four years older than me.

To determine the interjudge reliability of ratings, three independent judges rated the poll of 120 earliest memories of the sixty respondents on the five-point scale. For every memory at least two judges agreed. For 57% of the memories there was exact agreement of three judges, with a third judge disagreeing on the remaining 43% of the memories.

Institutionalization and the Earliest Memory

By comparing the distribution of scores for the three samples, it becomes possible to test the hypothesis that the current stressor is reflected in the reconstruction of the earliest memory. For example, a higher percentage of severe loss for the institutional sample than for the other community and waiting-list sample would suggest the impact of the institutional environment.

As shown in Table 1, the percentage of the severe losses of personal injury and death (levels 4 and 5 on the scale) is higher for the institutionalized sample (47%) than for either the community sample (28%) or the waiting-list sample (24%). Our interpretation of these data is that the earliest memory is being influenced by current concerns which are very stressful for the institutionalized aged. Of interest is the fact that the percentage for the waiting-list sample is comparable to the percentage for the community sample (24%) as compared to 28%. This suggests that it is the event of institutionalization *per se* that affects the reconstruction, rather than the disruptions that lead to application to the institutions.

Corroborative evidence for this institutional effect was found in a test-retest study where the same aged were followed from pre- to post-institutionalization. When shifts in loss level for this sample were compared to shifts for four matched control samples (community, waiting list, short-term and long-term institutionalized samples), 51% of the experimental sample manifested an increase in loss level as contrasted to only 20% of the control aged. Therefore, in the test-retest study, the increase in expressed loss in the earliest memory appears causally related to institutionalization *per se*. Of added interest, is that this study revealed that "shifts in loss level were invariably associated with the selection by a respondent of a different incident, rather than an elaboration of the same incident that would be clearly related to a breakthrough of repression." (Tobin & Etigson, 1968.)

Age and Loss in the Earliest Memory

A further question prompted by these data concerns the extent to which the community and waiting-list samples would be different from the samples of younger people in reporting earliest memories with severe loss. Could, for example, this measure of loss be used to determine age-related differences in the reconstruction of the earliest memory? To obtain leverage on this question, three adult-community samples were rather hastily collected. When it became apparent that each of these three samples manifested a comparable distribution of severe loss (e.g., a range of 14-19% of respondents manifesting severe loss in their earliest memory), the three samples were pooled to form an adult-community sample of 94, aged 31-51 years. The three subsamples comprising this adult-community sample are 50 jet pilots (30-45 years old), 31 social work students (21-33 years old) and 13 middle-aged persons (43-51 years old) who are not unlike the children of the aged in the matched samples.

While this adult-community sample is not at all matched with the aged sample, the percentage of severe loss memories is not appreciably less than the community and waiting-list aged. As shown in Table 1, this younger community sample manifests a severe loss rate of 16%, as compared to a 25% rate for the older non-institutionalized aged.

One question, among many, raised by this comparison was whether the difference of 9% reflects a valid age difference in affective experience. As an aid to clarification of potential age differences, the earliest memories of a sample of upper middle-class adolescents were scored on the loss scale. The distribution for this sample, revealed a percentage of severe loss of 27% which is remarkably similar to the aged noninstitutionalized samples. The adolescents and the noninstitutionalized aged are closer to each other than either are to the middle age group. One may speculate that the comparability of percentage of severe loss for the very old and for adolescents relates to heightened experience of crises at these pivotal developmental points. One would hypothesize less crises for the adult years.

Possibly a more systematic study would reveal age differences that could be related to current adaptation issues along the life line. The present exploratory study only whets the appetite; it offers no definite answers. That such a systematic analysis may be revealing of age associated differences was also suggested by a clinical inspection of the data in which it appeared that issues of aggression and separation were more prominent for the adolescents than for the other two samples. It would appear, therefore, that if a system were developed to assess these hypothesized differences, as was the case in the development of the present loss scale where specific content was assessed to relate to institutionalization, the probability of finding suspected age differences might be increased.

Early Trauma and Loss in the Earliest Memory

In matching samples of different ages one must control for initial differences in acculturation. When the researcher wishes to investigate intrinsic and systematic age-related developmental changes by cross-sectional methods, he confronts the impossibility of controlling for early experience. Historical differences certainly are factors to be considered in the analysis of earliest memories.

If a synthesis of a meaningful life event within current adaptive concerns is to be valid, an effort must be made to control for early life events so that the reportage of loss becomes more clearly related to present concerns. This inability to hold constant, or "partial out," early events is somewhat better controlled for the older samples which were matched. At least it is assumed that the older sample had comparable distributions of such early trauma as infant mortality, diseases, and pogromal attacks which were the common experience for the present aged who were reared in the *shtetls* of Eastern Europe.

It may be that the estimates reported above of severe loss in earliest memories for the younger samples is an underestimate because their early lives may, in actuality, not have been as traumatic. As a step toward exploring the relationship between actual early trauma and the expression of loss in the earliest memory, a special sample was gathered of adults who were traumatized when young.

This sample, homogeneous to the extent of all being so crippled when young that they had to attend a special grade school, was 25-35 years old when the earliest memory was gathered. As shown in Table 1, their percentage of extreme loss of 65% is appreciably higher than the 47% found for the institutionalized aged. Not surprising, therefore, is how the actual early trauma is reflected in the reportage.

The data for the younger samples, nontraumatized as well as traumatized, has relevance for the comparison among the three older samples. For example, the percentage of severe loss for the noninstitutionalized aged appears to be comparable to that found for nontraumatized younger samples. These stand in contrast to the responses of the institutionalized sample and the traumatized younger sample. These differences suggest that for the aged person who becomes institutionalized, a shift occurs toward an inner experience of narcissistic loss, or "self-mortification" (Goffman, 1961), as reflected in the intrusion of thema of morbidity and mortality. This inner experience of institutionalized aged may be not unlike that of respondents who were severely traumatized when young. That is, the experience associated with the severe stress of institutionalization in old age may resemble the hardship undergone by those who were traumatized when young.

Reminiscing and the Earliest Memory

The focus in this paper has been on the usefulness of the earliest memory as data for research. The theoretical position has been oriented to how the reconstruction reflects present covert affects in general and more specifically on the negative affect associated with institutional stress. In the literature on this aspect of aging, the focus has been more on the utilization of reminiscence as a means for meeting adaptive demands. Butler (1963), for example, postulates a spontaneous reminiscence process in the aged, which he has called the life review; a process that is "prompted by the realization of approaching dissolution and death;" characterized by the progressive return to consciousness of past experiences and, particularly, the resurgence of unresolved conflicts;" which can be "surveyed and reintegrated;" and if successfully reintegrated, can give "new significance and meaning to one's life" and "prepare one for death, mitigating one's fears (pp. 66-68)." He adds that the life review "is further shaped by contemporaneous experiences and its nature and outcome are affected by the life long unfolding of character (p. 66)." Thus, for Butler the focus is on how the spontaneous reminiscence in the aged may be useful for the adaptation to one's own death.

The earliest memory gathered by the direct question "What is the first thing you can remember—go as far back as you can?" is not very comparable to spontaneous reminiscence. Spontaneous reminiscence is assumed to occur in the privacy of one's own mind and may hold vague images that are difficult, or even impossible, to articulate verbally. Possibly the gathering of these reminiscences is facilitated by less structured means, such as psychoanalytic techniques that are designed to retrieve unconscious material. However, the data retrieved through these unstructured techniques still does not capture the spontaneous reminiscence in its entirety. The presence of another person, such as the psychoanalyst-interviewer, or the unfamiliarity of verbal reportage as a means of expressing the reminisced images, may somewhat contaminate the process of accurate retrieval of spontaneous reminiscence.

Intermediate between the related question on the earliest memory and the amnestic interview, as data-gathering procedures for reminiscence, are "guided-focused" types of interviews on the complete life line or on specific eopchs. Data were available for the comparison of the earliest memory and a focused interview on childhood. For this analysis, the other childhood reminiscences and earliest memories were available, both before and after institutionalization, for a sample of thirty-three aged respondents. While eighteen of these respondents manifested an increased loss on the earliest memory scale, comparable changes were not found in the other childhood reminiscences. Further analyses are now in progress to determine differences in these types of reminiscent reportage.

At present it appears that while both types of data show thematic consistency, the childhood reminiscence shows much greater thematic consistency in repeat gatherings. Thus, it would appear that the technique of gathering reminiscence data plays an important role in the nature and quality of the reportage; and that the more focused data such as the earliest memory may be quite distinct from the process of spontaneous reminiscence. Because of the researcher's need, however, to standardize the data collection procedure, and also to not be overwhelmed with a quantity of reminiscence that becomes unmanageable for measurement, the earliest memory data may prove helpful in clarifying the role of spontaneous reminiscence for adaptation.

Kastenbaum (1963), for example, is interested in how time perspective related to the maintenance of self-continuity; and, in a recent study of past memories, including the earliest memory, Costa and Kastenbaum (1967) have suggested that "the reservoirs of memories help sustain his present moment of existence and also aid him in creating a perspective in preparation for his eventual death (p. 15)." It appears quite possible, therefore, that the reconstruction of the earliest memory may help the investigator in the clarification of the role of the reminiscence process in aging.

The Perception of Reminiscence by the Aged

A rather different perspective on the role of reminiscence in the aged emerged from a psychopharmacological study of the effects of a "memory pill" on the aged. In this way it became possible to investigate how the process of spontaneous reminiscence may be perceived as maladaptive by the aged, rather than as an adaptive force at their disposal. In the pharamacological study, all the residents in the institution were asked to cooperate in a "memory pill" study; but, because not all volunteered to be in the study, it was possible to contrast the frequency of severe loss of earliest memories for a sample who agreed to be in the study (N = 99) and for a sample who refused to be in the study (N = 50). To elicit voluntary cooperation for this psycho-pharmacological study, residents were told the following at a meeting of residents and staff:

> "As we grow old we all begin to lose some of our ability to remember. For some people this loss of ability to remember begins when they are in their early adult years, and for others in their later adult years. In older people this loss can become quite severe and the older person, for example, may be unable to remember where he places his reading glasses or a newspaper that he had in his hand only a moment before."

As anticipated, many residents equated recent memory with remote memory. Indeed it was difficult for these residents to make a discrimination between recent and remote memory; and, thus, detect that a pill could be developed that principally related to amelioration of recent memory. For example, one elderly man arose three times at the meeting to tell us we were "crazy" to give pills that will help older people remember their early life because only "crazy people want to remember all those things."

Approximately half of the available population of residents agreed to be in the "memory pill" study; and for these residents, there was a 25% rate of severe loss in earliest memories, as shown in Table 1. This rate of 25% is considerably lower than the 47% for the previous institutional sample as reported earlier. While the samples were different (primarily because the rate of 47% applied to a sample in the institution who were interviewed four years earlier and most of those aged had died by the

TABLE1: Earliest memory (EM) descriptive statistics for the several samples

						EM loss level			
			Un-		Non-loss or		Severe	
			usable	Usable	minimal loss		loss	
	Total	Age	EMs	EMs	(L 1, 2 & 3)		(L 4 % 5)	
Sample	N	range	N	%	N	N	%	N	%
A. The Three Matched Samples of Aged Respondents									
Community	40	66-93	1	2	39	28	72	11	28
Waiting-List	100	68-87	11	11	89	68	76	21	24
Institutional	37	70-91	7	19	30	16	53	14	47
B. Younger Samples									
Adult-Com. **	94	21-51	13	14	81	68	84	13	16
Adolescent	60	14	0	0	60	44	73	16	27
Adult-CWY***	48	25-35	8	16	40	14	35	26	65
C. "Memory Pill" Study of Institutional Aged									
Agreed	99	62-94	24	25	75	56	75	19	25
Refused	50	68-99	20	40	30	17	57	13	43

* Uniformly, approximately two-thirds of unusable EMs are a result of refusals and one-third a result of vague images which are unscorable.

** The Adult-Community sample is composed of three subsamples with comparable descriptive statistics: 50 jet pilots (30-45 y.o.), 31 social work students (21-33 y.o.), and 13 middle-aged (43-51 y.o.).

*** CWY = crippled-when-young.

time of the psychopharmacology study), the characteristic of the resident population had remained rather constant, which suggests that the difference in rates was not accidental. That is, the lower rate (25%) for those who agreed to be in the study, as contrasted with a higher expected institutional (or population), rate (47%) suggested that those who refused would manifest a rather high rate of at least 50% and possibly 75%. The percentage of 43% for the refusal sample, however, is indeed higher than the 25% for the cooperative sample. While the rate for the refusal group was not as high as anticipated, it does support the hypothesis that those who did not volunteer to take a pill experienced more severe loss in their reminiscences of the past than those who volunteered.

A possible reason for the reduction in the rate of severe loss for the drug-study sample may relate to the interesting phenomenon of the "unusable," or unscorable earliest memory. Reasons for the latter were rather constant across samples. Invariably two-thirds of the unscorable memories were due to refusals and one-third due to vague images. A second observation, as shown in Table 1, is that the three aged samples (matched samples of community, waiting-list, and institutionalized aged) manifested different percentages of unusable earliest memories. These figures (2% for community aged, 11% for waiting list aged, and 19% for the institutionalized) show an increase in unusable memories with the process of institutionalization.

Based on the hypothesis that environmental stress affects the willingness to, or ability for, reconstructing the earliest memory, one would expect response patterns for the younger group that differ from the observed. To be specific, the percentage of unusable memories for the adult-community sample of 14% was appreciably higher than the 2% found for the community aged. However, the adolescent percentage of 0% is comparable to that found for community aged, and the percentage of 16% for the adults who were traumatized when young is comparable to that for institutionalized aged. It is the 14% rate for the adult-community sample that is indeed confusing. This observation remains unexplained and needs further analysis.

The data gathered in the drug study suggest another value in reporting nonusable memories. The rate for those who agreed to be in the study was 25% as compared to a rate of 40% for those who refused. Both rates are higher than the previous institutional sample which may be related to the data-gathering procedure in the drug study where the earliest memory question was embedded in a series of tasks designed to tap cognitive functioning, which is indeed quite taxing to the aged. Any tendency, therefore, to resist giving an earliest memory is probably heightened by the testing situation.

The relationship between usable memories and the percentage of severe loss remains to be explored. If, as these data suggest, a high percentage of unusable memories relates to a lessening of severe loss earliest memories, then the "true" comparison between the three aged samples might reveal an even greater percentage of severe loss memories for the aged institutionalized sample (19% unusable, 47% severe loss) as contrasted with the community sample (2% unusable, 28% loss). The waiting-list sample (11% unusable, 24% loss) stands intermediate between the community and institutionalized samples.

In an effort to clarify reasons for refusal, a sample of those refusing were interviewed. After asking why they did not wish to participate in the "memory pill" study, these fifty aged were asked whether they agreed or disagreed with the following statement: "Many old people do not want a memory pill because they don't like to think about the past. Is this true of you?"

While the principal reasons for nonparticipation were not wishing "any more pills," "too sick," and not wanting to be a "guinea pig," a frequent primary or secondary reason related to their attitudes toward reminiscence. For example, six in this Refusal sample mentioned their capacity to block out the past with statements like:

"My memory suits me all right. I remember the pleasant things. I never remember the unpleasant things."
"I have an excellent memory. Everything is well. If you want to forget, you forget."

"I just don't think about the past. I *know* what was."

"I don't feel the need of them now. I'm not in that category. Things that are past are past."

"Things that have been past, it's written off."

"I don't talk as much as other people. I don't remember nothing."

Three gave unqualified "yes" responses indicating they did not want to think about the past. Six aged gave responses suggesting a fear of reminiscing:

"I'm satisfied if my memory stays as good as it is. I'm not afraid of that!"

"No. Why should I remember. I'm too sick to remember."

"It's no good for old people to remember what was."

"No. I take my shave when I go to bed. I have my memories, but why burden other people with it."

An additional four aged who appear to have had a good past life, seemed not to wish to be reminded of the contrast with their present life:

"I hate to think about the past. I had a wonderful life, my married life."

"Don't want to compare the past with now."

In all, nineteen (or 38%) of the fifty aged who refused to participate in the "memory pill" study expressed a personal attitude toward reminiscing, best characterized as a wish to avoid a resurgence of a more vivid past. While this phenomenon has only been explored for a rather special subexample of the aged—institutionalized aged who refused to be in a psychopharmacological study—it is deserving of further investigation. Of importance is the fact that some institutionalized aged do appear aware of the resurgence of the past into their thoughts; and that for some aged there is a wish to control or avoid the resurgence. Several important questions are raised by these sparse results: How frequent is it for the general population of aged to perceive their spontaneous reminiscence as painful and maladaptive? To what extent is this type of perception related to personality characteristics and environmental stressors? Are there age-associated mechanisms for coping with the painful quality of reminiscence, such as the active inhibition of the affect associated with past memories?

Conclusions

The purpose of this paper has been to explore the usefulness of the earliest memory as data for research in aging. The usefulness of these data was first explored by comparing the earliest memories where content indicates severe loss of matched samples of community, waiting-list, and institutionalized aged. The higher percentage for the institutionalized sample suggests that the inner affective experience that is associated with the stress of institutionalization in the aged can be assessed by using the reconstruction of the earliest memory as data. Hopefully, the earliest memory will prove as useful in tapping the affective experience associated with other stressors among the aged.

Having demonstrated the usefulness of these data for the study of institutionalization in the aged, several additional uses were then explored. For example, by including samples of younger respondents, it became possible to ask questions related to age-associated differences in the earliest memory; and, by including a sample of adult respondents who were traumatized when young, to focus on the role of actual early life experiences in the reconstruction of the past.

In part, the usefulness of the earliest memory relates to the ease of gathering these data from aged respondents who are assumed to be engaged in a spontaneous process of reminiscing. The substantial issue was then explored, of the relationship between the earliest memory and the process of reminiscing; which in turn led to the exploration of the role of reminiscence of the past for current adaptation. Present data, for example, suggest that the aged may be quite aware of the resurgence of the past into consciousness, and that for some aged respondents such a resurgence is perceived as quite undesirable.

Thus the usefulness of the earliest memory for research in aging related not only to the assessment of the effects of the current ecology, but also to the process and adaptative functions of spontaneous reminiscence in aging.

REFERENCES

Adler, A. Significance of early recollections. *International Journal of Individual Psychology*, 1937, *3*, 283-287.

Aldrich, C. K., & Mendkoff, E. Relocation of the aged and disabled: A mortality study. *Journal of the American Geriatric Society*, 1963, *2*, 185-194.

Brodsky, P. Diagnostic importance of early recollections. *American Journal of Psychotherapy*, 1952, *6*, 484-493.

Burnell, G. M., & Solomon, G. F. Early memories and ego function. *Archives of General Psychiatry*, 1964, *2*, 556-567.

Butler, R. N. The life review: An interpretation of reminiscence in the aged. *Psychiatry*, 1963, *26*, 65-76.

Camargo, O., & Preston, G. H. What happens to patients who are hospitalized for the first time when over sixty-five? *American Journal of Psychiatry*, 1945, *102*, 168-173.

Chess, S. Utilization of childhood memories in psychoanalytic therapy. *Journal of Child Psychiatry*, 1951, *2*, 189-193.

Costa, P., & Kastenbaum, R. Some aspects of memories and ambitions in centenarians. *Journal of Genetic Psychology*, 1967, *110*, 3-16.

Fink, H. The relationship of time perspective to age, institutionalization, and activity. *Journal of Gerontology*, 1957, *12*, 414-417.

Freud, S. *General introduction to psychoanalysis*. Garden City, N.Y.: Garden City Publishing, 1938.

Friedman, A. Early childhood memories of mental patients. *Individual Psychology Bulletin*, 1950, *8*, 111-116.

Glover, E. The screening function of traumatic memories. *International Journal of Psychoanalysis*, 1929, *10*, 90-93.

Goffman, E. *Asylums: Essays on the social situation of mental patients and other inmates*. Garden City, N.Y.: Doubleday and Cox, 1961.

Greenacre, P. A contribution to the study of screen memories. *Psychoanalytic Study of the Child*, 1949, *314*, 73-84.

Hanawalt, N. G., & Gebhart, L. J. Childhood memories of single and recurrent incidents. *Journal of Genetic Psychology*, 1965, *107*, 85-89.

Holmes, D. S. Security feelings and affective tone of early recollections: A re-evaluation. *Journal of Projective Techniques and Personnel Assessment*, 1965, *29*, 314-318.

Ivimey, M. Childhood memories in psychoanalysis. *American Journal of Psychoanalysis*, 1950, *10*, 38-47.

Kahana, D., Weiland, I., & Snyder, T. Values of early memories in psychotherapy. *Psychiatric Quarterly*, 1953, *27*, 73-82.

Kastenbaum, R. The direction of time perspective. I: The influence of affective set. *Journal of Genetic Psychology*, 1965, *6*, 189-201.

Kay, D. W., Norris, K. V., & Post, F. Prognosis in psychiatric disorders of the elderly. *Journal of Mental Science*, 1956, *102*, 129-140.

Kris, E. Recovery of childhood memories in psychoanalysis. *Psychoanalytic Study of the Child*, 1956, *11*, 54-88.

Lakin, M. Formal characteristics of human figure drawings by institutionalized aged. *Journal of Gerontology*, 1960, *15*, 76-78.

Langs, R. Earliest memories and personality: A predictive study. *Archives of General Psychiatry*, 1965, *12*, 379-390.

Langs, R. First memories and characterological diagnosis. *Journal of Nervous and Mental Diseases*, 1965, *141*, 318-320. (a)

Langs, R., Rotherberg, B., & Fishman, J. A method for clinical and theoretical study of the earliest memory. *Archives of General Psychiatry*, 1960, *3*, 523-532.

Laverty, R. Nonresident aged-Community versus institutional care for older people. *Journal of Gerontology*, 1950, *5*, 370-374.

Levy, J., & Grigg, K. Early memories. *Archives of General Psychiatry*, 1962, *7*, 57-69.

Lieberman, M. A. Childhood memories as a projective technique. *Journal of Projective Techniques*, 1957, *21*, 32-36.

Lieberman, M. A. Relationship of mortality rates to entrance to a home for the aged. *Geriatrics*, 1961, *16*, 515-519.

Lieberman, M. A., & Lakin, M. On becoming an institutionalized aged person. In R. M. Williams, C. Tibbetts, & W. Donahue (Eds.), *Processes of Aging*. New York: Atherton Press, 1963.

Mason, E. P. Some correlates of self-judgments of the aged. *Journal of Gerontology* 1954, *9*, 314-337.

Mayman, M., & Faris, M. Early memories as expressions of relationship paradigms. *American Journal of Orthopsychiatry*, 1960, *30*, 507-520.

Mosak, H. Early recollections as a projective technique. *Journal of Projective Techniques,* 1958, *22,* 302-311.

Niederland, W. The ego in the recovery of early memories. *Psychoanalysis Quarterly,* 1965, *34,* 564-571.

Reider, N. Reconstruction and screen function. *Journal of American Psychoanalysis Association,* 1953, *1,* 389-405.

Reiff, R., & Scheerer, M. *Memory and hypnotic age regression.* New York: International Universities Press, 1959.

Roth, M. Natural history of mental disorder in old age. *Journal of Mental Science,* 1955, *101,* 281-301.

Saul, L., Snyder, T., & Sheppard, E. On earliest memories. *Psychoanalysis Quarterly,* 1956, *25,* 228-237.

Schactel, E. On memory and childhood amnesia. *Psychiatry,* 1947, *10,* 1-26.

Schrut, S. D. Attitudes toward old age and death. *Mental Hygiene,* 1958, *42,* 259-266.

Stern, E. Diagnostic value of children's early memories. *Archives of International Neurology,* 1935, *54,* 1-11.

Wynne, R. D., & Schaffzin, B. A technique for the analysis of affect in early memories. *Psychological Reports,* 1965, *17,* 933-934.

PART III

STUDIES IN RESEARCH AND THEORY

18:: PSYCHOANALYTIC VIEWPOINTS ON AGING —AN HISTORICAL SURVEY

STANLEY CATH

It is a long stride from Spartan society where the elderly were summarily disposed of to our American culture in which most elderly are regarded as capable of making a definite contribution to family and society. Few societies have overcome centuries of reluctance to think about preserving the meaningfulness of life for as long as possible (Cath, 1963). Rather, youth is idealized beyond measure. There seems to be an unconscious, if not conscious, repugnance for the aging process itself. There is something in each of us that results in an universal desire to avoid contact with the aging, the dying, and the dead. While the struggle against this repugnance has not yet been won in Western society, this paper presents one part of this struggle. It is limited to a consideration of the psychoanalytic thinkers of the past eighty years. This narrowed perspective reflects that about which I feel best informed, and does not imply others have not contributed a great deal.

Medicine early decided many of its procedures were not applicable to the aged. Only in retrospect, can one reassess how anxiety over "favorable results," often led to a selection of younger, better risk cases. We in the psychological fields have also been reluctant to apply our techniques for similar reasons.

Part of the explanation is that this period has not been considered as an age-specific phase of the life cycle with its own developmental tasks. In fact it poses the most difficult one of all for the ego—namely to face "not being" at all (Erickson, 1959). In truth, what better life stage to study the formation, integration, and dissolution of ego defenses? During the aging process one has the last chance to accomplish this task, or, in Kleinian (Klein, 1948) terms, to work through "the depressive position" and achieve some integrity. For many, this last task cannot be accomplished alone and dissolution of the ego begins with loss of significant people. Scientists, however, differ as to just how much of the decline is object-related and how much inevitable organic change. For those who subscribed to the theory of aging as being at least partly psychologically determined, the challenge remained how to help people through their climacteric years and to strengthen them for their last struggle. Outside of a few compassionate physicians who recognized this need in the eighteenth and nineteenth centuries, only in literature did the loneliness of aging and the chill of facing death without conscious discussion, receive the attention it deserved (Tolstoy, 1960).

A history of attitudes towards therapy of the aged needs reflect: 1) What techniques were available at the time; 2) The reluctance or enthusiasm of the therapist to invest time and energy in applying new techniques to elderly persons; 3) The willingness and receptivity of the elderly person to subject himself to those techniques; and 4) The overall applicability of these techniques to the aged.

I would like to suggest that psychoanalytic psychotherapy of the aged was first hindered by very early statements of Freud, and then gradually stimulated by Freud's own aging pattern and by other psychoanalytic thinkers who began to treat patients in their middle years. At first only a few dared to publish reports offering encourage- ment for others to try. Some became aware of a definite shortcoming or incompleteness in the theoretical models of the life cycle. For, in truth, life does not end with genital maturity. People do not walk off into a brilliant sunset of eternal bliss when they are married. When I first became aware of this gap in personality theory and therapeutic techniques, almost ten years ago, I decided to take a closer look, from a historical perspective, at the writings of those analysts who have most influenced the mainstreams of thought on psychotherapeutic procedures.

The Early Psychoanalytic Approach, 1890-1930

In *Sexuality and Aetiology,* Freud said (1898, p. 245):

> The psychoanalytic method is not at present applicable to all cases; I recognized the following limitations in regard to it . . . it demands a certain measure of clearsightedness and maturity in the patient and is therefore not suited for youthful persons or for adults who are feeble-minded or uneducated. *With persons who are too far advanced in years it fails because, owing to the accumulation of material, so much time would be required so that the end of the cure would be reached at a period of life in which much importance is no longer attached to nervous health.* And finally it is possible only if the patient is capable of a normal mental condition from the vantage-point of which he may overlook the pathological material. (Italics added)

Freud was then forty-two; analytic knowledge barely ten years of age and limited to findings from a small number of cases. Later, he qualified these statements by adding he had tried his treatment exclusively on severe cases of hysteria and obsessional neuroses, and could not tell about others as yet. It was characteristic of him "to attack the hardest tasks with imperfect instruments."

Twenty years passed without too much apparent change in attitude. But in 1919, Abraham (1927) reopened the issue of applicability of psychoanalytic techniques to patients of advanced age. It is apparent that he had been working with older people during this interval because 1919 was the first date of the publication. He began by quoting Freud's viewpoints cited above, but concluded that psychoanalytic techniques had been greatly developed—by experiences gathered over the ensuing twenty years. While Abraham had no doubt of the general correctness of Freud's view that, "with the beginning of psychical and physical involution, a person is less inclined to part with a neurosis which he has had most of his life," it seemed opportune to him to consider more carefully Freud's comment that analysis loses its effectiveness in patients of advanced years. It had been held that treatment in the forties was doubtful, and without effect in the fifties or beyond, but he wisely cautioned, "We cannot expect mental processes to be too uniform," and he recommended we "not approach the investigation or treatment of nervous conditions with *a priori* theories." He continued, "It would seem incorrect today to deny *a priori* the possibility of exercising a curative influence upon the neurosis in the period of involution and rather it is the task of psychoanalysis to inquire under what conditions the method of treatment can attain results in the later years (pp. 312-317)."

Abraham then had treated a number of chronic neuroses of persons aged forty to fifty-five and over, with the self-expectation at least that he could give them a better understanding of the trouble than a physician untrained in psychoanalysis might do. He first succeeded in analyzing an involutional melancholic man of fifty who had been institutionalized several times. Later he was successful in several cases of obsessional neurosis of severe magnitude, and again in a forty-one-year-old woman with street and traveling anxiety. When he described his failures, they had been particularly among those who retreated from any contact with their instinctual life and discontinued treatment lest they face "unwished for discoveries." Abraham concluded, "the age at which the neurosis breaks out is of greater importance than the age at which treatment has begun (p. 316)."

In 1921, another pioneer, Sandor Ferenczi (1955), published his findings in psychoanalyzing cases of "involutional psychoneurosis." He postulated psychoneurosis at this age was due to a failure to make a change in the distribution of libido, or of the individual to adapt himself to the new distributions of libidinal interests. Following closely upon Freud's ideas that quantitative libidinous interests were withdrawn from love objects and devoted to the ego, he described the aged as becoming increasingly narcissistic, losing their capacity for sublimation, particularly in the sphere of shame and disgust, and becoming characteristically cynical, malicious, and mean. Underdisguised anal and urethral eroticism, characteristic of pre-genital stages, linked with voyeurism, exhibitionism, and a tendency to masturbate, expressed themselves. Ferenczi commented, "in growing old, man has nearly as many awkward reefs to navigate if he is to avoid falling ill as he had in the transition from childhood to sexual maturity (p. 208)."

It is interesting to note that in those days of preoccupation by analysts with neurasthenia, the feeling of impoverishment was related primarily to the wasted libido theory and associated with excessive masturbation or fear of the same. Depression after coitus and in the elderly was linked with the narcissistic regret over the loss of man's precious bodily fluids. Ferenczi felt this tendency towards neurasthenia probably increases with age or at least is likely to in those who loose object ties. If it is excessive, it may result in more than just post-coital depression, and the extreme picture of guilt, self-damage and impoverishment.

For Ferenczi the idea of impoverishment always concealed fear of the consequences of masturbation, and the delusion of guilt always had been related to the expression of an incapacity for object love, that was constitutionally, or later became, defective. It is interesting to note that one of his other observations was to explain some of the symptoms of senile dementia as related to libido distribution or of the attempts to cope with alterations in libido distribution. He believed that the noticeable loss of receptivity to new sensory impressions in the aged, side by side with the retention of old memories, may be the result not of histopathological alterations in the brain, but of impoverishment of available object libido. Old memories spring to mind so readily because of the lively feeling tone or residue of still undiminished object libido which remains associated with them, while the present interest in the outside world is no longer sufficient for acquisition of new lasting memories.

In 1922 Ferenczi, in collaboration with Hollós (Hollós & Ferenczi, 1925), probably encouraged by his work with patients in the middle years, extended his research to the relationships between mental and physical illness from the psychoanalytic point of view. With the introduction of the concept of narcissism, Freud had been able to clarify human behavior during illness as well as health. In regression, the ailing individual withdraws narcissism from objects to the self, or parts of the self, as represented in the mind.

According to Freud, the "ego nucleus" behaves as a subject criticizing the rest of the ego, which remains narcissistic, and sets up new institutions of conscious reality and self-observations. Ferenczi followed patients through disintegrating process in the ego, along these regressive pathways, as the essential products of growth and development were destroyed as a consequence of paretic brain disease. When the pain of self-observation became too great, regression was found to be inevitable to earlier levels, which, although primitive, were once ego-syntonic.

Ferenczi was one of the first to point out how the course of organic disease was influenced and colored by the basic structure of the ego prior to the illness. He stressed that a person's past, his ego development, and his cultural level cannot be irrelevant to the manner and intensity of the pathoneurotic or psychotic reactions to organic stress. A cerebral process of disease altered the ego state but was in turn influenced by the ego structure at the time of onset. In fact, if the patient was asked his age, he would often give his age as that at the onset of his illness.

This early attempt to explain the psychotic phenomena of organic illness, psychoanalytically at least, led to a range of ideas which held out the promise of a solution of difficult problems both in psychiatry and psychology. The concept of libido served as a focal idea upon which later elaborations could be made.

1920-1940

In these years many analysts began to tackle the particular problems pointed out by Abraham and Ferenczi—namely, those of patients in the middle years. The Bibrings, the Deutsches, Robert Waelder, Ives Hendricks and many others took into their practices a limited number of forty-to-fifty-year-old men and women of whom most were depressed and paranoid.

In 1925, Helene Deutsch (1945), published a monumental paper in German, later to be included in *The Psychology of Women*, devoted to the climacterium. This period of life, when a woman no longer feels able to function as a childbearing biological unit and because of many other related factors, becomes a psychologically traumatic phase. With the regression of physiological functioning marking the end of her femininity, there may be a heightened compensatory "libidinal thrust" as the woman tries to act young again. This so-called "dangerous age" begins a phase of retrogression to abandon infantile libidinal positions. The genitals may become deprecated as an organ and the details of the puberty conflict are reproduced. However, "it is now too late," and this first phase of attempted compensation directed strongly towards objects, is followed by devaluation of the genitals with renewed masturbation and turning away from reality. Reversed oedipal fantasies may occur with the son taking the place of the father or the daughter of the mother. The work of sublimation of sexual and hostile feelings for children seems to disintegrate with resurgence of these older oedipal feelings. Anxiety over the loss of reproductivity or vaginal insufficiency is again mobilized and indicates grave injury to feminine narcissism.

During the corresponding period in the male the focus may also center about the sexual problem, but the difference is in the field of sublimation. The intensity of aggression which the reactionary old man displays towards youth indicates how revolutionary his whole attitude was during puberty. The frequency of agitated depression, so-called "involutional melancholia," and the various paranoid conditions is indicative of the type of regression which takes place. Following the lead suggested by Hollós and Ferenczi earlier, organic injury of the central nervous system is also included in her considerations.

The next year of particular interest to us is 1937. At this time two papers appeared. One by Freud (1959), "Analysis, Terminable and

Interminable," could not have increased enthusiasm for analysis or therapy with older patients because of the following relatively accurate statements . . .

> If the latter, that is the ego, becomes enfeebled whether through illness, exhaustion or some similar cause, all the instincts which have so far been successfully tamed may renew their demands and strive in abnormal ways for substitutive satisfaction. In another group of patients . . . , we were surprised by an attitude we could only put down to loss of plasticity, an exhaustion of a capacity for change and development. We are indeed prepared for a certain degree of physical inertia in analysis. When new paths are pointed out for the instinctual impulses, we almost invariably see an obvious hesitation entering upon them. We have described this attitude, although perhaps not quite rightly, as resistance from the id. But in the case which I have in mind all the mental processes, relations and distributions of energy are immutably fixed. *One finds the same state of affairs in very old people when it is explained by what is described as a force of habit—the exhaustion of a receptivity through a kind of physical entropy, but I think of people who are still young.* Our theoretical knowledge does not seem adequate to explain these types. Perhaps a mild matter of a temporal nature is at work here and changes when some rhythm in the development of a psychical life which we have not yet apprehended (p. 327). (Italics added)

A second paper, in the same year, by M. Ralph Kaufman (1937) was more encouraging. Later, in *Old Age and Aging: The Psychoanalytic Point of View,* Kaufman (1940), observed that psychoanalysis had had little to say concerning the matter of old age and aging.

Kaufman observed that Freud's statements about the elasticity of mental processes or the educability of elder people were impressionistic and not based on psychoanalytic studies. He pointed to Abraham's cautiously presented observations of several patients over fifty in which the prognosis seemed more favorable if the neurosis had been in full severity after a long period had elapsed since puberty, and after the patient had enjoyed, for at least several years, a sexual attitude approaching the normal. He gave Abraham credit for demonstrating that the personality of an individual may not be quite as rigid for the purposes of psychoanalytic investigation as one had been led to believe.

Kaufman reported on two female cases he had been analyzing, during the preceding few years, in which psychoanalytic technique with relatively little modification had been indeed applicable, partly as a therapeutic method and definitely as a research instrument. He pointed to the importance of reality factors, and noted that an aging individual, menaced by his own feelings of inadequacy and insecurity, might project his anxiety into the outside world and elaborate external threats, such as war or economic disaster. He felt it was a general and valid observation that, with increasing age, the majority of people tend to become fixed in their opinions and reactions, and wondered about the psychological significance of these changes. Does it mean that reality factors are more objectively evaluated and the earlier conflicts of childhood and the young adult years have lost their intensity? Rather the rigidity seems to be a type of dissociation and lack of elasticity, which really expresses a deeper repression of the anxieties, with an increasing fixity of reaction formation originally laid down as a character trait. This leads to a certain brittleness of the personality, and, rather than anxieties being dissipated with the climacteric, they may become more threatening.

Kaufman was one of the first to attempt analytic therapy with older patients and to believe advanced age was not necessarily a contra-indication. Still, the object of treatment was not to restore genital primacy, but to attempt symptomatic improvement. The two cases he treated with favorable outcomes might be called "transference cures" and this in his opinion was the most important aspect of the treatment.

1940-1960

In a survey of the literature of aging by Robert E. Moss (1965), much of what follows has been already summarized. For the purposes of this paper, I would like to repeat his emphasis on the need for continued reassessment of our attitudes toward the aging.

A major contributor to this reassessment, Dr. Maurice Linden (1953), initiated a new approach to the problems of the most deteriorated elderly patients back in the forties. It became known as "The Miracle in Building 53." (Dr. Linden's research at this time was conducted at the Pennsylvania State Hospital at Norristown). Here, by a combination of revised staff attitude, a humane and reasonable environmental setting, the use of an optimistic group therapy, and one-to-one relationship structured by members of the professional staff or volunteers, a new approach to the aged in mental hospitals was born. Working against social isolation, the loss of individual pride and social status, Linden tried to provide a meaningful present existence with personal gain for the individual. Rather than leaving older patients to their own devices, with increasingly deep feelings of anxiety and discomfort leading to ever deepening regression, he attempted to shift the balance by this approach to total care.

Through the following years, Linden (Linden & Courtney, 1953) published many papers, one of which attempted to redefine the human life cycle. "An individual at any time . . . is the aggregate and interaction of many functions—some in development—some at peak and some in decline . . . . Adult life is usually regarded as simple achievement of an ambiguous maturity followed by a general decline . . . (p. 906)" Linden considered the life cycle as divisible into halves—evolescence and senescence. The former referred to the younger side of the middle years during which the rebellion of the evolescents against the senescents reflected fighting for change. Currently, almost all cultural values have been placed in evolescence. The senescent counterrebellion may be regarded as a continuous restatement of old ideals, a tenacious attachment to established and proven solutions, and an awareness of the value of the past as a predictor of the future.

In Linden's life cycle, later maturity contains three segments, the first being social-political or cultural-organizational. With the progeny in the family-creating period, the elders shift to a "state-creative" period. Obviously, this is idealistic and not necessarily an achievement by a large number. The second segment, the "moral and ethical reaffirmative period," is one in which (hopefully) the judgmental functions of the human mind are most highly developed. It produces a rediscovery of old values with concern for system, meaning, and order in human experience and a newly found kinship with the past. The third segment, "a retrospective examination period," is characterized by a need to correlate the present with the past, and to evaluate life's meaning and purpose.

In old age, Linden suggests senility as a result of loss or impairment of psychic defenses related simultaneously to a similar impairment of physical resistances. Without therapy, organic deterioration will follow and finally dementia and death. The first stage of senility is senile latency, characterized by instinct dominated affects and ideation. Then there is a period of reparation with a return of better social functioning, but the partially restored psyche fails to endure. Social unlearning or de-education of the instincts is the next stage, as each gain made in psychosexual development progressively disappears. The latest acquired is the first lost. Language deteriorates. Adult sexuality is replaced by masturbation and then by loss of sphincter control. Partially controlled aggressiveness leads to impulsiveness and "acting out" with decreased motor coordination, ability to maintain erect posture, and lack of comprehension of spatial and temporal relations. Memory looses its acuity for the present. Food tolerance is altered by stages, from pap to milk. Now we have instinct supremacy resembling the period from birth to puberty in reverse.

Gitelson (1948) described the first task of the aging organism as survival. He theorized about many of the psychological burdens—dulling of recent memory and turning away from the painfulness of the present. The increasing incidents of illness or death of their peers leads to an increase in free-floating anxiety and psychological tension resulting in somatic tension, increased sensitivity to bodily functions, and revival of infantile body interests. This paper was based on the analysis of a sixty-six-year-old depressed woman with insomnia, difficulties in thinking clearly, and failing memory. Six months previously, her husband had died after several years of mental deterioration. Electric shock had been recommended for her depression, but Gitelson considered this patient a pure culture for a study of grief. While she seemed sad about a friend dying of a deteriorating cerebral process, she related her husband's death had meant nothing. Still, she felt concern because she didn't grieve, describing herself as empty and intellectually inadequate. Having been in analysis for two years in 1924, this patient fascinated Dr. Gitelson, giving him a chance to study not only the survival of the sexual impulse but also the fate of the neurotic transference in an elderly woman or the opportunity to make a relatively infrequent observation on the catamnesis of a psychoanalysis by extending the post-hoc view of a previous period of analysis.

So one of the most interesting "modified analyses" on record of a sixty-six-year-old woman began, and was quite successfully concluded. It was the beginning of the accumulation of clinical experience which would confirm or refute therapeutic accessibility. True, the case was not classical analytic work. Rather, it was one in which a "cold woman," who had struggled with sexual inhibitions all her life, had remained relatively unchanged after an initial period of brief analysis, and her conversion symptoms still occurred. At such an age, many such symptoms are disguised or considered psychosomatic. During twice-a-week, psychoanalytic therapy over eight months, the unresolved erotic attachment to her old analyst was finally resolved.

After termination of treatment, she had remained active in the family business for two years. Then, at seventy, she took her first winter vacation and met a new friend. She decided to remain in this new community where, for thirteen years, she has remained active in civic affairs with a host of friends. She became a highly respected group therapist and an instructor of other lay people interested in this work.

This, then, is the first case on record of a patient in her sixties successfully treated by an analytic method to resolve transference from a previous analysis and to develop even better integration with increased capacity to relate. This case was presented in 1963 at the third annual symposium of the Boston Society for Gerontologic Psychiatry and entitled "A Transference Reaction of a Sixty-Six-Year-Old Woman" (Gitelson, 1965).

During the fifties, the number of professionals working with the elderly increased greatly. Linden continued his excellent work and Alvin Goldfarb (1955) made other major contributions. To the latter, however, all behavior of the aged was designed "to secure help," and the therapist had to play the part of a dominant individual, giving sufficient strength to reduce the elder's anxiety thereby increasing hope. Most elders, he suggested, felt so worthless they could only envisage a relationship of power, with the secret belief the patient really dominated the therapist. One had to provide enough emotional gratification to raise self-esteem and it was essential to reach this point in the first few interviews. Particularly in the brain-damaged, this illusory mastery was fostered. His treatment was rather brief therapy frequently limited to fifteen minute interviews twice a week.

Grotjahn (1951), reaffirmed that prospects of treatment were better for those who were not psychotic, but commented the ego's resistance against unpleasant truth is lessened. The task is to integrate and accept life as lived, and a life-long struggle is sometimes good preparation for therapy. The neuroses of old age are defenses against the narcissistic trauma of growing old and the castration threat. Three different possible patterns were suggested: 1) The normal reaction to accept life as lived; 2) Increased conservatism and rigidity holding the line of defenses according to previous more or less neurotic adjustments; and 3) Neurotic or psychotic regression.

With age, people are often easier to deal with in psychotherapy because of their decreased resistance. Introspection modified to an attitude of retrospection is the basis of therapy. He further postulated that the success of shock treatment in melancholia might be because it provides the experience of death with a happy ending.

A young therapist may feel self-conscious and apologetic with the old. If the therapist is old, he may feel superior, so the need for the resolution of the countertransference to older patients is evident. A reversed oedipal relationship develops and may be utilized. For this reason, the transference may be stronger and more intensive than in younger people. The therapist needs to be able to withstand the patient's hostility without feeling guilty for being younger, and the patient learns the father should not submit to, or kill, the son.

In 1952 Hollender advised that deeper therapy only adds further stress and arouses uncontrollable emotions, particularly when a person turns to the past. He thought defenses should not be tampered with unless adequate substitutes could be found.

In 1953 Wayne, using a psychoanalytic approach, described the need to know historical background in order to understand the transference. He suggested that the therapist needs to be more active, not limit his goals, and attack crucial current problems as the mainstream for therapy. In his experience, one could interpret the transference or samples of behavior transfered outside therapy, and he suggested the patient sit up in order to decrease dependency. Seeing his patients one to three times a week for a period of about a year, it seemed appropriate to him to discuss physiology, cultural attitudes, and values, and aim at more realistic superego and ego ideals.

By 1955 other important writings appeared. Meerloo (1955) visited his patients at home and used whatever activities possible to counteract lost social contacts until the patient formed new relationships. He said, "Those who have no future must be brought to the past in order to accept the present (p. 585)." Using free association, he often encountered a spontaneous increase in childhood memories. He, too, felt resistance to therapy was now more related to anxiety over death. He used more intellectual interpretations unless he felt the patient was made suspicious and anxious when it might be bad strategy to stir things up by a deeper investigation of the unconscious. In such cases, he would explain enough to help the patient feel less critical or regretful. He considered introspection as an effort to repair, rather than as a narcissistic defense to prove how much life has failed, and attempted to convince his patient of this interpretation (Meerloo, 1961).

Rigidity was more related to fear or reduced organic adaption, and possibly to more direct contact with the unconscious. But it was this same contact that permitted less biased responses to interpretation. Certain "warning signals" of regression included increasing attention to the body, preoccupation with food "as a new ceremonial to evade death," and changes in the body image noted through dreams. He felt more than 50% of his patients were successful in psychotherapy in reaching a new pact with death. There was a lessened suggestibility, greater patience, and a new concept of time.

Once again, he agreed with those who felt the transference and countertransferences were extremely strong when working with older people. The analyst needs to become a benevolent superego but should not permit himself to be manipulated like a little child. The patient has to be guided to readapt to previously unexperienced bodily sensations. The therapist has to break through the block of isolation and overcome his countertransference or prejudice, related to the inner conviction of decay, revived conflicts with his own parents, and fear of death (Meerloo, 1955).

In the same year, Kurt Eissler (1955), published a book on the dying patient in which much of the same type of material is to be found. He suggested, in essence, the psychiatrist take over the role of priest and reduce the fear of death by establishing a transference which mobilizes "the archaic trust in the world." He indicated that the suffering of the dying can be reduced to a minimum even with the presence of extreme physical pain, if one revives a primordial feeling of protection by an omnipotent mother or parent. The analyst or therapist does this by providing sublimated love. This includes a readiness to help, sorrow, and pity, but not grieve nor despair.

Using the libido thesis, namely that the libido is totally drawn into the process of binding the death instinct leaving no surplus to maintain other essential functions, it becomes apparent the psychiatrist needs to provide optimal libidinal accretion to ease the patient's struggle. Grief and despair burden the patient and the psychiatrist must have a belief in the indestructibility of the patient's body and mind or at least that it cannot be converted into something dead. Only when the patient falls into terminal coma, or is unconscious, may the psychiatrist relinquish this magical belief.

The psychiatrist, on the one hand, gives the dying patient the feeling that he is dying with him, or, on the other, avoids the pain of impending death by turning memories back to re-experiencing successful danger situations in the past and denying the disaster faced in current reality. To do this, the therapist must partially identify with the patient but at the same time remain free enough of the identification to be able to relinquish it when the patient dies.

Rockwell (1956) felt that free association was less valuable for the aged and used a Meyerian approach, namely, trying to analyze all factors. At the end of each interview, he offered a constructive formulation in order to synthesize the material. He pointed to apathy due to hopelessness as one of the most serious possible symptoms leading to more or less lasting deterioration of behavior. It was his impression that those who develop simple arterioscleroric deterioration, with varying degrees of impairment of intellectual functions, emotional liability, and personality change, were best cared for at home, in order to keep them in familiar surroundings.

In 1958 Hannah Segal, a Kleinian, analyzed a man who started treatment at the age of seventy-three-and-a-half. To the best of my knowledge this is the only, and the purest, analytic case reported in the literature. The patient's treatment lasted for approximately a year and a half. When first seen, he suffered from psychotic depression, hypochondria, paranoid delusions, and attacks of insane rage. After eighteen months of analysis he could resume normal life. The cause of his breakdown was considered an unconscious fear of death precipitated by disillusionment in his son, when, after a lifetime of turning away from his family, he became lonely and returned with the expectation his son not only would accept him but provide a new lease on life. He learned simultaneously the remaining members of his family had died in concentration camps and suffered from the fear that his past bribery in business would be uncovered. For these reasons, among others, he perceived old age and death as persecution and punishment and used splitting, idealization, and denial as main defenses.

Hannah Segal divided the analysis into three phases: First, the complete denial of aging associated with fear of death and the resultant idealization of those who would restore his usefulness, structured by oral, homosexual fantasies. While idealization of the analyst remained his only protection for a while, gradually he admitted aggression towards her as well. In the third phase, persecution fantasies and idealizations gave way to overt ambivalence, a sense of psychic reality, and depressive anxiety. Now he could show anger when the analyst went away and realized some of his guilt at having left his family behind so many years ago when he ran away.

After a mourning phase he altered his idea about his own death. It was a reason for sorrow and mourning the loss of something he deeply appreciated—his life. Mourning can be differentiated from clinical depression and is needed in order to feel enjoyment of life. Now life was once again worth living, in spite of his age, and he no longer thought of children and grandchildren only as projections of himself, but as objects he could love. He enjoyed the thought of their going on and growing after his death.

This case represented an ideal version of how elderly patients should respond to therapy. While it is not possible to attain such a result in all old people, it remains the hallmark of the analytic method.

In marked contrast with such an intrapsychic approach, Sheps, an analyst, worked primarily with the environment, particularly in the borderline and schizophrenogenic families. He advocated (1959) changing family attitudes in that such people are often categorized as good or bad, and use denial predominantly. Whatever is not acceptable is not admitted by the family, even while fantasies of violence associated with fear and guilt exist. He observed children stopping communication with their ailing parents. Unable to accept their parents or themselves as weak and helpless, they retain magical omnipotent parental images. Therapy aims to get such children to accept their parents as children in need, rather than responding to past images of omnipotent parents who are now neglecting and disturbing their grown-up children. To do this, one must undo fear and denial of death, and work with all members of the family. Once the parents' new role as children of the family is established, a new equilibrium may be obtained. Children can be taught to gratify needs of their parents, when one has reduced their anxiety over weaknesses and hostility caused by feeling imposed upon.

Sheps (1957), stated the doctor must decide whether denial is desirable for the patient's peace of mind, and, if the fear of death breaks through this defense, to use whatever means possible to give the patient a feeling of lovability. This may require the doctor to assume the role of a substitute parent.

1960 to the Present

By the sixties, it had become apparent to many all over the world that the aged could no longer be excluded from the realm of psychotherapy and, in rare cases, were able to undergo modified analysis. Social workers, as well as psychiatric consultants to agencies or in homes for the aged, had accumulated a great deal of experience. State departments of aging increasingly used such consultants, some of whom were analytically trained. Duke and Michigan Universities set up departments to study both the biology and psychology of the aged from eclectic points of view. In a panel discussion on such psychotherapeutic measures in New York, psychoanalytic thinkers began to explore some of the rationale for dynamic therapeutic manipulation.

In 1960 in Boston, it dawned on a group of seven analysts that they were indeed doing analytic work with increasing numbers of older patients, and, led by Dr. Martin Berezin, formed the Boston Society for

Gerontologic Psychiatry. This was the first organization of its kind, devoted exclusively to the dynamic study of the aging and the application of psychoanalytic principles to therapeutic techniques.

It became obvious that psychoanalytic theory had much to offer, but even more apparent was the need to learn and a series of annual symposia was initiated to share experiences. In addition educational efforts were made to overcome psychotherapeutic prejudices and stereotyped viewpoints held in training programs and in other agencies—medical schools, hospitals, etc. We found aging was still regarded all too frequently by professional caretakers exclusively as a deteriorating process. Freud's comments about rigid, unresponsive older patients remained fixed in people's minds, so that therapeutic measures often came too late and were destined to be inadequate. Consistent coordination of the multidisciplinary efforts of the therapeutic potential of the community was needed to work with the complicated factors and the vastness of the geriatric problem.

In the sixties there came a number of important writings: *Growing Old,* by Elaine Cumming and William E. Henry (1961), and others by Martin Berezin (1963), Zinberg & Kaufman (1963), Sidney Levin (1963a), Stanley Cath (1965), and others too numerous to mention.

Cumming and Henry studied two hundred and fifty men and women over the age of sixty in Kansas City, and they suggested that old age is not merely a prolongation of middle years but has its own intrinsic properties. These include a reduction in ego energy and social interaction, lessening of emotional ties to other people, and increasing importance to the individual of his own inner thoughts and feelings. Furthermore, the individual's involvement in work and family, society's two focal demands, becomes less binding and relevant and he becomes free to adapt new goals. This is seen as a two-way process. Society cuts its demands on old people while they feel less committed to social involvement. In addition, there may be a resurgence of self-expression and self-indulgence. And so, for some, it may be a distressful time but for others it is a period of relief and personal enjoyment. If one can successfully reorganize one's goals and self-images, Dr. Henry commented, considerable satisfaction can be found. Satisfaction may be derived from having had satisfying experiences in these areas in the past and from adopting an altered present life style. All of this is acceptable theory, but it implies older people should not be encouraged to be more active, but to disengage.

Dr. Henry said the theory of disengagement was a theory of normal aging unrelated to therapeutic or activation techniques. However, he suggested programs which aimed to recreate social and emotional situations characteristic of middle life rather than old age must take disengagement into account or be apt to fail. This contradicted the long, dominant "activist's school" which held old people are happiest and best adjusted when busy.

It seems this theory has a true scientific validity which must be accepted and, as with Freud's comments, placed in context, rather than isolated and overgeneralized. If taken as a true observation, it reflects a need to change the goals and images of what many older persons should or be expected to do. If seen as a study to guide-planners, it is one matter, but if seen as a barometer for therapeutic effort it appears discouraging. In truth, not all need be active to be happy in old age. As with Hannah Segal's case, therapeutic goals may be high but individualized. One finds one can only deal with what is available and potentially possible, but conflict is ever present and can be alleviated.

In 1961 the first annual meeting of the Boston Society for Gerontologic Psychiatry was held. Some of the problems and rewards of experience in therapy with the aged began to emerge, as reported by Zinberg and Kaufman (1963). There are problems in communication. For example, taciturn or garrulous persons tend to become more so with age, and, this is complicated by feelings of dominance and submission. Many times older people pull themselves together when visiting a doctor, and conceal some of their problems. If the patient opens up to the physician, but says little or nothing to the family, the problem becomes one of diagnosis and to enlist their help requires revelation and interpretation of the true state of affairs to the family. The difficulties in diagnosis, the proper weight to be given to the role of organic illness, the wish to avoid hospitalization, to reduce regression— all must be communicated. The dynamic psychiatrist may have little interest in the aged because these are often additional tasks to insight therapy, and verbal communication may be so difficult. In general, older people tend to identify a psychiatrist with a familiar someone and relate better if they make a concrete identification with someone like mother, brother, old friend, previous doctor and so forth. This may help bridge the gap. A psychiatrist must modify some of his previously held notions about proper doctor-patient relationship because older people are more likely to hold one's hand, hug, or kiss their physicians. One has to be flexible enough to permit many changes in one's treatment routine. Ofttimes, a patient may not know why he is being seen and cannot identify his problem. Many come as more or less emergency cases and require an indefinite period to handle the crisis. The psychiatrist may be consulted about every aspect of an older person's life, not because of need, but to help him gain self-esteem and maintain narcissistic supplies. Thus insight may not be the initial therapeutic lever the analyst utilizes in his therapeutic approach.

At the same symposium, Alvin Goldfarb (1965) noted that the early establishment of self-assertive trends, a good early education, a setting in keeping with one's past, and a social atmosphere of interest and hope, in contrast to neglect and futility, have been demonstrated to preclude or minimize psychological complications in the aged.

Those experienced in psychotherapy often watch the selection of persons for therapy by new therapists, and are aware of their tendency to select young, attractive, articulate, and well-educated persons well-motivated to a conversational technique and who often have respect for, or a built-in transference, toward psychoanalysis. Aged persons are not generally viewed with such favor as candidates for psychotherapeutic techniques, or, for that matter, any techniques which bring the doctor into a direct or sustained relationship with them. It is probably true that the critical factor in selecting patients for psychotherapy is the communicative potential felt in the interaction between therapist and patient. These factors have been found at work on the choice of patients for individual therapy at the Hebrew Home for the Aged and Infirm in New York by Goldfarb.

Goldfarb (1965), also called attention to the cannibalistic fantasies associated with clinging in the aged. Some may have a conscious or unconscious idea that new strength in life can be obtained by processes of incorporation—sucking, eating, or magically taking in through bodily orifices. Emotions involved often lead to guilt with fear of retaliation, then attempting to repair, and wishing to be forgiven for these angry demanding fantasies. Respect for psychotherapy then may disguise a special elaboration of the search for a magical fountain of youth with a readiness to submit to authority. Yet, this "primitive transference" provides the greatest possible leverage for helping the patient in that it delegates to the therapist an influential parental role. In his opinion, we have evidence that psychotherapeutic experiences can be repeatedly reinforced and have revealed unsuspecting abilities of the aged for healthy adaption. Rationally, therapists should view the aged more happily and optimistically.

In the same volume, Zinberg (Zinberg & Kaufman, 1963), calls our attention to another unrecognized advantage in therapy with an older person, namely, the "gain of distance." By this he means the capacity "to take a long view of oneself and others." He found he could speak readily to the patient of "corrosive anger" or the "cutting biting nature of envy in human affairs" and meet with understanding (p. 153).

Zinberg never proposes anything new to older people, but rather asks them to use their intellectual distance to search for solutions that worked earlier in their lives. One thing he has already learned is economical, because so much energy is needed to just get through the day. He directly asks if he reminds the patient of anyone. There are specific vicissitudes to the oedipal triangle related to feelings about death, a frequent fantasy is one has outlived his father. Now one may become preoccupied with the meaning of survival, as Oedipus was at Colonus. A man may also feel he has replaced mother with wife, and have related guilt fantasies. This may lead to loss of ego boundaries and the re-emergence of the primacy of the archaic superego.

Dr. Sidney Levin (1963), focused upon distribution and depressive reactions with the waning of sexuality in the male. Increasing anxiety may have to do with lack of elasticity, due to deeper repression of this conflict. Following Kaufman's (1937) ideas Levin feels the individual is more vulnerable to regression, further contributed to by restriction in activity leading to losses of important satisfactions. Precautionary attitudes of relatives reinforce "fears of overdoing it." The functions of the genitals and the brain are very much involved in narcissistic equilibrium. If they are interfered with, feelings about mental infeeblement, loss of intellectual and/or sexual prowess (sometimes more apparent than real) appear in the forefront. With weakened ego functioning, there is a tendency to become more conservative, and many cultural factors are involved. He, also, pointed to the limited applications of psychotherapy influenced both by cultural attitudes and emotional reluctance to work with the aged. In his opinion, therapeutic nihilism is giving way.

Over the next five years, a series of symposiums confirmed and reaffirmed the therapeutic potential of older people. Attempts to study not only later years, but to clarify the dynamic balance between losses and ego resources experienced through the middle years, were evident in two papers—one by this author (Cath, 1965), and another by Elliot Jacques (1965). The age specific crises of mid-life were to be more than the previously well- recognized "involutional periods" in both male and female.

In my own paper, I suggested aging brought with it an accentuation of the role of the enteroceptive apparatus, so that messages from within the body were more quickly perceived, cogitated upon, and responded to than ever before, with the possible exception of childhood. This process is set in motion by a turning-in of libido in increasing quantities based upon somatic depletion, illness, or pain, and this phenomenon explains the increasing narcissistic position assumed as one ages.

I further hypothesized that anxiety took on age-specific quantitative and qualitative aspects in the face of the greatest reality threat of one's own emotional exile and/or annihilation. I conceptualized a "triad of recathexis" in which the individual then turned most of his attention (libido) to the past, his own body, and toward transitional objects.

Another concept was of omniconvergence, related to the summing effect of the combination of outer and inner losses and depletions, the latter term, "depletion," seemed most appropriate to describe the findings not only of psychoanalysts and psychologists, but of neurophysiologists as well. The latter confirmed a progressive shrinkage of body cells and substance at a designated rate of one to one-and-one-half percent of total structure each year after age thirty-five. For me, the middle and later years emerged as an age-specific crisis, a balance between factors of depletion and sources of restitution, both past and present each individual could summon in his response to the intensity and new dimension of "depletion anxiety." This depended to a surprising degree, on social or environmental supports that had been constructed, retained, or abandoned.

Reluctantly, I had to concede one other analogy to "second childhood." Homeostasis depends increasingly upon the environment as one ages, all too frequently. It also depends on the timing of losses, the ultimate effects of which could be significantly related to the availability of replacement objects and the subsequent degree of sensory isolation. Still, the "margin of safety" is far greater than people generally assume. The "lumping together" phenomenon, or tendency to retire people irrespective of their capacities, seems destructive. In these years then, people will pass through periodic self-assessments with increasingly severe phases of depression, through which they may gradually achieve a sense of integrity, with the final integration of an altered aged body-image.

Because of the increasing amounts of energy needed to maintain denial of reality and internal losses, and/or to repress violent rage, we may observe a state that from all external signs reflects apathy with decreased instinctual energy available to meet inner and outer demands. This is still a reversible state, readily accessible to therapy in which energetic depletion can, to some degree, be reversed, aggression neutralized, and restitution made, through the emotional refueling of the therapeutic relationship. One of the reasons the older person sometimes avoids problems is simply that he lacks the energy to deal with them. With the presence of a therapist, energy is borrowed temporarily—the problem is met and solved, and the aged person gradually can recoup sufficient force to carry on by himself.

Thus, the condition many aged demonstrate is not adequately described by the concept of depression. Rather, it is another entity complicated by depletion, in which self-reproach is rarely evident, introjections are not hated and other mechanisms characteristic of depression are not predominant features. Depletion, then, seems an intermediate step between depression and other complex conditions subsumed under the term "senility." As conscious and unconscious messages of depletion (one's hat suddenly seems to large, or the shirt size one has worn for fifty years no longer will do) received are unacceptable to the ego and because of omniconvergence, one observes intermittant partial or complete abandonment of external and internal reality. To abandon internal reality is the most difficult, but the thinking process itself may be decathected in the final stages. Still, the recognized capacity of one person to strengthen another permits an opportunity for regression to be worked through, and to begin a new identification in the therapeutic relationship. Treatment except in rare cases, does not focus on undoing neurotic character traits, or on the analysis of defenses, but rather on recent reactions to precipitating factors related to depletion. Good results may be obtained then by permitting the patient a significant reality relationship to assist his natural restorative potential.

The task of the psychiatric geriatrician is to utilize every possible means of developing each person's remaining potential while preserving the intactness of ego defenses for as long as possible. The rationale for therapy is based upon the reversability of the balance between depleting and refueling factors, a balance determined by the ego's capacity to tolerate loss and depletion anxiety.

The specific reaction by the ego to loss associated with the aging process has also been noted by Dr. Elizabeth Zetzel (1965). She suggested we consider, between primary and secondary anxiety, the interposition of an intermediate form of depressive anxiety. This anxiety increases with the passage of years and the individual response will be influenced by previous experiences of loss, and the quality of individual object relationships. She commented on the lack of guilt in many older patients and the multiple determinants involved.

Dr. Greta Bibring (1965), in discussing the paper by Dr. Gitelson, "The Transference Reaction in the Sixty-Six-Year-Old Woman," related how, in her study of older women, she could find the same persistence of sexual impulses and fantasies as in younger females. We need to review many accepted concepts of the aging individual.

Certain biological and endocrine changes are bound to affect the course of aging. In addition, there are inevitable emotional problems or traumata and a diminishing of psychic energy. Bibring suggests that regression can be understood from economic, as well as dynamic considerations, and that when strong central themes of of life recede, some of the peripheral less vital positions seem to be more in focus. She made the parallel of the stars emerging when the sun goes down. These changes are not necessarily pathological but rather within a normal range.

Through the succeeding years of the sixties, it became apparent that most analysts were treating older people for the first time in their lives. Gradually, not only the style of a person's life, but longitudinal aspects came into focus.

Many studies suggested that style was one of the most constant aspects of the expressive activity of an individual. Accordingly, one of the more important assets of therapy might be to help restore a certain style of life. Dr. Berezin (1965) reported a case of a hospitalized seventy-four-year-old woman with some organic brain disease who demanded a certain form of interplay with the hospital staff. When provided with this feedback, an oral narcissistic style of life was restored, sustaining her once again. In Levin's (1963) experience, depression in the aged was reversible with therapy and engagement rather than disengagement.

Dr. Weisman (1965) differentiated despair and depression. Despair refers more to an aimless apathy with detachment from purposeful existence or alienation from familiar values. Its antithesis is hope. Despair is like primary anxiety rather than like depression. He included under despair, syndromes of depression, delirium, or dementia which also may correlate with organic changes.

Weisman (1965) suggests that not to be able to take up the subject of death frankly may be due to our own anxiety, in that the person who is dying accepts the fact of imminent death much more readily than the doctors who are taking care of him. Reflecting common experience, Dr. Zinberg (1963) observed that as analysts we were often called upon to see the parents or older relatives of analytic colleagues. True, usually one has been called upon in a troubled or chaotic situation, rather than earlier in the game. Thus, in part, consultation in many instances is to relieve our colleagues' guilt, rather than to reflect training in terms of early referral and belief in early therapeutic potential. Old people experience a slow rate of change in themselves or a constant preparation for death in watching others die. Thus, we all die a little at a time. Every time we lose someone important, a reassessment of life is required. In his opinion, a third of the admissions to general hospitals are essentially in lieu of mental hospital admission.

Regardless of the age, Dr. Levin (1963) believed much of our psychotherapeutic endeavor is usually directed to removing excessive repression present since early life.

To Dr. Gregory Rochlin (1965) older people may appear to be

disengaging but there is no real intention to do so. It is a superficial compliance; rather there is a tenacious holding-on. The enormous value denial possesses may need reinforcement in many patients. While it is assumed old people may have the ability to cope with a confrontation with death, Rochlin doubted this is so. It was his impression only few really can. He did not believe the aged "wait for death," and that if they do it is pathological.

Gitelson (1968) feels that we cannot survive if we surrender objects, and, therefore, the concept of disengagement, if it implies this, needs further study. The man who goes to pieces immediately after retirement may do so because all object orientation has been channeled through his occupation, and he may die in remarkably short order. What is required rather than disengagement is a change of objects and of aims with respect to objects. Thus, there is a redistribution of energy, and those who are able to disengage themselves in this sense are the ones most likely to survive.

Jacques (1965) considers approximately age thirty-five as a crisis because at this time there is a reduction in the intensity of sexual behavior, a change in creativity, in the mode of expression of artistic work, and a peculiar awareness of one's own personal death. He considers the *Divine Comedy* an expression of working through of Dante's mid-life depression, following his banishment from Florence at the age of thirty-seven. He quotes the beginning of this poem:

> In the middle of our journey of our life, I came to myself within a dark wood where the straight way was lost. Ah, how hard it is to tell of that wood, savage and harsh and dense, the thought of which renews my fear. So bitter is it that death is hardly more.

Death at the conscious level, instead of being a general conception, becomes a personal matter, one's own and actual mortality. The individual has stopped growing up and has begun to grow old. A new set of circumstances has to be met. He suggests that one must work through what is generally considered in Kleinian theory, the infantile depressive position. This task is accomplished by the overcoming of grief, the resolution of ambivalence, and the regaining of that security in which good and bad objects can in some measure be synthesized. The ego becomes integrated and hope for the reestablishment intrapsychically of the good object is experienced. The latter process is called "reparation," love overcoming hate, life overcoming death.

But if this synthesis fails, the inner world is unconsciously felt to contain the persecuting, annihilating, devoured, and destroyed bad breast or object. The ego feels itself split into bits, and the chaotic situation thus experienced is the infantile equivalent of the notion of death. The evasion of awareness of death by manic defenses and the revival of unconscious memories of hate and destruction are all healed by loving grief. It is a task to be reworked and reexperienced but it results in an increase in confidence of one's capacity to love, or mourn what has been lost, and what has passed, rather than to hate and feel persecuted by it. Given such a resolution to the internal situation, the last half of life can be lived with conscious knowledge of eventual death. Acceptance of this knowledge is an integral part of living. If one can look back and confirm that one's lovingness has indeed outweighed infantile notions of destructiveness aroused by depletion and loss, there may be the enjoyment of mature creativeness and work in full awareness of death which lies beyond, resigned but not defeated.

In 1966 one particular contribution from a most objective observer emerged. It seemed to Dr. Greta Bibring, after seventy years of living, an appropriate time to move from the appreciation of dynamic pathology, and therefore of psychotherapeutic potential, to another vantage point—that of life itself. She viewed aging as a specific developmental and maturational sequence. Senescence, in her opinion, is a developmental phase, whose changes proceed in an orderly fashion and follow a genetically given pathway through which control is introduced into the changes. She wanted to correct certain common value judgments and determine what intrinsic characteristics of maturation or "ripening" had been overlooked. She suggested there were developmental gains, as well as losses, compared with the preceding period, and that there were age-related special forms of achievement.

We all have to prepare for death, and the closest each of us can come is a realization of the concept by experiencing the death of a person to whom we are strongly attached. Various forms of apprehension about death are determined by leading unconscious childhood anxieties. It represents the loss of oneself as the main recipient of narcissistic investment, the loss of all objects by being lost to them, and it evokes the earliest anxieties around an idea present from childhood as the greatest disaster that can happen. Yet, there is certainly more than one way of dealing with this perplexity. Dr. Bibring (1966) says, "We are not yet justified in the assumption that a state of equilibrium at the thought of death cannot be genuine but is achieved only by its denial." She requotes Freud—"If you want to endure life, prepare yourself for death."

The decisive roles in the resolution are played by a variety of factors: by a life that has a measure of instinctual gratification, by the ability to tolerate narcissistic injuries without serious regressive reaction, and a flexible superego structure, tolerant enough to permit some unavoidable modifications of the standards of the preceding years. There is a receding sexual drive that does not, by necessity, lead to intense anxiety or depression, nor does retirement objectively represent demotion and abandonment. All these challenges can be mastered. Old age can provide a freedom from outer and inner pressure which may never have existed before in this form.

While "psychometabolism" at any age can best be understood by physicians with a broad background, there is needed a long postponed reconciliation of medicine, psychiatry, and the social sciences, particularly appropriate to the field of geriatric psychiatry, in which these fields are absolutely interdependent and essential to the other. While we need to learn more about unique psychological features of aging, we are likely dealing with most of the psychological phenomena seen earlier.

However, the internal changes and real external losses of the aging process play an especially significant role and accordingly modify treatment techniques.

It would seem psychoanalytic theories of aging have made a major contribution to the therapeutic approaches. Let us return full circle to our starting point—Freud's cautions about aged patients—and examine his ideas from the vantage point of history, his history to be exact.

From an early age, Freud thought death was near at hand. It cannot be insignificant in considering his viewpoints on aging, that he was preoccupied with the realization that life or his creative powers might be suddenly terminated. It probably encouraged him both to renewed efforts and to premature synthesis or closure of his system of thought. Yet it was not strong enough to prevent him from blossoming again and again into creative production. While he continued to live in great pain and discomfort from 1923 to his death in 1939, he continued to be an active analyst whose writings increasingly influenced the course of man.

In the words of Phillip Reif (1961), he was burdened in youth with the wisdom of age. He was said to have had the "Weltanschauung" of an old man. But age did not alter him in any essential way; it merely gave him time to polish the intellectual instruments with which he expressed the greatness of his character. He had an attitude of cheerful pessimism or inveterate realism, as he was never particularly idealistic or optimistic about mankind. The war and his exile scarcely improved this estimation. He felt that the death instinct was literally hungering for his body. At age sixty-five, he said, "Seven organs are fighting for the honor of ending my life."

But this awareness was tempered by his intense desire to continue living and writing. As he aged, he made another most important comment:

> Do not make the mistake of thinking I am depressed. I regard it as a triumph to retain a clear judgment in all circumstances. I know too that were it not for the one trouble of possibly not

being able to work, I should deem myself a man to be envied. To grow old, to feel so much warm love in my family and life, so much expectation of success and such adventurous undertaking, if not success itself, who else has attained so much? . . . at the age of eighty and one-half, I fret at whether I shall reach the age of my father, or further still into my mother's age, tormented on one hand by the conflicts for the wish to rest and the dread of fresh suffering that further life brings, and the anticipation of a pain of separation. If I were alone, I should long ago have done with life (Schur, 1964).

While some people see his constant preoccupation with death and his fear of mental or physical breakdown as signs of despair, he showed none of this in his actual pattern during the final years. In general, his years were kind to him. His mind and body stood up well. His intellectual life remained intact. He survived thirty-three operations on his jaw bouyed by an indomitable spirit with a strong faith in life. He had a belief in the power of knowledge and the primacy of truth. His formulations became even more terse and his final work, *The Outline of Psychoanalysis,* is a fine example of his unwavering integrity. He also said:

I cannot face the idea of life without work, work and the free play of the imagination are for me the same thing. What would one do when ideas fail or words refuse to come? It is impossible not to shudder at the thought. Hence, in spite of all the acceptance of fate, I have one secret prayer, that I may be spared any wasting away and crippling of my ability to work because of serious physical deterioration. In the words of Macbeth, "Let us die in harness (Schur, 1964)."

So, he had a particular dislike of aging, especially if it meant a loss, or even a decline, of his creative activity. At no point did he reach that point in life "in which much importance is no longer attached to nervous health." When he discovered he had cancer, he was furious with his physicians for concealing it. Subsequently he told a new doctor, Dr.

Max Schur, he wanted a basic understanding—to be told the truth and nothing but the truth. Freud asked Dr. Schur to promise he would not let him suffer more than was necessary. At 82, almost legendary courage was revealed in the calm and dignified manner with which he met the Gestapo and psychologically triumphed over them. Before he died he became apathetic, lost weight, and developed a new lesion creating an opening between his oral cavity and the outside. He was not spared wasting deterioration. Still, he was considerate of his family to the end, wanting to spare them undue pain. He died in September, 1939. His life style was a direct repudiation of the idea that with normal aging one necessarily becomes less resilient, less well integrated, and less capable of meeting a crisis and adapting to it. Any such implications gleaned from his early writings on the criteria for analysis are a miscarriage of what was subsequently demonstrated by his life itself.

REFERENCES

Abraham, K. The applicability of psychoanalytic treatment to patients at an advanced age. In K. Abraham, *Selected papers on psychoanalysis.* London: Hogarth Press, 1927.

Berezin, M. A. Some intrapsychic aspects of aging. In N. E. Zinberg, & I. Kaufman (Eds.), *Normal psychology of the aging process.* New York: International Universities Press, 1963.

Berezin, M. A. Discussion of a transference reaction in a sixty-six-year-old woman. In M. A. Berezin, & S. H. Cath (Eds.), *Geriatric psychiatry: Grief, loss, and emotional disorders in the aging process.* New York: International Universities Press, 1965.

Bibring, G. L. Discussion of the transference reaction of a sixty-six-year-old woman. In M. A. Berezin, & S. H. Cath (Eds.), *Geriatric psychiatry: Grief, loss, and emotional disorders in the aging process.* New York: International Universities Press, 1965.

Bibring, G. L. Old age, its liabilities and assets, a psycho-biological discussion. Paper presented at the meeting of the Boston Psychoanalytic Society, February, 1966.

Cath, S. H. A survey of selected geriatric psychiatric facilities in Northern Europe. *Journal of the American Geriatric Society,* 1963, *11,* 679-698.

Cath, S. H. Some dynamics of middle and later years: A study in depletion and restitution. In M. A. Berezin, & S. H. Cath (Eds.), *Geriatric psychiatry: Grief, loss, and emotional disorders in the aging process.* New York: International Universities Press, 1965.

Cath, S. H. Beyond depression, the depleted state, a study in ego psychology in the aged. *Canadian Psychiatric Association Journal,* 1966, *2,* supplement, 329-339.

Cumming, E., & Henry, W. E. *Growing old: The process of disengagement.* New York: Basic Books, 1961.

Deutsch, H. *The psychology of women. Vol. II. Motherhood.* New York: Grune and Stratton, 1945.

Eissler, K. R. *The psychiatrist and the dying patient.* New York: International Universities Press, 1955.

Erikson. E. *Identity and the life cycle.* New York: International Universities press, 1959.

Ferenczi, S. A contribution to the understanding of the psychoneuroses of the age of involution, In S. Ferenczi, *Selected papers: Problems and methods of psychoanalysis. Vol. III. Final contributions to the problems and methods of psychoanalysis.* New York: Basic Books, 1955.

Freud, S. Sexuality and aetiology. In S. Freud, *Collected papers.* Vol. I. London: Hogarth Press, 1959.

Freud, S. Analysis, terminable and interminable. In S. Freud, *Collected papers.* Vol. 5. New York: Basic Books, 1959.

Gitelson, M. The emotional problems of elderly people. *Geriatrics,* 1948, *3,* 135-140.

Gitelson, M. A transference reaction in a sixty-six year-old woman. In M. Berezin, & S. Cath (Eds.), *Geriatric psychiatry: Grief, loss, and emotional disorders in the aging process.* New York: International Universities Press, 1965.

Goldfarb, A. I. Psychotherapy of aged persons. *Psychoanalytic Review,* 1955, *42,* 180-187.

Goldfarb, A. I. A psychological and sociophysiological approach to aging. In N. E. Zinberg, & I. Kaufman, *Normal psychology of the aging process.* New York: International Universities Press, 1963.

Grotjahn, M. Psychoanalytic investigation of a seventy-one-year-old man with senile dementia. *Psychoanalytic Quarterly,* 1940, *9,* 80-97.

Grotjahn, M. Some analytic observations about the process of growing old. In G. Roheim (Ed.), *Psychoanalysis and the social sciences.* Vol. 3. New York: International Universities Press, 1951.

Grotjahn, M. Analytic psychotherapy with the elderly. *Psychoanalytic Review,* 1955, *42,* 419-427.

Hollender, M. A. Individualizing the aged. *Social Casework,* 1952, *33,* 337-342.

Hóllos, S. & Ferenczi, S. *Psychoanalysis and the psychic disorder of general paresis.* New York: Nervous and Mental Disease Publishing, 1925.

Jacques, E. Death and the mid-life crises. *International Journal of Psychoanalysis,* 1965, *46,* 502-514.

Kaufman, M. R. Psychoanalysis in late life depressions. *Psychoanalytic Quarterly,* 1937, *7,* 308-335.

Kaufman, M. R. Old age and aging: Two psychoanalytic points of view. *The American Journal of Orthopsychiatry,* 1940, *10,* 73-79.

Klein, M. *Contributions to psychoanalysis 1921-1945.* London: Hogarth Press, 1948.

Levin S. Depression in the aged. *Geriatrics,* 1963, *18,* 302-307.

Levin S. Libido equilibrium. In N. E. Zinberg, & I. Kaufman (Eds.), *Normal psychology of the aging process.* New York: International Universities Press, 1963. (a)

Linden, M. E. Group psychotherapy with institutionalized senile women: Study in gerontologic human relations. *International Journal of Group Therapy,* 1953, *3,* 158-170.

Linden, M. E., & Courtney, S. D. The human life cycle and its interruptions: A psychological hypothesis. Studies in gerontologic human relations I. *American Journal of Psychiatry,* 1953, *109,* 906-915.

Meerloo, J. A. M. Psychotherapy with elderly people. *Geriatrics,* 1955, *10,* 583-587.

Meerlo, J. A. M. Transference and resistance in geriatric psychotherapy. *Psychoanalytic Review,* 1955, *10,* 583-587. (a)

Meerloo, J. A. M. Modes of psychotherapy in the aged. *Journal of the American Geriatric Society,* 1961, *9,* 225-234

Moss, R. E. Aging—A survey of psychiatric literature, 1950-1960. In M. Berezin, & S. H. Cath (Eds.), *Geriatric psychiatry: Grief, loss, and emotional disorders in the aging process.* New York: International Universities Press, 1965.

Reif, P. *Freud, the mind of a masochist.* Garden City, New York: Doubleday, 1961

Rochlin, G. Discussion of a transference reaction in a sixty-six-year-old woman. In M. A. Berezin, & S. H. Cath (Eds.), *Geriatric psychiatry: Grief, loss, and emotional disorders in the aging process.* New York: International Universities Press, 1965.

Rockwell, F. V. Psychotherapy and the older individual. In O. J. Kaplan (Ed.), *Mental disorders of later life.* Stanford: Stanford University Press, 1956.

Schur, M. The problem of death in Freud's writings and life. Fourteenth Freud anniversary lecture presented at the meeting of the New York Psychoanalytic Institute, 1964.

Segal, H. Fear of death: Notes on the analysis of an old man. *International Journal of Psychoanalysis*, 1958, *39*, 178-181.

Sheps, J. Management of fear of death in chronic disease. *Journal of the American Geriatric Society*, 1967, *5*, 793-797.

Sheps, J. New developments in family diagnosis in emotional disorders of old age. *Geriatrics*, 1959, *14*, 443-449.

Tolstoy, L. *The death of Ivan Ilyitch*. London: Oxford University Press, 1960.

Wayne, O. J. Modified psychoanalytic therapy in senescence. *Psychoanalytic Review*, 1953, *40*, 99-116.

Weisman, A. D. Discussion of a transference reaction in a sixty-six-year-old woman. In M. A. Berezin, & S. H. Cath (Eds.), *Geriatric psychiatry: Grief, loss, and emotional disorders in the aging process*. New York: International Universities Press, 1965.

Weyer, E. M. *The Eskimos*. New Haven: Yale University Press, 1952.

Zetzel, E. R. Dynamics of the metapsychology of the aging process. In M. A. Berezin, & S. H. Cath (Eds.), *Geriatric psychiatry: Grief, loss, and emotional disorders in the aging process*. New York: International Universities Press, 1965.

Zinberg, N. E., & Kaufman, I. *Normal psychology of the aging process*. New York: International Universities Press, 1963.

19:: SOCIOLOGICAL PERSPECTIVES IN GERONTOLOGICAL RESEARCH

GEORGE L. MADDOX

In the Foreword of Cumming & Henry's *Growing Old: The Process of Disengagement* (1961) Talcott Parsons described the book as:

> probably the most serious attempt so far to put forward a general theoretical interpretation of the social and psychological nature of the aging process in American society. It may be safely predicted that this study will serve as the most important focus of discussion of the problems on this level for some time (p. 5).

In the main, this evaluation has been confirmed by events in the past five years. Predictably disengagement theory has produced opponents as well as proponents; but no one in social gerontology has been indifferent to this sophisticated attempt to make theoretical sense out of aging processes and the conditions which lead to optimum aging. A review of the papers presented in the psychological and social sections of the Seventh International Congress of Gerontology indicates that disengagement theory remains a current concern among many European as well as American investigators.

Five years of research and discussion stimulated by disengagement theory have produced further thoughts on the part of the original proponents and numerous suggestions for modification of the theory

A paper presented at the 19th Annual Meeting of the Gerontological Society, New York City, November 3-5, 1966.

from others (for a summary of some of these developments, see Maddox, 1964, 1965; and Havighurst, Neugarten, & Tóbin, 1964). This is as it should be, since theories are ultimately judged by their utility, not their initial credibility. Within the next few years we may confidently expect systematic assessments of just how useful disengagement theory has proved to be. A review of relevant literature is not, however, the concern of this paper.

The concern here is to illustrate some relevant aspects of a sociological perspective in gerontological research. In this task the original statement of the theoretical orientation first outlined in *Growing Old* will be used as a foil. For, it will be argued, while Cumming & Henry (1961) did not preclude the relevance of a sociological perspective for understanding processes of aging, they specifically denied a direct interest in social structure (p. 11)—and personality structure, for that matter. And they were as good as their word. Their focus was, as they put it, on social psychological aspects of interaction and their analysis of interaction was existential. The possible effects of social structure and its patterned impact on past and current experience of individuals were not denied; but such effects did not figure prominently in their analyses. Social stratification, for example, which sociologists consider to have demonstrable effects on life chances, ways of thinking about oneself, and characteristic styles of relating to the environment, was handled primarily by implication. Cumming & Henry's subjects were, by definition, not economically deprived; otherwise, variations in socioeconomic status among them was ignored. Similarly, no interest was shown in whether a retired male in their sample had experienced an orderly career, to use Wilensky's term (1961), or had a disorderly work history. Retirement, one was invited to infer, is retirement and that is that. Cumming [1963] has had some further thoughts on retirement, but this is another matter.

In their deliberate nonuse of a sociological perspective in analyses of data, Cumming & Henry, in their initial theoretical formulation, were not antisociological. Their explicit denial, the blessings of a prominent sociologist in the Foreword, and an entire chapter (XII) which outlines sociologically relevant hypotheses for future research all argue against such a conclusion. Their initial posture is more adequately described as nonsociological. The admitted decision to be nonsociological has, nonetheless, had consequences for both the analysis of, and the conclusions drawn from, the data available to Cumming & Henry. These consequences, it will be argued, have been serious enough to require major modifications of disengagement theory as originally stated. But more important for our purposes here, a review of the central argument in *Growing Old* provides an excellent point of departure for discussing what a sociological perspective in social gerontology might involve.

For convenience, we may use as a point of departure the three *assumptions* announced by Cumming & Henry in the opening chapter of *Growing Old*. We should assume, they tell us, that aging is a developmental process; that an individual has access to his "whole culture" and exercises "some freedom of choice in selecting his contact with it (p. 12);" and that the total environment of an individual is relevant in understanding his behavior. These assumptions advertise a perspective not calculated to offend sociologists. But, since one investigator's assumption is another's hypothesis, let us look at each of these assumptions in the interest of exploring the relevance of a sociological perspective in research on aging as a biosocial process. This exploration will, in turn, lead to a brief consideration of some methodological implications of research on developmental phenomena.

Aging as Development

The notion that the human life cycle represents a complex process involving biological, psychological, and social factors in dynamic equilibrium has a certain obviousness about it. The man in the street probably needs neither the authority of a Freud nor of an Erikson to believe that life as it is observed and experienced by him illustrates continuity within change as well as the ways in which a man's past intrudes upon his present and constrains his future. Put formally, the life cycle may be thought of as a stochastic process in which any given event is conditioned by one or more previous events. In fact, it is just such obviousness which has led to what Cumming & Henry lable "the implicit theory of aging" which tends to equate busyness with happiness in the later years. The man in the street, as well as a number of sociologists, can believe that elderly individuals who developed and sustained conceptions of themselves as adequate human beings in an instrumentally oriented society in the early and middle years of life would continue this style into the later years insofar as possible. But the obvious is wrong, argue Cumming & Henry, because the observer too often reckons without biology.

Having paid respect to Erikson's emphasis on life as a biosocial process, Cumming & Henry choose to stress biology. In the long run, we are all dead and, with this realization, mortal men in their later years begin coming to terms with their finiteness, or more simply, begin to disengage. The imagery of disengagement as a Markovian process eventuating in death is invited by the principal argument in *Growing Old;* they make much, for example, of the intrinsic, hence inevitable, quality of the biological, psychological, and social decrements which characterize the later years. The growing perception of shortness of available time is attributed, characteristically, to all elderly persons and is given a negative interpretation. Interestingly, Wilbert Moore (1963), a sociologist, has proposed a "perceived scarcity of time" scale to measure social integration on the assumption that it is the socially integrated person who is most likely to perceive time as a scarce commodity. Moore's explanation of perceived scarcity of time is not presented as obviously correct or even preferable to the alternative explanation of Cumming & Henry. But Moore's explanation is an alternative explanation which grows out of a sociological perspective. Perceived scarcity of time, in his view, would reflect social factors. Hence, from this perspective, age and perceived scarcity of time might be correlated positively. Such a conclusion would not be inevitable, however, because it would depend on the degree of social integration experienced by an individual. The alternative explanations of Moore and of Cumming & Henry are not necessarily exclusive. Biological decrement and social integration may, and probably do, interact. However, in *Growing Old* this interaction is not explored and the conclusion that perceived scarcity of time is primarily a function of age and not of social integration is premature. Their assumption that perceived scarcity of time inevitably leads to disengagement is unwarranted. The interpretation of such variables as perceived scarcity of time in *Growing Old* calls to our attention a basic problem in the analysis of life cycle events. If we are to take seriously the notion that the human life cycle is a complex stochastic process which has social as well as biological elements, then the inclusion of social structural variables in the analysis of aging process is necessary and not to be treated implicitly in a network of assumptions.

The importance of viewing development as a process characterized by social contingencies, rather than as the expression of some intrinsic, inevitable organic changes, is also suggested by an analysis of retirement as a social event. Social structure and its patterned impact on experience make removal from the work force a very different experience for different individuals, even when health is assumed to be constant. For example, the voluntary retirement of a white collar worker who has experienced an orderly work career, the involuntary retirement of a blue collar worker who has experienced an orderly work career, and the involuntary retirement of a blue collar worker with a disorderly work history simply cannot be equated. Cumming & Henry surely would agree. But their original analysis does not reflect their agreement although Cumming (1963) more recently has taken specific note of such sociologically relevant distinctions. In a word, the original analysis of perceived scarcity of time and of retirement in *Growing Old* was inordinately preoccupied with aging as a function of biological decrement. This preoccupation was so extensive that the substantial variations in the process they described were minimized in the interest of highlighting similarities. The result is an over-biological view of aging process.

This sort of flirtation with biological determinism has had its parallel in sociology. In the past five years there has been a growing reaction to various forms of sociological determinism which can be summarized under the rubric of the "oversocialized conception of man in modern sociology."

The inadequacy of sociological determinism has been the specific concern of Dennis Wrong but has also appeared in the work of Erving Goffman, Howard S. Becker, Lewis Coser, Alvin Gouldner, and others. For convenient references to some relevant articles, see Rose L. Coser, "Role Distance, Sociological Ambivalence, and Transitional Status Systems," *American Journal of Sociology,* 72:2 (September 1966), pp. 173-187.

Determinism, whether biological or sociological, is suspect and for the same reasons. Several recent articles on adult socialization (Brim & Wheeler, 1966; Becker, 1964; and Rosow, 1965) help bring the issues into focus. Becker, for example, takes specific issue with both psychological and sociological theorists who place an inordinate emphasis on the unchanging qualities of adult life. Social structure has a patterned effect on human experience, but it does not follow that explanations of adult-behavior are reducible to childhood experiences or that available cultural values are perfectly internalized by most individuals. Observers of human behavior are frequently misled by what might be called *situational adjustment,* that is, the demonstrated capacity of individuals to live within the constraints of the available institutional arrangements. Medical students may display an appropriate cynicism in medical school; this situational adjustment is not, however, demonstrably predictive of either their attitudes or behavior subsequently. Or, while legally imprisoned individuals appear to think and behave more and more like prisoners the longer they are imprisoned, these characteristics appear to be reversible as prisoners approach release if they were not integrated into the underworld previously. Rosow (1965) makes a similar point in his discussion of a typology of value orientations and behavior theoretically observable among adults. If one excludes the "unsocialized" minority who have internalized neither the values nor the behavior appropriate to their situation, the remaining majority includes those who have internalized both appropriate value orientations and behavior patterns (the "socialized") and also those who deviate on one or the other characteristic (the "undersocialized"). That is, one may find an individual who subscribes to the dominant value orientations but is selective in conforming behaviorally, as well as one who conforms behaviorally but who has not internalized the dominant values. Rosow then notes how little we know about the distribution of individuals which would be observed if such a typology were applied to any given adult population and about the social circumstances under which behavioral conformity might be expected from the two "undersocialized" types in situations in which alternatives become feasible, as in a time of crisis or rapid social change.

Although neither Becker nor Rosow addresses his comments explicitly to the elderly, the argument in each article has an obvious relevance for understanding aging processes. Neither argument, for example, would preclude the possibility that disengagement theory is valid. Yet both arguments invite the inference that the observed adjustment of elderly individuals would typically have a substantial situational component and would reflect structural constraints. Thus the observed adjustment of a disengaged individual can hardly be considered to reflect an intrinsic, inevitable process in the absence of research which establishes that disengagement as a mode of adjustment is typically found even when situational constraints on the elderly person are minimal or permit alternative types of adaptation. Perhaps this is precisely what Cumming & Henry attempted to do in selecting subjects who were not excessively deprived economically or physiologically. If so, this was a move in the right direction, although an inadequate one. The central theme of the argument for disengagement as the modal process of aging remains biological and the relevant social contingencies remain largely implicit.

It is worth repeating here that the nonsociological perspective of *Growing Old* does not in itself invalidate disengagement theory. The argument here is rather that, in the absence of data analysis informed by a sociological perspective, it was grossly premature to advertise the behavior used to illustrate disengagement as though it represented an intrinsic, inevitable process. The argument was confounded, furthermore, when disengagement was described as functional not only for the individual but also for society. Rose (1964) has argued persuasively against the casual acceptance of such an argument in the absence of evidence which takes into consideration socially derived situational constraints. Taitez (1966) addresses this issue with research on "disengaged and engaged communities" as differential contexts within which the aging process must be observed before an adequate test of disengagement theory is possible.

Recent experimental evidence (Troyer, Eisdorfer, Wilkie, & Bogdonoff, 1966) also suggests the importance of assessing situational factors in explaining behavior which can be interpreted as evidence for disengagement. The speed required in learning experiments has been shown to influence the tendency of subjects to make no response to stimuli to which under less stressful conditions they can and do respond. See also Cloward and Ohlin (1960) for a discussion of the significance of differential opportunity structures in understanding social behavior.

Discussion of the first of Cumming & Henry's assumptions about aging processes has led to the conclusion that any adequate analysis of human development must include structural constraints as control variables. Social constraints, the argument here has been, must be included in the analysis of data purporting to test hypotheses derived from a particular theoretical perspective which clearly is primarily biological in its emphasis. In effect, Cumming & Henry, in their initial formulation, called attention to biological effects, that is, effects of organic changes which would be manifest regardless of the sociocultural context in which they appear. This is the implication of their heavy stress on disengagement as an intrinsic, inevitable process which, in the final analysis, is culture free. A sociological perspective suggests just the opposite emphasis; that is, an investigation of the extent to which the impact social structure is superimposed on biological processes (Z. Blau, 1961; P. Blau, 1960). The extent to which Cumming & Henry were not initially interested in the effects of social structure is also reflected in their assumption that individuals have free access to the "whole culture" of the social system in which they find themselves. We now turn attention to this second assumption.

Free Access and Social Constraints

Even in a democratically organized society the assumption of the free access for all individuals to the resources and rewards of their society cannot be taken seriously as a basis of understanding how societies are organized, how individuals are socialized, or how behavior and attitudes change in the later years. From a societal standpoint, social stratification, both as a social process and as a social fact, calls our attention to structured inequality of access to life chances, power, and prestige. Social class is, in fact, a shorthand designation for differential access of individuals to the opportunities and rewards probably available to members of a society. Interestingly, *social class* does not appear in the index of *Growing Old,* figures only nominally in the discussion of the sampling procedure used in the research reported, and does not appear as a crucial variable in the analysis of data. Whether the aging individual in fact does have free access to the resources and rewards is of some consequence if one is arguing that disengagement is an inevitable, intrinsic process. But this would seem to be a matter to be settled by empirical evidence rather than by assumption.

From the standpoint of the individual, differential access to opportunity and rewards, has, over time, a patterned effect which may be described variously in terms of differential perception of opportunity, differential personal and social resources, and differential personal commitments. The probability that an elderly individual will behave in a way consistent with past performance even in the face of situationally feasible alternatives, or that he will seek, perceive, and exploit alternatives is not independent of the individual's previous experience and commitments.

Becker (1964) uses *commitment* to indicate the externally related interests which become relevant when alternative courses of action are being considered and which constrain choice. Personal commitments constitute, in part, what might be designated as character (Cumming, 1963; Havighurst, Neugarten, & Tobin, 1964, and underlie personal consistency.

Consider, for example, the commitments associated with work force participation in our society. Wilensky (1961) has noted that some individuals have orderly careers and other have disorderly work histories. He defines an *orderly career* as a succession of related jobs arranged in an ordered, more or less predictable, sequence which is socially recognized, sanctioned, persistent, and which implies a life plan. Only a minority of the work force in the United States may be said to have orderly careers in this sense. Work force participation and, specifically, work force participation that may be described as *orderly,* affects, according to Wilensky, the vitality of social participation and the strength of social ties to the community and its major institutional arrangements, as well as the vitality and maintenance of primary relationships. Work history, he concludes, is a better predictor of social integration than either income or age and is equally as good a predictor as education. While systematic attempts to relate work history to the meaning of retirement for the individual and his reaction to it are unusual in the voluminous literature on retirement (an exception is Simpson & McKinney, 1966, Chapters II-VI; see also Maddox, 1966a), work history does appear to have a patterned effect on individual behavior in the later years. To the extent that this is the case, retirement *per se* cannot be treated as an event with the same meaning and the same consequences for individuals with different work histories. Individuals come to retirement with different interests and resources which, in turn, affect the opportunities they perceive and the opportunities which are, in fact, available to them. Put another way, the work history of an individual has as its correlate different personal and social resources which make a variety of adaptive maneuvers in retirement more or less feasible.

Variation in aging process as a result of factors such as those discussed here are perceived as relevant but are not integrated into the analysis of p. 325 data in *Growing Old* [See Chapter XII, Postulates 1 and 5; See also Cumming's (1963, p. 387). Cummings recognizes that the blue collar and white collar workers might need to be distinguished in terms of short run and long run reactions to retirement]. The blue collar worker, she guessed, might adapt well in the short run but not in the long run while the white collar worker would probably display the opposite pattern. Such variations would seem to be more amenable to a sociological than a biological explanation.

This brief consideration of the second assumption underlying the argument in *Growing Old* brings into clearer focus a crucial deficiency. Although the model of development presented acknowledges individual variations in the probability of change from one period of time to the next, the analysis of data from which disengagement theory is said to be induced treats individuals as though the probability of change is uniform. Significantly, in reporting disengagement to be the modal process, central tendencies but not standard deviations in the behavior and attitudes of their subjects are reported. The probability that such a style of analysis masks precisely the variations in the process of aging which a sociological perspective would predict has been discussed frequently and need only be noted again here (Maddox, 1963, 1965, 1966). The assumption of equal access to social resources and rewards for all elderly individuals begs a crucial question which, if left unanswered, confounds the evaluation of intrinsic and extrinsic factors in developmental processes.

The Total Environment

The third and final assumption called to our attention by Cumming & Henry may be treated briefly, largely because the sociological issues it poses have been anticipated in the discussion provoked by the two assumptions previously noted. Succinctly, the third assumption in the argument of *Growing Old* is that the total environment of man is relevant for understanding his behavior. This anti-reductionist sentiment is essentially nonpartisan, leaving some room for anyone interested in explaining aging process. But, at the same time, such an assumption leads to begging exactly the issues of most relevance to the sociologist.

Consider, for example, Cumming & Henry's view of the relevance of culture. On the one hand, they propose that the disengagement process is culture free. This is consistent with their emphasis on intrinsic, inevitable biological decrements which underlie age-related changes in an elderly individual's behavior. But, on the other hand, the possibility that patterning of the disengagement process may vary from culture to culture is also recognized (p. 15). In effect, this reminds us only that, in the end, all men experience decrement and die. The sociologist's interest in how cultural differences are reflected in culturally derived variations in the aging process, and with what effect, are not explored systematically.

One need not fault Cumming & Henry for not doing what they indeed inform the reader at the outset they are not going to do. While they do not utilize a sociological perspective extensively in their analysis of data, their assumptions do not preclude either the relevance or importance of introducing such a perspective. In fact, in their analysis of culturally determined differences in male and female roles which might be reflected in different patterns of disengagement, they make their strongest explicit case for a sociological perspective. Moreover, their work has already stimulated cross-cultural research (Havighurst & Thomas, 1966) and will certainly stimulate more. Increasingly, cultural variations in the processes of aging will be charted and the cultural variables associated with these variations will be specified. For a systematic statement of the logic of comparative research and a review of illustrative literature of interest to the gerontologist, see Marsh (1966); Cantril (1966), although not specifically interested in human aging, has recently presented comparative data on cross-cultural variations in patterns of human concerns, aspirations, and life satisfaction. Some of the analyses use age as a control variable and demonstrate substantial variations among older respondents in different cultures.

A Note on Strategies for Studying Social Aspects of Developmental Processes

Growing Old is methodologically as well as theoretically provocative. The detailed methodological statement appended to this sophisticated monograph illustrates almost all the research problems which continue to plague research in social gerontology. For example, selection of subjects combined stratified random sampling procedure with supplementary quota sampling. The representativeness of the resulting sample was compromised still further by a substantial refusal rate, a situation which is common in research involving older subjects (Maddox, 1962). Although Cumming & Henry's subjects constituted a panel and were seen a number of times, the data analysis presented in support of disengagement as the modal process of aging and as the process of optimum aging is essentially cross-sectional. Arrays of means ($\bar{X}$), ordered by age categories and unaccompanied by a measure of dispersion, are presented in support of the hypothesis that both social and psychological disengagement are a function of age. Similarly, the hypothesis that disengagement is a necessary condition for the reestablishment of equilibrium and, hence, morale in old age is tested by an array of individuals categorized by degree of disengagement along with mean morale scores.

In order to accept Cumming & Henry's evidence as supporting their hypotheses, however, one must assume that the subsample in each age category is representative of the implied population of comparable age, that the standard deviations from the reported means are small, and that individuals in the oldest and youngest age categories are theoretically interchangeable. In the face of their reported sampling procedure and their style of data analysis, such assumptions ask too much and we are well advised to think of the inducted theory of disengagement as provisional, which readers of *Growing Old* were in fact asked to do. The possibility that the evidence such as that presented in support of disengagement theory is an artifact of the research design is substantial (Maddox, 1962, 1963, 1965, 1966; Lowenthal, 1964).

Methodological problems encountered in *Growing Old* raise basic questions: Do the problems lie in faulty execution of a cross-sectional design or in cross-sectional research design *per se* when the phenomena to be studied are developmental? While the answer to these questions is certainly not obvious, as will be indicated below, longitudinal design would appear to be preferable to cross-sectional design in this study of developmental processes. Repeated observations of the same individuals permit an investigator to explore directly the antecedent and intervening factors as well as the consequences associated with change. In a cross-sectional design these issues can be studied only inferentially. Whether, for example, differences in behavior which appear to be age-related reflect developmental change or unreliability of observations, can be investigated most adequately within the framework of longitudinal design. Moreover, testing the utility of developmental models which do or do not assume homogeneity in the probability of change among aging individuals is best accomplished when multiple observations of the same individuals are available (Coleman, 1964).

Probably few methodologists would argue in the abstract that cross-sectional design is superior to longitudinal design in the study of life cycle processes. If this is so, the relative rarity of longitudinal research design in research on human aging calls for explanation. The answer appears to be disarmingly simple: Longitudinal research design is inordinately difficult to execute successfully. The practical problems are real, substantial, and fairly obvious (Sussman, 1964). For example, in cross-sectional, "one-shot" research, inadequate conceptualization and biased samples are unfortunate; in longitudinal research the consequences of such misfortunes are multiplied and, ironically, become increasingly obvious as the research progresses. New theoretical insights are frequently not easy to incorporate into panel studies and uncontrolled attrition of panelists accentuates sample biases, making generalizations of findings increasingly problematic. Moreover, maintenance of continuity in a core of investigators is difficult and maintaining the interest of investigators over a long period of time is as much a problem. Still another source of trouble for the investigator interested in longitudinal design is the relative poverty of established techniques currently available for measuring and analyzing change in human subjects (Harris, 1963; Coleman, 1964).

Primarily for practical reasons, then, cross-sectional studies of the elderly will continue to predominate in social gerontological research and will continue to provide useful descriptive information about the distribution of this or that characteristic among individuals of various ages. Yet, the development of models of aging process and of the process of optimum aging from research with a cross-sectional design has serious limitations, thus posing a dilemma. Fortunately the current work of Coleman (1964), of Riegel (1965), and of Harris and his associates (1963) suggests that the current impasse is under attack. Perhaps of greater significance in this regard is the recent proposal of Professor K. Warner Schaie (1965), which attempts to integrate into a single research model aspects of both cross-sectional and longitudinal design.

Although a review of Schaie's general model for the study of developmental problems is not possible here, its major feature can be indicated. In simplest terms, the model outlines a strategy which permits the effects of cohort and environmental differences, as distinct from age differences, to be partialled out. In the typical investigation of aging processes among social scientists, age, cohort, and environmental factors are confounded to such a degree that the developmental processes in the later years cannot be described; therefore, the crucial factors associated with variations in these processes cannot be identified with confidence. Schaie's model for the study of developmental aspects of aging will not be easy to implement since it requires the achievement of representative sampling. Representativeness is demonstrably difficult to achieve in the upper ranges of age (Maddox, 1962). Moreover, under the general reference to "environmental factors" in Schaie's model there must be a specification of the relevant factors to be controlled in analysis. Clear specification of relevant "environmental" variables in advance of the research would thus permit stratified sampling where random sampling might not permit an adequate distribution on one or another variable. In general, however, Schaie's model represents a substantial step in the direction of a research design which is adequate to research which purports to study developmental processes.

Summary

The initial statement of disengagement theory called attention to the uniform effects of intrinsic, age-related biological changes which help explain the modal course of human development in the later years. Sociological factors which might account for significant variations in how elderly individuals grow old successfully are acknowledged in a series of assumptions but do not figure prominently in the analysis of data. This paper has argued that the theoretical orientation of Cumming & Henry had as one of its practical effects a preoccupation with the biologically-derived aspects of aging processes; this preoccupation led them to treat variations in the social histories of individuals and in the social constraints they experience in different situations as non-problematic or as not warranting inclusion in the analysis of data. The result is that the assessment of intrinsic and extrinsic factors which contribute to the process of aging remain confounded; this confounding is further complicated by a cross-sectional research design and a style of data analysis which maximize the probability that the evidence introduced in support of disengagement theory initially is artifactual.

The theoretical and methodological limitations found in Cumming & Henry's *Growing Old,* however, illustrate some persistent research problems in social gerontology which have resisted solution. In the future, research designed to explore social dimensions of aging and of successful aging, variations in the social histories of the elderly and in the constraints which different environmental arrangement impose on them will be investigated explicitly. As this is done, the utility of disengagment theory in understanding human aging will be clarified. Such clarification will be aided by the development of research designs which provide a higher probability than has existed up until now to partial out the effects of aging as a biological process as distinct from social and cultural aspects of this process.

REFERENCES

Becker, H. S. Personal change in adult life. *Sociometry,* 1964, *27,* 40-53.

Blau, P. Structural effects. *American Sociological Review,* 1960, *25,* 178-193.

Blau, Z. Structural contraints on friendship in old age. *American Sociological Review,* 1961, *26,* 429-439.

Brim, O. G., Jr., & Wheeler, S. *Socialization after childhood: Two essays.* New York: Wiley, 1966.

Cantril, H. *The pattern of human concerns.* New Brunswick, N.J.: Rutgers University Press, 1966.

Cloward, R., & Ohlin, L. *Delinquency and opportunity.* Glencoe, Ill.: Free Press, 1960.

Coleman, J. S. *Models of change and response uncertainty.* Englewood Cliffs, N.J.: Prentice-Hall, 1964.

Coser, R. L. Role distance, sociological ambivalence, and transitional status systems. *American Journal of Sociology,* 1966, *72,* 173-187.

Cumming, E. & Henry, W. *Growing old: The process of disengagement.* New York: Basic Books, 1961.

Cumming, E. Further thoughts on the theory of disengagement. *International Social Science Journal,* 1963, *15,* 377-393.

Harris, C. W. (Ed.) *Problems in measuring change.* Madison: University of Wisconsin Press, 1963.

Havighurst, R., Neugarten, B., & Tobin, S. Disengagement, personality and life satisfaction in the later years. in P. F. Hansen (Ed.), *Age with a future.* Philadelphia: F. A. Davis, 1964.

Havighurst, R., & Thomae, H. A cross-national study of adjustment to retirement: A report on a pilot study of school teachers and steel workers. The nature of the research. *Proceedings 7th International Congress of Gerontology.* 1966, 6, 89-91.

Henry, W. The theory of intrinsic disengagement. In P. F. Hansen (Ed.), *Age with a future.* Philadelphia: F. A. Davis, 1964.

Lowenthal, M. F. Social isolation and mental illness in old age. *American Sociological Review,* 1964, 20, 54-70.

Maddox, G. L. A longitudinal multidisciplinary study of human aging: Selected methodological issues. *Proceedings Social Statistics Section,* American Statistical Association, 1962, 280-285.

Maddox, G. L. Activity and morale: A longitudinal study of selected elderly subjects. *Social Forces,* 1963, 42, 195-204.

Maddox, G. L. Disengagement theory: A critical evaluation. *The Gerontologist,* 1964, 4, 80-82.

Maddox, G. L. Fact and artifact: evidence bearing on disengagement theory from the Duke Geriatrics Project. *Human Development,* 1965, 8, 117-130.

Maddox, G. L. Persistence of life style among the elderly: A longitudinal study of patterns of social activity in relation to life satisfaction. *Proceedings 7th International Congress of Gerontology,* 1966, 6, 309-311.

Maddox, G. L. Retirement as a social event in the United States. In J. C. McKinney, & F. DeVyver (Eds.), *Aging and social policy.* New York: Appleton-Century-Croft, 1966. (a)

Marsh, R. Comparative sociology, 1950-1963, *Current Sociology,* 1966, 14, entire issue.

Moore, W. *Man, time and society.* New York: Wiley, 1963.

Riegel, K. F. Behavioral aspects of aging. Paper presented at the meeting of the Gerontological Society, Los Angeles, November 1965.

Rose, A. A current theoretical issue in social gerontology. *The Gerontologist,* 1964, 4, 46-50.

Rosow, I. *Forms and functions of adult socialization.* Social Forces, 1965, 44, 35-45.

Schaie, K. W. A general model for the study of developmental problems. *Psychological Bulletin,* 1965, 64, 92-107.

Simpson, I. H. & McKinney, J. *Social aspects of aging.* Durham, N.C.: Duke University Press, 1966.

Sussman, M. B. Methodology for studies of long-term care. Use of the longitudinal design in studies of long-term illness: Some advantages and limitations. *The Gerontologist,* 1964, *4,* 25-29.

Taitez, P. Community structure and aging. *Proceedings 7th International Congress of Gerontology.* 1966. *6.* 375-378.

Troyer, W. G., Jr., Eisdorfer, C., Wilkie, F., & Bogdonoff, M. D. Free fatty acid responses in the aged individual during performance of learning tasks. *Journal of Gerontology,* 1966, *4,* 415-419.

Wilensky, H. Orderly careers and social participation: The impact of work history of the middle mass. *American Sociological Review,* 1961, *26,* 521-539.

20::GERONTOLOGICAL THEORY
AND EMPIRICAL RESEARCH

S. J. MILLER and K. K. SCHOOLER

The occupational, political, educational, and welfare structures of our society attempt to develop policy and to implement programs for the old. These past efforts have emphasized the problems confronting the old living on reduced incomes in an expanding economy. Attention has been focused on the material aspects of creation. However, program planners increasingly are recognizing that a material concern is not enough. We must approach problems in terms of the social implications of aging. Services are no longer planned to meet an anticipated need without accompanying efforts to employ social determinants of participation and utilization as a stimulus for the desired response of older people. Our best contemporary efforts at assistance are based on the assumption that men live not only in a physical environment with material implications but also in a social environment with its more subtle implications. It is these implications which must be considered when evolving a policy for old age, providing a program of service, or attempting an explanation of aging.

"Social Gerontology," writes Philibert (1965, p. 4), "has been more and more widely used in the United States to designate a set of problems and studies concerning the social processes of human aging." Philibert's definition suggests that social gerontology in America excludes all but sociological and psychological phenomena from the content of its theories of aging. Needless to say, there are social researchers who recognize but do not include physiological phenomena in their explanations of aging, and for some this would be a serious

334

criticism of their work. This inevitably poses the question: To what extent should a theory for social gerontology employ biologically based explanations of aging?

In this paper we do not propose that biological explanation be excluded from theories of aging; in fact we would argue that social scientists must make greater efforts to include *the influence* of such factors on the sociological and psychological processes which they utilize in their explanations of aging. There are no notable examples of conceptualizations which do just that without becoming unduly concerned with the biological mechanics of growing old. For example: Birren's (1959, pp. 3-42) discussion of three kinds of aging; Rose (1965, pp. 201-209) has hypothesized a scheme of physical disability and/or infirmity which is "associated with differences in outlook on life and relationship with others (p. 201)." On the other hand, theories based on biological explanations often tell the social scientist more than he needs to know for a meaningful consideration of the influence of those factors on the sociological and psychological dimensions of growing old. For that reason, we shall not attempt a theory based on biological explanation; but rather we shall limit conceptualization and research to the influences of the biological on the social processes which, by definition, are the concerns of social gerontology.

An eventual goal of social gerontology *may be,* as Kastenbaum (1965) has suggested, to document and describe the association between the physiological processes and the social processes of aging; however, it would seem plausible first to attempt some statement of the social processes which would include both the sociological and psychological dimensions of aging. By limiting theory and research to the social processes in this way, the biological dimensions may be included without unduly encumbering the next logical development in social gerontology—that is, a statement of a theoretical scheme which would provide, at least, a mutually acceptable language and possibly a common framework for the variety of contemporary social explanations of aging.

Since social gerontology is an emerging field of research with relatively little evidence in demonstrable support of its explanations of aging, an explicit statement at this time attempting complete theoretical integration would be not only ambitious but presumptuous. Many current explanations are undergoing revision or have only recently been stated. For example, Cumming (1963) has had further thoughts on the theory of disengagement, and Rose (1965, pp. 3-16, 19-36) has stated an addition to the interactionist approach by postulating an "aging group consciousness" and "the aging subculture." Synoptic analysis of the various approaches would result in documentation of their many agreements in concept and method; but, being the result of information about explanations which are undergoing modification, it would not serve as a framework for social gerontology. If the statement is to be useful, it must, in our opinion, document the nature and direction of theoretical modifications; it must capture the spirit of the change in social explanations of aging.

What Kastenbaum (1965) has called "a great divergence between biological and psychosocial emphases (p. 23)" is, by our definition of the problem, not a crucial issue for a theory of social gerontology. Of crucial importance *is the divergence* between approaches emphasizing the social and those stressing personal explanations of aging.

A common framework must make maximum use of theoretical formulations presently employed in explanations of aging. The processes of reciprocal influence and social labeling are discernable in the explanations of aging which dominate contemporary social gerontology. Rose hypothesized an emerging subculture of the aging by assuming the reciprocal influence of older people and society. In the process of interaction the aged and non-aged evaluate their respective social circumstances and attribute characteristics to each other as categories of people. This results in older people being excluded from interacting with young people and the old excluding the young because of a positive affinity the old feel for each other in our society. The Cumming & Henry explanation hypothesizes a mutually satisfying withdrawal of the old from society by assuming the interdependent character of people and the structures of society. Older people are preparing for the ultimate withdrawal by disengaging from associations and functions well in advance of death; in order to reduce the impact of losing its members, the disengagement of the old is facilitated by society. When examined as social explanations of aging, Rose and Cumming & Henry do not appear to differ significantly; but their thoughts are based on varying theoretical predilections, both of which are significant for sociological theory. The question is, however, how critical are the nuances of sociological theory for social gerontology?

We suggest that the current theoretical issues of sociology are of relatively little importance for social gerontology. What is important is a definition of the social environment and an examination of its implications for growing old. The processes by which people influence each other and distinguish between others and themselves provide a beginning for the definition of "social environment." No matter to what sociological theory the data are ultimately referred, these processes and the ways in which they influence behavior must be considered critical for an explanation of aging in our society.

The purpose of the present paper is to present and discuss the social theories which underlie approaches to the study of aging and to discuss the limitations of these theories. We will also propose what appears to be a tenable theoretical perspective, which can combine the more salient aspects of the major current theoretical positions. Finally, we will suggest what we consider the necessary lines of research to test such a theory.

The approach to aging as a process-of-disengagement conceptualizes aging as "an inevitable mutual withdrawal" of society and the aging person. The formal statement of the theory contained in the Cumming & Henry book, *Growing Old* (1961), does not imply a direct relationship between morale or other measures of adjustment *and* disengagement. But the findings reported make explicit a bi-model relationship, showing high morale at both extremes of the disengagement continuum. Cumming (1963), in her further thoughts on the theory of disengagement, enlarged upon the theory through a discussion of the differential aspects of disengagement, relating them to differences in biologically determined temperament, differences in societal constraints, and differences arising from changing roles. Subsequent to the publication of *Growing Old,* Henry, on the basis of additional analysis, also modified the earlier position of disengagement. In his theory of intrinsic disengagement, Henry (1963) implies that "engagement and disengagement are a general form of personality dynamic and the disengagement of the aged, a special case (p. 417)." The crux of his presentation lies in his speculation on the question of the extent to which disengagement is an intrinsic process, " . . . the processes of disengagement . . . are intrinsic in the sense that societal and environmental events are not sufficient to predict them and that they appear clearly related to various personality processes generally understood to be of long duration (pp. 417-418)."

The purpose of noting that point in this paper is to call attention to the inference that the intrinsic nature of the disengagement process persists as a basic tenet of that theory. Others associated with the Kansas City study of adult life have also addressed themselves to the question of adjustment of the disengaged elderly. Havighurst, Neugarten, & Tobin (1963), have summarized their analysis of the Kansas City data with the inference that "those older persons who are highly engaged in various social roles, generally have greater life satisfaction than those who have lower levels of engagement. At the same time the relationship is not a consistent one . . . presumably there are certain personality types who as they age disengage with relative comfort . . . others disengage with great discomfort and show a drop in life satisfaction (p. 422)."

Still others, we may assume, for a large part of their lives have been relatively disengaged and are quite satisfied with that state; in this respect, aging brings no noticeable change. This leads to the inference that neither the activity nor the disengagement theory of successful aging accounts for the empirical findings. The inference of Neugarten as just cited, of Maddox & Eisdorfer (1962) and of others, is that satisfaction or adjustment in later years is positively associated with engagement for some persons and negatively associated for others. For these investigators, the answers to the difficult questions of life satisfaction or adjustment lie in the development and test of theories of personality, theories which purport to account for adjustment in the later years of life on the basis of lifelong patterns of behavior subsumed by the term personality.

To the extent that disengagement theory continues intact it remains a theory about intrinsic and, therefore, inevitable phenomena. As theory and speculation have evolved from the earlier statement of disengagement, the concept of mutual withdrawal by society and the individual has received little or no attention. Clearly in the context of the personality approach of Neugarten, such a concept is almost unnecessary. "Society" appears to be simply a part of the environment to be coped with, acted on, or responded to, but not necessarily to be interacted with. The definition by Henry (1963) of the term "intrinsic," quoted previously, continues: "[the various personality processes] are thus ego processes having a developmental history, a discoverable course of their own, and a positive power that can influence reaction to external events and choice of response to them (p. 418)." The response to the environment is suggested, but interaction with or impact on the environment does not appear to have been considered. While the activity theory versus disengagement theory conflict seems to have been resolved by saying "it all depends," we now find that the explanations for adjustment and well-being of the elderly are still in terms of developmental or personalistic, that is, intrinsic processes.

But what of that which Cumming refers to as "societal constraint" or response to changing role? And what of the even earlier statements about mutual withdrawal of society and the individual? The intrinsic theorists apparently do not account for the withdrawal of society, nor the recent evidence that society may be initiating re-engagement with the old. A considerably different theoretical perspective is required to account for the phenomena of successful aging in the context of an interactive environment, an environment of people as well as of objects, an environment that can withdraw but that can also reengage and be reengaged. Rose and his collaborators, as well as other symbolic interactionists, offer such a theoretical perspective.

Many individual statements of the interactionist theory in sociology have been made, but of particular interest are the articles collected by Rose (1962), attempting to systematically state and present empirical support of that theory. The articles on interactionist theory by Rose and others present concepts and approaches to social research which were, for most part, the rationale for subsequent researches conducted by the Midwest Council for Social Research on Aging and reported in *Older People and Their Social World* (1965).

The papers by Cavan (1962, pp. 526-536) and Deutscher (1962, pp. 506-525) are particularly illustrative of the assumptions underlying interactionist theory—more particularly, the interactionist conceptualization of growing old. These two separate researches deal with different phases of the life cycle. Cavan concerns herself with the effects of compulsory retirement or the loss of a spouse during old age, and Deutscher examines the adjustment of parents to the departure of children during middle age. Both focus on a central theme of interactionist analysis; that is, life changes which require major adjustments of people. The theoretical point of both papers is that life is a series of incidents, some more critical than others, and all requiring a learning of new ways or alternative ways of playing roles in society. Both Cavan and Deutscher conceptualize the respective phases of life with which they are concerned as transitional points in a lifelong process of social learning—that is, an occasion of adult socialization.

A man's social identity is a function of his membership in groups and the accompanying statuses which establish his place in society. These allow other people to evaluate his status and provide a context for his social activity. The life cycle, theoretically, is a succession of conventional identities, progressing from that of childhood to the multiple identities of adulthood. However, no matter what the phases of the life cycle, people are constantly undergoing a process of socialization which is preparing them for particular group memberships and appropriate social roles. For the adult, socialization is necessitated by a change in social circumstances—for example, an empty nest, widowhood, or compulsory retirement—a change requiring an adjustment in the ways of participating in society. The change in circumstances is the turning point, but the actual transition from an old to a new identity is accomplished by the continuing process of socialization. The work of Cavan is also an interactionist contribution to social gerontology, and the influence of this approach is equally obvious in the work of the members of the Midwest Council for Social Research on Aging, e.g., the articles by Miller (1965) and Christ (1965) which deal only with age-related changes in statuses and accompanying redefinitions of social roles.

People who grow old may or may not be able to maintain their conventional identities, but those who do not maintain an identity with accompanying roles are assumed to suffer a socially debilitating loss of roles. To compensate they must seek a substitute identity with new social roles. This conceptualization is not unlike those sociological theories utilizing the concepts of social role and socialization, but Rose (1965) proposed a framework for research in social gerontology which was more than this traditional way of thinking about aging. His proposal, however, either was not fully adopted or only partially understood by his collaborators. For example, Miller (1965) made note of the "cultural trend which sets the old apart from the young [and] may well result in the formation of a social group of the aging which will provide them with a meaningful social audience, a frame of reference, and a range of participation which will help them to develop a new identity, role and self-concept (p. 83)." But this was no more than an attempt to include the concept of aging subculture proposed by

Rose in a somewhat more sophisticated, but no more rewarding, conceptualization of aging than the traditional role-loss-social adjustment paradigm so popular in social gerontology.

To this point we have described two major current approaches to the study of aging. One of them gives major emphasis to the personalistic, intrinsic aspects of the aging process, and relatively little attention, if any, to the characteristics of the social or cultural milieu. The other, accounting for the phenomena of aging on the basis of culture and interaction, overlooks the developmental, individual aspects of the aging process. We assert that these views are not competitive but complementary; and the meeting ground between them is to be found in the concepts of socialization and social role.

Society is a system of reciprocal influences which are patterned by the common values and beliefs of people sharing a particular social environment of society. The values and beliefs which accompany a particular environment are the referents for acts and responses of others as well as the basis for expectations of others—that is, the social facts which facilitate the predicting of behavior. Conceptually, values and beliefs which serve as a context for behavior constitute a culture. People learn sets of values and beliefs and by so doing are prepared or prepare themselves for places in particular cultures of society. The concept of culture and the processes by which people are prepared, in our opinion, are critical for an explanation of aging.

The subculture of the aging postulated by Rose (1965), for example, implies a general set rather than particular sets of values and beliefs available to those who are growing old:

> The aging subculture is a general one that cuts across other subcultures—those based on occupation, religion, sex, and possibly even ethnic identification—which are characteristic of the middle-aged population. Insofar as older people are somewhat more likely to unite on the basis of age than on the basis of these other divisions, relatively speaking, they are likely to weaken the other subcultures as they substitute a new one for them.

We agree with the implicit assumption that people of the same social category or generation will face more or less similar problems which precipitate like adjustments, but we are reluctant to generalize a general subculture of the aging. This is not to say that we deny the concept of a general culture; there are values, beliefs, and behaviors which must be learned by all, or significant, populations of society. Rather, we suggest that the generic character of the problems and adjustments of the old, advanced by Rose, et al., purports more of a culture peculiar to the old than actually exists in our society. The social conditions under which a subculture emerges is of importance to sociology and to social gerontology; however, that is not as critical as the implications of the various arrangements of group affiliation and accompanying roles which constitute an immediate social environment for people who are growing old.

Social research based on the framework proposed by Rose would focus on the aging as an emerging subculture rather than a category of people in American society. Unquestionably implicit assumptions of contemporary explanations of aging set the old apart from the young and to some extent alter social participation of the aged. However, there are few reasons for *limiting* conceptualization of growing old to the ways in which the old identify with, and participate in, a subculture of the aging. The substitution of one subculture for another may well be characteristic of the mechanisms by which the old adjust to their loss of roles in society. The crucial question then becomes: need the subculture which is substituted be one of the aging? We think not, and we suggest here a simple modification of the Rose framework. We postulate that as alternative substitutes for the subcultures from which the old are excluded or retired, the aged may turn to any one of the variety of subcultures with their numerous role sets that do exist in society.

The concept of aging subculture explains but part of the social participation of the old in society; also, as Rose has noted, the number of people who retain their middle-age identification and roles is increasing and the social factors which set the old apart from the young are declining. If these are the facts, and they appear to be, the subculture concept as elaborated by Rose appears to be a limited framework for research in social gerontology. This is not to say that the study of the process by which a category of people become a social group is not important for the theoretical rewards for sociology would be great. Rather, it is to say that the simple elaboration we propose provides a framework for gerontological as well as sociological research.

Our modification of the Rose conceptualization of growing old is simply an extension of the role loss-adjustment paradigm to permit substitution by the old of any one of a variety of new subcultures rather than a specific subculture of the aging. The implication of the conceptual modification is that the aging might play a part in any one of a number of subcultures based on a new occupation, religion, and/or regression to earlier ethnic or class characteristics which had been temporarily superseded in middle age. We then have a system of subcultures, any one of which may have meaning and value for the individual. The individual may have to learn the requirements of participating in the new subculture and, if he does, that learning is accomplished by the process of socialization. This conceptualization, in our opinion, readily lends itself to social psychological statement and is in accord with other theoretical positions utilizing the concepts of interaction and social role, while making allowance for individual differences. This affords a framework for gerontological research which takes into account the personal as well as the social influences on the behavior of the aging.

Although customarily socialization has been thought of as a process of childhood through which the infant and child incorporate the values of the general culture as well as those of a variety of subcultures, it is now recognized that the process of socialization is ongoing throughout life: through the school years, adolescence, young adulthood and the later years. Conceptualizing socialization as an exchange between the individual and society, it can be seen that not only does the social environment have impact on the individual, shaping and modifying that complex of attitudes, values, and behaviors that we call personality, but also personality will influence what relationships are entered into, how responses of others are perceived, and which of a repertoire of responses—behavioral and attitudinal—are evoked, reinforced, or modified. Moreover, given continuity with respect to culture, the individual will enter many new relationships with some understanding of what is expected of him.

Thus when people cross a rather ambiguous threshold into a new status called "old," they bring with them a repertoire of personal attributes, values, behaviors, and attitudes subsumed by the term personality as well as a set of beliefs about what will be expected of them as older persons by others. There is no reason to assume, however, that the process by which the old are socialized into a new constellation of roles comprising the role set of the elderly will differ significantly from the process of transition at adolescence, adulthood, parenthood, or other significant periods of the life cycle.

Needless to say, the transition to the status of older person need not be marked by a complete substitution of one role set for another. For example the role behavior of a merchant aged seventy may not, or need not, be different from that which was appropriate at age fifty-five, nor must the scholarly activities of the professor emeritus necessarily be different from those engaged in when he was professor. On the other hand, certain discontinuities in role sets accompanying chronological or physical aging are commonplace. Compulsory retirement, widowhood, physical infirmity are but a few circumstances resulting in loss of roles, in some cases the loss being total. We might posit then a continuum of continuity of role sets. At one extreme, old age results in no discontinuity at all; at the other extreme, an entirely new set of roles may be substituted. Positions between these extremes represent varying discontinuity of role sets. (Cf. Rosow, 1963.) While a role or aspect of a role remains continuous insofar as content is concerned, the frequency with which the appropriate role behavior is evoked may change. Thus, for example, the frequency with which behavior appropriate to the role of grandparent or parent is required may diminish if there is a geographic separation between the elderly and their children. Similarly the role of patient, in the doctor-patient dyad may be acted more frequently with advancing years, even though the content of such roles remains constant.

Becoming old may then be conceptualized within this framework, as a process of becoming socialized to a new status and acquiring, to a greater or lesser extent, new role sets (either with respect to content or intensity or both). The observed process of disengagement may then be described as a process in which the complexity of the role set diminishes. While using different words to describe the concept does not necessarily explain it or add to its usefulness, by attempting to view the phenomenon within the framework of role theory, we may reduce the apparent differences between current explanations of aging.

Consider the implications of the concepts of socialization and role for the analysis of adjustment to the aging process. We may thus see the elderly person as an individual whose self-concept at that point in time is a product of developmental factors. And this self-concept is conveyed through and by interaction with significant others. Each role enacted throughout a lifetime makes its impact in the shaping and molding of the individual's concept of himself; and in turn one's concept of self determines in part those roles which will be occupied and the way in which they will be played. Now, in this, which may be the last crucial transition period in the individual's life, one of several situations may obtain. First, there may be no appreciable change in the role sets of old people. Secondly, there may be a diminishing of the complexity of the role set; that is, fewer roles may be performed. Thirdly, there may be modification of the role set; and finally, there may be actual substitution of new roles.

In the first instance where the role set remains constant, we might expect to find the well-adjusted elderly of two types: 1) those who are and have been fully engaged and those who are and have been relatively disengaged; 2) where the role set is found to be diminished, we find those who are, in conventional terms, "disengaging." Within this latter class, we may further discern two types: 1) those who are disengaging voluntarily; and 2) those who are disengaging involuntarily.

For those who are disengaging voluntarily, role theory leads us to predict that the individual has arrived at this stage with a set of beliefs about what is expected of him and that these beliefs are compatible with the expectations of those around him. Specifically, one might expect that the values of significant others and reference groups are conducive to, or compatible with, withdrawal. In those instances where the individual chooses to disengage or withdraw, but significant others in his life space expect a person of his status to continue at the same level of activity, one might predict that the older person is subject to some stress which will be ultimately resolved by his continued withdrawal, but not without cost to his self-esteem.

Others will be found to be disengaging involuntarily, that is to say, through forced retirement, widowhood, physical infirmity, and geographic isolation. The desire to maintain existing role relationships notwithstanding, the older person may be stripped of those meaningful relationships that give significance to his life and to his image of himself. In such cases, one might speculate that a satisfactory resolution never takes place and a price is paid in the form of continued insult to the individual's self-esteem.

In the case where the role set is modified, one might expect, in view of the reciprocal nature of role expectation, the individual to be subject to considerable role strain. We might speculate that the modification in the role set is a result of bargain and compromise in order to bring balance or congruence into the situation where incompatible expectations impinge upon the individual. For example, in the role of parent the elderly person may find that his children define the status of growing old in terms of diminished activity, whereas, the members of some other reference group, say, for example, the deacons of his church, expect that now that he is retired from business he can devote more time to the fund raising or charitable works of his church. One reference group expects less activity and another expects more. In such situations role strain is produced and the individual has at his disposal a number of ways of reducing the strain. He may establish a priority among the conflicting role expectations on the basis of a perceived hierarchy of reward for him. Ultimately, this may be expected to lead to a gradual diminishing of low priority roles. Alternately, he may accommodate himself to the conflict or competition by altering his perception of the expectations themselves and/or altering his perception of the consequent change in behavior of his role partners. He may also not resolve the strain or conflict but live with it. We may anticipate the consequences of these circumstances to be reflected in various degrees of emotional disturbance.

Finally, let us consider those elderly who are characterized by having substituted new role sets for the previously existent role sets. This condition may be considered characteristic of what Rose terms "the aging group conscious." They are "those elderly persons aware not merely that they are old but that they are subject to certain deprivations because they are old, and they react to these deprivations with resentment and with some positive effort to overcome the deprivations (Rose, 1965)." Rose goes on to identify several patterns of response to the changing roles. One of these classes of elderly persons consists of "those who succeed in creating new independent roles," that is, who become reengaged. Another class is "those who create new roles for themselves in an aging subsociety which is different from larger general society." While in Rose's conception the aging subculture would appear to be those who have substituted a new role set voluntarily, he has also spoken of those who are forced into new role sets. The distinction between voluntary and involuntary acquisition of new roles would seem to be critical in terms of the consequences for the individual's self-concept and feelings of social worth.

In summary, we have attempted to offer an explanation which would accommodate the intrinsic, developmental, personalistic view of the aging process with the interactionist view of that process through a social psychological approach relying largely on the concepts of socialization and role theory. Within this view the intrapersonal processes may be seen as accounting for beliefs regarding the expectations of significant others, choice of significant others, and the mode of response to lack of congruence between the individual's and the others' expectations of behavior. The phenomena of interaction on the other hand produce the signals and stimuli through which the individual acquires and modifies his sense of self. It is our contention that through an analysis of role behavior and interaction we can produce an understanding of the phenomena of the aging process in such a way as to permit recommendations for social policy pertaining to the health and welfare of the aging community.

Research to support such a view should in our opinion follow along these lines:

First, a program of methodological research should be undertaken prior to substantive research. The outline of such a program has already been presented in the paper by Schooler & Estes (1966, Part I). Briefly, that paper presented four methodological problems: 1) the problem of methods of analyses of longitudinal data; 2) the problem of defining the qualitative aspects of social interaction; 3) the problem of defining the limits of the life space; and 4) the problem of using the reports of significant others in the analysis of the elderly person's role.

Following the completion of such methodological studies, research programs should be addressed to the problem of the definition of the category or status called "old." That is to say, how is that category defined by "others" and how is it defined by older persons themselves? The specific questions to be answered are: What are the characteristics attributed in general to the elderly by others, and then, given a particular and specific older person, what are the characteristics attributed to him by others? We are then in a position to determine what factors account for the differences in those cases where any given person of advanced years is defined or described differently from the stereotyped definitions of older people. Subsequently, we would be able to determine what factors are associated with discrepancies between a specific older person's definition of himself and the definition attributed to him by significant others in his social environment.

There are at present a number of studies in which perceived or expected attributes of elderly persons are recorded (cf. Aaronson, 1966). These studies are significant not only because they reveal the degree of the disagreement on some attributes but also because they point up the fact that there is indeed disagreement and lack of concordance about the characteristics of the old. Going beyond the documentation of the disagreement would not only lend support to the notion that the elderly are indeed subject to conflicting or competing expectations with respect to their behavior, but also, and perhaps more importantly, would show the relationship between the degree of concordance among expectations and the consequent physical and emotional dysfunction of the old. Such an investigation would then lead naturally into a study focused on the resolution of role strain in which the differential effects of intrapersonal and social events would be pursued.

A second basic line of investigation would necessitate the longitudinal study of changes in role repertoires of the elderly, not simply to document what is already known, but rather to relate the specific qualitative changes in the role repertoire to various measurable intrapsychic processes on the one one hand and to the measurable opportunities for interaction on the other.

REFERENCES

Aaronson, B. S. Personality stereotypes of aging. *Journal of Gerontology*, 1966, *21*, 458-462.

Birren, J. E. Principles of research on aging. in J. E. Birren (Ed.), *Handbook of aging and the individual.* Chicago: University of Chicago Press, 1959.

Cavan, R. S. Self and role in adjustment during old age. In A. M. Rose

(Ed.), *Human behavior and social processes: An interactionist approach.* Boston: Houghton Mifflin, 1962.

Christ, E. A. Economic and other functions of systematized leisure activity. In A. M. Rose, & W. A. Peterson (Eds.), *Older people and their social world.* Philadelphia: F. A. Davis, 1965.

Cumming, E., & Henry, W. E. *Growing old: The process of disengagement.* New York: Basic Books, 1961.

Cumming, E. Further thoughts on the theory of disengagement. *International Social Science Journal,* 1963, *15,* 377-394.

Deutscher, I. Socialization for post-parental life. In A. M. Rose (Ed.), *Human behavior and social processes: An interactionist approach.* Boston: Houghton Mifflin, 1962.

Havighurst, R. J., Neugarten, B., & Tobin, S. Disengagement, personality, and life satisfaction in the later years. In P. F. Hansen (Ed.), *Age with a future: Proceedings of the Sixth International Congress of Gerontology, Copenhagen, 1963.* Copenhagen: Munksgaard, 1964.

Henry, W. E. The theory of intrinsic disengagement. In P. F. Hansen (Ed.), *Age with a future: Proceedings of the Sixth International Congress of Gerontology, Copenhagen, 1963.* Copenhagen: Munksgaard, 1964.

Kastenbaum, R. Theories of human aging: The search for a conceptual framework. *Journal of Social Issues,* 1965, *21* (4), 13-35.

Maddox, G., & Eisdorfer, C. Some correlates of activity and morale among the elderly. *Social Forces,* 1962, *40,* 254-260.

Miller, S. J. The social dilemma of the aging leisure participant. In A. M. Rose, & W. A. Peterson (Eds.), *Older people and their social world.* Philadelphia: F. A. Davis, 1965.

Philibert, M. The emergence of social gerontology. *Journal of Social Issues,* 1965, *4,* 4.

Rose, A. M. (Ed.). *Human behavior and social processes: An interactionist approach.* Boston: Houghton Mifflin, 1962.

Rose, A. M. Physical health and mental outlook among the aging. In A. M. Rose, & W. A. Peterson (Eds.), *Older people and their social world.* Philadelphia: F. A. Davis, 1965.

Rose, A. M. The subculture of the aging: A framework for research in social gerontology, and group consciousness among the aging. In A. M. Rose, & W. A. Peterson (Eds.), *Older people and their social world.* Philadelphia: F. A. Davis, 1965. (a)

Rosow, I. Adjustment of the normal aged. In R. H. Williams, C. Tibbitts, & W. Donahue (Eds.), *Processes of aging.* Vol. II. New York: Atherton Press, 1963.

Schooler, K. K., & Estes, C. L. Differences between current gerontological theories: Implications for research methodology. *Proceedings of the 7th International Congress of Gerontology,* 1966, *6,* 259-261.

21:: A CROSS-CULTURAL PERSPECTIVE

MALCOLM ARTH

This paper is concerned broadly with the role of the aged in nonwestern cultures, but focuses mainly on the Ibo people of southeastern Nigeria. The author resided in a village in the Nsukka Division of the Eastern Region* of Nigeria from October, 1964 through June, 1965, and again during the summer of 1966.[1] At first it may seem a long leap from institutionalized geriatric patients in the urban United States, discussed in the other chapters, to community-dwelling elders in a West African village. Indeed, there are differences of which even the anthropologist who identifies closely with "his" village is aware. However, it is a working assumption of those engaged in cross-cultural research that studies of tribal groups provide insights into the nature of urban-industrial societies. Hopefully this paper reflects the validity of that assumption.

In one sense, anthropologists have been concerned with the aged for a long time. Elderly members of tribes have frequently served as informants, and as the sources of revealing life-histories. One rarely finds in the anthropological literature, however, a focus on aging. Recently, Margaret Clark (1967) surveyed the limited anthropological literature on this topic. There are penetrating insights about the role of the aged in occasional monographs, for example in Kluckhohn's *Navaho*

*What is now the East Central State.

[1] The author expresses appreciation to Adelphi University for a research grant enabling him to pursue his study during the summer of 1966.

Witchcraft (1944), though the focus of such studies lies elsewhere. In a few societies where there is what might loosely be termed a gerontocracy, the subject is extensively dealt with (e.g., Hart & Pilling, 1960). Occasionally an anthropologist has examined aging in American culture (e.g., Arth, 1961). By and large, however, anthropologists have been late arrivals in the field of gerontology. It is noteworthy that the earliest major cross-cultural study of the aged was done by a sociologist (Simmons, 1945), and that the first session devoted to aging at the annual meetings of the American Anthropological Association took place only in 1965.

There is some rationale, one almost says rationalization, for the relative neglect of this topic. The explanation for the scarcity is often that life expectancy is short in tribal societies or that the elderly there are too small a segment to warrant special inquiry. Yet Leighton, Lambo, Hughes, Leighton, Murphy, & Macklin (1963) comment, in a recent study of the Yoruba, on the fact that the relative proportion of the aged in Nigerian communities they studied was comparable with that encountered in a Canadian community investigated previously (Leighton, et al., 1963). The author's own experience with the Ibo suggests that there, also, are older people in numbers worth studying. The crucial question is not whether old people exist in the same proportion as in industrialized societies where better standards of health and medical care prevail, but whether there are enough aged people in tribal societies to warrant investigation. There is little doubt that in many places there are.

Another explanation for the dearth of studies of the aged in tribal cultures is cited by Clark (1967). She calls attention to the implicit assumption of many field workers, particularly those in the area of culture and personality, that the earliest years are the crucial determinants of adult behavior, thus introducing a bias against gerontological studies (pp. 56-57). One also suspects that the psycho-dynamic factors involved in studying parental figures, and facing the topics of decline and death are involved in the omission, anthropologists being subject to the same anxieties as others. Whatever the reasons, historical, psychological, or in terms of theoretical assumptions, it is clear that the neglect of the aged as a category is more than accidental. The increasing number of studies of aging in the past decade has undoubtedly been stimulated by the increasing sociological significance of that growing proportion of the population. The proportion of persons over 65 in the United States almost doubled between 1890 and the mid-twentieth century (von Mering and Weniger, 1959). However, there were enough subjects for study even in 1890.

The Aged in Ibo Culture

Before discussing the role of the aged among the Ibo, a brief description of some of the important elements of the culture is presented (cf. also Green, 1947; Forde & Jones, 1950; Uchendu, 1965; Ottenberg, 1965). The Ibo number about six million, and constitute a single tribe, although there is considerable variation in dialect and custom within the territory they occupy. The economy is basically agricultural, the staple crops being yam, cassava and cocoyam. Some families raise goats, chickens, or pigs, and other food products such as rice and dried fish are obtainable in local marketplaces. The village studied is located in the countryside with flat grasslands, abrupt hills, and small clumps of forest, making for a varied and handsome landscape. The year is divided into two major seasons, wet and dry, and the climate, though tropical is not unpleasantly hot most of the year. Ibo political organization contrasts with that of kingdoms in some other parts of Nigeria. Ibo villages by and large are autonomous units, and operate on a democratic basis. However, at the same time, there are important bonds tying some villages to others, these connections growing out of origin myths and finding expression in the kinship system. The traditional religious belief system focuses on placating spiritual forces by perpetual sacrifice, and contains a good deal of protective magic to help in warding off the work of evil-doers. Ancestors figure prominently in the supernatural world and act as protectors of the living. Christianity, particularly Roman Catholicism, has made considerable inroads with the younger generation by virtue of the fact that the churches operated most of the schools until 1960.

The village studied contains twenty-three compounds, each compound ideally representing an extended family, though in practice this is not always the case. The population is almost evenly divided between those over eighteen and those under, and there are six persons over the age of sixty, four men and two women. It is several of these elders who are cited later in this chapter, but many older persons in neighboring villages were also observed and contributed to the analysis presented by the author. A word is in order as to how age estimates were made, since written records were rare. Relative ages were well known to older people in the village; that is, different persons were able to agree independently as to who was older than whom. Absolute dating was a bit more of a problem, though such well remembered events as the influenza epidemic of 1918, and the year of the construction of the mission hospital a few miles away, served as good markers.

The village has a resident population of about 150, this figure varying seasonally as some villagers travel to or return from work in other parts of the country. The resident population figure does not count the women of the village who have married out, but does include the women from other villages who have married in. The society is patrilocal, polygynous, and has a strong patrilineal emphasis.

As mentioned earlier, Ibo culture contains regional variations. Nevertheless, there has been substantial agreement by observers regarding central values (Ottenberg, 1959; Ottenberg, 1965; Uchendu, 1965). One of these core values is reflected in the dual emphasis on achievement and status. They are extremely hardworking, enterprising, and emphasize "getting ahead" to such a degree that the adjustment to many Western patterns has been relatively simple (Ottenberg, 1959). Individualism too is highly valued and so is physical strength.

Ibo personality is a subject too complex to outline in a chapter such as this (as indeed are the topics already cited, such as political organization and religious beliefs). But, briefly, they may be characterized as an energetic people with a capacity on the one hand for great restraint and formality, and on the other hand the ability to burst forth periodically with little inhibition of impulses.

There is little doubt that the Ibo demand respect for the elderly, and that the elders play important roles in the society. In one of the few sources dealing with the role of the aged among the Ibo, Shelton (1965) expresses this clearly. Lineage elders have important ritual functions to perform. Compound elders are required to make daily sacrifices to household shrines. It is the old who often control the knowledge of midwifery, of curing, and of divining the future. Respect is seen in the fact that the funerals of the aged are the most elaborate; the list could be extended. In the village studied, all these functions of the aged persist, though modern medical practices and the introduction of Christianity have lessened their exclusiveness.

Still, one does not find among the Ibo the intense respect pattern reported in some cultures, for example, village Thailand (Cowgill, 1965). Among tribal peoples, the degree of respect-deference varies enormously, an important fact for gerontologists to note. Too often one finds reference in the literature to respect patterns in non-Western cultures as if all such patterns were the same. There is a broad range of attitudes and behaviors on this dimension in non-Western societies too. The author's own observations suggest that though the ideal of respect holds in Ibo culture, behavior often indicates a highly ambivalent attitude. Furthermore, the acculturation process seems to be contributing to increasing the stress and conflict between generations. The kinds of behavior observed vary, but the following three cases serve to illustrate the intensity of feelings involved.

Case: Richard

Richard, thirty years of age, is an unpredictable young man. At times he is the life of the party, stimulating laughter and spirit in a group.

However, his mood changes abruptly and an almost uncontrollable rage might break through. Although usually this occurs when he has been drinking heavily, the mood shifts are not confined to such times. Richard was in the process of marrying and had begun the exchange of gifts with the family of his intended, but had not yet brought her to live in his compound. His father, a wealthy man by village standards, had had five wives, though only two were currently with him. Richard's own mother died some years before and he seems unresigned to his father's present marriages. He argues constantly with his father's wives, blackened the eye of the younger of them, and on another occasion cut the older one with a knife. On one occasion he beat a village elder and on another physically attacked his father. Richard is a junior son, and his elder brother who is married and lives away is better educated, calmer, and has achieved greater financial success. Richard himself has only a sixth-grade education. He is nominally a Protestant, though the majority of youths his age are Roman Catholics, most of the schools in the area being sponsored by the latter church.

Psychodynamically, there are many suggestions in this brief case history to explain Richard's hostility towards his father and his father's wives. There are strong suggestions that his behavior might warrant labeling him a serious psychiatric problem. However, the case demonstrates that outbursts against elders occur, and that the observed behavior is far from the ideal respect pattern called for in the culture.

Case: Father and son

The father in this case is a part-time diviner, a perceptive man about sixty who often emerges informally as a peacemaker in minor disputes. He is not without the ability to strike out verbally, especially if intoxicated, but such outbursts are rare and usually provoked. He has had only one year of formal schooling and speaks little English.

His younger son is twenty-six years old, a small person which the youth himself attributes to his premature birth. The son is fluent in English, has completed six years of schooling and two years of clerical training beyond that. He is responsible and mature for his years and, like most Ibo youths his age, is eager to find work. He has some of the qualities of his father, such as acting as a mediator among his peers. The son drinks less and seems somewhat less motivated to seek out girls than his agemates, which may relate to his church commitment; he is a devout Roman Catholic.

Several situations arose in which this father and son had strong arguments, but perhaps none so vocal and vituperative as the Sunday morning when they argued violently over whether a young member of the compound should cut grass for the goats or go to Sunday school. This situation in part grows out of the acculturation process taking place, but illustrates nonetheless the capacity for ideals to yield markedly.

Case: The lineage elder

This man, in his late sixties, has certain ritual obligations to perform for the benefit of his lineage. He is mild mannered, shorter than most men his age, and rather frail, though not feeble by any means. He is poor by village standards, though he had two wives, one of them now deceased. He has only one child, a young man of twenty-two, with whom he argues frequently about money and the youth's laziness. The son, like most other youths I observed, does not sit quietly by on such occasions, but defends and retaliates with accusation for accusation.

On one particular occasion the lineage elder was scheduled to perform a ritual which only he was empowered to carry out. For some hours previously he had been participating in the celebrating which accompanies many religious occasions: music-making, dancing, and drinking. A word of explanation about the drinking pattern is perhaps needed. There are two principal alcoholic beverages consumed, both of local manufacture: palm wine and gin. Palm wine has an alcoholic content ranging from 3% to 14%; locally distilled gin has about the same strength as the Western product (a taste estimate), and both are imbibed in large quantities on festive occasions. An adult may consume five quarts of palm wine and six ounces of gin over three or four hours. On such occasions the threshold of impulse control is considerably lowered, arguments occur, and there can be overt fighting, though others present usually intervene to keep the peace.

The lineage elder had been drinking and eventually passed out. Despite all attempts to revive him, he remained unconscious, and was unable to perform the needed ritual. Criticism of him was long and loud that day and the next. Outspoken criticism bordering on ridicule was made both by his peers and by younger men. Young men for the most part did not direct their remarks to the elder himself but did speak freely in front of other village elders.

Discussion

These three cases are merely intended to be illustrative. The intensity and extent of the outbursts could hardly be overemphasized, though in fairness one must acknowledge that Ibo arguments generally tend to be raucous. Others could be cited, but the point that the aged are not revered to the extent implied in some of the literature seems clear. How might one account for such outbursts towards the aged in a society where deference is the rule? There are insights to be gained from examining this question from psychological, structural, and cultural perspectives.

As remarked earlier, the aged have been generally avoided as subjects of study, in part because they serve as reminders of mortality; they are the nearest to death, an ever-present source of anxiety. In addition, they represent parental figures for younger adults, and the negative side of ambivalent feelings for parents still finds expression. If anthropologists and other social scientists have ambivalent attitudes for the aged growing out of such psychological concerns, the Ibo are probably not exempt from them either. Perhaps here is a psychological basis for beginning to understand the latent hostility which bursts through in case situations such as those cited.

Robert LeVine (1965) has recently provided a sharp analysis of the extended family in a number of African societies, though his discussion does not include the Ibo. LeVine suggests that the extended family system itself, so common in many cultures including the Ibo, has built-in strains. He notes that some societies have developed institutions to cope with these strains, and cites father-son avoidance patterns and emigration as examples. Neither of these institutions is present among the Ibo, although some migration to seek employment occurs, and whatever stresses grow out of extended family demands must find expression in other forms. One might hypothesize that the kinds of outbursts described above would be less frequent if either the avoidance patterns or mass emigration were present.

In the traditional Ibo marriage a sizeable amount of wealth in the form of cash and goods must be given by the bridegroom to the family of the bride. Traditionally, a young man's father was instrumental in helping the youth to accumulate such a bridewealth. This meant that young men tended to marry relatively late, and that older men could afford young wives. The potential for intergenerational stress here is obvious, particularly in a society in which marriage and multiple wives are avenues to higher status. This normal stress between generations evolving out of the institution of marriage has been accentuated, rather than eased, by the acculturation process. As the Ibo economy shifts from a subsistence pattern toward a wage-cash one, young men are finding it increasingly possible to acquire substantial sums of money and are thus able to compete with older men for younger wives. This has tended to decrease the dependency which young men formerly had on their fathers.

It has often been observed that the focus on youth and activity in American culture places a special series of stresses on the aging individual in the United States (Parsons, 1954). There is a comparable though different value emphasis in Ibo culture which provides Ibo elders with a source of anxiety, namely, the focus on physical strength. Here one must distinguish a pattern which has only moderate importance from a central one. Ottenberg (1965) designates the emphasis on physical strength as one of three core values in Ibo culture; it is a point also illustrated in a literary work by Ibo author Chinua Achebe (1958). For members of such a society, aging could well prove extremely stressful. Although one might look at physical decline as potentially traumatic in any society, where the culture highly prizes physical strength there will be an even higher tension level. There is some support for this in the village data. The one crippled man in the village is a source of amusement because of his affliction, and the one elderly man who manifests a conscious concern about aging harps on his arthritis which prevents him from engaging in agriculture, roofing, and other tasks which men of all ages perform. He continually came to me for medication, complaining of his inability to work, and of pain. The focus was not so much on the discomfort but rather on the inability to perform. Other people were ill with dysentery or malaria but complained little, for they knew they would recover.

In other Ibo values, one also sees points at which the aged find themselves challenged. As stated earlier, the Ibo are achievement-oriented and status conscious. Most observers are impressed with their willingness to work and their entrepreneurial spirit. As Slater (1964, p. 234) points out, in systems which value change and mobility the aged may necessarily be devalued. They would constitute a dysfunctional element in the system. This may provide a clue to the underlying basis for conflict between the generations. That is, there may be a noncongruence of values, and a noncongruence of certain values with structural demands of the system.

Not all values and customs in Ibo culture work toward making the process of adjusting to aging difficult. There are some which make the Ibo elder's task easier than that of his American counterpart. For example, mild memory loss and confusion, even a tendency to wander, are less acute problems for a community where compounds are fenced or walled and in which physical hazards such as automobile traffic are minimal. Different attitudes toward body excrement present another instance. For the elderly person who has lost bladder or bowel control, the social implications are less drastic with an earth or a rough cement floor, in contrast with the practical problems presented by wall-to-wall carpeting. Also, there is a more permissive attitude toward contact with urine and feces than is true in middle-class American culture. Thus, some traditional attitudes and customs make the aging process less stressful, while others create potential stresses for the individual and frictions between generations.

One of the steadying aspects which tends to make Ibo aging adjustment smoother is a continuity of activity as long as the person is physically able. The oldest woman in the village, near 80, continues to cook, to work in the garden, to care for young children, or simply to keep an eye on the compound while others are away. For elderly men there are often curing or ceremonial functions, or light gardening. There is a continuity to existence not easily found in an urban-industrial society with compulsory retirement. The maintenance of active roles for the elderly helps to insure the respect in which they are held.

In summary, this paper suggests that the aged, at least in some tribal societies, do constitute a sufficient segment of the population to warrant study by gerontologists. The data suggest that the stereotyped view that the aged occupy venerated positions in tribal cultures needs refinement. Clearly, a culture with respect as an ideal pattern, may on the behavioral level display strong ambivalence. This ambivalence is viewed as deriving from certain near universal psychological concerns and structural factors such as the nature of the family and the marriage institution. Ibo values and customs are also seen as relevant, some tending to create stress points while others help ease the adjustment to old age. The changes resulting from acculturation add another dimension to the problem. One topic which might have been explored is the possible relevance of historical changes altering previously established patterned outlets for hostility. With the suppression of inter- village hostilities, and the added frustrations of life under colonial rule, it is possible that aggressive impulses sought new channels and broke through to the surface at points of give in the social structure and value system.

An intensification of cross-cultural studies by gerontologists is needed. Theories of aging cannot ignore the majority of the world's cultures, a fact recognized by anthropoligists, but too little appreciated by other disciplines which too often content themselves with a footnote recognizing that the "human" behavior referred to is really Western behavior. Up to now, anthropology has not done well by gerontology. There is a sizeable collection of data, but the quality is spotty. There is a need for anthropological studies of aging in depth. This preliminary report of a brief encounter in one society is not such a study. Hopefully, it may stimulate some.

Some writers have observed that the aged represent a dysfunctional element in systems which value change and where high-level performance skills are essential. Perhaps it is nonrational to provide for such a dysfunctional element in the system. However, there is no culture known which operates only in terms of functional-rational considerations. There seems reason to hope, therefore, that care and concern for the aged might flourish as a product of cultural learning, if not out of functional necessity.

REFERENCES

Achebe, C. *Things fall apart.* London: William Heinemann, 1958.

Arth, M. J. American culture and the phenomenon of friendship in the aged. *The Gerontologist*, 1961, *1*, 168-170.

Arth, M. J. Ideals and behavior, a comment on Ibo respect patterns. *The Gerontologist*, 1968, *8*, 242-244.

Clark, M. The anthropology of aging, a new area for studies of culture and personality. *The Gerontologist*, 1967, *7*, 55-64.

Cowgill, D. O. Social life of the aging in Thailand. Paper presented at the meeting of the Gerontological Society, Los Angeles, November 1965.

Forde, D., & Jones, G. I. *The Ibo and Ibibio-speaking peoples of southeastern Nigeria.* London: International African Institute, 1950.

Green, M. M. *Ibo village affairs.* New York: Praeger, 1964.

Hart, C. W. M., & Pilling, A. R. *The Tiwi of North Australia.* New York: Holt, Rinehart & Winston, 1960.

Kluckhohn, C. *Navaho witchcraft.* Boston: Beacon Press, 1962.

Leighton, A. H., Lambo, A., Hughes, C. C., Leighton, D. C., Murphy, J. M., & Macklin, D. B. *Pyschiatric disorder among the Yoruba.* Ithaca, New York: Cornell University Press, 1963.

Levine, R. A. Intergenerational tensions and extended family structures in Africa. In E. Shanas, & G. F. Streib (Eds.), *Social structure and the family.* Englewood Cliffs, N.J.: Prentice-Hall, 1965.

Ottenberg, S. Ibo receptivity to change. In W. J. Bascom, & N. J. Herskovits (Eds.), *Continuity and change in African cultures.* Chicago: University of Chicago Press, 1959.

Ottenberg, P. The Afikop Ibo of eastern Nigeria. In J. L. Gibbs (Eds.,), *People of Africa.* New York: Holt, Rinehart and Winston, 1965.

Parsons, T. Age and sex in the social structure of the United States. In T. Parsons, *Essays in sociological theory: Pure and applied.* Free Press, 1954.

Shelton, A. J. Ibo aging and eldership: Notes for gerontologists and others. *The Gerontologist,* 1965, *5* 20-23.

Simmons, L. *The role of the aged in primitive society.* New Haven: Yale University Press, 1945.

Slater, P. Cross-cultural view of the aged. In R. Kastenbaum (Eds.), *New thoughts on old age.* New York: Springer, 1964.

Uchendu, V. C. *The Ibo of southeast Nigeria.* New York: Holt, Rinehart and Winston, 1965.

Von Mering, O., & Weniger, F. Socio-cultural background of the aging individual. In J. Birren (Eds.), *Handbook of aging and the individual.* Chicago: University of Chicago Press, 1959.

22:: BEER, WINE, AND MUTUAL GRATIFICATION IN THE GERONTOPOLIS

ROBERT KASTENBAUM

Child-watching can be a refreshing and instructive pastime for the gerontologist. Consider, for example, the patterns of injury and therapy that come into being when a generous assortment of preschool children are cavorting about. Young Kevin receives a blow to both knee and ego as he tumbles from a rock. Tears begin to blubber up. Younger David moves to his side, places his arm around the victim's shoulder and bestows a therapeutic kiss, along with the supportive message, "It's aw wight. Don't cwy." In a twinkling and a half Kevin has recovered his sense of psychobiological integrity. The physician-patient dyad dissolves; play continues in its freewheeling way. A few minutes later it is David who tumbles into the prickly blackberry bush and emerges in distress. Elizabeth and Kevin are soon with him, offering verbal and tactual tokens of their support. Again a therapeutic kiss is bestowed. And again, the mutual aid scene dissolves. Individual and group play resume as though had ever happened.

Kiss-and-make-better is a superb form of short-term therapy, not only between parent and young child but also between young child and his peers. What we wish to emphasize is that the relationship of helper to helped is occasional, fleeting. Role-reversal occurs easily. Both partici-

The studies reported here were supported in part by USPHS mental health project grant MHO-1520, and supplemented by contributions from the Wine Advisory Board of the State of California and the United States Brewers Association.

pants quickly become free agents once the therapeutic scene has been enacted. This fluid pattern does not persist into adult life. It is replaced by a rigid, formalized one-way relationship that leaves its marks both on the helper and the helped. The physician does not expect his patient to minister to him when it is his turn to suffer distress. And when physician and patient encounter each other away from the medical office it is likely that their relationship still pivots around the therapeutic situation. One can say approximately the same thing for the psychotherapist-client relationship. Whatever passes between these two people must be filtered by the non-reversible role they have accepted in one particular situation.

Most of us have experienced the patient or helped role from time to time. Many of us have also served as therapists or helpers in some sense of the term. Let us concentrate upon the patient role specifically. Medical and nursing attention exacts a certain psychological cost along with the monetary. For "our own good" we must obey the explicit instructions and prohibitions placed upon our behavior; additionally, we are expected to obey certain implicit rules, e.g., don't ask too many questions, don't gripe, etc. The combination of illness and medical-nursing regime can reduce our customary activities rather drastically. Along with such physical changes as restricted mobility and such social changes as restricted visitors and interpersonal contacts we may also experience a more general sense of transformation. Our life does not seem to be in our own hands as much as we usually like to think it is. We are being treated differently; we begin to regard ourselves differently. "Here am I, a something to be helped."

Our prized sense of selfhood might be strained and buffeted by the patient role, but ordinarily it proves strong and resilient enough to survive the experience. The time factor is very important here. We can usually regard the illness and confinement as an episode. Soon we will be on our feet again, resuming our normal lives. This time perspective enables us to be relatively tolerant of our current plight. We can submit to the discomforts of a medical regime and even to the correlated sense of being treated as something less than the full person we are, for it is just a matter of time until we are once again captains of our own souls. Furthermore, we are likely to have frequent reminders that we are still part of a family, still part of the work force, still part of a world that is larger than a hospital ward.

But the problem intensifies for the person who is suffering from a debilitating chronic illness. It is especially threatening to the elderly-and-impaired individual. He is likely to experience more difficulty in convincing himself that he will be able to return to the semblance of a normal life, and is likely to have fewer tokens of his current membership in society at large. In short, he faces the prospect of *permanent captivity* in the sick role. There was a time when he was a person who was many things to many people, including himself. He gave and received. He participated in a variety of relationships encompassing the spontaneous and informal as well as the rigid and ritualistic. Today he is merely One-Who-Is-To-Be-Helped. And tomorrow will be very much like today.

The wheel has come full circle from the spontaneous, reversible, ephemeral kiss-and-make-better therapy practiced by the preschool child. In fact, the wheel has lodged itself in a deep rut where it spins and spins but takes the individual precisely no place. It is an alarming and incongruous thought that the spontaneous child for whom helping or being helped is merely one incident among others might some day become totally absorbed into the impoverished identity of One-Who-Is-To-Be-Helped.

"Us" and "Them" in the Gerontopolis

The distinction between "Them" and "Us" is one of the obvious facts of institutional life. "Us" comes first—the staff whose training, skills, and dedicated efforts are devoted to "Them," the recipients. "Us" wear uniforms when we can, and find many ways to make it clear that we are not to be mistaken for "Them." Relationships between "Us" and "Them" are not necessarily lacking in human sympathy. But the power and control resides in "Us," and there is a definite double-standard to guide behavior toward "one of 'Us' " and "one of 'Them'."

Even apart from institutional life, "Us" and "Them" distinctions keep the young and the old in their places. What is exciting for "Us" is improper for "Them," although certain weaknesses and indulgences can be excused in "Them" more easily than in "Us." Studies have shown over and again that younger people tend to regard elders as being quite different from themselves, a view that some elders also share (Kastenbaum & Durkee 1964; 1964a). Right now we are less concerned with the accuracy or inaccuracy of attitudes toward the elderly than we are about the fact that it has become so commonplace to regard older people as occupying a separate category of existence.

The person who is both elderly and institutionalized is nailed into place by both hammers. Clearly, he is expected to follow, not to lead, to receive, not to give. Just a shade less obviously, the staff is also bolted into position. Most of "Us" make a determined effort to be helpful to "Them." We do not expect "Them" to help "Us." Both sides have allowed themselves (ourselves) to be trapped, and at least half-persuaded that this is the best, if not the only, possible arrangement.

One of the most striking effects of the "Us"/"Them" distinction is the sheer dullness of life in the gerontopolis. It tends to be dull for the patient and dull for the staff. In search of material for the heart and mind to feed on, the patient is likely to totter into only moderately rewarding musings on his past, or into outright hallucinations. The staff must generate its intramural rivalries and scandals if there is to be something worth talking and thinking about. The staff-patient interface may provide sporadic incidents to enliven the day, but in general these transactions are so constricted and predictable that they can be walked through with very little thought or fresh experiencing.

We are implying that glorious self-actualization is not the rule for staff members in a gerontopolis. Efficient management of routine, interspersed with occasional heroics, and an end-of-the-day grim self-satisfaction that the necessary has again been accomplished—this is a little closer to the mark. The patient is even less to be envied. Each day of exposure to a constricted and ritualized environment (even though it may be this environment that is keeping him alive) tends to reinforce further those regressive or primitivizing processes that age has a way of foisting on us. The aging brain that requires *more* salient and appealing stimulation receives *less*—and so, powers of attention and concentration continue to decline. The uprooted citizen who needs appropriate challenges and demands to maintain his sense of interpersonal potency is given few such opportunities or none. It is not surprising that increasingly he comes to resemble the stereotype of apathetic, disconnected old age. Moreover, as the habit and motivation structure of adult life decay, the elderly patient finds less and less point in doing *anything*. Reduction of behavioral output is an invitation to the entire organism: physiological processes also slow down. Possessing only the function of being a recipient of medical-nursing-custodial services, the elder eventually may comply by acting as though even his body were no longer his own. Almost any stray infection or psychobiological stress can overwhelm the semi-abandoned body. The constricted role of patienthood, coupled with actual age-related changes, can squeeze the life out of the elderly institutionalized patient even before it hastens him to an unnecessarily early grave.

The "Us"/"Them" distinction is encountered in the low-level and marginal gerontopolis, such as the undermanned, underfinanced nursing home or the neglected geriatric unit of a large and somnolent mental hospital. But it is also encountered with some frequency in the bustling facility that offers numerous specific services to its residents. Energetic, trained and well-motivated staff members may do a great deal *for* the elderly resident, but these therapeutic actions nevertheless can have the effect of reinforcing the distinction between helper and helped. As enlightened people plan the new gerontopolis or seek to upgrade existing facilities it is possible that innovations will also fail to avoid the "Us"/"Them" dichotomy. We will comment upon some of these proposed innovations later.

Mutual Gratification

It is probably not realistic or even desirable to contemplate a thorough dissolution of the "Us"/"Them" distinction in the gerontopolis. But might it not be possible to lessen the significance of this distinction, perhaps by making it subordinate to a broader outlook? No doubt there are many ways in which a reorientation might be attempted, many theoretical models that might be devised to guide the program. We will be discussing just one particular approach here. Other procedures and other theoretical models might be as effective or more effective. We are simply trying to indicate that the gerontopolis does not have to be the way it usually is, that ideas generated by social science research can be applied here.

Mutual gratification has become a central concept in the series of small clinical studies that will be summarized below, as well as several that are now in early stages of development. The notion of mutual gratification unfurled itself from several years of clinical and research experience in one sort of gerontopolis, an all-geriatric hospital, and from a conceptual approach known as developmental-field theory (Kastenbaum, 1965; 1966). A brief description of the institutional setting might be useful at this point.

The hospital in which these studies were made is one of the few all-geriatric hospitals in the United States. It offers the full range of medical and nursing services one would expect from an accredited general hospital (which it is). There are usually eight house physicians, supplemented by part-time physicians and a broad array of consultants in various specialties. In these days of rugged competition for nurses and other trained health personnel, this hospital has been rather successful in recruiting and retaining registered nurses, licensed practical nurses, and attendants. The nursing service has been conducting an inservice training program for years, and recently added a more specialized and innovative inservice program with Federal support. There are social workers to advise and process potential new admissions as well as to assist those who are already residents. There are occupational therapists to provide a large range of supervised activities, both individual and group. There are recreation therapists. There are psychologists. There are community volunteers whose participation in the life of the hospital is directed by a full-time staff member. There are Catholic, Greek, Orthodox, Protestant, and Jewish chaplains. There are skilled personnel to maintain the facilities, to man the hospital's own fire department, security force, greenhouse, etc. In short, the hospital has many features of a self-contained community; it is a hospital and then some.

Elderly people are admitted to the hospital for treatment of medical conditions that frequently are complicated with social or behavioral problems. Patients come from their own homes, from nursing homes, from general hospitals, from almost every conceivable source. There is a broad spectrum of medical and psychological conditions represented in the patient population—some elders are severely ill or impaired; others can be maintained on a relatively high level of functioning. There is a live discharge rate, but, as one might expect in a population with an average age of eighty-three, the rate is low. More often than not, the hospital is the patient's dwelling for the remainder of his life. The approximately 650 patients are all voluntary admissions, even those who have had a history of hospitalization for mental illness or who may now be showing signs of psychological deterioration or pathology. The whole enterprise is operated by the State Department of Mental Health.

Naturally enough, the hospital functions largely within a medical-nursing model. There is a broader range of activities and greater flexibility than one customarily finds in a geriatric or 'chronic' hospital, but hospital it remains. The elder who was once a citizen with a complex set of interlocking roles, a subtle and varied phenomenological life, and a relatively secure sense of identity, tends to shrink into the narrow confines of permanent patienthood. He becomes a set of symptoms to be managed and a set of administrative papers to be shuffled. Fortunately, the symptoms are usually well managed, the papers well shuffled. Compassion and affection frequently endow the situation with a warmer tone than might have been anticipated. But the "Us"/"Them" distinction continues to prevail.

Analysis of this situation in terms of the developmental-field theory (Kastenbaum & Slater, 1964) led to the general impression that three related phenomena should be modified: (a) the gross discontinuity (overdifferentiation) between the former self and his present, institutionalized self; (b) the gross discontinuity (overdifferentiation) between himself and other humans, especially staff members; and (c) the underdifferentiation of the elder's interpersonal and phenomenological life in the hospital. Application of a mutual gratification model was then proposed. Interpersonal pleasure—even more crucial, the *expectation* of *possible* interpersonal pleasure—tends to become one of the major casualties in the transition from independent adult to geriatric patient. Perhaps the staff-patient and patient-patient relationship could be altered in such a way that expectations of mutual gratification predominate. Could staff and patients be enticed to seek each other out *not* because they "have to" or "should," but simply because the contacts might be enjoyable? In a way, this was a prescription for "selfish" instead of "dutiful" behavior. As it has been expressed elsewhere: "Estrangement from the "old" self and submergence in an inadequate new role could be avoided and/or counteracted by encouraging expectations for mutual gratification. The expectation of mutual gratification should allow both the patient and the staff member to step out of their narrow roles and interact as ordinary human beings. Moments of mutual pleasure would brighten the long day of Mr. Oldman and the staff members who serve him, but of no less importance would be the sense of underlying continuity that is preserved for Mr. Oldman. He is now an older and sicker man, but his relationships with his fellow humans remains predicated on the expectation of appropriate mutual gratifications" (Kastenbaum, 1965a).

Four Little Studies

An exploratory action program was derived from the mutual gratification model. Four little clinical studies have been completed to date. As the title of this paper suggests, all of these ventures involved the use of beer or wine. Why?

The decision to initiate an action program that centers around the serving of wine was based upon several considerations:

1. A new program that makes great demands upon staff time and effort is unlikely to become a permanent aspect of institutional practice even if it does gain acceptance at first;

2. Preferably, the program should not make a frontal onslaught upon established customs—or more significantly, perhaps should not *appear* to be making an onslaught;

3. The mutual gratification model implies that a program should succeed not because it has been added as another grim duty of an already-burdened staff, but rather because the personnel feel like doing it, feel more able to give and receive;

4. The program should not be very expensive to begin or maintain;

5. It should not require specialized skills or rare "personality types" for its effective implementation;

6. Any specific materials or procedures that are introduced to foster the mutual gratification effect should also have their own specific merits to contribute to the welfare of the patient, staff, or institution; and

7. The explicit rationale should be reinforced by existing cultural habits or symbols that work favorably beneath the surface, requiring scarcely a mention.

Accordingly, wine was selected as a reasonably close analog of a type of treatment program that is ultra-familiar to hospital personnel: drug administration. It seemed related more particularly to the administration of psychotropic drugs, and also had something in common with the serving of juice and other refreshments. Wine itself can be regarded as a psychotropic drug *and* a food (Leake & Silverman, 1966). Therefore it was possible to introduce wine as a quasi-medical or nutritional item that is prescribed and administered under specified conditions. Consternation is held in check by the familiar pattern into which the new element has been added.

Furthermore, wine brings along a multitude of connotative meanings that support its more direct psychophysiological effects. "Candlelight and wine" elicit thoughts of mutual gratification on an intimate adult level. Occasions of group solidarity, family togetherness, and social intimacy frequently are accompanied by the sanguine "blood of the grape." Sacred rituals in many cultures, including our own, often involve wine. The connotations of wine are not equally salient and positive for all individuals, or for members of all ethnic groups. However, when there is an ethnic tradition, as among persons of Italian background (Lolli, Serianni, Banissoni, Golder, Mariani, McCarthy, & Toner, 1953; Sadoun, Lolli, and Silverman, 1965), the serving of wine can be a powerful impetus to developing a renewed sense of adult-individuality-within-a-loving-context.

It is worth noting that the studies to be described briefly below were preceded by several years of research on the behavioral effects of conventional psychotropic drugs. Among other things, this line of research suggested that the outcome of psychotropic drug administration to elderly patients can be influenced markedly by personality and ethnic factors, sometimes in an adverse or "paradoxical" direction (Slater & Kastenbaum, 1966). Wine appeared to be an agent whose social connotations would facilitate rather than impede its physiological effectiveness.

The First Study

Our attention was directed first to a male ward whose patients were among the least impaired in the hospital. Medically and mentally, these men were capable of leading relatively normal lives within the protective environs of the institution. In point of fact, however, they tended to constrict themselves to parallel, isolated existence. Patterns of patient-patient interaction had been found to be minimal both on and off the ward. Conversation and other forms of socializing were seldom observed, nor did more than a handful involve themselves in solitary activities (e.g., painting, gardening) that seemed to yield satisfaction. Clinical experience with these patients indicated that they felt they had little that was worth communicating to each other. They regarded each other as being equally powerless to affect the course of life in the institution. Furthermore, there were signs of a definite intragroup prejudice, elderly men speaking disparagingly of their peers *because* of their age (e.g., "What do I want to talk with that old crock for? I got my own troubles."). Affectionate coaxings on the part of the ward staff and repeated contacts on the part of occupational therapists were largely responsible for whatever glimmerings of social and physical action one could discern in most of these patients.

This first study was designed to explore the general response of the institution to the introduction of wine as well as test the practicality of the mutual gratification model in producing favorable changes in patient-patient and patient-staff behavior. Twenty male patients (mean age: 76.6) were approached to participate in this study. All agreed to take part. The hospital's medical director personally checked into each case and indicated that wine posed no likely health problem for any of these patients. The participants were divided randomly into two groups of ten patients each. These groups met each weekday at 3 p.m. in separate day rooms on opposite ends of the ward. A participant observer (PO) on the staff of the Psychological Research Unit was assigned to each group.

For the first three weeks, members of Group A received servings of red port wine (1 1/2 oz., one refill available), while members of Group B received servings of grape juice. Appropriate glassware was introduced for this purpose instead of the usual paper cup or plasticware familiar in the administration of liquid drugs and juices. During the subsequent three-week period the beverages were reversed. The thirty-first session for each group was devised as a critical free-choice period in which all patients had their choice of either or both beverages.

The participants had agreed merely to come to the specified place at the specified time each day. No patient was required to accept the beverage that was offered to him, nor was he required to remain in the area—still less was he required to become "groupy" and sociable. It was entirely possible, then, that the participants would regard wine within the conventional drug-administration framework and not alter their solitary habits. The PO had been instructed simply to be available for mutual, equalitarian interactions if the patients showed an inclination to use him in that way. The PO was not to turn himself inside out to please or sitmulate the patients (i.e., to be completely a giver), nor to be a sort of group therapist. He was just to be with them as a person (apart from his record-keeping functions).

Results of this study have been published elsewhere (Kastenbaum 1965a; Kastenbaum & Slater, 1964). The major findings and impressions can be summarized as follows:

1. For the first time in the history of the hospital, patients spontaneously formed themselves into groups. The simple beverage-administration situation became elaborated into something of a social club. The "members" increasingly stepped outside of the patient role to function in an equalitarian manner as adults who enjoyed each other's company, the company of the PO, and of those staff members who dropped in from time to time;

2. The daily "club meetings" persisted for more than a year after the

termination point of the wine study *per se.* This continuation was entirely voluntary on the part of the patients, in fact, was engendered by their interest and insistence. The "charter members" occasionally admitted new members and maintained a mutually supportive group fabric. The group became a place where pleasures and complaints could be aired and shared with little fear of rejection or reprisal. Members whose medical condition worsened were given more than the usual amount of emotional support by their fellows, including regular visits to the "sick ward;"

3. Within the structure of the original study itself, wine was decisively preferred to the control beverage both in the critical free-choice session as the extended free-choice period that followed;

4. Group involvement was significantly greater under wine than under juice conditions during the first thirty sessions;

5. Patient behavior with the group improved markedly—more communication, more positive in spirit, more varied. Yet patients tended to return to their usual roles when on the ward. There were many flashes of what might be termed adult mutual gratification between patients and staff when the latter visited the groups, but not much obvious carry-over on the ward; and

6. The project was accepted by the hospital informally as well as administratively. Ears perked up. Staff members on other wards as well as the project ward expressed curiosity and enthusiasm. Invitations came to "do something like that on my ward." This reception was in some contrast to the more grudging, dutiful institutional response typically forthcoming when we attempted to initiate an applied or research-oriented psychological project.

The Second Study

Next, we accepted the invitation of the physician responsible for the rehabilitation unit. This unit consisted of adjoining male and female wards. Many, but not all, of the patients were involved in programs of intensive treatment for such purposes as rehabilitation of mobility, manual dexterity, and speech. The initial level of interaction on this unit was higher than in the first project ward, but there was also a greater sense of tension and pressure. Many patients felt that what happened on the rehabilitation unit would either "make them or break them." Fear of unsuccessful rehabilitation and fear of success (leading perhaps to a hoped-for-and-dreaded return to the community) aroused strong competing sentiments.

Goals of this project included the involvement of nursing personnel as key participants, broadening the participation of patients (female as well as male, including many with marked physical impairments), and diversifying the setting (intensive treatment on a bustling ward to add to the previous experience on a relatively quiet ward).

Three groups of patients were established: all-female, all-male, coed. Two members of the ward nursing staff accepted assignments as PO's, with the third PO provided by the research unit. A social group worker affiliated with the research unit provided preliminary training and continuous supervision for the PO's. Red port wine was served in appropriate stemware by the PO in each group; as before, the groups met every weekday afternoon. Patients could request juice in place of wine. After fifty sessions (ten weeks), analyses were made based upon direct observations in the group situation, follow-up interviews with the participating patients, and ratings made by the registered nurses on the rehabilitation unit before and after the project. Results have been presented elsewhere (Kastenbaum, 1965a; Kastenbaum & Simon, 1964) and are summarized below.

1. A core of involved, interacting patients developed within each of the three groups.

2. The all-male group showed the most rapid rate of development. From all indications it became the most cohesive and mutually gratifying group. In this case we were able to observe that the enhanced social interaction and self-esteem carried over beyond the group sessions *per se.*

3. The all-female group appeared to be the least cohesive and least gratifying. In general, the women consumed less wine than the men, and some displayed hesitation in accepting any wine at all.

4. The coed group did not flow as smoothly as the male-only, but seemed to produce more unusual and intense experiences. For example, one man with a history of mental hospitalization with dominant paranoid symptomatology had been on the verge of being transferred back to a mental hospital because of his uncooperative and idiosyncratic behavior. The coed wine group not only "saved" him, but elevated him into the role of a celebrated raconteur, an unfailing source of enlivenment for the group. Participants in this group quickly began to resemble alert, self-respecting citizens more than troubled, preoccupied geriatric patients.

Several hypotheses had been entertained while planning this study, but problems associated with repeated behavioral ratings by a panel of untrained and partially trained observers made it impossible to arrive at clear-cut conclusions. The general effect of this second study was to encourage the nursing service to develop social activation programs on their own. Several nurses and attendants now had tasted a bit of the satisfaction that can derive from patient-staff interactions that are predicated upon mutual pleasure. One of these new programs developed into the fourth study cited below.

The Third Study

These two modest successes were followed by a disaster. It was a constructive and instructive disaster to be sure, but, withal, a disaster. As part of a training and research project concerned with dying and death in later life, we had been devoting much attention to the hospital's intensive treatment unit. Several months were given to observation and to building rapport with patients and staff. Gradually and cooperatively a program was evolved with the aims of fostering alertness and sociability among patients on the intensive treatment unit.

It had been observed that a number of patients drifted into states of disorientation, "blankness," and isolation during their period of passive existence. Some patients who pulled through their crises and returned to their home wards seemed to have lost something: they appeared more shallow emotionally, less alert and interested mentally. Furthermore, we speculated that a general psychological decline induced not only by illness but also by decreased activity and stimulation might in some cases have contributed to death. It appeared worthwhile to develop, if possible, a more stimulating and rewarding psychosocial atmosphere to supplement the attentive and thorough medical-nursing care.

One aspect of this program was intended to increase the ward staff's knowledge of each patient. Increased knowledge, in turn, might be expected to enable the staff to enter into a more individualized relationship with the patient. Instead of labeling the patient primarily as "the new kidney in the first cubicle," the nurse would know that here was a retired schoolteacher from her own town, or a very proud man reluctant to admit any impairments but who had to be addressed via his left ear only. Ward staff below the registered nurse echelon were not permitted to acquaint themselves with the patient's history by consulting the medical records (hospital policy), and so were the least prepared to converse with or understand the individual patient although they generally devoted the greatest amount of time to actual contact (serving meals, giving bed-baths, etc.).

A simple procedure was developed to give ward personnel access to basic information regarding their patients, without running into conflict with hospital policy on confidentiality of medical records. Thumbnail sketches of all patients on the ward were prepared by the project staff and placed in a file box on the ward (with permission of hospital authorities). This file box was available for use at any time by any member of the staff. Cards were prepared for new admissions to the ward and both project and ward staff were asked to cooperate in adding to our knowledge of each patient.

This procedure is typical of the several small innovations that were gradually introduced after discussions with ward personnel. Let us turn directly to the most relevant innovation. Favorable advance reaction by three members of the ward staff and our previous experience with wine made it seem worthwhile to explore the possible value of beer in promoting the desired individual and ward changes. It was the consensus that beer seemed to be more appropriate that wine on this ward, both because this beverage was more familiar to most of the patients and because it seemed to possess one or two medical advantages. Accordingly, we made the necessary arrangements, talked it over with ward and project staff, then initiated the program which is described below in the information sheet distributed to ward personnel:

Fact Sheet: Beer

1. Beer is of medical value to some elderly people who do not have enough fluids in their body. Drinking beer, then, is one of the most pleasant ways of battling against dehydration.
2. Beer is of social value to those elderly people who enjoy it:
   a. It is an adult form of pleasure, and so encourages the patients to continue to feel and behave as responsible adults.
   b. It relaxes tensions, and so increases the sense of comfort, and makes it easier for the body to carry out its natural healing functions.
3. Beer is of particular value on an intensive care unit such as Ward X.
   a. Some patients feel they have come "to the end of the road" when they go to the "sick ward."
   b. Some other patients feel that they must just grimly endure their period of illness and lessened activity while on the "sick ward."
   c. Friends from the "home ward" are sometimes reluctant to visit their friends on the "sick ward" because they are afraid of becoming depressed and discouraged themselves.

(For reasons such as these, the serving of beer on Ward X was expected to be a visible indication that life was not necessarily in suspended animation while a person was receiving intensive medical-nursing treatment. Some patients would use the serving of beer as a clue that they were still expected to think, feel, and behave as responsible adults who could both give and receive pleasure. This attitude would attract more patient-visitors to the ward (more staff visitors, too?), perhaps reduce some of the complaints and demands made to the X staff, and almost certainly relieve some of the apathy and depression from which some Ward X patients suffer.)

4. Where is the beer coming from?

   The MHO-1520 project is financing a supply of beer for a sufficient period of time to permit an evaluation of how much benefit is produced. Long-range availability of beer will require other arrangements.

5. Who can have the beer?

   Those Ward X patients who have been given medical clearance and had prescriptions written by the ward physician. Drinking beer, of course, is completely voluntary, and is not forced upon any patient.

6. When will the beer be served?

   To begin with, beer will be served in the afternoon from approximately 1:45 to approximately 3:00 p.m. These starting and finishing times are *not* to be followed in a rigid way; they merely indicate the general range of time during which beer will be served. The beer will be served *daily,* including weekends (this was later amended to exclude Sundays). Beer-serving is a separate procedure—*not* to be carried out at the same time as dispensation of medications.

7. Lots of other questions will probably occur to you (and to us). Please bring these questions up as they occur. We will have to work out many of the answers as we go along. We expect you to have some of the answers for us, as well as the questions!

The beer phase of the program began in a slow, tentative way. The ward staff appeared somewhat unsure of the entire operation. "It will never work," went some of the mutterings. The self-conscious, stilted beginning was far from auspicious. But within a week there was response from the patients—favorable response. The staff began to smile and relax. Daily reports indicated an upsurge in patient-patient and patient-staff interaction and a general acceptance of the beer.

In less than three weeks it was evident that Ward X had a new look. Patients who had been wan, listless and "blank" now took interest in themselves, their fellow patients, and the outside world. There was a new undercurrent of conversation around the ward where previously silence had reigned. Although the "action" was concentrated in a particular place at a particular hour, patients and staff were enlivened throughout the day. The beer hour itself attracted an influx of visitors to the ward. These visitors included staff members, other patients, and friends and relations of the Ward X patients, all of whom added much to the general sense of enlivenment. The invisible "out of bounds" sign had been removed.

The resourcefulness of the ward staff produced a number of embellishments. One afternoon a phonograph and a stack of "old-timey" records appeared on the scene. The next day saw the appearance of beer steins and red-and-white checkered tablecloths. An attendant showed up with his polaroid camera to make snapshots that he gave to the patients and their visitors. Women and men were now sitting together during the afternoon "socials," conversing quietly or singing melodies remembered from years past. Staff members found the time to mingle with the patients on a social basis, and this seemed to strengthen their relationships in general.

Most of the important personages in the hospital visited the ward to see these new developments with their own eyes. A particularly significant visitor was a senior member of the nursing service who was famous as a "no-nonsense, hard-nosed babe." She planted her feet in the doorway of the "beer room" and gave the proceedings a long, severe scrutiny. Finally she rendered her judgment: "Say, this is the greatest!" Her broad smile seemed to dispel most of the lingering doubts that this program had succeeded in proving and establishing itself. It appeared that the project had succeeded with patients, ward staff, administration, and visitors.

The way up had been slow—but the descent was almost instantaneous. One influential member of the professional staff objected strongly. Essentially his position was that such a development was unprecedented, unnecessary, and improper. There should not be such goings-on in a medical setting; it lacked dignity. Furthermore, such a program invited the wrath of relatives, and there were relatives who know how to make trouble for a public institution if they so chose. One member of the ward staff concurred. She felt that it "wasn't right" in general, and that it might lead her personnel to neglect their other and more important responsibilities.

Naturally, the emergence of a determined opposition put a number of people on the spot. The hospital director reviewed the situation and decided in favor of continuing the project, recommending several steps that might lead to reconciliation of viewpoints and minimize further difficulties. But the ward personnel remained on the spot. They knew all too well that influential people in the hospital hierarchy had taken opposite positions. Whatever they did, and no matter how they did it, the ward staff was likely to incur the displeasure of somebody they would prefer to please. A sort of "freeze" resulted. Self-conscious and stilted actions returned; the spontaneity and overflowing good will suddenly evaporated.

There was only one alternative that promised to take the patients and the ward staff off the spot. Reluctantly, we contributed to the peaceable diminution and termination of the program on Ward X.

There are no villains in this piece. None of us wished to create an undignified atmosphere, interfere with the essential work of the unit, or stir up trouble for the hospital. And the "opposition" did not mean to slap down all attempts to introduce modifications. In retrospect it seems fairly clear that there are human potentials among both staff and patients which can be liberated for mutual benefit. And it also seems clear that ordinary preparation and effort are not adequate to ensure acceptance of a program—even a program that "works." One side might express alarm at the revolutionary happenings that seem to be generating disorder and disrepute on medical-nursing turf, while the other side might bemoan dogmatism, intolerance, rigidity, and whatnot on the part of the establishment. Neither doleful chorus is likely to improve matters. Somewhere along the line I neglected to consider sufficiently the possible case in which a mutual gratification situation brings about its own demise. Experience may be the best, but it is certainly not the most gentle of teachers.

The Fourth Study

The next incarnation of the beer-wine-mutual gratification theme made use of the increasing realization that an enduring program is most likely to result if it begins from the inside. Most personnel on the intensive treatment unit did not feel any pressing need to change the situation, especially in its psychosocial aspects. We had attempted to stimulate the need as well as develop a solution. Wouldn't it be more sensible to identify a need that had already impressed itself upon the staff?

Ward Z posed obvious difficulties. To this ward came the most severely incapacitated male patients, men who were grossly disoriented, who could not control their bodily functions, who required total care twenty-four hours a day. Medication was required around the clock and even the most elementary services were difficult to perform. It was a ward that made great demands on personnel while offering relatively few rewards. One of the supervisory nurses judged that Ward Z was ripe for a change. And so this fourth study came into being, this time in the form of close collaboration with Anne Volpe, R.N. The severely impaired patients, thirty-four of them, were transferred to a larger ward which was then provided with a phonograph, bulletin board, games, cards, checkers, and puzzles, as well as with tables for meals and activities.

Once again the beer bottles came out of the pharmacy. Six afternoons a week the patients were served beer, crackers and cheese. The men were attired in white shirts with ties every day.

The response to these innovations was immediate and favorable. The beer was greeted with special delight: "This is the real stuff!" "Ah, the golden drink!" These pleased remarks marked only the beginning of the behavioral effects. Within a one-month period the atmosphere of the ward in general and the behavior of individual patients had undergone a remarkable transformation. These just didn't seem to be the same patients who had been described for years as "confused, hostile, agitated, incontinent."

Before initiation of this project, twenty-six of the thirty-four patients had been incontinent and also had to be restrained by means of safety aprons to avoid self-inflicted injuries (i.e., tumbling out of a chair). By the end of the first month these conditions applied to only seventeen patients, and by the end of the second month all but nine men were free both from incontinence and from the necessity of wearing safety restraints. A similar pattern prevailed with the other behaviors and conditions—favorable changes occurred rapidly, persisted, and, in some instances, spread more widely through the ward (Volpe & Kastenbaum, 1967). For example, the number of patients who could ambulate increased from seven to twenty-five and remained at that level. Another example: while only two patients could be allowed to leave the ward to participate in social activities elsewhere in the hospital before the project started, the number of "exportable" men increased to five within one month, and to sixteen within two months. Some of the behavior changes associated with the treatment program are summarized in Table I.

Another index of improvement is the amount of psychotropic

BEHAVIOR CHANGE ASSOCIATED WITH TREATMENT PROGRAM						
BEHAVIOR	BASELINE		1 MONTH		2 MONTHS	
	N	%	N	%	N	%
Incontinent	26	76%	17	50%	9	27%
Jacket-Restraint	26	76%	9	27%	4	12%
Ambulatory	7	21%	25	74%	25	74%
Individual Activity	10	29%	26	76%	26	76%
Group Activity	7	21%	17	50%	24	71%
Music Responsivity	16	48%	16	48%	30	88%
Off-Ward Social Activities	2	6%	5	15%	16	48%

Number equals 34

medication required. Baseline data show that Thorazine (50 mg. q.i.d.) and Mellaril (75 mg. q.i.d.) were being administered to approximately three-fourths of the ward population. Within a month there was an appreciable shrinkage in both the number of patients receiving these drugs and the dosage levels: Thorazine administration was reduced to one-fourth of the population and Mellaril lowered in dosage to 10 mg. b.i.d. (prn) and now given only to one-tenth of the population. By the end of the second month all Thorazine administration had terminated, and Mellaril usage continued at the same low level that had been reached after the end of the first month (See Table 2).

This rather disheartening collection of grossly-impaired old men and their heavily-burdened caretakers had become transformed into something resembling a community of human beings. Less was done *to* and *for* the patients; more could be done *with* them, e.g., ward parties, including "mixers" with female patients (on the initiative of the men themselves). Conversation among patients and between patients and staff no longer was a rarity. Men who had a long history of being "totally confused and disoriented" were playing checkers and cards,

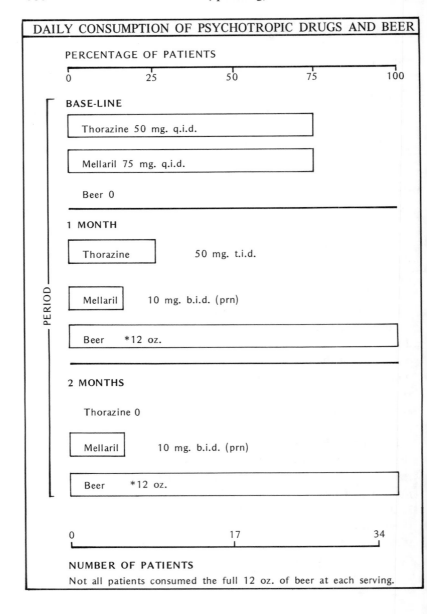

DAILY CONSUMPTION OF PSYCHOTROPIC DRUGS AND BEER

PERCENTAGE OF PATIENTS

0   25   50   75   100

BASE-LINE

Thorazine 50 mg. q.i.d.

Mellaril 75 mg. q.i.d.

Beer 0

1 MONTH

Thorazine   50 mg. t.i.d.

Mellaril   10 mg. b.i.d. (prn)

Beer   *12 oz.

2 MONTHS

Thorazine 0

Mellaril   10 mg. b.i.d. (prn)

Beer   *12 oz.

PERIOD

0   17   34

NUMBER OF PATIENTS
Not all patients consumed the full 12 oz. of beer at each serving.

helping to decorate the ward to mark changing seasons or holidays, making their own beds, and generally helping to keep their quarters in shape. Time began to mean something again. The day no longer stretched out endlessly, and needs no longer demanded instant fulfillment. Thus, patients now could wait their turn in the barber shop, and could remind the nurses that "It's beer time, isn't it?"

Perhaps the best illustration of the changes observed in the "Us"/"Them" relationship was a spontaneous action on the part of the ward staff. Ordinarily the half-hour lunch break is a most welcome opportunity for the personnel to get away from the patients they are "servicing" all day. This is especially the case when the patients are as impaired as those on Ward Z. But the Ward Z personnel decided to take their lunch breaks right on the ward, eating side by side with the patients. This action seemed to make a profound impression on the men. One scarcely could have planned a more effective or authentic way of conveying the sentiment that these forgotten old men were still part of the human race. Yet it is important to remember that this action was not required or asked of the staff; it just developed naturally with the new interpersonal climate.

A Few Things to Mull Over

What is to be learned from these small ventures? Here are some of the points that we are continuing to mull over:

1. It does seem possible to go all the way from an abstract general theory (in this case, developmental-field) to action programs in gerontology. Why isn't this attempted more often? Do the "theory-spinners" and "do-gooders" have to remain discreetly apart from each other ("Us"/"Them")? What a pity, if true! Perhaps we should require that gerontologists interested in both theory and action should grow separate heads so that these inclinations remain in separate containers—but it may be a little late in the evolutionary process to comply with

this demand. Although we have not sorted out all the implications of these experiences for theory and application, we do have the strong impression that we have learned more than would have been the case had ideas and action not banged heads together.

2. Bruises and bumps are the natural consequences of banging heads together. In attempting to read our own bumps (a neo-Gallian self-analysis), it has become obvious that we are deficient in certain mental faculties. Cool, dispassionate perspective appears to be one of the deficiencies—at least, we did not have enough of this faculty when a conflict situation developed on Ward X. From the role of an "objective" researcher we slipped into the battling togs of a partisan. Accordingly, we probably were more inadequate in both roles than would have been the case if we had restricted ourselves to either one or the other. Furthermore, it is entirely possible that the pressure to meet daily problems in the various projects distracted us from adequate elaboration of the conceptual rationale. Better theory could have produced more effective action. The reverse could also have been true: perhaps our need to tinker with theory led us to neglect some operations in the field. Better practical management could have yielded more satisfactory results even with the drag of a mediocre theory. In short, a formidable range of talents is required to sustain an applied project within a systematic conceptual structure. These talents include both creative and critical mentalities, flexibility, energy, and a highly developed gift for devising and carrying through strategies of implementation. Few individuals possess in themselves all these talents. And it is probably even more rare to possess the art to use these talents with the proper balance and timing. It is the fortunate research staff that collectively possesses the full range of necessary talents, and also the knack of using them well. With growing uneasiness we begin to suspect that most gerontologists veer away from theoretical-action programs simply because they know what dangers lurk. Perhaps, then, we should be mulling over the education and training of future gerontologists. Can more be done to develop the necessary range of talents for planning and

conducting action studies that are intimately linked with theory? Can we develop new models for research teams that might be able to get the job done?

3. Granted that this series of small ventures had its deficiencies in both conception and execution, it remains true that some favorable results were observed. The extent of favorable social and behavioral change seems to have been directly proportional to the pleasure which was engendered among the patients and staff, separately and jointly. Gratification, rather than obligation, was the basis for change, and this does tend to support the conceptual rationale.

4. Behavior change that is predicated upon expectations for mutual gratification can be distinguished from that which is brought about by more traditional means. *Spontaneity* is one of the best examples of this difference. In each of the four studies the participants (patients and staff) introduced a number of constructive innovations. Some of these innovations could have been introduced by the project staff, others, (such as Ward Z personnel lunching with their patients) would probably not have occurred to the project staff and could not have been requested or demanded in any event. The innovations "worked" because they grew out of the situation. Basically, all that had to be accomplished experimentally was to gain initial acceptance for the project and help the participants to develop the perception that the situation had changed and was amenable to still further change. The details then took care of themselves. This procedure contrasts with conventional programs aimed at step-by-step therapeutic attainments. When one objective seems to be reached, then the next is attacked. In each onslaught the research or innovation staff must once again muster its own ideas and energies to encounter the resistance ahead. Spontaneity is likely to be an intrusion rather than an asset once the plan has been forged. The full resources of "Them" (including their intimate knowledge of the situational microstructure) are not engaged. They are still being done-for by "Us," and may even be ungrateful enough to feel done-in, even though we are nothing but goodhearted and efficient. Is it

not more thorough, natural, and enjoyable simply to develop a mutual gratification situation that is capable of playing out its own destiny?

5. This is really the same point as above, faintly disguised and looking for a second chance to express itself. The person who enacts the role of expert in planning or modifying the gerontopolis is in some danger of working against the very results he seeks to achieve. The elder is not necessarily being stubborn and ungrateful if he fails to enthuse over the charming new arrangements that have been made for him; perhaps he is simply expressing his recognition that the expert programming has the effect of reinforcing his shrunken identity as One-Who-Is-To-Be-Helped. An example is needed here, so we will make it a gentle one.

Cautela (Chapter 5) has observed that the environment of the institutionalized elder is likely to offer minimal stimulus variability. He suggests that we will be helping the geriatric patient if we can bring about an increase in stimulus variability. To achieve this and other goals, Cautela proposes the application of behavior therapy principles as embodied, for example, in the token economy, programmed instruction ("teaching machines"), desensitization and shaping-by-reinforcement approaches. It is almost unnecessary to state that I am sympathetic with this approach because Cautela and I have, in fact, been working together on some of these projects. However, a behavior therapy approach that is adept on its own terms could miss the point when it is applied in the gerontopolis. Assume, for example, that such a program is successful in producing heightened stimulus variability. Can we be entirely confident that this effect will be a favorable one from the elder's viewpoint? No, indeed. I would contend that "stimulus variability" can make the life of the institutionalized elder more intolerable and frustrating unless it is perceived as occurring within a meaningful situation. "Meaningful" is, of course, an overworked term in psychology and psychiatry; but it is used here in a fairly specific sense. I am referring to the perception of myself-as-active-agent- in-a situation-where-it-makes-a-difference-what-I-do-and-how-I-do-it.   This perception often is lacking in the institutionalized elder who senses that he is existing neither in his own time nor his own place. Consequently, he has little eye for possible stimuli. To cause more lights to flash on and off, more bells to ring, more happenings of various sorts, is not necessarily to open an enriched world to him. Rather the elder might be distracted and dismayed by *an increase in stimulation that has no intrinsic relationship to himself.* If he is already estranged from the *situation* and the situation becomes more salient, active, and complex, then the individual may feel an even greater need to overcontrol, "distanciate" himself, withdraw.

Furthermore, we should examine more closely the observation that the institutional environment lacks stimulus variability. It is this observation that makes it appear necessary to introduce new phenomena into the environment. Is it perhaps the case that the observed lack of variability is effect as well as cause? In other words, does the elderly patient (and the staff, to a lesser degree) inhabit an oversimplified, constricted perceptual world because they have not learned to appreciate the variability that actually exists in and around them? Even within the special, limited framework of the gerontopolis there is usually a fairly complex mixture of personalities (to touch upon only the human components of the environment). If the inhabitants seem blank or two-dimensional to each other, then the cause is as much to be sought in the area of perceptual and cognitive differentiation as in the "actual" properties of the individuals themselves. Why don't "They" (i.e., "We") see each other in a richer, more varied way?

This question brings us back to the dreadfully persistent theme that has been spinning itself out since page one: the basis upon which interpersonal relationships are predicated is perhaps the single most important factor to consider in understanding or attempt to modify the life situation of the elderly person. Once the expectation of *mutual gratification* has been established as the primary basis for the relationship, most of the other benefits have an opportunity to flow as naturally as brew from the keg, or wine from the bottle.

REFERENCES

Kastenbaum, R. Engrossment and perspective in later life: A developmental field approach. In R. Kastenbaum (Ed.), *Contributions to the psychobiology of aging.* New York: Springer, 1965.

Kastenbaum, R. Wine and fellowship in aging: An exploratory action program. *Journal of Human Relations* 1965, *13*, 266-276. (a)

Kastenbaum, R. Developmental-field theory and the aged person's inner experience. *The Gerontologist,* 1966, *6,* 10-13.

Kastenbaum, R. Multiple perspectives on a geriatric "Death Valley." *Community Mental Health Journal,* 1967, *3,* 21-29.

Kastenbaum, R. *Humans . . .Aging.* New York: Free Press, in press.

Kastenbaum, R., & Durkee, N. Elderly people view old age. In R. Kastenbaum (Ed.), *New thoughts on old age.* New York: Springer, 1964.

Kastenbaum, R. & Durkee, N. Young people view old age. In R. Kastenbaum (Ed.), *New thoughts on old age.* New York: Springer, 1964. (a)

Kastenbaum, R., & Simon, W. Wine and morale in the rehabilitation of elderly patients. Unpublished manuscript, Cushing Hospital, Framingham, Mass., 1964.

Kastenbaum, R., & Slater, P. E. Effects of wine on the interpersonal behavior of geriatric patients: An exploratory study. In R. Kastenbaum (Ed.), *New thoughts on old age.* New York: Springer, 1964.

Leake, C. D., & Silverman, M. *Alcoholic beverages in clinical medicine.* Chicago: Year Book Medical, 1966.

Lolli, G., Serianni, E., Banissoni, F., Golder, G. Mariani, A., McCarthy, R. G., & Toner, M. The use of wine and other alcoholic beverages by Italians and Americans of Italian extraction. *Quarterly Journal of Studies on Alcohol,* 1953, *14,* 395-405.

Sadoun, R., Lolli, G., & Silverman, M. *Drinking in French culture.* New Brunswick, N.J.: Publications Division, Rutgers Center of Alcohol Studies, 1965.

Slater, P. E., & Kastenbaum, R. Paradoxical effects of drugs: Some personality and ethnic correlates. *Journal of the American Geriatrics Association,* 1966, *14,* 1016-1034.

Volpe, A., & Kastenbaum, R. Beer & "TLC" in a geriatric hospital. *American Journal of Nursing,* 1967, *67,* 100-103.

23:: THE PAVLOVIAN BASIS OF OLD AGE*

JOSEPH CAUTELA

The Pavlovian analysis of old age has relevance for a number of reasons:

1. Some investigators hold that from a developmental viewpoint the aged individual can be viewed as functioning on a primitive level. Behavior is more apt to be determined by the formation of conditioned reflexes.

2. The geriatric individual is likely to have some kind of cerebral malfunctioning. Pavlov's work on brain damage and its effect on the formation of conditioned reflexes is particularly relevant in this regard.

3. The usual environment of the geriatric patient is one of repetition of monotonous stimulation and sensory isolation.

4. The learning deficits of the aged, such as the loss of previously-established habits and the difficulty of forming new habits, are the kinds of behaviors investigated in the Pavlovian laboratories.

Accordingly, it is the purpose of this paper to: 1) develop a Pavlovian theory of the aged which is consistent with his speculations and empirical findings; 2) try to relate present knowledge about the aged, especially research on learning, to the Pavlovian system; and 3) generate new hypotheses about the aged that can be verified empirically.

The Pavlovian analysis of old age is derived from information provided by Pavlov concerning old age, brain damage, development of inhibition and sleep, and the acquisition and extinction of reflexes.

Based on a paper presented at the 19th annual meeting of the Gerontological Society. New York City, November 5, 1966.

Pavlov's Speculation About Old Age

In Pavlov's extensive writings and empirical research relatively little direct mention is made of the aged. A careful scrutiny of Pavlov's works, however, does reveal certain characteristics attributed by him to the aged individual. The senile individual is viewed as declining in activity and the inhibitory process is impossible or greatly weakened (1928, p. 293). In some cases, only a strong US can provoke the inhibitory processes (1957, p. 241). There is also very weak excitability in the cortex of aged animals (1928, p. 293; 1957, p. 241). In the aged individual conditioned reflexes previously produced in a regular and stereotyped way often become irregular and chaotic (1957, pp. 337). For this reason the nervous system of the aged individual is considered "the weak type." The mobility of the nervous system can then be said to decline as the result of old age.

To put the above statements relative to old age in proper perspective, it is necessary to present a brief review of Pavlov's theoretical speculations concerning the nervous system.

In discussing the properties of the nervous system, Pavlov assigns great importance to the excitatory and inhibitory functions of the cortex. At any one time, the balance of excitation and inhibitation in the nervous system can be on a continuum from the total inhibition of sleep to an excitable stage in which conditioned reflexes are formed rapidly while it is difficult to obtain negative reflexes (or inhibition). On the bases of the balance between the excitability and inhibitory states in a particular individual and the mobility (i.e. excitability of the N.S.), Pavlov (1957, pp. 313-341) distinguishes four types of nervous systems: 1) strong equilibrated labile type; 2) strong equilibrated calm type; 3) strong unequilibrated type; and 4) weak type. The strong Equilibrated Nervous System is characterized by an almost equal balance between excitation and inhibition. The organism forms positive conditioned reflexes in a steady, rapid manner and inhibition can be developed in a similar way. The Strong Equilibrated Nervous System is divided into two types according to its mobility. Strong Equilibrated type *labile* in activity (analogous to Hippocrates' sanguine type) and the Strong Equilibrated type characterized by *calmness and inertness* (analogous to Hippocrates' phlegmatic type).

In the Strong Unequilibrated type of nervous system the organism has high cortex excitability and very low inhibitory processes. Conditioned reflexes form very rapidly, but extinguish slowly. Inhibitory states are not stable. In the Hippocratic classification, this would be labeled the choleric (impetuous) type.

The Weak Type of nervous system is characterized by a "manifest weakness both of the excitatory and inhibitory processes;" these people never fully adapt themselves to the conditions of life, are easily broken, often and quickly become ill and neurotic as a result of difficult life situations or of the difficult nervous tasks which we place before them ... this type, as a rule, cannot be improved to any considerable degree by training and discipline; it becomes fit only under particularly favourable, deliberately created conditions, or, as we usually say, in "hothouse conditions (1957, pp. 338-339)."

Pavlov also notes that extreme external inhibition readily occurs in the weak personality type (i.e., the conditioned reflexes in the process of acquisition are easily disrupted by extra stimuli) (1957, p. 260).

From Pavlov's comments concerning the aged and his discussion of the weak type of nervous system, it is clear that this type is applicable to the personality of the geriatric patient (1957, p. 241). An examination of the recent literature in the geriatric field tends to support the characteristics attributed by Pavlov to the aged individual. In a study using electric shock as a US and tone as a CS, Botwinick & Kornetsky (1960) found that older *S*s conditioned less readily and extinguished earlier than young control *S*s.

Other studies show that reaction time in the geriatric individual is poor and can fluctuate easily (Koga, 1923); his attention span is poor (Doppelt & Wallace, 1955); and he is easily distracted from his ongoing task. It has been observed, too, that it is difficult to extinguish old and inappropriate habits of the aged individual (Ruch, 1934). In other words, a decline in the inhibitory process is evident.

This decline in the inhibitory process of the aged is clearly demonstrated in an experiment by Pollack & Kastenbaum (1964). They compared young and old Ss in their ability to slow down a writing task. Pollack & Kastenbaum concluded that elderly men (mean age: 72.2 years) have less inhibition ability than young men (mean age: 19.1 years). After completing the inhibition task, a number of elderly Ss volunteered introspective remarks such as, "I didn't want to slow down—I'm used to doing things quickly," while others said, "I can't slow down, even if you ask me to. I think of how little time I have left!" An interpretation of the verbal reports of the aged Ss could be postulated in terms of their attempts to reduce dissonance created by poor performance.

If there is some validity in Pavlov's classification of the aged individuals into weak personality types, an interesting problem emerges. In young adulthood the aged individuals were distributed among four personality types. Unless one assumes that the weak personality types are constitutionally more suited to live longer than the other personality types, which is unlikely since Pavlov emphasizes the frailty of the nervous system and the total organism of the "weak types," the emergence of this type must be a correlate of age. Assuming that some of the aged individuals were other than weak personality types earlier in their lives, their adjustment to old age with its decline of excitatory and inhibitory processes might be more difficult. On the other hand, the individual with a weak personality type has less adjustment to make in old age since his excitatory and inhibitory processes will involve relatively less change than that encountered in the other personality types. The non-weak types, in all probability, have a greater sense of loss, as compared to the other types, upon reaching old age. On the other hand, since the aging process is a gradual one, the transition to the "weak type" may not involve any greater adjustment than that encountered by the individuals who are weak types before old age occurs. If the pre-aged personality type can be determined from case records and interviews, then one could compare the effect of personality type on the behavior of the aged individual.

Cortical Damage and Conditioned Reflexes

Pavlov studied unconditioned and conditioned reflexes only as a means of achieving more understanding of the higher nervous system (for Pavlov this meant the cortex). It was evident to Pavlov, as it is to present day investigators, that a great deal could be learned about the cortex by examining it under normal and pathological conditions. Besides studying the intact normal animal, Pavlov and his associates performed many experiments designed to determine the relationship between cortical damage caused by extirpation of different parts of the cerebral hemispheres.

Pavlov (1957, p. 304) considered the cerebral hemispheres as representing a system of analyzers, which decompose the complexity of external and internal worlds into separate elements and moments and then connect the phenomena thus analyzed with one or another activity of the organism. In this regard the visual and auditory systems are "analyzers." The effect of extirpations on formation and elimination of conditioned reflexes depended primarily on the analyzers involved. Since Pavlov's methods of determining precisely what part of the nervous system was involved by extirpation were crude by present day standards, he worked backwards by inferring the nature and extent of the analyzers extirpated from the behavioral phenomena. In general, Pavlov observed that by fully extirpating the cerebral hemispheres or removing certain parts of them either all, or certain groups of, conditioned reflexes disappeared (1957, p. 291). He concluded from these studies that the cerebral hemispheres are, in effect, the organs of temporary connections, the birthplace of conditioned reflexes.

Extirpating part or all of a particular analyzer not only affects the conditioned reflexes of that analyzer, but often causes damage to irradiate to other parts of the cortex. One can deduce from this observation that the effect of some slight brain damage on the formation of conditioned reflexes may involve more than one analyzer and thus lead to an extensive loss of already established conditional reflexes, as well as great impairment to the function of new conditioned reflexes. The damage does not, of course, always irradiate to other parts of the cortex, so that sometimes the ability to form new conditioned responses may be only slightly impaired, especially if the conditioned reflexes do not involve the analyzer damaged by extirpation.

Gantt (1964) has demonstrated that many individuals (humans), with severe organic impairment cannot form conditioned reflexes (crs). Gantt has developed a conditioned reflex test as an aid to studying various psychiatric patients. The test involves the ability to generalize crs and the ability to form differentiated crs as well as simple crs. Gantt's work (1964, p. 38) with dogs and with human patients has led him to develop a hierarchy of the aspects of the adaptive cr function. These, when arranged in order from the least to the most serious, are: 1) Disturbance of the latent period of the cr; 2) Speed of formation of the cr; 3) Ability to form differentiated crs, (i.e. to positive and negative signals); 4) Disturbance of the function of generalization; 5) Ability to form spontaneous, but not integrated, crs; 6) Failure to obtain previously formed crs; 7) Inability to form an experimental cr; 8) Lack of retention of very old crs, including those to word signals, and failure of the ability to carry out orders; and 9) Failure of forming some unconditioned reflexes, e.g., the orienting reflex—seen only in severe organic cases.

As can be seen from the hierarchy, one could expect that senile patients with minor organic impairment will show impairment of the ability to form new habits and some impairment of the ability to retain some recently learned habits and, unless they are severely damaged, they will retain old habits (crs). Most gerontologists have observed that geriatric patients find it difficult to learn new habits easily and often fail to retain recently learned habits. Also it is plausible that old habits, which are no longer appropriate in terms of the patients' physiological functioning and immediate surroundings, interfere with the acquisition of new habits (Birren, 1964, p. 158).

Gantt's conditioned reflex test can be used as an aid in differential diagnosis when a question of brain damage is involved. In a study concerned with the application of conditioning procedures to the investigation of aging, Whitman, Brown, & Gantt (1964) found that all aged patients (median age, 67.5 years) with chronic brain syndrome failed on the conditioned reflex test (received a "D" score), as compared to more than half of the patients, without a diagnosis of CNS damage who received an "A" rating (good). An interesting feature of this study is that some of the patients not diagnosed as having CNS damage received a "D" score. This led the authors to conclude that impairment in the ability to form conditioned reflexes may be a precursor of chronic brain syndrome.

The Pavlovian Theory of Hypnosis and Sleep

In a number of his experiments, Pavlov observed that at times a dog would become drowsy and fall asleep (1928, p. 250). Since the dog in this state interrupted the ongoing experiment, and because Pavlov saw this as an interesting phenomenon in its own right, he set out to systematically investigate sleep during the experimental session. His investigations in this regard led him to conclude that monotonous and continuous stimulation together with conditions of confinement and isolation are prime factors in producing the phenomenon of sleep and drowsiness in the experimental session. Pavlov found that various procedures could prevent what he called "hypnotic behavior" and sleep during the experimental session. These included: reinforcing the animal by food (Pavlov 1928, p. 253); short experimental sessions spaced long intervals apart (Pavlov, 1928, p. 253); calling, stroking, and slapping during the experimental session; changing stimulation or introducing new stimuli (Pavlov, 1928, p. 252). Pavlov considered sleep as an irradiation of inhibition throughout the cortex (1957, p. 273). Hypnosis is a form of sleep in which inhibition develops slowly and is not complete inhibition. Hypnosis is the state between normal wakefulness and sleep.

Using human Ss, Das (1965) was able to produce a state of drowsiness and sleep similar to that of Pavlov's dogs by presenting some of the same conditions used by Pavlov to the Ss (a monotonous stimulus while Ss sat in a confining dentist-type chair).

Geriatric patients are often observed to be lethargic, drowsy, asleep, or in a coma. They often seem to have a hypnotic-like stare similar to the "hypnotic trances" observed by Pavlov as occurring between normal wakefulness and sleep. Geriatric patients are often confined to their beds, rooms, or wards under conditions of isolation where stimulus variability is minimal. Little or no reinforcement is presented to the patient other than that which may occur accidentally either by the staff or generated by the patients' own behavior. For the most part, this lack of activity and sleep-like behavior is attributed usually to the patients' old age or some kind of brain damage. One could make as good an interpretation of the behavior by calling it a result of the lack of adequate stimulus variability, isolation, and minimal reinforcement. Isolation is enhanced by poor sensory acuity, often found in geriatric patients. It is possible that brain damage could exacerbate the manifestation of minimal behavior.

If we follow Pavlov's methods of eliminating drowsiness and sleep during the experimental sessions in the manipulation of the behavior of the geriatric patient, stimulus variability should be increased and more reinforcements should be introduced, especially if they follow any kind of activity on the part of the patient. One must be very cautious in doing so, however, with the geriatric patient. Overloading the central nervous system through stimulus variability and reinforcement can produce a deleterious effect. As was discussed above, the geriatric patient is quite susceptible to external inhibition.

Stimulus variability should only be introduced in a systematic way, so that the useful and ongoing behaviors are not inhibited. Also, too strong a conditioned stimulus can actually produce inhibitory states in the organism. Pavlov labeled this "transmarginal inhibition," (1957, p. 277). In discussing transmarginal inhibition, Pavlov says: "The cortical cell possesses a certain limit of efficiency, and beyond this point there arises inhibition which results from excessive functional exhaustion of the cell. The limit of efficiency is not constant; it undergoes both acute and chronic changes in cases of inaction, hypnosis, disease and in old age. This inhibition arises sometimes instantaneously and sometimes manifests itself only when the super-powerful stimuli are repeated."

It is evident from the above that a carefully planned research program is needed to determine the maximum amount of stimulus variability (quantitative and qualitative) that can be tolerated by geriatric patients without increasing disorganization in the patient. Pavlov (1957, pp. 328-334) and others (Gantt, 1964); Teplov (Gray, 1964) have developed methods of determining the toleration level of the nervous system of particular individuals to excessive stimulation and protracted states of inhibition. These procedures can be used in individual patients and a specific program developed for each individual. Although this is a valuable procedure, it can be time-consuming and costly. Procedures have to be developed aimed at the manipulation of the total environmental situation of geriatric patients and which will take into account the toleration level of the "typical" geriatric patient.

The above statements concerning Pavlov's views toward old age, brain damage, hypnosis, and sleep can be analyzed and developed into a more explicit Pavlovian theory of the aged than is presented by Pavlov himself.

According to Pavlov, the development of old age is a process whereby the efficiency of the cortical cells is reduced so that these cells can be easily exhausted. If monotonous stimulation is presented, this means that the stimulation is repeatedly affecting the same cortical cells. This results in an exhaustion of the excitatory substance and inhibition occurs. Since the cortical cells have already lost some efficiency due to aging, then less monotonous stimulation is needed to produce inhibition than in younger individuals. Also with old age, the mobility of the nervous system declines. This means that the speed with which excitatory states are reinstated is hampered under normal conditions. This is seen behaviorally in the lack of ability of the aged population to adjust to change in a rapid manner.

Since the aged individual has a "weak" personality, it is difficult for him to learn new responses. What new responses are learned can be easily inhibited by distracting stimuli (external inhibition) or very strong stimulation (transmarginal inhibition). As a result of the aged individual's poor inhibitory processes, it is difficult to extinguish old habits that interfere with the present adjustment of the aged to new demands brought about by reduction of physical capability and new social adjustment. For the geriatric patient who has some kind of central nervous system damage, it is even more difficult to form new conditioned reflexes and maintain them. Also it is more difficult to eliminate undesirable habits.

The Implications of Pavlovian Theory for Research

Tests, such as those devised by Gantt (1964), can be used as an aid in the diagnosis of brain damage. Many times central nervous system damage is inferred because some behavior appears stereotyped and bizarre. Often this behavior is due to faculty conditioning and reinforcement contingencies. The conditioning of individual subjects can be tested to determine the subject's ability to profit from certain learning procedures. These conditioning tests should include the most effective analyzer (or sensory modality) for learning new tasks. In other words, if it is found that the use of conditioned stimuli of a visual nature leads to more rapid and stable conditioning than stimuli of an auditory nature, then visual aids should be primarily used in teaching that particular geriatric patient. An attempt should be made to find a balance between sensory isolation and overloading of stimulation. Pavlov had developed tests to determine the ability of organisms to withstand strong stimulation and protracted inhibition (1957, p. 331). If a project is conducted studying many geriatric patients, then perhaps some data will emerge pointing to the general range of stimulus change and the stimulus intensity needed to shape productive activity.

Pavlov has suggested that the aged individual has a weak personality type. Pavlov (1957, pp. 313-341) and Teplov (Gray, 1964) have developed methods of determining personality types. It would be interesting to test a number of geriatric patients to validate the Pavlovian hypothesis.

For example, Pavlov observed that in the strong equilibrated type, caffeine increases the effect of the excitatory processes and diminishes it in the weak type (1957, pp. 228-230). Pavlov was one of the first investigators to notice the paradoxical effect of drugs. A recent controlled study of tranquilizer and stimulant effects on geriatric patients seems to provide clear support for Pavlov's observations concerning the relationship of drugs to personality types. Slater & Kastenbaum (1966) found that many geriatric patients respond in a paradoxical way to both tranquilizers and stimulants and that the patients exhibiting these paradoxical responses were functioning on a lower behavioral level than those Ss who responded in the expected manner (i.e., if they were given a tranquilizer, the drug had tranquilizing effects and if given a stimulant, the drug had stimulating effects).

It would be interesting to compare the frequency and duration of dreams of the aged with those of younger subjects. According to Pavlov, one would predict that the aged would have a lower frequency of dreams with less duration than younger subjects. According to Kleitman (1960), dreaming involves excitation in certain parts of the cortex (e.g., the visual area). Since aged individuals have low excitability of the cortex, one would predict that they would be apt to dream less than younger subjects who usually have greater overall excitability of the cortex.

Another interesting speculation concerns the effect of tactual stimulation on learning. As mentioned above, Pavlov found that stroking the animal tended to prevent lethargy and sleep during the experimental session. This result was probably due to the increased excitation caused by stroking. In the aged individual, since the general excitability level of the cortex is low, conditioning is hindered. If the aged individual is hugged or caressed, or even kissed, this will increase the excitability of the cortex and facilitate learning. An experiment could be designed in which a group of aged individuals receive tactual stimulation and then are given simple learning tasks, such as paired associative learning. This group can be compared to a control group not receiving the tactual stimulation. It would also be interesting to compare the tactual group with a group whose cortical excitability is increased by another means (e.g., drugs).

The kinds of research programs just outlined may appear at first to invade the privacy of the geriatric individual, as well as place some stress on him. However, if the tests are administered slowly, it has been my experience that the geriatric patients welcome a change from the routine of the hospital. In other words, the experimenters become a source of stimulation change.

REFERENCES

Birren, J. E. *The psychology of aging.* Englewood Cliffs, N. J.: Prentice-Hall 1964.

Botwinik, J., & Kornetsky, C. Age differences in the acquisition and extenction of the GSR. *Journal of Gerontology,* 1960, *15,* 83-84.

Das, J. P. The Pavlovian theory of hypnosis: An evaluation. In R. E. Shor, & M. Orne (Eds.), *The nature of hypnosis.* New York: Holt, Rinehart and Winston, 1965.

Doppelt, J. E., & Wallace, W. L. The performance of older people on the Wechsler adult intelligence scale. *American Psychology,* 1955, *10,* 338-339.

Gantt, W. H. The conditional reflex as an aid in the study of the psychiatric patient. In C. Franks (Ed.), *Conditioning techniques in clinical practice and research.* New York: Springer, 1964.

Gray, J. A. *Pavlov's typology.* New York: Pergamon, 1964.

Kleitman, N. Patterns of dreaming. *Scientific American,* 1960, *203,* 82-88.

Koga, Y., & Morant, G. M. On the degree of association between reaction times in the case of different senses. *Biometrika,* 1923, *15,* 346-372.

Pavlov, I. P. *Lectures on conditioned reflexes.* New York: International Publications, 1928.

Pavlov, I. P. *Experimental psychology and other essays.* New York: Philosophical Library, 1957.

Pollock, K., & Kastenbaum, R. Delay of gratification in later life: An experimental analog. In R. Kastenbaum (Ed.), *New thoughts on old age.* New York: Springer, 1964.

Ruch, F. L. The differentiative effect of age upon learning. *Journal of Psychology,* 1934, *11,* 261-286.

Slater, P. E., & Kastenbaum, R. Paradoxical reactions to drugs: Some personality and ethnic correlates. *Journal of the American Geriatrics Association,* 1966, *14,* 1016-1034.

24:: ALTERNATE PREDICTIONS CONCERNING DESPAIR IN OLD AGE

S. SHERWOOD and T. NADELSON

Since the preliminary aspect of theory making in the field of human behavior often derives from personal reflection and insight into one's own phenomenology, the student of psychology has the advantage of easy but not untrammeled access into the subject he investigates. That which may provide both the spark and richness to formulations concerning behavior may also serve as a block to objective verification. The clinician-therapist, gathering data and impressions primarily from contact with patients, has additional problems in creating theoretical models. The "pathological" conditions he observes may not always present a rounded picture of existing conditions; furthermore he interacts with, and thus may affect, the data he observes. For the clinician, the general theory of human behavior he evolves may be "internally" validated. That is, by observing similar phenomena repeatedly, he checks for himself the goodness of fit of his model.

Such theory, perhaps, is satisfying and valuable without the application of the usual empirical procedures, but it can by no means be considered scientifically verified. At times such theory may seem closed to the usual empirical procedures employed by researchers. Such

This paper is expanded from a presentation made at the 21st annual meeting of The Gerontological Society, Inc., Denver, Colorado, November 1, 1968. The research reported here was supported in part by USPHS grants CH23-26 and HS00470 (formerly CH00436).

theory, we would contend, may only "seem" closed to empirical testing. It is the contention of this paper that often it may be possible to redefine terms operationally and bring to bear critical tests on such social psychological formulations. Furthermore, the attempt to delineate on logical grounds both the empirical conditions that, if observed, would tend to support the theory as well as those that, if observed, would tend to refute the theory can reveal whether the theory is potentially useful for "predicting" behavior. Even when there is some question concerning the interpretation of theory, the empirical investigation of the suggested formulations may bear fruitful results.

Whether a theory is clinically derived or otherwise, such tests not only yield support or negative evidence for it, but also contribute to knowledge of the specific subject area being investigated. Indeed, a major assumption of this paper is that better understanding of the problems of the aged will obtain not only from deriving implications regarding the aging process from general theories of behavior, including clinically developed theories, but also subjecting them to empirical test. (Indeed, the value of exploring theories of behavior for implications regarding the aged is well illustrated by a number of papers appearing in this volume. In "The Pavlovian Basis of Old Age," and "Manipulation of the Psychosocial Environment of the Geriatric Patient," for example, Cautela deals with applications of learning theory to old age. In "A Developmental-Field Approach to Aging and Its Implications for Practice," and in "Beer, Wine, and Mutual Gratification in the Gerontopolis," Kastenbaum explores a number of implications of developmental-field theory for problems of the aged. In "Applications of Psychological Research to Social Action," Gottesman deals with applications of ego-psychology to problems of old age. In these papers, both testable derivations from the theoretical models as well as implications for social action are discussed.) It is further maintained that advances in the field will be made by "organizing the best available evidence for and against" (Cohen & Nagel, 1934, p. 192) alternate theories of behavior allowing us to determine the relative predictive power of each of the alternative theoretical models.

The investigation being reported in this paper can be considered a methodological exercise towards these ends. It attempts to compare two general theories of behavior that yield predictions concerning despair in old age in terms of implications for data gathered from a population of elderly applicants to a long-term care facility. Specifically this paper deals with the clinically derived developmental theory of Erik H. Erikson versus that of relative deprivation theory, a non-clinically derived sociological theory of behavior.

Implications for the Aged of Erikson's Theory of Behavior

In *Childhood and Society* (1950) and later in *Identity and the Life Cycle* (1959), Erikson presents the concept of different crises that occur at separate stages of the individual's life. Table 1 summarizes Erikson's conceptualization of successful versus unsuccessful resolution of the associated crises for each stage in the life cycle.

The eight stages and the psychological consequences of successful versus unsuccessful resolution of crises appear to be postulated as "universals." From his writings, however, it would seem that the content or the specific kind of behavior required for successful

TABLE 1:   Erikson's conceptualization of sequence of psychosocial crises in the life space

Stage	Successful vs. unsuccessful resolution of crisis	
	Successful	Unsuccessful
Infancy	Trust	Mistrust
Early childhood	Autonomy	Shame, doubt
Play age	Initiative	Guilt
School age	Industry	Inferiority
Adolescence	Identity	Identity diffusion
Young adult	Intimacy	Isolation
Adulthood	Generativity (Productivity)	Self-absorption
Mature age	Integrity	Disgust, despair

Derived from Figure I in *Identity and the Life Cycle* (Erikson, 1959), p. 120.

resolution of crises will vary to some extent from culture to culture. Erikson views behavioral acts in terms of the historical context within which a person has been reared. He links successful resolution of crises to appropriate solutions in line with the particular culture's values and normative framework. Erikson (1959) points out that:

> The growing child must derive a vitalizing sense of reality from the awareness that his individual way of mastering experience (his ego synthesis) is a successful variant of a group identity and is in accord with its space-time and life plan (p. 22).

As an example of the importance of the cultural context even for the acquisition of what might be considered "natural" human physical skills, he cites the child who is learning to walk (Erikson, 1959):

> To be "one who can walk" becomes one of the many steps in child development which through the coincidence of physical mastery and cultural meaning, of functional pleasure and social recognition, contributes to a more realistic self-esteem. By no means only a narcissistic corroboration of infantile omnipotence (that can be had more cheaply), this self-esteem grows to be a conviction that the ego is learning effective steps toward a tangible collective future, that it is developing into a defined ego within a social reality (p. 23).

Although specific behaviors required for successful resolutions may differ depending upon role prescriptions and expectations of the society, the eight stages appear to be postulated not only as universals but as unilateral stages of development. Success in a stage is not possible unless the individual has resolved successfully the crises of the previous stage. Success in coping with previous crises will not guarantee success during the present and/or future stages, but it is a prerequisite for such success.

The eighth and last stage of development (called by Erikson "Mature

Age") differs from previous stages in that the essential task is mainly reflective in nature. Erikson (1959) states:

> Only he who is in some way taking care of things and people and has adapted himself to the triumphs and disappointments of being, by necessity, the originator of others and the generator of things and ideas—only he may gradually grow the fruit of the seven stages. I know no better word for it than *integrity* . . . . It is the acceptance of one's own and only life cycle and of the people who have become significant to it as something that had to be and that, by necessity, permitted of no substitutions . . . . But I can add, clinically, that the lack or loss of this accrued ego integration is signified by despair and an often unconscious fear of death . . . (p. 98).

Apparently the major "crisis" that must be "resolved" in mature age involves the development of a state of mind in which the individual sees himself as having been a "success." He must experience a sense of accepting his own life, of having done all that he could have done with it; he must not wish for any other life nor any changes nor, seemingly, for any new paths in which to wander. Unsuccessful resolution of this "crisis" results in despair.

Erikson's formulations concerning old age, then, can be seen as having direct implications for predicting despair in old age. According to his theoretical position there are at least two requisites to "lack of despair" in old age without which despair is the resultant: 1) previous successful resolution of the crises of adulthood, including "generativity" (productivity); and 2) successful resolution of the crisis of old age—more specifically the perception of success and the feeling of self-acceptance on reflection of one's past years.

In testing implications of Erikson's approach, then, "despair" can be considered the "dependent" variable, and the two requisites—previous success and perception of success—can be considered the "independent" variables. Of the three dimensions, "despair" perhaps presents the least difficulties for research. Assuming optimal interview conditions, responses of elderly persons to questions concerning life satisfaction, whether life is worth living, state of happiness, and other morale questions can be used as an index of despair. Clinical judgments can also be used as a measure of the degree of despair.

Erikson's second requisite—perception of elderly persons concerning their past—also appears to present little difficulty. The elderly person can be asked directly about how he feels about his past, whether he regrets the chances he missed to do something else with his life, etc. Ordinarily there is a serious problem in using the life review method in research undertakings—particularly if one is interested in valid knowledge concerning external reality for the subject. However, according to this requisite, what matters is the way the individual perceives the situation—that is, how he thinks of his previous life, whether he thinks it was successful, whether he accepts his own past history. Therefore, questioning the subject *now* about *then* is appropriate.

The same presumption does not hold for the "reality" picture since valid knowledge of the individual's past is paramount here. Unless pertinent longitudinal data have been collected, for the most part the experimenter is forced to depend on indirect measures such as: rating successful resolution of adult life crises in terms of specified assumptions concerning societal definitions of success for certain social groups; using financial status or material evidence of other types of achievement during the previous life stage as indicators of successful resolution of crises; and perceptions of others concerning the elderly person's past life and successes.

A further difficulty concerning the "reality picture" is rooted in the way in which Erikson discusses "generativity," the successful resolution of the crises of the seventh (the immediately previous) life stage. According to Erikson (1959):

> The problem of genitality is intimately related to the seventh criterion of mental health, which concerns parenthood . . .

generativity . . . concerns the establishment (by way of genitality
and genes) of the next generation . . . Generativity is primarily
the interest in establishing and guiding the next generation,
although there are people who, from misfortune or because of
special and genuine gifts in other directions, do not apply this
drive to offspring but to other forms of altruistic concern and of
creativity, which may absorb their kind of parental responsibility
(p. 97).

Erikson disclaims mere "parenthood" or wanting to have children as
necessarily indicating generativity. He leaves the impression that the
development of generativity is intimately tied to involvement of the
individual with the well-being and continuity of his cultural group,
whether by "guiding" the next generation or creative contributions to
his culture. But he does little to clarify at what point "successful"
development of "generativity" takes place.

For the reasons given above, then, definitions of the "reality picture"
present a more difficult problem for research. Such a picture depends
to a large extent upon the researcher's own ability to interpret
Erikson's writings and to make operational definitions in line with
research steps that enable empirical testing of this interpretation of his
theory.

Implications for the Aged of Relative Deprivation Theory

Relative deprivation theory, a tenet of the more general formulation
of reference group theory takes a position differing from Erikson's. It
suggests that behavior is more situationally derived. The basic postulate
of relative deprivation theory is that the greater the perceived
differences between current circumstances and more favorable circumstances of peers in one's reference group, the greater the feelings of
deprivation leading to despair, low morale and misery (Merton & Kitt,
1950; Hyman, 1942; Chapman & Volkman, 1939). Conversely, if a

person is experiencing unfavorable life circumstances but he believes he is better off than most of the group with whom he identifies (his reference group), then he is likely to view his situation as better than can be expected and be relatively satisfied with his lot.

Pertinent both for Erikson's early formulation and for relative deprivation theory is the importance of inner thoughts and introspection as related to life satisfaction and lack of despair in the elderly. However for Erikson the resolution of the psychosocial crisis depends upon the introspective process in the final stage of life more than in any of the other stages. The theory of relative deprivation, on the other hand, postulates the importance of introspection at almost every point in a person's life.

For Erikson the final stage involves more of an assessment of the elderly person's past life than do the other stages. It involves more of a review of life than action. This is not to say that introspection is not important in any of the other seven stages, but merely that it is more important in the final stage. For example, in the adolescent state the crisis involves one of ego identity (successful resolution) versus ego diffusion (unsuccessful resolution). But the adolescent state also involves concurrent active identification with peer groups through activity and achievement.

As relative deprivation theory is described in the literature, the major time perspective is the present—here and now. Extending the concept in another direction, it is possible to postulate feelings of relative deprivation not only in terms of the comparison between circumstances of self and others, but in terms of the perceived difference between one's own present unfavorable circumstances and previous success. Rather than his peer group as the anchorage, *then* against *now* is the frame of reference against which the individual makes a self-judgment. The greater the perceived disparity between present circumstances and previous success, the greater the feelings of deprivation leading to despair, low morale, and general misery. From this point of view, persons whose life experiences in old age are not substantially different from middle age are *not* likely to develop feelings of deprivation leading to despair; those who remain relatively "successful" as well as elderly persons whose present life circumstances are not good . . . not substantially different from the past (they were "bad" before but are not particularly worse now) do not suffer from feelings of deprivation. Furthermore, elderly persons whose present life circumstances are not good now but are better than they were during middle age are likely to perceive present circumstances as better than expected and thus be relatively satisfied with their current status.

Contrary to Erikson's position concerning the elderly, according to this postulate, if the elderly person perceives his present life to be favorable as compared with an unfavorable past, he can indeed achieve contentment; furthermore, such perceptions will hinder the development of feelings of despair.

Extending the theory of relative deprivation one step further, it is also possible to postulate the development of feelings of deprivation leading to despair in old age in terms of life developments relative to "expections." Some losses in old age—particularly bodily deterioration, death of friends and spouse, etc.—are undoubtedly anticipated by most persons. Expectation of loss therefore may act as a mechanism for warding off pervading misery and despair when losses are actually experienced. According to the additional postulates to relative deprivation theory being suggested here, however, the greater the disparity between anticipated degree of loss and actual perceived loss, the greater the impact on feelings of deprivation and resultant despair. Life circumstances which turn out worse than anticipated are likely to result in feelings of deprivation leading to low morale, misery and despair. Despite unfavorable circumstances, however, if they turn out to be better than expectations, such developments are likely to promote feelings of life satisfaction and hinder the development of feelings of despair.

The postulates derived from the relative deprivation model described above do not by themselves attempt to predict the content of the expectations nor the significant values held by the individual. As in the Erikson approach, it is assumed that societal values in the development of norms and values of the individual are important. The theory contains the presumption that comparisons with others, or with one's self at a previous time, or life developments compared with expectations are related to feelings of relative deprivation only for areas of life that have meaning. For such areas the postulates are being asserted as "universals," applying cross-culturally and to all age groups capable of introspection. The fact that many aged persons face severely deteriorating life circumstances, however, makes the theory perhaps of unusual interest as a predictor of despair in the final stage of life.

In testing implications of the relative deprivation postulates, "despair" can be considered the "dependent" variable as in Erikson's approach. Each of the conditions outlined above can be considered the "independent" variables—self-judgments based on comparisons of self with peer group, self in middle age as compared with now, and the current state of events relative to anticipations or expectations.

Each of the relative deprivation postulates is defined in terms of perceptions of the elderly person. Therefore the same general conditions obtain for relative deprivation as for Erikson's postulate concerning perceptions of success. Responses to questions concerning the relevant dimensions can be used as measures of relative deprivation. That is, the elderly person can be asked directly about how he feels compared with his peer group, how he is doing now as compared with before, and whether conditions are worse or better than expected.

Comparing Predictions of the Two Theories

It is possible to examine, at least on an exploratory level, some of the implications of these theories with data gathered as part of a demonstration project concerning applicants to the Hebrew Rehabilitation Center for Aged, a long-term care facility in Boston. The objectives of the demonstration project (CH 23-26) were focused on learning about the needs of the applicants and on testing the effectiveness of a program to help maintain them in the community. During the post-testing phase a number of pre-coded questions were included on the interview schedule that tapped dimensions relevant to the testing of the two theories.

Two types of items suitable for measuring despair were available from the home interview: 1) pre-coded responses of elderly persons to direct questions, and 2) pre-coded home interviewer judgments. (The home interviews were conducted by a social worker or a Public Health nurse with special training for making such assessments.) Two separate despair scales were developed: 1) a twelve-item scale that combines direct response items and home interviewer judgment items; and 2) a six-item home interviewer judgment scale. Adequate data that permitted the computation of scores for the despair scales were available for 172 elderly persons.

The twelve-item scale consists of ten direct response items (six of which were taken from the Lawton morale scale) and two home interviewer judgments. Responses to each item were dichotomized to indicate a greater or lesser degree of despair. The total Combined Direct Response and Home Interviewer Judgment scale score equals the number of responses indicating a greater degree of despair. The Kuder Richardson 20 alpha reliability coefficient computed for this scale was .831. (For further explication of this technique, see: Cronbach, 1951.) Since the alpha reliability is the mean of all possible split-half reliability coefficients, this indicates a high reliability for this scale.

Table 2 presents the individual despair items and scoring system for the Combined Direct Response and Home Interviewer Judgment despair scale.

The six-item scale consists of the same two home interviewer judgment items as in the twelve-item scale plus four additional judgments. Each judgment was coded on a five-point scale, with five indicating the highest degree of despair. The total Home Interviewer Judgment scale score equals the sum of the six items. The Kuder Richardson 20 alpha reliability was .893, indicating a high reliability also for this scale.

TABLE 2:   Scoring system for the twelve-item combined direct response and
home interviewer judgment despair scale[1]

	Scoring system	
Despair items[2]	Greater degree of despair (Scored as 1)	Lesser degree of despair (Scored as 0)
1. I sometimes feel that life isn't worth living	Yes	No
2. I have a lot to be sad about	Yes	No
3. How satisifed are you with your life today?	Not satisfied	Satisfied
4. Little things bother me more this year	Yes	No
5. I sometimes worry so much that I can't sleep	Yes	No
6. Life is hard for me most of the time	Yes	No
7. Considering yourself now as compared with then, would you say you are	Much less happy now	Much happier now; less happy now
8. All in all, how much unhappiness would you say you find in life today?	A good deal	Some (but not very much) or almost none
9. On the whole, life gives me a lot of pleasure	Disagree	Agree
10. Nothing ever turns out for me the way I want it to	Agree	Disagree
11. Attitude toward self: rating of elderly person as perceived by interviewer	Depreciating somewhat accepting	Accepting
12. Emotional state: rating elderly person as perceived by interviewer	Somewhat depressed; very depressed	Exuberant even mood

[1] The scoring system is based on "logic" (for direction) plus distribution of responses.

[2] The first six items are from the Lawton Morale Scale (see "The Dimensions of Morale" in this volume).

Table 3 presents the individual despair items and scoring system for the Home Interviewer Judgment despair scale.

Other relevant pre-coded items on the home interview schedule include perceptions of the work role and feelings of success and satisfaction with middle years, relevant background factors (having

TABLE 3:   Six-item home interviewer judgment despair scale scoring system*

1. Emotional state:	Scored as
Very depressed	5
Somewhat depressed	4
Even mood	3
Quite cheerful	2
Exuberant	1

2.-6. Other general ratings of applicant by interviewer (each on a five-point scale)
Highest degree of despair scored as 5   Least degree of despair scored as 1

2. Self-depreciating	_____	Self-accepting
3. Extremely embittered	_____	Not at all embittered
4. Extremely depressed	_____	Not at all depressed
5. Not at all satisfied	_____	Satisfied
6. Not at all happy	_____	Happy

*Total scale score—sum of item scores (6 = least despair; 30 = most despair)

children, for example, throws light on "generativity"), attitudinal responses and perceptions in connection with current circumstances compared with peer group members and whether conditions are worse or better than expected. Responses to these pre-coded items constitute the bulk of the data being used as measures of the independent variables in this investigation.

Because a number of the relevant questions were added to the interview schedule after post-testing had begun, responses to some of the items were not obtained for all of the 172 elderly persons for whom despair scores are available. Furthermore, not all of the items are equally relevant to persons in the study population. For example, questions pertaining to treatment by children and parental role are not applicable to persons who have never married or have no children; questions concerning retirement and enjoyment of the "work" role are applicable only to men and "working" women; likewise questions pertaining to the role of housewife and housekeeper are, for the most part, applicable only to married women. Accordingly the size of the sample available for analysis varies depending upon the item under examination.

It should also be pointed out that the "relevant" items are not necessarily "relevant" to both theories. In fact, when the relationship between each of the items and despair is considered by itself, only two of the available pre-coded items from this home interview apply to both theories. This general problem in theory testing emerges clearly when two theories are contrasted. There are times when one of the theories may have predictive implications for a set of facts while the other does not. The situation may be reversed for another set of data. For example, the relative deprivation model predicts that elderly persons who feel they are in better health than most people their age are less likely to have feelings of despair than persons who believe they are in worse health than the rest of their peer group. While the Erikson position does not stand in refutation of such a possibility, the model has no direct implications given only this set of facts. The Erikson model predicts that if an elderly person feels that he was unsuccessful in business during his middle years (assuming the American value system), he is likely to suffer during his old age from feelings of despair since he has not achieved the necessary requisite "integrity." Thus elderly persons who feel that they were successful during their middle years have a greater chance of attaining integrity and lack of despair than elderly persons who feel that they were not successful during middle age. While the relative deprivation position would not deny that perceptions of elderly persons concerning success in business during middle age may be important for an individual in old age, the model has no direct implications given this set of facts alone.

A total of twenty-three items were available for testing the theories, eleven items pertaining to the Erikson theory, ten items to the relative deprivation theory, and two items pertaining to both theories. For the two overlapping items the Erikson and relative deprivation theories predicted despair *in the opposite direction*. For this exercise, then, these two items can be considered to constitute a form of crucial "experiment" that throws light on the relative predictive power of each of the alternative theoretical models.

By attempting to verify alternate theories of human behavior, the researcher throws into sharper relief differences between theories. Of necessity when one operationalizes concepts, one makes them more specific and exposes basic assumptions. This is illustrated by the measures used here, for two factors yield directly opposite predictions depending upon the theory used.

One of these factors centers about having had children. According to the theory of Erikson the aged person who has raised children presumably would have been successful in fulfilling the generativity demands of the adult stage. Conversely the elderly who have not had children are more likely to develop despair in old age since they are likely to have failed to meet the "generativity" requisite.

However, if one uses the theory of relative deprivation, a very different line of reasoning is necessary and yields an opposite prediction for the sample being used here—a group who found it necessary to apply for admission to a home for the aged. Those aged who have children are more likely to feel deprived upon finding themselves in the position of having to apply to a "home for the aged" than those elderly who do not have children. The aged seeking admission to the home probably have peers who are living quite independently and this unfavorable comparison could well lead to despair. All of this could be heightened by comparing their present position with their former independence. Obviously this interpretation assumes certain negative feelings about institutionalization. The result is that from the single datum of having children, two quite different predictions regarding probable despair emerge depending upon the use of either Erikson's or the relative deprivation theory.

A similar difference occurs when we consider the feelings about success as parents. Erikson's theory leads one to predict that those who feel they have been excellent parents will have less despair than those who feel that they were less adequate as parents. The contrary is likely to be the case if we follow the logic of relative deprivation. The elderly applicant to a home for the aged who feels he has been a very good parent probably will be more downcast by the "perceived rejection" of a child than those who make more modest claims. The same differences hold for items relative to whether there are children nearby. However, the latter set of facts does not apply directly to Erikson's theory.

Table 4 presents the items and the scoring system used in testing the theories. Items that apply primarily to the Erikson model have the prefix E, and those applying to the relative deprivation model have the prefix R, and the two items applying to both theories have E and R prefixes.

Correlation was used as the method for testing the theories—correlation between each of the selected items and the measurements of despair. For convenience of interpretation—except for the two items applying to both theories—the items were scored in such a way that a positive correlation would result if the relationship between the variables was in the direction predicted by the theory to which it applied. For example, (see Table 4) in item E-1, (satisfaction with marital life history), an Erikson item, the score (*0*) was assigned to that response (very glad or very satisfied with marital status) which Erikson's theory would expect from elderly persons with minimum despair. Since despair is scored in the same way (the lower the score the less the despair, the higher the score the greater the despair), a positive correlation will result if Erikson's prediction is borne out by the data.

As can be seen in Table 4, in the case of the two items (12 and 13) that applied to both theories, one item was scored in line with the Erikson model, the other in line with the relative deprivation model. Item ER-12 (satisfaction with the parental role) was scored in line with the Erikson prediction (accordingly, the prefix appears as ER). Thus, a positive correlation will result if Erikson's prediction is borne out by the data. Since the relative deprivation model predicts in the opposite direction, a negative correlation will result if the relative deprivation prediction is borne out by the data. Item 13 (whether the elderly person has children) on the other hand was scored in line with relative deprivation prediction (thus the prefix appears as RE). Therefore a positive correlation will result if the relative deprivation prediction is

TABLE 4: Scoring system for Erikson and relative deprivation items

A. Scored in line with Erikson's theory (predicts a positive correlation with despair)

Erikson items	Scoring system	
	"Good" past life (Scored as 0)	"Not so good" past life (Scored as 1)
E-1 Satisfaction with marital life history	very satisfied	other than very satisfied
E-2 Happiness during middle age	happy or happier than anticipated	unhappy or worse than anticipated
E-3 Acceptance of own past efforts	yes	no
E-4 Success in work role	very successful	other than very successful
E-5 Enjoyment of work role	very much	other than very much
E-6 Enjoyment of housewife role	very much	other than very much
E-7 Success as housekeeper	very successful	other than very successful
E-8 Enjoyment in keeping house	very much	other than very much
E-9 Excellence in cooking	very good, excellent	other than very good, excellent
E-10 Enjoyment in cooking	very much	other than very much
E-11 Missed opportunities	no regret	great regret or some regret
ER-12 Satisfaction with parental role[1]	very good parent	other than very good parent

B. Scored in line with relative deprivation theory (predicts a positive correlation with despair)

Relative deprivation items	Scoring system		
	From relatively least deprived (scored as 0)	. . . to . . . (Scored as 1)	Relatively most deprived (Scored as 2)

	Relatively not deprived (Scored as 0)		Relatively deprived (Scored as 1)
R-13 Parental status	no children		have children
R-14 Health compared to peers	better	same; better than some, worse than others	worse
R-15 Present finances—past success	getting along well although unsuccessful past	getting along well and very successful past; or not getting along well and unsuccessful past	not getting along well although very successful past
R-16 Present money control—past success	yes, although unsuccessful past	yes, and very successful past; or no, and unsuccessful past	no, although very successful past
R-17 Fulfillment of retirement expectations	better	about as expected	worse
R-18 Circumstances relative to expectations	better	same	worse
R-19 Children living up to expectations	much above call of duty	somewhat more than can be expected	not more than can be expected
R-10 Treatment by children compared to others	very well	better than most	not better than most
	Relatively not deprived (Scored as 0)		**Relatively deprived (Scored as 1)**
R-21 General comparison	much better or better than most		other than much better or better than most
R-22 Children in area	no		yes
R-23 Preferred choice of non-independent residence	in a home for the aged		with children

The scoring system is based on "logic" (for direction) plus distribution of responses.

[1] This item applies to both the Erikson and relative deprivation theories. However, relative deprivation theory predicts a negative correlation of this item with despair.

[2] This item applies to both the Erikson and relative deprivation theories. However, Erikson's theory predicts a negative correlation with despair. For convenience in the multiple correlation tables, this item has been left in this position. Actually, as one of the dichotomized variables, it should be listed at the end of this table.

borne out by the data and a negative correlation if the Erikson position is borne out by the data.

Because of the varying size of the population for which data were available on many of the items and also because the Erikson and the relative deprivation theories each consisted of a number of distinctly different dimensions, the twenty-three items are being correlated on an individual basis with the despair scores rather than adding scores and developing multiple-item Erikson and relative deprivation scales. (Originally an exploratory attempt was made to develop an "Erikson Scale" using only those Erikson items that apply to the entire sample. However the Kuder 20 alpha reliability coefficient for this scale was only .322. It was decided therefore to abandon the attempt to continue along these lines with this data.) Furthermore, since the size of the sample available for analysis varies for different items, a missing data correlation matrix was employed in testing the theories.

Correlations were computed for the entire sample and also, because of the specialized nature of some of the items, for three separate subsamples: 1) men and women who had worked (for whom retirement had meaning); 2) housewives; and 3) persons having one or more children. First, zero-order correlations were computed between the twenty-three items representing the independent variables and the two measurements of despair (the dependent variables). A series of multiple correlations were then computed using step-up regression techniques. Specifically, the procedure involved the selection of independent variables to be included in the multiple correlation equation on the basis of the magnitude of their correlations (either zero-order or partial) with the dependent variable. It is called "step-up" because one independent variable enters the formula at a time. The actual independent variable chosen at each step is the one with the highest correlation with the dependent variable of all those not already in the equation. This procedure mechanically can go through the entire list of independent variables and add them to the equation, irrespective of significance levels, increases in explained variance, and the redundancy of the independent variable to be entered when compared with others already in the formula. In order to overcome the limitations resulting from such a mechanical procedure, three criteria were employed to indicate when the equation would be considered complete: 1) The probability level for the entire equation was ≤.05; 2) The probability level for the Beta of the next variable to enter was ≤.10 (Note: the probability values for the Betas were based on the total N for the sample or the subsample involved); 3) The determinant (Harmon, 1969) of the inverted portion of the correlation matrix ≤.10.

A multiple correlation for the entire sample and for each of the subsamples was computed for Erikson items considered by themselves; likewise a multiple correlation was computed for relative deprivation items considered by themselves; finally, a multiple correlation was computed in which both Erikson and relative deprivation items were included. (See Blalock, 1960, p. 346 for an explanation of the zero order and the multiple correlation techniques.)

Unfortunately, with the exception of the item concerning whether the elderly person has one or more children, all of the Erikson items under investigation here refer to Erikson's second requisite described previously—*perception* of one's past and not to the "reality" picture (Was in fact the elderly person "successful" during middle age?). Therefore the correlations computed here barely test the postulate that successful resolution of the crisis of adulthood is a necessary requisite for the development of "integrity" and lack of despair in old age.

In addition to the relevant pre-coded items, data potentially useful for making judgments of the reality dimension ("actual" rather than "perceived" success during middle age) for this sample exist from a variety of sources including responses to open-ended questions on the home interview, consultation reports by the home interviewer and members of the interdisciplinary team assessing the needs of these applicants (a psychiatrist, physiatrist, internist, social worker and nurse) and a telephone interview with a family member. It is planned to utilize these data for further testing of both the Erikson and the relative deprivation theories. In fact, such data for a random sample of some 112 of the total group of 172 persons have already been used in a Boston University School of Social Work group thesis to test Erikson's theory. (This was conducted under the direction of S. Sherwood, Adjunct Professor at the Boston University School of Social Work for the 1969-70 academic year, who acted as Thesis Advisor to the group. The group thesis attempted to compare Erikson's theory with that of Peck as predictors of despair in old age [Esselstyn, J. Glass, T. Glass, Kleinhaus, Marsh, McTeague, Schoenecker, Smith, Strachan, Van Strien, & Weaver, 1970].)

After any items or references to despair were deleted from the available data, the social work students read the case material and made assessments for three separate dimensions:

The first assessment consisted of a two-point "generativity" scale. The higher score was given to persons thought to be "generative"—they raised their own or an adopted child, niece or nephew, or made a contribution to society through a service profession such as teacher, physician, social worker, etc.

The second assessment consisted of a five-point "reality picture concerning middle age" scale. The highest score was given to persons who, from the case history material available, were in the social work students' judgment, satisfied with their marital status, work role, and parental status in middle age.

The third assessment consisted of a five-point scale concerning the elderly persons "self-perception of middle age." The highest score was given to persons who were judged by the social work students from the case history material available to perceive themselves as being happy in middle age, good parents, and doing the best they could under the circumstances.

The twelve-item Combined Direct Response and Home Interviewer Judgment Despair Scale was used in the group thesis as the measurement of despair for zero-order and multiple correlation analyses. A brief report of the results of these efforts will be included among the findings of the investigation being reported here.

TABLE 5: Descriptive characteristics of the entire sample[1]

Age	(N = 172)	Place of birth	% (N = 171)
Mean	78.8 years	East Europe	79.53
Median	79.1 years	Other	20.47
Standard deviation	5.4 years		
Education in years	% (N = 139)	*Primary spoken*	
None	19.42	*language*	% (N = 154)
Four or less	20.14	English	29.87
Five-six	15.83	Other	70.13
Seven-eight	18.71		
Nine-eleven	14.39	*Sex*	% (N = 172)
Twelve	5.76	Male	37.21
Some college	5.76	Female	62.79

Family occupation % (N = 168)

White collar	37.50
Other	62.50

Note: The distribution for the subsample of males and working females is: % (N = 107)

Males	56.07
Females	43.93

Receiving financial assistance % (N = 159)

No	13.84
Yes	86.16

Marital status	% (N = 172)
Married	22.67
Widowed, divorced, separated, single	77.33

[1] These distributions are based on the sample having real scores for the twelve-item Combined Direct Response and Interviewer Judgment Despair Scale. The distribution for the 171 persons having real scores for the six-item Home Interviewer Judgment Despair Scale and for all sub-samples are quite similar to these, except where not relevant. It should also be pointed out that the categories of the subsamples being analyzed (Males and Working Females; Housewives; People with Children) are not mutually exclusive.

Findings

Table 5 presents some basic characteristics of the sample under investigation. As can be seen, the average age of this group of elderly applicants to a long-term facility is over seventy-eight years. Almost two-thirds of the sample are female. Although most members of this group (150 of these 172 persons have children) have been married at one time, the majority are now widowed. Less than one-fourth of the group are presently living with their spouses. The majority of this group are immigrants and English is the primary language spoken for only one-third of the sample. The median education is five to six years. Most

TABLE 6: Zero-order correlations of despair scales with Erikson and relative deprivation items—a missing information correlation matrix (blanks indicate that the independent variable is not applicable to the subsample)

Erikson and relative deprivation items	Twelve-item combined direct response and interviewer judgment despair scale				Six-item home interviewer judgment despair scale			
	Entire sample	Males & working females	House-wives	People with children	Entire sample	Males & working females	House-wives	People with children
E-1 Satisfaction with marital life history	.222[2]	.180	.260[2]	.226[2]	.185[1]	.107	.236[1]	.203[1]
E-2 Happiness during middle age	.245[2]	.215[1]	.251[1]	.288[2]	.187[1]	.135	.216[1]	.212[1]
E-3 Acceptance of own past efforts	.074	.044	.045	.067	.059	.078	.048	.052
E-4 Success in work role	.078	.078		.154	.037	.037		.116
E-5 Enjoyment of work role	.018	.018		-.001	.040	.040		.035
E-6 Enjoyment of housewife role	.017		.017	.080	.165		.165	.216[1]
E-7 Success as housekeeper	.058		.058	.141	.102		.102	.155
E-8 Enjoyment in keeping house	-.040		-.040	-.011	.037		.037	.050
E-9 Excellence in cooking	.005		.005	.047	.024		.024	.056
E-10 Enjoyment in cooking	-.008		-.008	.015	.039		.039	.052
E-11 Missed opportunities	.265[2]	.162	.391[2]	.323[2]	.255[2]	.127	.357[2]	.330[2]
ER-12 Satisfaction with parental role	-.041	.069	-.112	-.002	-.014	-.003	-.051	.046
RE-13 Parental status	.091	.178	.131		.127	.205[1]	.121	
R-14 Health compared with peers	.205[2]	.180	.251[1]	.169[1]	.106	.089	.180	.117
R-15 Present finances—past success	-.055	-.055		-.112	.080	.080		.072
R-16 Present money control—past success	-.032	-.032		-.130	.096	.096		.012
R-17 Fulfillment of retirement expectations	.269[2]	.299[2]		.238[1]	.207[1]	.226[1]		.208

TABLE 6 (continued)

Erikson and relative deprivation items	Twelve-item combined direct response and interviewer judgment despair scale				Six-item home interviewer judgment despair scale			
	Males & Entire sample	working females	House-wives	People with children	Males & Entire sample	working females	House-wives	People with children
R-18 Circumstances relative to expectations	.530[2]	.545[2]	.542[2]	.559[2]	.473[2]	.469[2]	.435[2]	.528[2]
R-19 Children living up to expectations	.213[1]		.161	.213[1]	.287[2]		.255[1]	.287[2]
R-20 Treatment by children compared to others	.254[2]		.199	.254[2]	.330[2]		.273[1]	.330[2]
R-21 General comparison with peers	.296[2]	.301[2]	.319[2]	.299[2]	.354[2]	.309[2]	.433[2]	.340[2]
R-22 Children in area	.068		.107	.005	.092		.104	-.025
R-23 Preferred choice of nonindependent residence	.179[1]		.184	.184[1]	.249[2]		.232[1]	.247[2]

[1] $p \leqslant .05$
[2] $p \leqslant .01$

of the applicants in this sample find themselves in the position of depending upon some sort of outside financial assistance (in the form of old age assistance, medicaid or, at the very least, financial aid from their children).

Table 6 presents the zero-order correlations of the twenty-three items with each of the two measures of despair—the twelve-item Combined Direct Response and Interviewer Judgment Despair Scale and the six-item Home Interviewer Judgment Despair Scale. It should be kept in mind that, with the exception of the two items pertaining to both theories, a positive correlation indicates support for the theory to which the item pertains. For the two items pertaining to both theories: 1) a positive correlation for item ER-12 (Satisfaction with Parental Role) indicates support for the Erikson model, a negative correlation indicating support for the relative deprivation model; but 2) a positive correlation for item RE-13 (Parental Status—whether the elderly persons have children), indicates support for the relative deprivation model, a negative correlation indicating support for the Erikson model. Of the eleven variables relevant to the Erikson model only, as few as three appear rather consistently as significantly correlated with the two measures of despair in the direction predicted by the model: E-1 (Satisfaction with marital life history); E-2 (Happiness during middle age); and E-11 (Missed opportunities). Such is the case for the entire sample and for the Housewives and People with Children subsamples. Except in one case, E-2 (Happiness during middle age), in the set of correlations with the twelve-item Combined Direct Response and Interviewer Judgment Despair Scale, none of these three variables is significantly correlated with despair for the Males and Working Females subsample. In fact, the Erikson theory is most inadequate with respect to the Males and Working Females subsample. In the six-item Home Interview Judgment Despair Scale analysis, E-6 (Enjoyment of the housewife role) for the People with Children subsample is also significantly correlated with despair in the direction predicted by the Erikson model. Although the direction of a few of the remaining items in the twelve-item Combined Direct Response and Interviewer Judgment Despair Scale analyses is opposite to that predicted by the Erikson theory, the correlations are extremely small and none is statistically significant. All of the remaining items, although only to a slight extent and not statistically significant, are correlated with despair in the direction predicted by the theory in the six-item Home Interviewer Judgment Despair Scale analyses.

Of the ten items relevant to the relative deprivation model only, six in the entire sample are significantly correlated with the two measures of despair in the direction predicted by the model: R-17 (Fulfillment of retirement expectations); R-18 (Circumstances relative to expectations); R-19 (Children living up to expectations); R-20 (Treatment by children compared to others); R-21 (General comparison with peers); and R-23 (Preferred choice of non-independent residence). With the exception of R-19 and R-20 for the Housewives subsample in the twelve-item despair scale correlations and R-17 for the People with Children subsample in the six-item scale correlations, these items are significantly correlated in the direction predicted by the model for each of the subsamples as well. In the twelve-item despair scale analysis, R-14 (Health compared with peers) is also significantly correlated with despair in the direction predicted by the relative deprivation model for the entire sample, and the Housewives and People with Children subsamples. Two of the remaining items in the twelve-item despair scale correlations, albeit only to a small extent and not statistically significant, are not in the direction predicted by the theory. However, the remaining items (although not statistically significant) are all in the direction predicted by relative deprivation theory.

As can be seen from Table 6, with one exception (the Males and Working Women subsample when the six-item Home Interviewer Judgment Despair Scale is used to measure the dependent variable), none of the correlations is statistically significant for the two items that are relevant to both the Erikson and the relative deprivation models. However, all the correlations are in the direction predicted by the relative deprivation model.

Tables 7 and 8 present the results of the multiple correlation analyses. All items were used to test either one or the other or both theories for the entire sample. All items but RE-13 (Parental Status) applied to the People with Children subsample. For the Males and Working Women subsample, however, ten items were eliminated from the testing situation—E-6, E-7, E-8, E-9, E-10, E-12, R-19, R-22, and R-23. These were the items pertaining to housekeeping and parental roles other than parental status itself (see Table 4). For the Housewives subsample, items pertaining to the work role, financial success, and retirement were eliminated from the testing situation—five in all: E-4, E-5, R-15, R-16, and R-17.

It should be kept in mind that according to the criteria set up for inclusion in the multiple correlation equation, the standard partial regression coefficient of an item had to be statistically significant at or less than the .10 level. (In a few instances variables are included when the significance level of the standard partial regression coefficient was just above the .10 level.) In Tables 7 and 8, only those items that contributed significantly at this level to at least one multiple correlation equation have been listed. Blanks in Table 7 and 8 in the spaces for variables that potentially could have entered the equation indicate that these variables (although contributing to some other multiple correlation equation) would not contribute significantly to this equation once the correlations between these items and those which have already entered this equation have been taken into consideration.

It can be seen that when the twelve-item despair scale was used to test the alternate theories (see Table 7), of the Erikson items (E-1 through E-11, ER-12 and RE-13) that could have entered multiple correlation equations, only six in fact entered into any of the equations. Erikson items 3 through 8 and E-10 (seven items in all) contributed significantly to *none* of the equations and are therefore not listed in Table 7. Of the relative deprivation items (ER-12, RE-13, R-14 through 23) that could have entered, nine items contributed significantly to one or more of the multiple correlation equations. Three items (R-17, R-22, and R-23) entered into *none* of the equations and are therefore not listed in Table 7.

Similar results obtained when the six-item despair scale was used to test the theories (see Table 8). Of the Erikson items that could have contributed, seven entered into one or more of the multiple correlation equations. However, Erikson items 2, 3, 5, 7, 8, 10 and ER-12 entered into *none* of the multiple correlation equations and are therefore not listed. Of the relative deprivation items, six contributed significantly to one or more of the multiple correlation equations. However, ER-12, R-16, R-17, R-19, R-22, and R-23 entered into *none* of the equations and are therefore not listed in Table 8.

It should be noted that, regardless of which measure of the dependent variable was used (the twelve-item or the six-item despair scale) to test the theories, Erikson items 3, 5, 7, 8 and 10 and relative deprivation items 17, 22 and 23 never contributed significantly to a multiple correlation equation.

A comparison of Tables 7 and 8 reveals that the overall results for the two measures of despair are very similar. This is true not only for the entire sample, but for each of the subsamples. For the multiple correlation analyses dealing with the Erikson items (including items relevant to both theories), the multiple correlation squared (R^2) was approximately .12 for the entire sample and .07 for the Males and Working Women, between .18 and .22 for the Housewives and between .14 and .15 for the People with Children subsamples. For the multiple correlation analyses dealing with the relative deprivation items (again including the two items relevant to both theories), R^2 was between .35 and .40 for the entire sample and approximately .40 for the Males and Working Women, between .37 and .38 for the Housewives and between .35 and .43 for the People with Children subsamples.

In each instance R^2 for the relative deprivation items is much higher (that is, explains a much greater proportion of the despair measurement variance) than for the Erikson items. As is the case for the zero-order correlations, the Erikson model seems to apply least for the Males and Working Females subsample.

It should further be pointed out that when the two variables that are relevant to both theories entered into the multiple correlation equation, the direction of the standard partial regression coefficient supported the relative deprivation mode. This, of course, constitutes negative evidence for the Erikson model. If we wish to know how much of the variance (in despair) can be explained by the Erikson theory *per se*, technically this variable should have been excluded from the equation when dealing with the Erikson multiple correlations since the R^2 is higher than it would have been if only items supporting the theory had been entered into the equation. Therefore it should be realized that whenever this variable enters the Erikson multiple correlations, the actual R^2 of the supporting items is less than the R^2 reported here.

TABLE 7:   Final multiple correlation equations for various samples using the twelve including beta weights (the standard partial regression coefficients) for v

Independent variables[2]	Entire sample			Males and working wom		
	Erikson items	Deprivation items	Erikson and deprivation	Erikson items	Deprivation items	Eriks depri
E-1 Satisfaction with marital life history	.1458°	NA			NA	
E-2 Happiness during middle age	.1536*	NA NA	.1645†	.1994*	NA NA	.13
E-9 Excellence in cooking		NA	-.1437*	NA	NA	N
E-11 Missed opportunities	.1899*	NA	.2374†		NA	.17
ER-12 Satisfaction with parental role	-.1059			NA	NA	N
RE-13 Parental status		.1466*	.1446*	.1581°	.2534†	.25
R-14 Health compared with peers	NA		.1090°	NA		
R-15 Present finances—past success	NA		.1096°	NA		.11
R-16 Present money control—past success	NA			NA		
R-18 Circumstances relative to expectations	NA	.4882†	.4341†	NA	.5352†	.55
R-19 Children living up to expectations	NA	.1284*		NA	NA	N
R-20 Treatment by children compared to others	NA		.2117†	NA	NA	N
R-21 General comparison with peers	NA	.1796†	.2017†	NA	.2002†	.21
No. of persons in sample	172	172	172	107	107	1
Multiple correlation squared	.1247	.3472	.4755	.0709	.3969	.46
Probability of multiple correlation	≤ .001	≤ .001	≤ .001	≤ .022	≤.001	≤.

[1] Key to symbols for probability levels: °≤.10; *≤.05; †≤.01. When the indep Deprivation theory), or in any case not used in testing a theory for a particular subs
[2] Erikson items have an E prefix. Relative Deprivation items have an R prefix. Two it scored in line with the Erikson position. Item 13 is labeled RE-13 since it is scored
Multiple correlations for columns labeled "Erikson Items" deal only with the multiple correlation equation. Likewise, multiple correlations for columns labeled ' cates that the item did not enter into the multiple correlation equation.

combined direct response and Home Interviewer Judgment Despair Scale,
bles in the final multiple regression equation[1]

Housewives			People with Children		
Erikson items	Deprivation items	Erikson and deprivation	Erikson items	Deprivation items	Erikson and deprivation
.1794˙	NA			NA	
	NA	.1306	.2086†	NA	.1975†
	NA	-.1552*		NA	
.3783†	NA	.3953†	.2592†	NA	.2615†
.1954*	.2087†	.2265†	NA	NA	-.1131˙ NA
NA			NA		
NA	NA	NA	NA		.2044†
NA	NA	NA	NA		.1265˙
NA	.5114†	.3665†	NA	.4989†	.5106†
NA		-.2311*	NA	.1280˙	
NA		.3928†	NA		.1305*
NA	.2228†	.2450†	NA	.1472*	.1512*
101	101	101	149	149	149
.2200	.3758	.5691	.1439	.3502	.4989
≤.001	≤.001	≤.001	≤.001	≤.001	≤.001

variable is not applicable (as, for example, E items for the testing of Relative
it has been indicated by the "NA" notation.
relevant for both and have E and R prefixes. Item 12 is labeled ER-12 since it is
with the Relative Deprivation position.
and RE items. A blank in an E space indicates that the item did not enter into the
vation Items" deal only with the R, RE, and ER items. A blank in an R space indi-

Table 8: Final multiple correlation equations (for various samples using the six-item regression coefficients) for variables in the final multiple regression equation[1]

Independent variables[2]	Entire sample		
	Erikson items	Depriva- tion items	Erikson and depri- vation
E-1 Satisfaction with marital life history		NA	
E-4 Success in work role		NA	
E-6 Enjoyment of housewife role	.1558*	NA	.1438
E-9 Excellence in cooking		NA	−.2423†
E-11 Missed opportunities	.2627†	NA	.3013†
RE-13 Parental status	.1789*	.1662†	.2036†
R-14 Health compared with peers	NA		
R-15 Present finances–past success	NA	.2054†	.2435†
R-18 Circumstances relative to expectations	NA	.4153†	.4071†
R-20 Treatment by children compared to others	NA	.2171†	.2922†
R-21 General comparison with peers	NA	.2745†	.3023†
No. of persons in sample	171	171	171
Multiple correlation squared	.1153	.4028	.5360
Probability of multiple correlation	⩽.001	⩽.001	⩽.001

[1] Key to symbols for probability levels: ⩽ .10; * ⩽ .05; † ⩽.01. When the inde-
privation theory), or in any case not used in testing a theory for a particular sub-
[2] Erikson items have an E prefix. Relative Deprivation items have an R prefix.One
in line with the Relative Deprivation position. Multiple correlations for columns la-
dicates that the item did not enter into the multiple correlation equation. Likewise,
and ER items. A blank in an R space indicates that the item did not enter into the

Home Interviewer Judgement Despair Scale, including beta weights (the standard partial

Males and Working Women			Housewives			People with Children		
Erikson items	Depriva-tion items	Erikson and depri-vation	Erikson items	Depriva-tion item	Erikson and depri-vation	Erikson items	Depriva-tion items	Erikson and depri-vation
	NA	.1552°	NA			NA		
	NA	NA	NA	NA		NA		.2209†
NA	NA	NA	NA	.1308°	.1963†	NA		.2575†
NA	NA	NA	NA	−.2186†		NA		−.2990†
.1536	NA	.2248†	.3503†	NA	.3977†	.3177†	NA	.3245†
.2231*	.2385†	.2624†	.1924*	.1762*	.2387†	NA	NA	NA
NA	.1455°	.1672*	NA			NA		
NA	.2287†	.2609†	NA	NA	NA	NA	.2762†	.4581†
NA	.5464†	.5599†	NA	.3644†	.2876†	NA	.4981†	.4757†
NA	NA	NA	NA	.1443°	.2857†	NA	.2045†	.2245†
NA	.2737†	.2991†	NA	.3394†	.3442†	NA	.2485†	.2632†
109	109	109	103	103	103	150	150	150
.0653	.3951	.4434	.1849	.3662	.5392	.1473	.4348	.6194
≤.028	≤.001	≤.001	≤.001	≤.001	≤.001	≤.001	≤.001	≤.001

pendent variable is not applicable (as, for example, E items for the testing of Relative Dep-
sample, it has been indicated by the "NA" notation.
item is relevant for both and has an RE prefix. Item 13 is labeled RE-13 since it is scored
beled "Erikson Items" deal only with the E, ER, and RE items. A blank in an E space in-
multiple correlations for columns labeled "Deprivation Items" deal only with the R, RE,
multiple correlation equation.

This caution, of course, holds as well for the two other items for which partial regressions not in the direction predicted are entered into the multiple correlation equation—i.e., to the R-9 (Excellence in Cooking) Erikson item and, in the case of the Housewives subsample for the twelve-item despair scale, to the R-19 (Children Living Up to Expectations) relative deprivation item (for the combined Erikson and Deprivation multiple correlation analysis).

Although not directly pertinent to the central focus of the paper, the multiple correlations computed in which both the Erikson and the relative deprivation items were included are of interest. It should be noted that the Erikson and relative deprivation items, when combined in a multiple correlation analysis, explain not only a greater proportion of the variance (in despair) than either of the sets alone but an even greater proportion of the variance than the two added together. In line with the general conclusion of this analysis, it should again be noted that the combined equation includes more deprivation items than Erikson items.

Table 9 presents findings from the Boston University group thesis that have pertinence to the testing of the Erikson model, and in particular, to the testing of the "reality picture" requisite—actual successful resolution of the crises of the previous stage—for the

Table 9: Correlations between despair and the assessments of Erikson theoretical dimensions by Boston University School of Social Work students

Erikson dimensions	Standardized correlation coefficient	Zero-order correlations with despair
Generativity	0.2150*	0.170
Reality picture of success in middle age	− 0.1469	0.194
Self-perception of success in middle age	− 0.2441*	0.258*
Number of persons in sample: 112		
Multiple correlation squared: .128		
Probability of multiple correlation: .02		

Despair is measured by the Twelve-item Combined Direct Response and Home Interviewer Judgment Scale.
*$P \leqslant .05$

development of "integrity" and lack of despair in old age. It should be noted that in the group thesis study negative correlations *support* the theory and positive correlations *negate* the theory. It should also be kept in mind that the elderly persons in the group thesis study represent a random sample of the population in the investigation being reported here.

From Table 9 it can be seen that assessments based on the rich case material available for these elderly persons yield similar results to those based on the pre-coded responses. In particular it should be noted that "Generativity" is in the opposite direction to that predicted by the Erikson model. Therefore the R^2 of .12 overrepresents the variance (in despair) being explained by the theory. A subsequent multiple correlation in which only the reality picture and the self-perception dimensions were entered into the equation yielded an R^2 of .08.

What is most interesting from the point of view of therapy is the fact that the self-perception of previous success dimension was more highly correlated with despair and contributed more to the variance (in despair) than the reality picture during middle age. Certainly, this presents a challenge to Erikson's postulate concerning unilateral development.

Conclusions:

The substantive findings of this paper are presented not primarily as a guide to practice but as support for the prime purposes of the study which were: 1) to demonstrate that general theories of behavior can be applied to the specific concerns of those working with an aged population; 2) to press for validation of current theory by operationalizing concepts; and 3) to support the feasibility of utilizing available data to aid in assessing the predictive power of alternative theoretical models.

In this paper theoretical constructs of Erikson and relative deprivation were used to predict "despair" in an aged population applying for admission to a long-term care facility. By the techniques used, relative deprivation proved to be a better predictor than the Erikson theory. This contention received additional support from a further study of a random sample of this population by graduate students of Boston University.

This conclusion, of course, cannot be regarded as definitive. The study population was a "special" one; and this is a single study. The problems of obtaining accurate records of an individual's perceptions are well-known and recognized by the authors of this paper. The even greater problems of determining "reality" are equally recognized. Furthermore, even what appears to be the better of the two theories, by itself, explains less than 50% of the variance in the dependent variable, "despair." On the other hand, it is known that measurement errors tend to lead to underestimation of correlation coefficients. Since there are undoubtedly measurement-error problems in this study, it may be that the true multiple correlations squared are higher than those computed.

Needless to say, not only are more studies needed but also a testing of other models. There are other theories that might well be applied and tested. Even so, it seems obvious that more and better theories are needed to explore the area of aging. An approach might include a combination of the theories considered in this paper; for example, that people in old age focus on whatever is best in their lives. If the past is better than the present, reminiscence may be the key to lack of despair; if the present is better, continued involvement may be the key. The results of this study in fact lend some support to this approach. Certainly the inclusion of Erikson items with relative deprivation items added to the explanation of the variance in despair found for this study population—for the entire sample as well as for each of the subsamples and regardless of the measure of despair employed. Indeed, in each case the multiple correlation squared of the Erikson and relative deprivation items combined equals approximately the sum of the multiple correlation squared of the set of Erikson and the set of relative deprivation items when each set is considered separately. It would appear that the distinctly Erikson items have independent information to add on their own to the explanation of the variance in despair over and above the contribution of the relative deprivation items.

In any event, more research and better theories are needed. The latter, however, will be of little value if we do not consistently devise testable propositions from them and subject them to validation. This in turn calls for a refinement of our present research procedures.

While research of the kind envisioned here is an indispensable element of good practice, the clinician cannot delay action pending definitive evaluations. The partial success of both theories tested in this paper indicates their viability depending upon given situations. For the researcher they present the challenge of more clearly defining the situational limits within which they, and other theories, function best.

REFERENCES

Blalock, H. M. *Social statistics*. New York: McGraw-Hill, 1960.

Chapman, D. W., & Volkmann, J. A Social determinant of the level of aspiration. *Journal of Abnormal and Social Psychology*, 1939, *34*, 225-238.

Cohen, M. R., & Nagel, E. *An introduction to logic and the scientific method*. New York: Harcourt, Brace & Company, 1934.

Cronbach, L. J. Coefficient alpha and the internal structure of tests. *Psychometrika*, 1951, *16*, 297-334.

Erikson, E. H. *Childhood and society*. New York: W. W. Norton, 1950.

Erikson, E. H. *Identity and the life cycle*. New York: International Universities Press, 1959.

Esselstyn, J., Glass, J., Glass, T., Kleinhaus, P., Marsh, N., McTeague, C., Schoenecker, J., Smith, G., Strachan, D., Strien, K., & Weaver, L. A comparison of the theories of Erikson and Peck as predictors of lack of despair in old age. Unpublished master's thesis, Boston University School of Social Work, 1970.

Harmon, H. H. *Modern factor analysis*. Chicago: University of Chicago Press, 1969.

Hyman, H. H. The psychology of status. *Archives of Psychology,* 1942, *38,* entire issue.

Merton, R. K., & Kitt, A. S. Contributions to the theory of reference group behavior. In R. K. Merton, & P. F. Lazarsfeld (Eds.), *Continuities in social research; Studies in the scope and method of "The American soldier".* Glencoe, Ill.: Free Press, 1950.

25:: SOCIAL CONSEQUENCES
OF PHYSICAL IMPAIRMENT
IN AN AGING POPULATION

PARKER G. MARDEN and ROBERT G. BURNIGHT

Several recent appraisals of sociological research concerning health and medicine have noted the strong tendency of the researchers to view social factors only as variables in their analyses that explain differences in health (Feldman, 1958; Freeman, Levine, & Reeder, 1963). Feldman's (1958) discussion of research on the relationship between social class measures and health status illustrates this point. He notes that there is always a tendency to regard the former as *independent* variables and the latter as dependent ones. Neglected is the possibility that the pattern of influence can also be in the opposite direction in that health condition may influence class and status or social behavior more generally. The message is quite clear.

It is unfortunate that social scientists working in the field of health should devote all their energies in trying to explain medical phenomena in terms of social processes. . . . It might benefit both social science and medicine if more frequently the orientations were reversed and attention was paid to the physiological factors bearing on the social environment (p. 218).

This investigation was supported by United States Public Health Service Grant No. HD-00671 from the National Institute of Child Health and Human Development. This is the expanded version of a paper presented at the Nineteenth Annual Meeting of the Gerontological Society, New York, N.Y., September, 1966.

445

Clearly, there is a need to view health measures as independent variables in sociological analysis.

The present research follows this recommendation by seeking to determine the social consequences of physical impairments in an aging population. Presence (or absence) of such medically diagnosed impairments is viewed as an independent variable accounting for certain variations in such social or socio-psychological conditions as participation in certain activities and life satisfaction. Data are drawn from a longitudinal study of a probability sample of white, married couples living in Providence, Rhode Island, in 1962 in which the husband was 60 to 64 years of age. One goal of this study has been the detailed investigation of the important changes in health that take place during the seventh decade of life and their consequences for the individuals and families involved (Burnight, 1965; Burnight & Marden, 1967).

The fact that the study population is composed of "aging" couples h?s particular relevance for the analysis of the consequences of physical impairments in two respects. First, National Health Survey (1966) statistics indicate that impairments increase in prevalence with advancing years, and it is generally accepted that loss of motor and sensory abilities are important components of the aging process. Focus upon their effect on an individual's behavior and attitudes is important. But not all older persons are infirm or impaired. So, second, the question arises as to how much public or personal reaction to someone who is "aged" or even the person's own self-appraisal is determined by (a) chronological advancement in years or (b) possible deterioration of health. Suspicion persists that the two are frequently confused (Brown, 1966). Discovery of attitudinal or behavioral differentials between impaired and non-impaired persons of the same age might serve to underline the fact that the aged are not a homogeneous group. It should also call for additional research to resolve this confusion.

Study Design

Because of the dependence of the present analysis upon the design of the longitudinal study from which it was developed, several general observations about the larger study are in order. More complete details have been presented elsewhere (Burnight, 1965). The general study population consisted of non-institutionalized white married couples who were residents of Providence, Rhode Island, on May 1, 1962 in which husband and wife were living together and the male was between the ages of 60 and 64. The purpose of the longitudinal study was to follow these persons through a period during which most of them would face important changes: withdrawal from the labor force with changed economic circumstances, an increased probability of becoming ill or even dying, and changes in family situations, including possible widowhood. Through a series of interviews with the same study population, these changes are being assessed. The present study is drawn from the first interviews, conducted between May and December, 1962.

Since all eligible couples in Providence, a city with a 1960 population of 207,000, could not be interviewed, a detailed sample design was developed. Following Deming's (1960) replicated area sampling technique, Providence was divided into eleven independent and non-duplicating area samples. Three of these, representing 27% of the study universe, were randomly drawn. To identify qualified respondents, a screening operation was undertaken. An "age-sex-race-marital status" census of the 18,000 households in the sample units was carried out and 668 eligible couples were identified. Interviewers visited these potential respondents and obtained completed schedules of information from both husbands and wives for 605, or 90.5% of the qualified couples.

A variety of health information was obtained from the respondents, including their identification of health problems that had been medically attended. This information was obtained by procedures that were similar to those developed by the United States National Household Health Survey (1964). Although information on all medical conditions present at the time of interview was collected (Burnight,

1965), attention in the present study is focused on physical impairments as classified by the National Health Survey's adaptation of the International Classification of Diseases. Of the 1,210 respondents (605 couples) interviewed, 105, or 17.4% of the males and 92, or 15.2% of the females had one or more impairments. The vast majority of these impairments involved motor or sensory abilities. For males, 37% involved an orthopedic difficulty or partial or full paralysis. An additional 52% of the impairments involved blindness, deafness, or other difficulties with vision or hearing. The comparable figures for females were 41 and 39%, respectively.

The concern of the present study, however, is not with the prevalence of such impairments in the study population. Rather, it is designed to consider the impact of the impairment on a person's attitudes and behavior, i.e., viewing it as an independent variable in this analysis. In doing so, one obstacle must be overcome. The social or dependent variables in this study (e.g., life satisfaction, social participation) can in turn be associated with other biosocial and social factors such as sex, ethnicity, marital status, and social class. To take but one example, marked differences in life satisfaction have been demonstrated between the married and the non-married (Neugarten, Havighurst, & Tobin, 1961). Similar relationships are well documented in the sociological literature. It is imperative that such influence, known or suspected, be held constant in the present context.

Such control was accomplished by taking the 105 males and 92 females in the general study population who had medically diagnosed impairments and matching each with a person from the study group who did not have an impairment. Matching was on the basis of the following eight charactersitics: sex, age, race, marital status, presence of spouse, urban residence, religion-ethnicity, and socio-economic status. Matching on the first six of these variables could easily be accomplished because of the nature of the study population—urban white married couples in which the husband was 60 to 64 years old. The wives, varying more in age, were matched on the basis of whether they were under 55 or 55 and over. In addition, each impaired respondent was matched with a non-impaired member of the study population according to a five-category religion-ethnicity grouping—Italian Catholic, Irish Catholic, other Catholic, Protestant, and Jewish (Burnight & Marden, 1967)—and on the three-level measure of socio-economic status used by the Bureau of Census that combines income, education, and occupation (1962). The non-impaired mates in the matching process were randomly selected in a computer operation and at no time was the choice limited to only one potential match. Statistical techniques that are appropriate to dependent samples of this type were employed (Blalock, 1960).

In summary, the present analysis focuses upon the 105 male and 92 female pairs that were drawn from the general study population. In each pair, one person was impaired and the partner was not. Matching procedures were employed to minimize the differences between the two with respect to variables that predictably might distort the relationships under study. This has been accomplished without the loss of cases that is generally characteristic of studies where matching techniques are used.

Chronic Illness

Each of the pairs derived from this matching process was studied with respect to a variety of factors in the attempt to examine possible differences between the impaired and non-impaired partners. The first variable to be considered was another medical condition: presence of a chronic illness. The relationship between impairment status and chronic illness is summarized in Table 1. Unlike the National Health Survey in which some impairments can also be coded as chronic conditions, procedures employed in this study made impairment and chronic illness distinct categories and eliminated the possibility that a statistically significant relationship could result simply by definition.

As Table 1 shows, chronic illness is positively associated with physical impairments. This relationship is statistically significant in the case of

Table 1. Presence of Chronic Illness
in Matched Pairs (Impaired—Non-Impaired)
of an Aging Population.

	Non-Impaired Matched Partner		
MALES	No Chronic	1+ Chronic	
Impaired Person	Illness	Illness	Total
No chronic illness	12 (11.4%)	10 (9.5%)	22 (20.9%)
1+ chronic illness	36 (34.3%)	47 (44.8%)	83 (79.1%)
Total	48 (45.7%)	57 (54.3%)	105 (100.0%)

$t=4.114$ $P<0.001$.

	Non-Impaired Matched Partner		
FEMALES	No Chronic	1+ Chronic	
Impaired Person	Illness	Illness	Total
No chronic illness	5 (5.4%)	9 (9.8%)	14 (15.2%)
1+ chronic illness	29 (31.5%)	49 (53.3%)	78 (84.8%)
Total	34 (36.9%)	58 (63.1%)	92 (100.0%)

$t=3.429$ $P>0.001$.

both males and females. For both sexes, there are high number of pairs in which both partners have chronic illnesses—a pattern that is to expected given the age composition of the study group. But the discovery that the number of pairs where only the impaired partner had a chronic illness (34.3% for men and 31.5% for women) greatly exceeded the number of pairs in which the opposite is true (9.5 and 9.8%, respectively) is of particular interest and permits the observation that was made above.

The presence of this strong relationship, however, means that the remainder of the discussion must consider the independent variable to be a "syndrome" of impairments and chronic illness. No specification of the exact contribution of each factor is possible at this time, but discovery of this very strong association is important and it points to some interesting possibilities for additional epidemiological analysis.

Life Satisfaction

One social consequence of medical condition is demonstrated in Table 2. Here the association is shown between impairments (to which

Table 2. Life-Satisfaction Score of Matched Pairs (Impaired—Non-Impaired) of an Aging Population.

MALES

Impaired Person Rating	Non-Impaired Matched Partner				Total
	1-5	6-10	11-15	16-20	
1- 5	0	3 (3.2%)	5 (5.2%)	0	8 (8.4%)
6-10	0	4 (4.2%)	17 (17.9%)	10 (10.5%)	31 (32.6%)
11-15	0	3 (3.2%)	23 (24.2%)	10 (10.5%)	36 (37.9%)
16-20	0	2 (2.1%)	9 (9.5%)	9 (9.5%)	20 (21.1%)
Total		12 (12.7%)	54 (56.8%)	29 (30.5%)	95 (100.0%)

$t = 4.623$ $P < 0.001$.

FEMALES

Impaired Person Rating	Non-Impaired Matched Partner				Total
	1-5	6-10	11-15	16-20	
1- 5	0	1 (1.1%)	2 (2.3%)	2 (2.3%)	5 (5.7%)
6-10	0	2 (2.3%)	4 (4.5%)	10 (11.4%)	16 (18.2%)
11-15	4 (4.5%)	6 (6.8%)	20 (22.7%)	14 (15.9%)	44 (49.9%)
16-20	0	2 (2.3%)	11 (12.5%)	10 (11.4%)	23 (26.2%)
Total	4 (4.5%)	11 (12.5%)	37 (42.0%)	36 (41.0%)	88 (100.0%)

$t = 1.804$, N.S.

one must hereafter mentally add the words "and chronic illness") and the Life Satisfaction Index developed in the Kansas City Study of Adult Life by Neugarten et al. (1961). Familiar to most gerontologists, the Life Satisfaction Index is a measure of psychological well-being that is relatively independent of the level of activity or social participation of the respondents. It includes assessments of zest versus apathy; resolution and fortitude; congruence between desired and achived goals; self-concept; and mood. Since the measurement instrument uses the individual's own evaluations as the point of reference, it is appropriate for use in household interview studies.

Table 2 presents the respondents' scores on the Life Satisfaction Index as arranged in four categories ranging from low (1-5) to high (16-20) psychological well-being or general life satisfaction. In general, the impaired males had lower scores on this measure than did their non-impaired counterparts. Table 2 shows that 15% of the impaired males had higher scores, 38% had the same scores, and 47% had lower scores than their partners who were not impaired. For females, however, the same relationship did not hold. The comparable figures were 26, 36, and 37%, respectively.

Several Explanatory "Mechanisms"

Reasons for this differential response to impairments by sex when life satisfaction is studied can be found by examining the information summarized in Tables 3 and 4. Table 3 presents the relationship between the presence of an impairment and the respondent's position in the labor force. Table 4 shows the relationship between impairments and the respondent's evaluation of his health. A case can be made for identifying these variables as mechanisms by which impairments (and the presence of chronic illness among those who are impaired) affect the dependent or social variables, including life satisfaction.

For example, there is a strong, statistically significant relationship

Table 3. Labor Force Status of Matched Pairs
(Impaired—Non-Impaired) of an Aging Population.

MALES Impaired Person Status	Employed	Non-Impaired Matched Partner Unemployed, Out of Labor Force	Total
Employed	53 (50.5%)	14 (13.3%)	67 (63.8%)
Unemployed, out of labor force	36 (34.3%)	2 (1.9%)	38 (36.2%)
Total	89 (84.8%)	16 (15.2%)	105 (100.0%)

$t = 3.250$ $P < 0.01$.

FEMALES Impaired Person Status	Employed	Non-Impaired Matched Partner Unemployed, Out of Labor Force	Total
Employed	8 (8.7%)	14 (15.2%)	22 (23.9%)
Unemployed, out of labor force	19 (20.7%)	51 (55.4%)	70 (76.1%)
Total	27 (29.4%)	65 (70.6%)	92 (100.0%)

$t = 0.869$, N.S.

Table 4. Comparison of Health with Others by
Matched Pairs (Impaired—Non-Impaired)
of an Aging Population.

MALES Impaired Person	Non-Impaired Matched Partner Better, Same	Worse	Total
Better, same	67 (69.1%)	5 (5.2%)	72 (74.3%)
Worse	24 (24.7%)	1 (1.0%)	25 (25.7%)
Total	91 (93.8%)	6 (6.2%)	97 (100.0%)

$t = 3.759$ $P < 0.001$.

FEMALES Impaired Person	Non-Impaired Matched Partner Better, Same	Worse	Total
Better, same	60 (68.2%)	4 (4.5%)	64 (72.7%)
Worse	23 (26.1%)	1 (1.2%)	24 (27.3%)
Total	83 (94.3%)	5 (5.7%)	88 (100.0%)

$t = 3.948$ $P < 0.001$.

between impairment and male participation in the labor force. As Table 3 indicates, one-half of the 105 pairs of males were still in the labor force. Of the remaining one-half, however, 34% of the impaired persons in the pairs had left the labor force while his non-impaired partner continued to work. In only 13% of the cases was the opposite pattern discovered. These findings suggest that presence of a physical impairment may cause withdrawal from the labor force prior to usual retirement age. This premature separation from what is socially defined as normal activity for males could influence the results of measurements of life satisfaction and other such social psychological conditions. Conversely, the fact that over 70% of both the impaired and non-impaired women were out of the labor force suggests that leaving work may not be perceived as the same discontinuity as for males, although an impairment may have been a reason for the actual withdrawal from the labor force.

Information on the evaluation of health is also insightful. Respondents were asked to evaluate their health in two ways: (a) in comparison with others their age and (b) without any reference to others. Table 4 presents the first set of evaluations as to whether the respondents felt that their health was better, the same, or worse than that of others who were their own age. Statistically significant relationships were found between impairments and these evaluations for both males and females. Indeed, a striking uniformity exists between the tables for men and for women that summarize this relationship. For both sexes, pairs in which the impaired person evaluated his health more pessimistically than that of his partner were five times more numerous than pairs in which the non-impaired person viewed his health as worse than that of persons his own age and the impaired partner did not.

But when the same respondents were asked to evaluate their health without reference to others (i.e., rate it as good, fair, or poor), a different pattern was found. While the relationship continued to hold for males, it did not for females. Women apparently do not evaluate their own health as negatively in the presence of impairments as do men, although they recognize that they are not in as good health as others of their own age. This pattern brings to mind the discussions of the sick role in the sociological literature (King, 1963) and those of mortality differentials by sex in the literature of demography (Madigan, 1957; Sowder, 1954). These discussions combine to suggest that women are "better and more frequent customers of modern medical science than are men" and adopt the sick role with more ease. As a result, an impairment again may not represent as important a discontinuity in life for women as for men.

Both of the above mechanisms help to explain sex differences in life satisfaction in the presence of a physical impairment. The disruptions in life that are produced by withdrawal from the labor force and by developing medical difficulties are relatively more important for males. These changes affect their psychological well-being as measured by the Life Satisfaction Index more than is the case with females. Through a knowledge of these mechanisms, the social consequences of a physical impairment can best be understood.

In the absence of knowledge about these mechanisms, comparisons between males and females might be more difficult, given the differences in age. The women in the study population, on the average, are slightly younger than the men, and control by matching could not be as exacting because of the greater range in their ages. Nevertheless, the average difference in age between the two groups is less than three years and, while further research on this variable is necessary, the information on labor force participation and evaluation of health suggests that this factor is not a crucial one.

Family Responsibility and Enjoyment

Given the point at which the respondents were in the life cycle, questions concerning attitudes toward family relationships are of considerable interest. Two questions were asked to measure the way in which the individual viewed his participation within the family. One involved the time of greatest family *responsibility* and the other concerned the time of greatest family *enjoyment*. The respondents were asked whether the time of greatest responsibility or enjoyment was behind them, ahead of them, at the present (now), or the same as it always had been.[1]

Predictably, the presence of a physical impairment was a factor in shaping these attitudes. As Table 5 indicated, when the answers to the question concerning the timing of greatest family responsibility were tabulated, little difference between the impaired and non-impaired persons, male or female, was found. But when the responses to the question of family enjoyment were analyzed (Table 6), significant differences by impairment status appeared. But again there was a variation by sex in this regard.

The impaired and non-impaired partners in most matched pairs of women saw the time of greatest family enjoyment as being the same as it always had been, or at the present, or ahead of them. Those pairs in which the answers did differ were almost evenly split with respect to which member of the pair—impaired or non-impaired—saw this enjoyment as being behind her. In the case of men, the percentage of male pairs in which both partners saw the time of this enjoyment as being unchanged, at the present, or ahead of them was the same as for women (75.0% compared to 79.8%). But in those cases where the partners differed, it was the impaired one who consistently took the more pessimistic view that the greatest enjoyment of his family was behind him. This pattern was statistically significant. While there are several questions here that are best left to students of the family, it would appear that the "discontinuity" interpretation that was offered in discussing life satisfaction can explain this sex differential in assessments of the time of family enjoyment as well.

---

[1] The authors would like to acknowledge the work of Eugene A. Friedman, who developed this distinction and those that follow concerning the separation of participation or activity and the enjoyment of that activity in certain role areas of adult life. His contribution is greatly appreciated.

Activity and Satisfaction in Role Areas

A series of questions was also asked in order to determine the significance that respondents of the particular age group under study assigned to several role areas of adult life in addition to the family. These questions, relating specifically to participation in church, with friends, and in clubs and organizations, were of two types: 1) the extent of participation or activity in each area: whether it is seen as in the past, at present, or in the future; 2) the satisfaction or enjoyment derived from participation: whether this is seen as being in the past, the present, or the future.

Thus, the measures distinguish between activity or involvement and the satisfaction derived from participation in the belief that satisfaction may not vary directly with activity. This distinction is especially relevant to considerations of the impact of a physical impairment upon social activity. An impairment may or may not reduce a person's participation in the three role areas mentioned, but it most certainly can affect the enjoyment of that activity. For example, a person with impaired hearing may still retain the habits of years by attending church regularly, but the "enjoyment" of that attendance may have diminished greatly.

The information summarized in Tables 7 and 8 support this contention. Once again differences by sex were found. Table 7 indicates that there are no significant differences between the impaired and non-impaired partners, male or female, with respect to perceptions on the time of greatest *activity* in the church. When satisfaction or *enjoyment* of this participation is assessed, however, statistically significant differences are found for the males. Table 8 indicates that the view that the greatest enjoyment of church activities was behind them is more commonly held by the impaired members of the matched pairs when attitudes with the pairs differ.

A similar pattern was found concerning relationships with friends.

Table 5. Time of Greatest Family Responsibility
in Matched Pairs (Impaired—Non-Impaired)
of an Aging Population.

MALES

| Impaired Person | Non-Impaired Matched Partner | | |
	Ahead, Now, Same	Behind	Total
Ahead, now, same	24 (25.0%)	22 (22.9%)	46 (47.9%)
Behind	29 (30.2%)	21 (21.9%)	50 (52.1%)
Total	53 (55.2%)	43 (44.8%)	96 (100.0%)

$t=0.980$, N.S.

FEMALES

| Impaired Person | Non-Impaired Matched Partner | | |
	Ahead, Now, Same	Behind	Total
Ahead, now, same	22 (24.4%)	22 (24.4%)	44 (48.8%)
Behind	19 (21.2%)	27 (30.0%)	46 (51.2%)
Total	41 (45.6%)	49 (54.4%)	90 (100.0%)

$t=-0.466$, N.S.

Table 6. Time of Greatest Family Enjoyment
in Matched Pairs (Impaired—Non-Impaired)
of an Aging Population.

MALES

| Impaired Person | Non-Impaired Matched Partner | | |
	Ahead, Now, Same	Behind	Total
Ahead, now, same	72 (75.0%)	5 (5.2%)	77 (80.2%)
Behind	18 (18.8%)	1 (1.0%)	19 (19.8%)
Total	90 (93.8%)	6 (6.2%)	96 (100.0%)

$t=2.806$ $P<0.01$.

FEMALES

| Impaired Person | Non-Impaired Matched Partner | | |
	Ahead, Now, Same	Behind	Total
Ahead, now, same	71 (79.8%)	8 (9.0%)	79 (88.8%)
Behind	10 (11.2%)	0 (0.0%)	10 (11.2%)
Total	81 (91.0%)	8 (9.0%)	89 (100.0%)

$t=0.469$, N.S.

There were no significant differences between impaired and non-impaired persons in the matched pairs when they were asked to assess the time of greatest *activity* with friends (Table 9). This was true for both males and females. But when they were asked to assess the time of greatest *enjoyment* of these friends, pairs of males in which the impaired and non-impaired partners disagreed about the timing and where the person with the impairment viewed the greatest enjoyment as being behind him were twice as numerous as those in which it was the non-impaired person who took the pessimistic view. While this pattern for males was found to be statistically significant, the same difference was not present in the case of females (Table 10).

Investigation of the third role area, participation in clubs and organizations, revealed a somewhat similar pattern. For men, statistically significant relationships were found (a) between impairments and the time of greatest *activity* being perceived as behind the respondent *and* (b) between impairments and the perception that the time of

Table 7. Time of Greatest Activity in Church
in Matched Pairs (Impaired—Non-Impaired)
of an Aging Population.

MALES

Impaired Person	Non-Impaired Matched Partner		
	Ahead, Now, Same	Behind	Total
Ahead, now, same	35 (36.1%)	17 (17.5%)	52 (53.6%)
Behind	29 (29.9%)	16 (16.5%)	45 (46.4%)
Total	64 (66.0%)	33 (34.0%)	97 (100.0%).

$t = 1.789$, N.S.

FEMALES

Impaired Person	Non-Impaired Matched Partner		
	Ahead, Now, Same	Behind	Total
Ahead, now, same	32 (36.0%)	19 (21.3%)	51 (57.3%)
Behind	22 (24.7%)	16 (18.0%)	38 (42.7%)
Total	54 (60.7%)	35 (39.3%)	89 (100.0%)

$t = 0.466$, N.S.

Table 8. Time of Greatest Enjoyment in Church
in Matched Pairs (Impaired—Non-Impaired)
of an Aging Population.

MALES

Impaired Person	Non-Impaired Matched Partner		
	Ahead, Now, Same	Behind	Total
Ahead, now, same	43 (44.3%)	11 (11.3%)	54 (55.6%)
Behind	28 (28.9%)	15 (15.5%)	43 (44.4%)
Total	71 (72.7%)	26 (26.8%)	97 (100.0%)

$t = 2.818$ $P < 0.01$.

FEMALES

Impaired Person	Non-Impaired Matched Partner		
	Ahead, Now, Same	Behind	Total
Ahead, now, same	40 (45.5%)	15 (17.0%)	55 (62.5%)
Behind	23 (26.1%)	10 (11.4%)	33 (37.5%)
Total	63 (71.6%)	25 (28.4%)	88 (100.0%)

$t = 1.303$, N.S.

Table 9. Time of Greatest Activity with Friends
by Matched Pairs (Impaired—Non-Impaired)
of an Aging Population.

MALES

Impaired Person	Non-Impaired Matched Partner		
	Ahead, Now, Same	Behind	Total
Ahead, now, same	33 (34.8%)	18 (18.9%)	51 (53.7%)
Behind	26 (27.4%)	18 (18.9%)	44 (46.3%)
Total	59 (62.2%)	36 (37.8%)	95 (100.0%)

$t = 1.209$, N.S.

FEMALES

Impaired Person	Non-Impaired Matched Partner		
	Ahead, Now, Same	Behind	Total
Ahead, now, same	20 (22.5%)	24 (27.0%)	44 (49.5%)
Behind	22 (24.7%)	23 (25.8%)	45 (50.5%)
Total	42 (47.2%)	47 (52.8%)	89 (100.0%)

$t = 0.293$, N.S.

Table 10. Time of Greatest Enjoyment of Friends
by Matched Pairs (Impaired—Non-Impaired)
of an Aging Population.

MALES

Impaired Person	Non-Impaired Matched Partner		
	Ahead, Now, Same	Behind	Total
Ahead, now, same	46 (48.9%)	12 (12.8%)	58 (61.7%)
Behind	26 (27.7%)	10 (10.6%)	36 (38.3%)
Total	72 (76.6%)	22 (23.4%)	94 (100.0%)

$t = 2.324$ $P < 0.05$.

FEMALES

Impaired Person	Non-Impaired Matched Partner		
	Ahead, Now, Same	Behind	Total
Ahead, now, same	40 (45.5%)	18 (20.5%)	58 (66.0%)
Behind	20 (22.7%)	10 (11.3%)	30 (34.0%)
Total	60 (68.2%)	28 (31.8%)	88 (100.0%)

$t = 0.323$, N.S.

greatest *enjoyment* of clubs and organizations had passed. Such relationships were not found in the case of women. The life discontinuity interpretation developed to explain the differential impact of impairment by sex at earlier points in this discussion can be employed here as well. Apparently impaired women possess more "insulation" which keeps the enjoyment derived from activity in church, with friends, and in clubs and organizations from being reduced. Men appear to lack such insulation.

The fact that there is an association for males between impairment status and the perception that the time of greatest activity is behind the respondent when clubs and organizations are considered permits some additional speculation. This relationship was not found when activity in church and activity with friends were analyzed. Perhaps the strength of commitment to the latter two role areas is stronger and participation in clubs and organizations is reduced first when an impairment becomes a limitation to activity. Certainly there is a suggestion for additional research in this area.

Conclusions

Although the results of the research presented above must be regarded as tentative and require qualification, they do demonstrate the value of conducting studies where health is the independent variable rather than the more usual way in which it is the factor to be explained. The analysis clearly demonstrates that impairments have important social consequences. This is true whether males and females are viewed separately or whether comparisons are made between the two sexes. Several points deserve review.

1. It was discovered that it was impossible to discuss impairments separately from chronic illness because of the high positive association between the two. Thus, the independent variable under discussion is more accurately identified as a "syndrome" of impairments and chronic condition.

2. This syndrome's impact upon social factors occurs through certain mechanisms. These can be summarized by talking of life discontinuity in that withdrawal from the labor force or becoming ill are events for which persons may lack the proper insulation. This is particularly true of men and presents one explanation for the differences by sex that were found throughout the study.

3. Areas in which impairments had a particular impact concerned (a) general psychological well-being as measured by the Life Satisfaction

Index, (b) attitudes toward family relationships, and (c) perception of activity and enjoyment of that activity within certain important role areas of adult life: church, friends, and clubs and organizations.

4. With respect to the latter area, it was discovered that *enjoyment* of church, friends, clubs and organizations was independent of the respondents' perceptions of their activity in these role areas. Where activity was viewed as remaining the same, enjoyment of that activity by impaired males was perceived as being behind them. Use of this distinction could be profitably extended to problems other than the present one concerning impairments.

Perhaps as important as these results, however, are the problems that can be identified for additional study. In part, this list represents some of the qualifications that should be applied to the present analysis. For example, work should be done to assess the role that severity of impairment might play in influencing social participation and the other dependent variables in this study. The principal focus has been upon pairs in which the impaired and non-impaired partners differed with respect to the factors being studied; but, both the impaired respondents and their non-impaired mates frequently had identical attitudes or responses. The question can be raised as to how the agreeing and disagreeing matched pairs themselves differed. Perhaps severity of impairment is one factor. To assess this fully, however, a larger study population would be required.

Likewise, the results are qualified by the fact that impairments and chronic illness were so closely related. Additional work should be done that could permit an assessment of the relative impact of each on the social factors under study. The same observation can be applied to the possible effects of the slight average difference in age between the males and the females. In both cases, however, expansion of the study population would be required to permit the inttoduction of additional controls in the analysis.

Other potential extensions of the research are also suggested from the results presented. Presence of the controls through the matching process, for example, raises the question as to what the effects of each of the control variables has in the association between presence of impairments and its social consequences. Examination of each would greatly add to knowledge of this relationship. Similarly, the males and females have been analyzed in a manner that disregards the fact that each is the member of a marriage partnership in which the spouse also may or may not be impaired. Consideration of the role of impairments in the family context would be an interesting endeavor. Finally, the fact that the present analysis is developed from a larger, longitudinal study suggests that the timing of impairments should be reviewed. This can be done in the re-interview of the 605 couples in the study to see how the development of an impaired condition affects future assessments of attitudes and behavior. But it might also be useful to distinguish between those impairments that are already present to see which are long standing and which developed comparatively recently since the consequences of each might be different.

One other point deserves re-emphasis. As noted in the introduction, this study distinguishes between members of an aging population who are impaired and those who are not. This distinction is one which deserves to be made with greater regularity in the gerontological literature since it separates the results of the aging process from the process of deterioration in health—processes that commonly become blurred in general analysis.

REFERENCES

Blalock, H. M. *Social statistics*. New York: McGraw-Hill, 1960.
Brown, M. I. Attitudes of nursing personnel toward aged patients. Paper presented at the meeting of the Gerontological Society, New York, November 1966.
Burnight, R. G. Chronic morbidity and the socio-economic characteristics of older urban males. *Milbank Memorial Fund Quarterly*, 1965, *43*, 311-322.

Burnight, R. G., & Marden, P. G. Social correlates of weight in an aging population. *Milbank Memorial Fund Quarterly.* 1967, *45,* 75-92.

Deming, W. E. *Sample design in business research.* New York: Wiley, 1960

Feldman, J. J. Barriers to the use of health survey data in demographic analysis. *Milbank Memorial Fund Quarterly,* 1958, *36,* 203-219.

Freeman, H. E., Levine, S., & Reeder, L. G. (Eds.) *Handbook of medical sociology.* Englewood Cliffs, N.J.: Prentice-Hall, 1963.

King S. H. Social psychological factors in illness. In H. E. Freeman, S. Levine, & L. G. Reeder (Eds.), *Handbook of medical sociology.* Englewood Cliffs, N.J.: Prentice-Hall, 1963.

Madigan, F. Are sex differentials in mortality biologically caused? *Milbank Memorial Fund Quarterly,* 1957, *35,* 1-22.

Neugarten, B. I., Havighurst, R. J., & Tobin, S. S. The measurement of life satisfaction. *Journal of Gerontology,* 1961, *16,* 134-143.

Sowder, W. Why is the sex difference in mortality increasing? *Public Health Reports,* 1954, *69,* 860-864.

United States Bureau of the Census. *Methodology and sources of socio-economic status.* Working Paper No. 15, 1962. Technical paper series.

United States National Center for Health Statistics. *Health survey procedures: Concepts, questionnaire development, and definitions in the health interview survey.* (Public Health Service Publication No. 1000-Series 10-No. 32) Bethesda, Md.: U.S. Public Health Service, 1964.

United States National Center for Health Statistics. *Age patterns in medical care, illness, and disability, United States-July, 1963-June, 1965.* (Public Health Service Publication No. 1000-Series 10-No. 32) Bethesda, Md.: U.S. Public Health Service, 1966.

26:: AGE, ANOMIE, AND THE INMATE'S DEFINITION OF AGING IN PRISON: AN EXPLORATORY STUDY*

MICHAEL W. GILLESPIE and JOHN F. GALLIHER

The "retreatist" variant of anomie involves the rejection of both socially valued goals and the conventional means used to attain these goals (Merton, 1957). This rejection, however, is a passive one. Neither goals nor means are devalued. Instead, the person withdraws from most meaningful activity because he despairs of ever achieving his goals. This point is illustrated by a number of studies. Joel Nelson (1968), for example, compares the responses of owners and managers to economic failure. Owners are more anomic than managers, but the differences occur mainly among the lower-income segments of the sample. Nelson suggests that the owners' reaction to economic deprivation is greater because the nature of their work reduces the prospects for improvement. Less mobile than managers, owners are unable to regard their financial situation as temporary. In partial support of his argument, Nelson's data show: 1) that owners are more locked in to their present situation; and 2) when the anomie scores are standardized according to the respondent's level of commitment, the differences between owners and managers are reduced.

Two other studies cited by Nelson also underscore the importance of the person's orientation toward the future. One, by Wilensky &

*The research on which this paper is based was supported in part by a postdoctoral training grant in social gerontology administered by the Midwest Council for Social Research on Aging.

Edwards (1959), reveals that downwardly mobile workers show little dissatisfaction with the American social structure because they view their setbacks as temporary. More relevant for our research is Chinoy's (1965) study of automobile workers. He discovered that the young and middle-aged workers he interviewed were unaffected by the poor pay schedule and boring work routine, again because they anticipated moving on to a better job. On the other hand, these same working conditions produced anomie among the older workers who, due to their age, realized that they could not escape the assembly line. The theme common to all three studies, then, is that persons who become anomic do so because some feature of their situation reduces the subjective probability of improvement.

The above line of reasoning is useful in explaining some data collected in a study of the inmates of a midwestern state penitentiary for men. The data consist of the inmates' impressions of aging in prison. Seventy-seven usable interviews were obtained. The interviews, approximately a half-hour in length, were conducted by ourselves and James Cain, a graduate assistant. Drawn from the prison records, the sample was stratified with respect to age, race, length of sentence served, and length of sentence remaining. (Race was ultimately dropped from the analysis because simple cross-tabulations revealed no race-linked differences in the inmates' definitions of aging in prison.) Because a large segment of the elderly inmates selected for the sample were either confined to the prison hospital or located on work farms scattered throughout the state, we were forced to substitute additional elderly inmates to obtain a sample size sufficient for analysis. As a result, this sample cannot be considered a random sample and no statistical generalizations can be made. In particular, the high substitution of elderly inmates biases this segment of the sample toward the more healthy and alert members of this age-range of inmates. The two main questions asked were whether inmates generally age faster or slower than they would "on the streets" and whether each respondent thought he personally had aged faster or slower in prison. (Since the two questions tended to elicit the same response, the responses to both questions were combined.

Recent literature on prison life depicts a situation akin to Hobbes' image of the "war of each against all," and our respondents' statements during some phases of the interview verified this image.

Davis (1968) has documented a number of homosexual assaults in the Philadelphia prison system. Apparently, these assaults are not sexually motivated but are attempts to degrade systematically certain types of inmates. We did not explore the subject of homosexuality in any detail, and when the topic arose in the course of an interview, the discussion generally centered on consensual activities. Nevertheless, some references were made to the violent nature of homosexuality in prison. One respondent, for example, claimed that a recent knifing was in retribution for an attempted assault. Moreover, an inmate of one of the work farms is currently appealing a conviction for prison escape on the grounds that he was the victim of a series of homosexual assaults. In addition, violence other than homosexual assaults was alluded to by our respondents. According to their reports, most of the advice and favors they exchange consist of attempts to keep one another out of fights or associating with the wrong kind of people—i.e., people who "mean you no good." Thus, the high probability of violence and the exploitation of personal relationships reveal a situation which is less than idyllic.

In reply to our questions about aging in prison, however, the majority of the inmates were optimistic and often idealistic about the effect that prison had on them. For the most part, they claimed that prison retarded the aging process. Our interpretation of this optimism is that it reflects a more inclusive orientation to prison life, an orientation which, like that of the young and middle-aged automobile worker, blunts the anomic features of prison life and makes them bearable.[1] Again, like the automobile workers studied by Chinoy, this optimism is concen-

[1] We are indebted to Howard A. Rosencranz for bringing this interpretation to our attention.

trated among the young and middle-aged inmates. Extending our interpretation, the role of age in these two studies suggests that old age heightens a person's sensitivity to alienating situations by reducing his prospects for a better future.

The remainder of this paper elaborates this interpretation. The paper is divided into three parts: the first compares the parallel decline of optimism among the automobile workers and the prison inmates; the second examines the relationship between the various definitions of aging in prison and some rough indicators of anomie; the third considers these findings in the context of a more general question concerning the relationship between age and anomie.

THE DECLINE OF OPTIMISM AMONG
THE AUTOMOBILE WORKERS AND THE PRISON INMATES

The parallel decline of optimism among the automobile workers and the prison inmates is illustrated best by comparing the two groups at the early, middle, and late states of the adult life cycle.

Young Adulthood

Discussing automobile workers still in their twenties, Chinoy (1965) notes that they were well aware of the low pay increases and the generally "dead-end" future that a career in the assembly plant offered. Nevertheless, these conditions had little effect on them, for most saw their jobs as temporary. In fact, those in their early twenties seemed unconcerned about the future and viewed their jobs as the means of obtaining money for the day-to-day pleasures of cars, girls, and general "good times." The workers in their late twenties, having acquired a wife and children, showed more concern about the future and began making plans to leave the assembly line for a better-paying and more satisfying job. Both groups, however, were generally optimistic about the future since neither had experienced the futility of attempting to put their plans into practice.

Like the young automobile workers, the inmates in their twenties were considerably more optimistic about their situation than the rest of the inmate population. Although the majority of the respondents in their twenties said they had aged faster in prison, probing indicates that they were referring to the attainment of adult status, or maturity, rather than to aging as senescence. For example, when asked why he thought he aged faster in prison, one inmate said, "I don't think I would have been confronted with the things that I have been in here. [What kinds of things?] Different people and different kinds of attitudes . . . you learn more about the give and take of life . . . getting along with people." Another said, "I haven't aged fast physically; I've aged fast mentally—as far as wisdom and knowledge go. At least I think I've learned some things. [What kinds of things?] I think I've gotten a little more intelligence—I think I've gotten better, as a matter of fact."

The point which these men appear to be making is that prison life has enabled them to attain an "adult" outlook on life earlier than they would have on the streets. This achievement occurs not because of any attempts at rehabilitation by the prison staff—at least according to the inmates—but because the inmates have been forced to get along with a large number of men under conditions of stress. The optimism of this claim is reflected in the implication that they have gained in prison the qualities of character which will enable them to make good on the streets and to stay out of prison in the future. Consequently, viewing prison life almost as an educational experience, the younger inmates are able to discount its anomic aspects and give a negative experience some positive value.

It is quite possible that our respondents were "conning us, telling us what they thought we wanted to hear rather than what they believed. This interpretation has merit since inmates appear to lump all representatives of the middle class—whether prison officials, lawyers, sociologists, whatever—into the category of "square" or "square John." Clearly the statements that a young man matures faster in prison or that a middle-aged man grows old more slowly on the streets are geared to a square audience, particularly one composed of a warden, social workers, parole officials, etc. Nevertheless, the fact remains that the content of the inmates' replies varied with age. Thus, even if the majority of our respondents were conning us, this variation still indicates a decline of optimism. However, whether this optimism had to do with 1) the likelihood that their interview would affect their chances for parole, or 2) their basic orientation toward prison, is a moot point. Only more careful research can resolve this problem.

Middle Age

Chinoy found that though the middle-aged automobile workers were still optimistic, they were less optimistic than the younger workers. The alternatives to work on the assembly line were not given such serious consideration by the middle-aged workers. They had built up too much seniority to lose by taking a chance on a farm or a small business, and too many of their co-workers had failed at such attempts for them to be confident about their chances for success. Nor did they hope any longer for the possibility of being promoted to supervisory positions, for they also were too old for that. Nevertheless, they rationalized the loss of these options by focusing on more tenable goals such as the automatic wage increases or a move to an easier job in the factory away from the assembly line.

The middle-aged inmates' view of aging in prison implies that they too had grown somewhat less optimistic or at least that their optimism had taken a different form. They claimed that prison retards the aging process, or, as they put it, prison "preserves" them. The inmates supported their claim in two ways: First, from the standpoint of their physical well-being, they argued that life in prison offers some advantages over life on the streets. Prison, they said, removed them from the temptations of liquor, drugs, prostitution, and the other attractions of an active night life. On a more positive side, prison offered regular meals, sleep, and the opportunity to keep physically fit by participating in varied sports programs. Second, many inmates argued that prison maintained their mental health by freeing them from the worries and responsibilities which were confronted on the streets. As one respondent remarked, "In prison you don't have to worry about paying bills and taking care of your family." Another said, "Everything's regular in here. You just eat, sleep, do your job, and play sports if you want. Out on the streets things are 'messy'; inside, everyone knows what's coming next. Everything's planned, and there's no worry."

The belief that people grow old slower in prison than on the streets is reinforced by a number of features of prison life. First, this belief appears to be part of the prison lore and, in fact, extends beyond the inmates to members of the prison staff. Consequently, a new inmate is likely to be exposed to this idea early in his prison career. Second, evidence contrary to this belief is obscured from the inmates by the residential segregation of the elderly inmates. The majority of the elderly inmates reside either in the geriatric ward of the prison hospital, on one of the work farms, or in the prison's honor dorm. Third, what inter-generational interaction does occur is of such a selective nature that the younger inmates are able to maintain their definition of aging in prison. Based on the respondents' reports of the ages of their best friends, we found that strong friendships tend to be age-graded, while exceptions typically involve the more active and alert aged inmates. Because of this selective interaction, a number of younger inmates supported their views of aging in prison with anecdotes about the exploits of certain elderly inmates. Interviews with these older men revealed that both their age and liveliness were exaggerated.

The optimism of the viewpoint that the aging process is retarded by prison life should be apparent. A prison sentence—even a fairly long one—can be regarded as a temporary state relative to the same amount of time spent on the streets. It is as if the inmates believe that they can return to the streets unchanged, ready to begin life where they "left off." However, considered from the younger inmates' point of view, it also indicates a reduction in optimism; for unlike the viewpoint of the younger inmates, prison is no longer seen as a source of self-improvement. Prison neither increases nor decreases the probability of future success on the streets. Instead, the future seems to be viewed as holding the same options it did when the inmate left. Thus, although the middle-aged inmates are still able to discount the anomci aspects of prison life, in comparison with the younger inmates their interpretation of the prison experience is a more neutral one.

Old Age

With increasing age, the automobile workers became more pessimistic about their future. Even the reduced aspirations which had sustained their hopes through middle age no longer provided any hope. Reaching the top of their pay schedule, the older workers were still economically depressed, but this time with no pay increase to which they could look forward. In terms of a better job in the factory, the future was even more bleak; for with the onset of old age, they faced the possibility of being relegated to a low-paying menial, "make-work" task. Thus, with the bulk of their lives behind them and with no future ahead, the older workers' final realization that they could not escape the factory led to a "bitterness and resentment aimed at themselves, at others, and at the world in general (Chinoy, 1965 p. 122)."

This bitterness and resentment is apparent in many of the older inmates' statement that prison life has aged them. Already old—even older than the oldest automobile workers—the inmates in their sixties and seventies are unable to maintain the view the prison preserves them. Apparently seeing what little future they have slip away while imprisoned, they blame the penitentiary for their physical and mental deterioration. For example, when asked why they grow old faster in prison, many older inmates refer to the anxiety which they say results from being confined with men who are "trouble-makers." As one inmate explained, "The main problem in here is that prisoners are no good. They are always trying to start something, and you don't have any means of protection in here." Other inmates argue that the regimentation and routine of confinement cause them to grow old faster. For instance, one said, "Prison's a confined place. When you're out, you can have your pleasures, and time passes quicker." Another said, "In prison you don't have no space to travel in, no freedom. It cuts off your thoughts. Outside, you can come and go as you please, visit friends, and keep yourself well-regulated."

The contrast between the older inmates and the two groups of younger inmates, then, is marked. Seeing prison life as temporary, the latter two have some hope for the future. The inmates in their twenties foresee a better life out on the streets, while the middle-aged inmates at least hope to return to the way of life they left. Only the older inmate's statement that prison has aged him suggests a lack of hope. Indeed, it suggests that he has no future in any meaningful sense of the term, but instead sees himself either spending the rest of his life in prison or returning to the streets too old either to do the things he used to do or to start a new life. In sum, the older inmates are in the same position as the older automobile workers. Deprived of any hope for the future, they receive the full impact of the negative features of prison life.

The relationship between the inmate's age and his definition of aging in prison is presented more systematically in Table 1. As indicated above, the majority of the inmates in their twenties say that prison has matured them, most of the middle-aged group claim that prison has preserved them, while the bulk of the older inmates state that prison has aged them. The respondents were classified mainly on the basis of their replies to the question asking whether they had grown old faster or slower in prison. The question concerning the rate at which the respondents believe inmates in general grow old was used when there

TABLE 1: The inmate's definition of aging in prison by age

The inmate's definition	Age		
	20-29	30-59	60+
Prison has matured him	12	3	0
Prison has preserved him	5	17	8
Prison has aged him	3	8	16
Prison has made no difference	0	1	4

was no response to the other question or when the response was "no difference." The classification of a definition of aging in prison as one which says that inmates mature is based on the content of the inmate's reply to the probe of why he thought he had "aged" faster in prison (or why he thought inmates in general age faster in prison).

Before accepting the interpretation that these age differences indicate a change in the inmate's attitude over time, we should consider the possibility of other interpretations. First, there is the usual problem with inferring temporal processes from cross-sectional data—a problem which cannot be resolved here. Second, the relationship in Table 1 could be masking the operation of other variables. For example, the longer inmates have been exposed to the conditions of prison life, the more these conditions may wear on them. Equally likely is the alternative possibility that as the inmates approach release, the conditions may bother them less. Due to differences in sentencing, one or both may be related to age and thereby may be responsible for the distribution of responses in Table 1. However, the data in Tables 2 and 3 indicate that neither the number of years served, nor the number of years left to serve, directly affect the inmate's definition of aging in prison. Moreover, neither of these variables appears to interact with age. The best interpretation of our data, then, is that the inmate's definition of aging in prison is related to his age.

Possibly a more refined measure of these two variables would yield different results. In studies of imprisonment (e.g., Clemmer, 1958), the practice is to trichotomize the time spent in prison in terms of six

TABLE 2: The inmate's definition of aging in prison by age with length of
sentence served controlled

	Sentence served five years or less			Sentence served more than five years		
Inmate's definition	Age 20-29	Age 30-59	Age 60+	Age 20-39	Age 30-59	Age 60+
Prison has matured or preserved him	70%	75%	18%	100%	62%	29%
Prison has aged him or made no difference	30%	25%	82%	0%	48%	71%
n	10	13	11	10	16	17

months or less served, six months or less remaining, and the time in between. There are two reasons why we did not use this scheme: First, the bulk of our sample fell into the middle category, leaving too few cases in the two extreme categories for a meaningful analysis. Second, precise measures of these variables were difficult to obtain. Although length of present sentence served is easy to determine, this does not represent the total time spent in prison by recidivists. To total their prison sentences, however, would ignore the intervening time spent on the streets and lump together possibly different types of prison experiences, (e.g., other state and federal penitentiaries, city and county jails, reform schools, etc.). Length of sentence remaining was equally difficult to ascertain because of the different types of life sentences and the possibility of parole and/or time off for good behavior.

THE RELATIONSHIP BETWEEN THE INMATE'S DEFINITION OF AGING IN PRISON AND THREE CORRELATES OF ANOMIE

According to our interpretation of these different definitions of aging in prison, the two optimistic ones serve to buffer the inmate against the anomic effects of prison life. Inmates with an optimistic viewpoint, therefore, should be less anomic than those with a pessimistic outlook. Because of the exploratory nature of this study, none of the standard anomie scales were used in the interview schedule. However, we can test the credibility of this interpretation by relating the different definitions of aging to three correlates of anomie: the inmate's participation in leisure-time activities, his association with other inmates, and the extent of his boredom. Brief discussions of each of these correlates may clarify their utility.

First, although participation in leisure-time activities does not automatically make a person's life meaningful or give it purpose, research on the aged, at least, indicates that the absence of such activities is associated with anomie (Tobin & Neugarten, 1961). Supporting the use of participation as an indicator of anomie are the resignation and apathy conveyed in many of the inactive inmates' responses to our questions about their use of leisure time. As one inmate said, "I walk about in the yard once in a while . . . That's all I do. [Anything else?] Nothing but lay on the bed." Another, though more active, still expresses the same sense of resignation. "I don't do too much . . . I play a little guitar, a little pool, I read a little bit, and that's about it." Generally, only inmates who said they participated in no activities at all were classified as inactive. However, in borderline cases where the respondent indicated minimal participation in one or more activities (e.g., the case just cited), we considered his answer to

TABLE 3: The inmate's definition of aging in prison by age with length of sentence remaining controlled

	Sentence remaining: five years or less			Sentence remaining: more than five years		
Inmate's definition	Age 20-29	Age 30-59	Age 60+	Age 20-29	Age 30-59	Age 60+
Prison has matured or preserved him	80%	73%	16%	90%	67%	30%
Prison has aged him or made no difference	20%	27%	84%	10%	33%	70%
n	10	11	8	10	18	20

the question asking whether his participation in these activities had increased or decreased during his sentence. Those whose participation had decreased were also classified as inactive.

Second, much of what has been said about participation in leisure-time activities can be applied to the respondent's contacts with other inmates. Friends do not necessarily make life more meaningful or purposeful; yet research—again limited to the aged—also shows that anomie is associated with social isolation (Rosow, 1967). To determine the inmate's social isolation, three questions were asked: "How many inmates do you know by their first name or nickname?", "How many of the inmates are close friends of yours?", and, "Do you ever give one another advice?" (The responses to each of these questions were dichotomized. The cut point for the first question is fifty inmates or less, while the cut point for the second question is four men or less. In both cases these cut points are "natural breaks." A simple "yes-no" scheme was used with the third question.) Based on the responses to these three questions, our respondents were split into two categories: one consisted of those with minimal or no contact with the other inmates (those with at most one positive response to the three questions), the other consisted of those with more extensive contacts.

To get at the extent of the respondent's association with the other inmates, three questions were asked: "How many inmates do you know on a 'first-name' basis?", "How many of these men are 'close friends'?", and, "Do you ever give one another advice?" The responses to each of these questions were dichotomized. The cut point for the first question is fifty inmates or less, while the cut point for the second question is four men or less. In both cases these cut points are "natural breaks." A simple "yes-no" scheme was used with the third question. The respondents were divided in two groups in the following manner: those with two or more positive responses to the three questions were put in one group, while those with one or more were put in the other group.

Finally, to determine which inmates were bored, we asked our respondents, "Would you say that time is passing faster or more slowly than it did during your first years (months) of prison life?" Again, this item has also been used in research on the aged (Shanas, Townsend, Wedderburn, Friis, Milhø, & Stehouwer, 1968). Its usage seems to be based on the following rationale: People whose lives are full do not notice the passage of time and perceive time as passing quickly. On the other hand, people whose lives are empty and meaningless have nothing to occupy their time; consequently, time seems to drag. Among prison inmates this distinction is particularly critical since it is part of the difference between what inmates refer to as "doing good time" and "doing bad time." (That is, good time is time which passes quickly, while bad time is that which passes slowly.) As with the two previous items, the inmates were divided into two groups: those who said that time was passing more quickly than at the beginning of their sentence, and those who said either that time was passing more slowly or that there was no difference.

In relating these correlates of anomie to the inmates' definition of aging in prison we have controlled for age and considered only the middle-aged and older groups of inmates. We controlled for age because age is related both to the inmate's definition of aging in prison and to the correlates of anomie. Failure to control for age would have confounded the relationships between these other two variables. The inmates in their twenties were dropped from the analysis because too few of them had a pessimistic view of aging in prison. Combining them with the middle-aged inmates would have reduced the precision of our control for age.

Although the small sample size requires cautious interpretation, the data in Table 4 show that, regardless of age, inmates who have an optimistic definition of aging in prison are more likely to participate in leisure-time activities, associate with other inmates, and see time as passing rapidly. The significance of these data is their implication that the inmate's definition of aging in prison is not just an isolated or casual reply to an interviewer's question but, instead, is part of a broader response to the prison experience.

SUMMARY AND DISCUSSION

Interviews with the inmates of a large midwestern state penitentiary show that young and middle-aged inmates tend to give optimistic definitions of aging in prison, claiming either that prison "matures" them or that it "preserves" them, while the inmates in their sixties and seventies offer a more pessimistic view, saying that prison has made them age faster than is normal. Our interpretation of these data is that the inmates' susceptibility to the anomic features of prison life increases with age. Three factors enhance the validity of this interpretation. First, these age-related differences parallel the dissipation of the "American dream" among the automobile workers studied by Chinoy (1965). Second, such variables as the length of time served and the length of time left to serve affect neither the inmate's definition of aging in prison nor the relationship between this definition and age. Third, the inmate's orientation is correlated, independently of age, with three additional aspects of his life. Inmates who say that they have aged faster than normal in prison also participate less in leisure-time activities, have fewer contacts among the other inmates, and are less likely to see their prison sentences as passing quickly. However, because the linkage between age and anomie occurred to us after the preliminary data analysis, and because of the small sample, this interpretation must be regarded as strictly tentative. Before more definite conclusions can be drawn, other inmate populations must be sampled, more direct indicators of both anomie and its behavioral correlates should be used, and additional and more refined control variables must be introduced.

Operating as if this linkage does occur, however, we will discuss it in terms of a more general relationship between age and anomie. In the development of their disengagement hypothesis, Cumming & Henry (1961) present a series of findings which relate old age to various psychological and social psychological variables. Our interpretation of

TABLE 4: Correlates of anomie by the inmate's definition of aging in prison with age controlled

	Age 30-59		Age 60+	
Correlate	Prison matures or preserves	Ages	Prison matures or preserves	ages
% active	80%	25%	62%	20%
% who have friends	75%	25%	75%	33
% who say time passes quickly	79%	14%	88%	25%
n	20	8	8	15

these findings is that with increasing age people adopt a retreatist orientation to the world.

As the two terms suggest, disengagement is similar to retreatism. The difference lies in the greater emphasis placed by Cumming & Henry on the voluntary nature of the older person's withdrawal from society. From the retreatist standpoint, this withdrawal is voluntary only in a technical sense. Whereas Cumming & Henry see it as a normal "developmental stage" in the life cycle, we see it as symptomatic of the resignation and despair which result from the special circumstances of many older Americans.

For example, the TAT protocols of a subsample of their respondents show that older respondents tend to be passive and withdrawn. Typically, their stories are less likely to be embellished with characters not portrayed in the picture; less likely to contain conflict, controversy, or situations requiring decision-making; more likely to consist of passive rather than active themes; and less likely to report strong emotional states as the motive for action. As Cumming & Henry state (1961, p. 127), "[the older person] tends to respond to inner rather than outer stimuli, to withdraw emotional investment, to give up self-assertiveness, and to avoid rather than embrace challenge." The retreatist orientation implied in these TAT protocols is also evident in the older respondents' low morale scores on such items as: "How satisfied would you say you are with your life today?", "As you get older would you say things seem to be better or worse than you thought they would be?", and "How often do you feel that there's just no point in living?"

Other research points directly to the older person's pessimistic outlook on the future. Spence (1967), for example, finds that the "very old" are less likely to plan for the future than the "old." Similarly, in one study Kogan & Wallach (1961) find that the "very old" and the "old" are more likely to devalue the future than a group of college-age respondents. In another study they find that both chronological and subjective age are related to an avoidance of risk and a lack of self-confidence in task-performance situations (1961 a).

Of course, the prevalence of anomie among the aged can be blamed partially on circumstances which often accompany old age. These include reduced economic status, bereavement, social isolation, the assignment of a socially devalued identity—circumstances which can produce anomie in adults of all ages. Yet, as with prison life or work on the automobile assembly line, these factors probably have a greater effect on the aged. The young person has most of his life ahead of him. Anything seems possible; therefore present difficulties can be regarded as temporary. In contrast, as a person ages the bulk of his life increasingly lies in a past whose failures and commitments have impressed upon him the limits of the possible. Thus, with the future holding little promise—except perhaps that of death—the older person experiences the full force of present difficulties. The result is disillusionment, despair, and apathy.

We have illustrated the development of this disillusionment in the case of the automobile worker and that of the prison inmate. In his short novel, *Seize the Day*, Saul Bellow (1965) provides a more sensitive portrayal of this process. At the end of the novel the main character, Tommy Wilhelm, confronts his mediocrity and failure while watching his youth slip away. Unsuccessful in his careers as movie actor and salesman, he is rejected by his wife, separated from his children, and scorned by his father to whom he turns for financial and emotional support. In a desperate attempt to salvage his version of the American dream, Wilhelm entrusts his remaining two hundred dollars to a confidence man. In search of the swindler on the streets of New York, he blunders into the funeral of a stranger. Passing by the coffin, Wilhelm sees in the corpse the death of his youth and his dreams. He is overcome by the futility of his situation and, as Alfred Kazin remarks (1968), "mourns himself as if he were dead." Although Wilhelm represents a special social milieu, Bellow's book has universal appeal. Wilhelm's despair is the despair that, in varying degrees, most men eventually must face. As man grows older, he watches his dreams die and realizes that his aspirations will remain unfulfilled. The horizon of his world narrows to the walls of his own particular prison.

REFERENCES

Bellow, S. *Seize the day*. New York: Fawcett Publications, 1965.

Chinoy, E. *Automobile workers and the American dream*. New York: Random House, 1965.

Clemmer, D. *The prison community*. New York: Holt, Rinehart, and Winston, 1958.

Cumming, E., & Henry, W. *Growing old: The process of disengagement*. New York: Basic Books, 1961.

Davis, A. J. Sexual assaults in the Philadelphia prison system and sheriffs' vans. *Trans-actions*, 1968, *6*, 8-16.

Kazin, A. Bellow's purgatory. *The New York Review of Books*, 1968, *10*, 32-36.

Kogan, N., & Wallach, M. A. Age changes in values and attitudes. *Journal of Gerontology*, 1961, *16*, 272-281.

Kogan, N., & Wallach, M. A. The effect of anxiety on relations between subjective age and caution in an older sample. In P. H. Hoch & J. Zubin (Eds.), *Psychopathology of aging*. New York: Grune and Stratton, 1961. (a)

Merton, R. K. *Social theory and social structure*. Glencoe, Ill.: Free Press, 1957.

Nelson, J. I. Anomie: Comparisons between the old and new middle-class. *American Journal of Sociology*, 1968, *74*, 184-192.

Rosow, I. *Social integration of the aged*. New York: Free Press, 1967.

Shanas, E., Townsend, P., Wedderburn, D., Friis, M., Milhø, P., & Stehouwer, J. *Old people in three industrial societies*. New York: Atherton Press, 1968.

Spence, D. L. The role of futurity in aging adaptation. Paper presented at the meeting of the Gerontological Society, St. Petersburg, Florida, 1967.

Tobin, S., & Neugarten, B. Life satisfaction and social interaction in the aging. *Journal of Gerontology*, 1961, *16*, 344-347.

Wilensky, H., & Edwards, H. The skidder: Ideological adjustments of downward mobile workers. *American Sociological Review*, 1959, *24*, 215-231.

27:: HOMOGENEITY AND HETEROGENEITY AMONG LOW–INCOME NEGRO AND WHITE AGED*

CARL HIRSCH, DONALD P. KENT,
SUZANNE L. SILVERMAN

In her review (1967) of gerontologic knowledge concerning the Negro aged, Jacquelyne Jackson (1967) pointed to past gaps and present "proliferating research interest (p. 168)" and suggested that there are many reasons for this proliferation. To place both this paper and the research study on which it is based in proper perspective we should emphasize the purposes for which the latter was begun.

The study is being conducted in Philadelphia at the suggestion of several Negro agencies and the State Department of Public Welfare. It is being conducted by staff of the Pennsylvania State University under a research grant from the Administration on Aging.

Many working with the Negro aged, prompted by the assertions of the National Urban League's publication *Double Jeopardy* (1964), have felt the need to appraise differentials between the major race-color, low income groups. The basic approach of the Urban League is that "Today's Negro is different from today's aged white because he is Negro ... and this alone should be enough basis for differential treatment (p. 1)." We have controlled, through sample selection, for socioeconomic status; and with that important control we are looking for indications of homogeneity and heterogeneity both within and

*Based on a paper presented at the 21st Annual Meeting of the Gerontological Society, November 1, 1968, Denver, Colorado.

between racial groups. Following Jackson's call for sensitivity to variations within white and Negro subgroups we have chosen to work with the low-income aged, recognizing that our data will make possible only restricted comments on patterns of living at other class levels.

The overall objectives of the study include assessing the needs of this segment of the elderly, measuring their knowledge and use of existing resources, and isolating the social and personal correlates of need and of the utilization of social services. In this paper we have purposely aimed at a descriptive report of characteristics, recognizing that careful description of the subgroups is a necessary prerequisite to analyses of process. We will be examining characteristics of family structure and interaction, group affiliations, housing and mobility, income maintenance, health and use of health services, and religious affiliation.

Method

A Socioeconomic scale (Pennsylvania Department of Public Health, 1963) was used to rank the two-hundred census tracts of Philadelphia county. From the quartiles ranked lowest by this SES measure, 923 block segments were randomly selected. Home interviews (averaging two hours in length) were conducted with more than one thousand persons over sixty-five who were residing in these low income areas. (The Refusal Rate was 18% with a total loss rate somewhat higher.)

Of the 1,039 persons interviewed, 74% were Negro and 26% white. (See Table 1) while census data on the racial composition by age for the black segments selected are not available, there are reasons to believe that the sample underrepresents whites.

Comparisons with census data for the nation as a whole (Brotman, 1968) indicate that the study sample is underrepresented in the 65-74 age category for white males. This may in part reflect the fact that, nationally, the white male is the most frequently employed (30.6%) of all persons 65 and over, and when employed, most frequently working on a full-time year-round job. It is likely that this would be equally true for our sample. Although two callbacks were required of interviewers,

TABLE 1: Homogeneity and heterogeneity among low-income Negro and White aged

		Age 65-74		Age 75-84		Age 85 & over		Total	
		No.	%	No.	%	No.	%	No.	%
Negro	Total	540		182		38		758	
	Males	225	70	81	25	16	5	322	100
	Females	315	72	101	23	20	5	436	100
White	Total	158		87		20		264	
	Males	59	51	45	39	11	0	115	100
	Females	99	66	41	28	9	6	149	100
Grand total		698		268		56		1,022 [1]	
1960 National Census									
Non-white	Males		69.5		25		5		
	Females		68.5		25		6		
White	Males		68		27		5		
	Females		65		29		6		

[1] Total N. = 1,039. Seventeen cases have been temporarily removed for data correction.

TABLE 2: Homogeneity and heterogeneity among low-income Negro aged

	Male				Female				Row
	Total	65-74	75-84	85+	Total	65-74	75-84	85+	Total
Married	178	139	34	5	98	63	11	2	269
%	55	62	42	31	22	26	11	10	
Separated-divorced	30	21	9	0	33	27	6	0	63
%	9	9	11	0	8	9	6	0	63
Widowed	95	51	34	10	234	192	74	18	379
%	30	23	42	63	65	61	73	90	
Never married	19	14	4	1	23	13	10	0	42
%	6	6	5	6	5	4	10	0	
Column totals	317	220	81	16	436	315	101	20	753
%	100	100	100	100	100	100	100	100	

Total male-total female: χ^2 = 105.12; d.f. = 3; Significance level = .0000; Contingency coefficient: C. = .349

this strategy apparently was not successful in gaining adequate representation of this group.

Familial Structure and Function

Actuarial data have long revealed substantial differences in death rates between Negroes and whites. At all ages, except among the very old, the Negro fares less well. This fact refelcts itself in the family structure of the aged. (See Tables 2, 3) At the same time, the family patterns of both racial groups reflect the biological fact that women outlive men and the social fact that men tend to marry women younger than themselves and to remarry at more advanced ages. Thus we find less than one-quarter of the females in the study group living with a spouse while more than half of the men are with a spouse. This pattern reflects significant differences between males and females within each race group. Differences between the racial group are not significant, although at each age level more whites than Negroes are living with a spouse.

Living without a spouse is, of course, a common experience for large numbers of older persons of both races and in all economic circumstances. However, it is interesting to note the length of time individuals have been living without spouse (See Table 4). One-half of all these living alone have been without spouse for fifteen years or more. Even among the "young old," (i.e., the 65-75 age group) the proportion of those once married who have now lived alone for fifteen years or more comes close to 40%. There are only minor differences between the races in this regard as seen in Table 4.

The raw figures associating widowhood with old age obscure the fact that for large numbers of persons the loss of spouse occurs during the middle years. We know relatively little about this "adjustment to singleness" as a function of age; however, it is reasonable to speculate that the problems of adjusting to the ordinary decrements of old age are magnified by the loss of spouse. If this hypothesis is correct, then the Negro aged again fare less well than the white, since at all age levels

TABLE 3:   Homogeneity and heterogenity among low-income White aged

	Male				Female				Row Total
	Total	65-74	75-84	85+	Total	65-74	75-84	85+	
Married	67	41	22	4	44	33	10		111
%	58	70	49	36	30	33	25	11	
Separated-divorced	4	4	0	0	8	3	3	2	12
%	4	7	0	0	5	3	7	22	
Widowed	36	11	19	6	86	54	26	6	122
%	31	18	42	55	58	55	63	67	
Never married	8	3	4	1	11	9	2	0	19
%	7	5	9	9	7	9	5	0	
Column totals	115	59	45	11	149	99	41	9	264
%	100	100	100	100	100	100	100	100	

Total male-total female: X^2 = 23.17, d.f. = 3; Significance level = .0001; Contingency coefficient: C. = .284

TABLE 4:   Homogeneity and heterogeneity among low-income Negro and White age

Number of years with-	Negro						White					
	Male			Female			Male			Female		
out spouse	65-74	75-84	85+	65-74	75-84	85+	65-74	75-84	85+	65-74	75-84	85+
0-4 years, 11 months	19	6	5	40	5	1	1	6	0	13	3	0
%	26	14	50	19	7	6	6	38	0	29	12	0
5-14 years, 11 months	23	9	0	67	19	4	9	4	2	15	10	1
%	32	22	0	33	25	27	56	25	67	33	40	20
15 years +	30	26	5	99	52	10	6	6	1	17	12	4
%	42	64	50	48	68	67	38	37	33	38	48	80
Column totals	72	41	10	206	76	15	16	16	32	45	25	5
%	100	100	100	100	100	100	100	100	100	100	100	100

more Negroes than whites have been without a spouse for fifteen years or more.

The essence of the family lies in the network of kin relationships and the interaction of its members. Most of the study sample had children; however, there are significant differences in size of family by race (See Table 5). Forty-two percent of the Negroes had no living children in contrast to only 27% of the whites, while 68% of the whites had two or more children compared with only 39% of the Negro aged. Remarkable homogeneity between sexes within racial groups can be seen in Table 5. Although we did not control for number of children by migration status we found that only 13% of the Negroes in the sample were born in Philadelphia. The influence of migration in depressing family size for this generation of the elderly Negro, as suggested by Dr. Jackson (during discussion of this paper), will be investigated.

While Negroes had significantly fewer children of their own, a significantly greater number raised children other than their own. Almost one-quarter (23.4%) of the Negroes compared to 8% of white respondents indicated that they had done so (See Table 6). Our data show a smaller but still significant difference between Negro males and females in this regard; however, we expect that greater light will be thrown on the nature of this difference by further analysis of the role of unmarried Negro women and grandmothers as foster mothers. As with the size of family, age is not significantly related to this variable which indicates that these patterns have been constant for all over 65.

Most of the elderly within the study reported frequent visits with and from their children (See Table 7). More than half reported seeing their children daily. Of the aged low income group who have living children, only five in one hundred "never saw them," while 21% saw them "less than once a month," and 20% saw them "at least once a month."

Not only were the elderly frequently in contact with their children, but they saw their grandchildren with surprising frequency (See Table 8). Almost half of the respondents saw their grandchildren at least weekly; and one in five grandparents saw a grandchild daily. While the

Negroes reported a daily contact with grandchildren more frequently, the differences are not statistically significant, nor are there differences by age or sex. The high frequency of visiting between parents and children and between grandparents and grandchildren, among both Negroes and whites in this sample, supports previous findings of assistance and visiting patterns associated with lower socioeconomic status and indicates greater homogeneity by class than by race in this regard. (Dotson, 1951; Montgomery, 1965)

This pattern of similarity between Negro and white is also apparent with regard to visiting between relatives other than children, grandchildren and siblings. χ^2 = 14.72, d.f. = 4, significance level = .02, contingency coefficient = .155. Among siblings, however, we found that the Negro aged had more contact that did the white. This difference mainly results from the higher number of whites who never see siblings. When we control for the foreign-born status of whites in this sample, whose siblings may still be in Europe, this difference disappears.

In the Babchuk & Thompson study of "Voluntary Association of Negroes (1962)," evidence was found for a higher rate of affiliation with voluntary associations among low income Negroes than among low income whites. Our data strongly supports this finding. ("Do you belong to groups other than church congregation?" χ^2 = 11.25 [Yates Correction] d.f. = 1, significance level = .001.) However, their assertion that this greater group affiliation replaced social contact and participation with kin is not supported. Our data indicate greater group affiliation among Negro subjects and homogeneity between races in family and kin interaction.

Housing and Mobility

It has been noted by others that the present generation of old people places great value upon home ownership. They received their early

TABLE 5:   Homogeneity and heterogeneity among low-income Negro and White aged

Number of Children	Negro			White			All Total
	Total	Male	Female	Total	Male	Female	
None	316	133	183	71	31	40	387
%	41	41	42	27	27	27	
One	157	62	95	38	15	23	195
%	21	19	22	14	13	15	
Two-four	189	80	109	107	48	59	296
%	25	25	25	40	41	39	
Five +	97	47	50	50	22	28	147
%	13	15	11	19	19	19	
Column total	759	322	437	266	116	150	1,025
%	100	100	100	100	100	100	100

Negro-White: x^2 = 36.74, d.f. = 3; Significance level: .0001; Contingency Coefficient: C. = .195.

TABLE 6: Homogeneity and heterogeneity among low-income Negro and White aged

Raised children other than own	Negro			White		
	Total	Male	Female	Total	Male	Female
Yes	171	59	112	20	9	11
%	23	20	26	7	8	8
No	560	249	311	235	102	133
%	77	80	74	93	92	92
Column totals	731	308	423	255	111	144
%	100	100	100	100	100	100

Negro-White: x^2 = 19.29, (Yates correction), d.f. = 1; Significance level = .0000; Contingency Coefficient: C. = .14. Negro Male-Female: x^2 = 4.9, (Yates correction), d.f. = 1; Significance level = .05; Contingency Coefficient: C. = .08.

TABLE 7: Homogeneity and heterogeneity among low-income Negro and White aged

Frequency of children's visits	Negro			White			Total sample
	Total	Male	Female	Total	Male	Female	
Daily	68	21	47	39	18	21	107
%	16	12	20	24	25	22	18
At least once per week	143	65	78	63	23	40	106
%	34	34	35	38	32	41	35
At least once per month	82	40	42	34	17	17	117
%	20	22	18	20	24	17	20
Less than once per month	97	50	47	25	9	16	122
%	23	26	21	14	13	17	21
Never	23	10	13	7	4	3	30
%	6	6	5	4	5	3	5
Column totals	413	186	227	168	71	97	582
%	99	100	100	100	99	100	99

TABLE 8: Homogeneity and heterogeneity among low-income Negro and White aged

How often visit grandchildren	Negro			White			Total sample
	Total	Male	Female	Total	Male	Female	
Daily	86	23	63	28	8	20	114
%	23	15	28	19	12	24	22
At least once per week	94	45	49	36	18	18	130
%	25	30	23	24	28	22	25
At least once per month	72	32	40	42	19	23	114
%	19	21	18	29	30	28	22
Less than once per month	95	42	53	35	18	17	136
%	26	27	24	24	28	20	26
Never	26	12	14	6	1	5	26
%	7	7	7	4	2	6	5
Column totals	373	154	219	147	64	83	520
%	100	100	100	100	100	100	100

socialization at a time when to own one's home was one of the major goals of American people. That this value is deeply held is readily seen in the fact that well over half of the low-income aged of this study owned their own homes (See Table 9). Differences between Negroes and whites are significant. Black subjects divided evenly between those living in owned and rented houses, while more than three-quarters of the white subjects reported home ownership.

These figures do not give the full meaning of home ownership. They fail to convey the pride of ownership—the fact that for many this represents one of life's major accomplishments. So strong are these feelings that many older people studied will not accept old-age assistance because a lien is then placed against the house, clouding individual ownership.

Links to the environment, such as the owned home, have been referred to as "basic anchorages" by Cath (1965). Another possible example of such an anchorage may be the neighborhood of residence. More than one-third of Negro respondents and nearly one-half of whites had always lived in the same neighborhood (See Table 9). Of those who had lived in different neighborhoods (Table 9E) nearly one-half of Negroes and more than three-fifths of whites had been residing in their present neighborhood for twenty years or more. Still, a significantly greater number of whites than Negroes were anchored to the present neighborhood, as seen by length of residence.

This same relationship held for length of residence in the city. While 50% of the whites were born in Philadelphia, only 13% of the aged Negroes were born in the city (Table 9B). A significantly greater number of Negro subjects came to Philadelphia as adults, compared to whites (Table 9C). The degree to which neighborhood stability and length of residence in the city was related to the ability of the aged person to meet needs by using resources in the environment will be a crucial variable in further analysis of the data. In a partial analysis of

TABLE 9:   Homogeneity and heterogeneity among low-income Negro and
            White aged housing and mobility patterns

	Negro		White	
	N	%	N	%
A. Home ownership				
Owns home (and lives with				
home owner)	380	51	209	80
Rents (and lives with renter)	366	49	54	20
Total	746	100	263	100

x^2 = 63.92 (Yates Correction), d.f. = 1; Contingency Coefficient = .24; Significance Level = .0000

B. Born in Philadelphia	99	13[1]	135	50[2]
C. Arrived in Philadelphia–age				
0-18 years	138	21	60	46
19-64 years	487	73	67	51
65+ years	39	6	4	3
Total	664	100	131	100

x^2 = 34.40, d.f. = 3; Contingency Coefficient = .203; Significance Level = .0001

D. Always lived in same				
neighborhood	279	37[1]	126	47[2]
E. Time in present neighborhood				
0-5 years	63	13	12	9
6-20 years	198	41	36	26
20 years +	223	46	92	65
Total	484	100	140	100

x^2 = 30.40; d.f. = 3; Contingency Coefficient = .215; Significance Level = .0001

[1] Of all Negro
[2] Of all White

TABLE 10:   Homogeneity and heterogeneity among low-income Negro and
            White aged

Source of income	Percent reporting income	
	Negro	White
Wages	16.5	11.5
Social security	77.9	85.3
Veteran's pension	0.1	9.0
Private disability pension	0.9	0.8
Private pension	14.8	21.5
Savings	5.8	13.6
Relatives' contribution	8.0	10.3
Welfare	23.8	10.0
Other sources	1.5	1.7

11% of respondents with severe unmet needs, no relationship was found between ignorance of potential resources and variables concerning residential stability.

Income Maintenance

During the mid-thirties when our present Social Security program took form, its architects envisioned a time when all older people would have a monetary income. This objective has been almost completely achieved. Less than 2% of the study group reported no income at all (See Table 10). Needless to say, this does not mean that the level of income is adequate.

Social Security is far and away the most frequently mentioned source of income for both Negroes and whites with 78% of the black subjects and 85% of the whites receiving benefits. Company and union pensions provided additional money for 15% of the Negroes and 21% of the whites. For neither racial group were wages and salaries a major factor—only 16% of Negro subjects and 12% of white reported income from employment.

There were marked racial differences with regard to receiving assistance. More than 20% of the Negro respondents received old age assistance benefits while 10% of the white did. There are a number of factors at play here, but chief among these is the fact that the average social security benefit for Negroes was somewhat less than for whites; consequently more Negroes were eligible for supplementary assistance.

Attitudes toward welfare are complex and will not be reported in this paper. It would be an oversimplification to state that "welfare has a bad image." Undeniably many feel this way; however there were too many reports of a positive nature to permit facile generalizing. Our data indicate that twice as many Negroes as whites had at some time in their life been on "the welfare." More Negroes than whites had applied for old age assistance but were not receiving it; and more blacks than whites felt they should be receiving assistance. However, the desire for independence, the pride in being self supporting, and the sacrifices made to maintain this position were manifested by both racial groups.

TABLE 11: Homogeneity and heterogeneity among low-income Negro and White aged

Religious activities	Total		Male		Female		For total Negro - White
	Negro	White	Negro	White	Negro	White	
Attends services							$\chi^2 = 12.04$; C. = .11; Sig. level = .0007; d.f. = 3
Regularly or often	372	110	139	42	231	68	
%	50	43	45	37	54	48	
Sometimes or never	370	146	172	72	196	74	
%	50	57	55	63	46	52	
Prays							$\chi^2 = 42.4$; C. = .20; Sig. level = .0001; d.f. = 3
Regularly or often	638	198	274	69	406	119	
%	91	76	87	60	95	89	
Sometimes or never	65	62	41	46	23	16	
%	9	24	13	40	5	11	
Religious programs							$\chi^2 = 132.2$; C. = .34; Sig. level = .0000; d.f. = 3
Regularly or often	402	42	159	17	240	25	
%	54	16	50	15	56	17	
Sometimes or never	347	217	158	98	188	119	
%	46	84	50	85	44	83	
Reads Bible							$\chi^2 = 131.9$; C. = .34; Sig. level = .0000; d.f. = 3
Regularly or often	440	65	165	21	273	44	
%	59	25	52	18	64	31	
Sometimes or never	307	191	151	92	154	99	
%	41	75	48	82	36	69	

Health

Often the obvious eludes us and goes unnoted. One of the major and obvious changes of the twentieth century is the vast improvement in health and health care. Not only has there been a remarkable increase in life expectancy, but there have been dramatic improvements in personal health and vigor. These advantages, which at the beginning of this century were limited to the affluent few, are now being extended to virtually all.

Only six out of each one hundred respondents were housebound, and there were virtually no differences by racial groups. And among the housebound, only a small fraction were confined to bed or wheelchair. Some 60% of the respondents indicated that they were not at all limited by health conditions. Again there were no differences by race.

Almost one-half of the Negro and three-quarters of the white respondents had family physicians on whom they felt they could call when needed. However, the lack of a family physician does not mean a lack of medical care. Of these without a family doctor, one-half of the white and one-fifth of the Negro respondents reported going to a physician at least once during the preceding year. Although this difference is significant χ^2 = 38.2 [Yates Correction] d.f. = 1, significance level = .001, C. = 275.) with whites having greater access to private physicians, there was significantly greater use of clinics by Negro respondents. χ^2 = 27.1 [Yates Correction] d.f. = 1, significance level = .0001, C. = .16.) There were no differences in utilization rates for overnight stays in hospitals.

As a measure of unmet need, respondents who had not received medical attention during the prior year were asked if they had felt a need for medical services during this period. Only 14% of the Negro and 8% of the white respondents so indicated. These data would seem to indicate that there is still a significant number of low income older persons needing medical care who are not receiving it. The plus side of this is that the group is relatively small and shows no significant difference by racial group.

The availability of medical care to low-income aged in a metropolitan setting is well documented by the data from this study. More than one-third of the study group (again, no racial differences) had had an eye examination during the previous year. More than 80% wore glasses. While only a fifth had visited a dentist during the preceeding year, 60% had dentures. Again, difference between the races was slight.

These data give too favorable a picture. A contextual analysis and the case material collected bring to light less favorable aspects. Clinics and hospitals often are located too far from the neighborhoods of the low-income aged. Public transportation is frequently nonexistent, often inconvenient, and almost always too expensive. Health personnel at times fail to communicate with the old. At times the health professional assumes a greater medical sophistication on the part of the aged patient than exists; and at other times the health workers are amazingly blind to the social needs of the elderly patient. His medical needs will be well diagnosed and the appropriate prophylactic prescribed; but at the same time his social needs will be completely disregarded with the result that the latter quite negate the hoped-for medical therapy.

Religion

Very early in the study it became apparent that religion plays a role for the Negro that is quantitatively and qualitatively different from its role for the average white.

One indicator of this difference is church attendance (See Table 11). While females of both races were more apt to attend church than males, the black male attended almost as frequently as the white female. The same pattern obtained for prayer. Again the black female was the most religious, and again the black male approximated the behavior of the white female. The white male lagged far behind.

When the measure was listening to religious services on the radio, the racial differences became even more pronounced. More than half of the

Negro respondents regularly listened to religious services broadcast on radio; less than one-fifth of the whites reported doing so. And twice as many Negroes as whites reported regularly reading the Bible.

Time does not permit an analysis of the differential meaning of the religious experience. However, in general the denominational affiliations and beliefs of the Negro respondents had a strong Pentecostal nature. This is perhaps explainable in terms of a hard working, underprivileged group seeking, and ultimately receiving, a triumphal reward. Since, in many respects, the Negro church follows a traditional pattern, it may more nearly meet the cultural expectations of the present group of elderly. Conceivably, the greater interest of the Negro aged in religion reflects not a greater inner need but rather a greater adaptability of the Negro church to the desires of the aged. Perhaps the white church in its open efforts to reach the young, has developed a service and message less congenial to the white aged.

Summary and Conclusions

This paper purposely has been descriptive. While the authors well recognize that analysis at a different level is necessary if we are to obtain an understanding of the process at work, we also recognize that careful description of subgroups is a necessary prerequisite to such analysis. The absence of adequate descriptive studies makes it almost inevitable that our theories and our programs will be equally inadequate.

We have examined differences by race and sex and found both heterogeneity and homogeneity between and among members of both racial groups. Age has only been introduced into discussion occasionally although we have some indication that the importance of age varies by race-sex group according to the characteristic being considered. Further analysis of age differences among the aged group is certainly planned.

The view expressed in *Double Jeopardy* (National Urban League, 1964) that race identity alone is " ... enough basis for differential treatment," is an oversimplification because it obviates the search for differentials among persons with the same racial identification, as well as ignoring the interplay of these within group qualities and the aging process. In addition, age can be a great leveler. The differences that derive from prior social class position, racial grouping, and environmental circumstances may be blurred by the decrements of age, the problems incident to the later years, and by the social and personal mechanisms developed to cope with them. To stress only the differences and ignore the similarities both within and between racial groupings would be to distort our vision and to defeat our efforts to develop effective approaches.

REFERENCES

Babchuk, N., & Thompson, R. V. The voluntary associations of Negroes. *American Sociological Review*, 1962, *27*, 647-655.

Brotman, H. B. Who are the aged: A demographic view. *Useful Facts No. 42*, August 9, 1968, 15-17

Cath, S. H. Some dynamics of middle and later years: A study in depletion and restitution. In M. A. Berezin, & S. H. Cath (Eds.), *Geriatric psychiatry: Grief, loss, and emotional disorders in the aging process*. New York: International Universities Press, 1965.

Dotson, F. L. Patterns of voluntary associations among urban working class families. *American Sociological Review*, 1951, *16*, 689-693.

Jackson, J. Social gerontology and the Negro: A review. *The Gerontologist*, 1967, 7, 168-178.

Montgomery, J. E. *Social characteristics of the aged in a small Pennsylvania community*. (Publication No. 233) University Park, Pa.: College of Home Economics Research, 1965.

National Urban League. *Double jeopardy: The older Negro in America today*. New York: Author, 1964.

Pennsylvania Department of Health, Community Health Services, Division of Statistics and Research. *Census tracts in socio-economic rank order for the city and within health districts, 1960*. October 29, 1963.

28:: AGED NEGROES: THEIR CULTURAL DEPARTURES FROM STATISTICAL STEREOTYPES AND RURAL–URBAN DIFFERENCES

JACQUELYNE JOHNSON JACKSON

That which follows (sans vocal inflections, arched eyebrows, *et cetera*) is largely a replication of a presentation in conjunction with a panel on "Cultural departures from statistical stereotypes," one of a series in a symposium on the "Adequacy of programs, planning, and evaluation for meeting the needs of the elderly."

This paper is concerned with the two specifically assigned tasks of that oral presentation. The first part contains a general discussion of some cultural departures from statistical stereotypes by aged Negroes; the second focuses upon some specific rural-urban differences found among several samples of Negro aged.

CULTURAL DEPARTURES FROM STATISTICAL STEREOTYPES

Needless to say, the operational definitions of "cultural departures" and "statistical stereotypes" used, as well as judgments made about the "adequacy" of programs, planning, and evaluation for meeting the

An oral version of this paper was presented at the annual meeting of the Gerontological Society, 30 October 1968, Denver, Colorado. Reprinted through the courtesy of *The Gerontologist*, the professional practitioner journal of the Gerontological Society.

needs of Negro elderly, were directly affected by my interpretations of the current status of knowledge about and programs and planning for aged Negroes.

As has been noted elsewhere (Jackson, 1967, 1968), very little is known about aged Negroes. Yet, if one essential criterion in determining the adequacy of programs, planning, and evaluation for meeting the needs of the elderly is that crystallized by Eisdorfer (1968) in another context as that of "basic information on the aging process and the impact of aging upon the individual and his community," it would follow that most such programs designed for or to include aged Negroes are inadequate. In fact, most such programs, planning, and evaluation for most aged, regardless of race and ethnicity, are, no doubt, yet inadequate.

(An incidental—incidental in the sense of falling without the realm of this paper—point is that of the "touchy" issue of racial segregation or of racial desegregation for programs in which aged persons would be expected to interact face-to-face. Should there be racial desegregation or segregation in "X" program? If so, why so, when so, where so, and how so? Although this may be more pronounced in the South, it is probably an "itchy" issue in the North as well. It is certainly an issue much influenced by various stereotypes regarding the Negro and other aged groups.)

Since so little is known about aged Negroes, no exhaustive nor precise delineation of cultural departures by aged Negroes from statistical stereotypes can now be proffered. However, a general discussion of some of their cultural departures may be especially useful for program, planning, and evaluation personnel for the elderly.

Three general areas which may be focused upon are: 1) statistical stereotypes derived largely from data collected by the U.S. Bureau of Census and variously interpreted by that agency and others; 2) statistical stereotypes obtained from empirical findings in social gerontological and other related studies; and 3) what may be termed the "laymen's 'statistical stereotypes.' "

One example of a cultural departure by aged nonwhites (i.e., 60+ years of age, 92% of whom were Negroes in the 1960 census) from a statistical stereotype of nonwhites generally is that nonwhites did *not* differ significantly by marital status from aged whites in 1960.

Since this fact may startle some, chi-square results are provided in Table 1 below. Overall, the largest proportional difference by marital status between these nonwhites and whites was that more nonwhites than whites were widowed. The second largest such difference for males was that more nonwhites were in the category of "spouse absent" than were whites: for females, more whites were "single" than were nonwhites.

The trend toward an increasing significant difference between the marital statuses of nonwhites and whites for younger age groups, however, suggests that as the younger nonwhite population becomes older, the marital statuses of aged nonwhites (or at least of aged Negroes) will vary from the 1960 pattern. If so, significant racial differences by marital status may appear among a future older population. Especially may more older Negro males be spouseless— increasing, perhaps, the need for even more institutionalized and other secondary supportive and protective services.

In 1965, Negro aged (i.e., 65+ years of age) were 6.1% of the total Negro population, a smaller proportion than that of all aged in the total population of the United States, because they tend to die earlier than whites. But, contrary to the usual statistical stereotype, it appears that whites do *not* have *lower* mortality rates or life expectancies in every age group.

Thornton & Nam (1968) examined mortality rates for whites and nonwhites in seven age groups (commencing with 25-34 years, and proceeding, by $i = 10$, to 85+ years) roughly between the years 1900 and 1961 (specifically 1900-02, 1909-11, 1919-21, 1929-31, 1939-41, 1949-51, and 1959-61). They concluded that "By age seventy-five, however, the life expectancy differential had reversed itself with whites having a life expectancy of 8.7 years and nonwhites one of 9.5 years.

TABLE 1: x^2 results for white - nonwhite marital statuses by sex, 1960[1]

Marital status	White-nonwhite males			White-nonwhite females		
	x^2	df	p	x^2	df	p
Single	0.6261	5	$<.98$	1.2477	5	$<.90$
Spouse present	1.1455	5	$<.90$	0.3863	5	$<.99$
Spouse absent	2.4179	5	$<.70$	0.4038	5	$<.99$
Divorced	0.0324	5	$<.99$	0.0098	5	$<.99$
Widowed	4.3987	5	$<.30$	2.2725	5	$<.80$

[1] Source of raw data: U.S. Bureau of the Census. *U.S. Census of Population*: 1960. Detailed Characteristics, U.S. Summary. Final Report PC (1) - 1D. U.S. Government Printing Office, Washington, D.C., 1963. Table 176, pp. 1-425 - 1-428.

This crossing seemed to have occurred at about the age of sixty-eight."

They contended that this phenomenon of racial reversal of life expectancy is probably not related to such factors as sex, cause of death, point in time, mortality measure, nor data error. Rather, the causal model "which appears most consistent with the data is one which does not rely on a biological explanation alone but which depends upon the interaction of biological and social variables." Calloway's emphasis on socioenvironmental variables to explain this reversal (Jackson, 1967) tends to support this conclusion.

However, Herman Brotman (in a private conversation with the author, 1968) suggested that data are too sparse and reporting too faulty to be able to even demonstrate such a pattern of racial reversal of mortality rates or life expectancies. He believes that, just as there is no significant difference by marital statuses between older whites and nonwhites, there is also *no* significant difference in their mortality rates or life expectancies. This, too, may be an issue in need of resolution. It is also highly probable that if older Negroes obtain significantly better preventive and other health care under Medicare, and if Medicaid is also extended significantly to the younger Negro population, this racial reversal, if it does exist, may well be erased.

Racial reversal or not, it is now the case that 1) most Negroes die earlier; 2) perceive of themselves as being "old" earlier; and 3) are, in fact, *old* earlier than are whites. Hence, this serious and highly pragmatic proposal: The minimum age-eligibility for retirement benefits should be racially differentiated to reflect present racial differences in life expectancies. Remaining life expectancy at age forty-five may be an appropriate base for computing such differentials. The following formula might be employed. At least it could be modified:

$$NMAE_{m/f} = AgMAE - (Wler_{m/f,45} - Nler_{m/f,45})$$

Where NMAE = Negro minimum age eligibility, AgMAE = Agency (e.g., Social Security Administration, State Department of Welfare) minimum age eligibility, $Wler_{m/f,45}$ = White expectancy rate for male or female cohorts at age 45, and $Nler_{m/f,45}$ = Negro life expectancy rate for male or female cohorts at age 45.

As an aggregate, aged Negroes depart from census-type statistical stereotypes of all aged in several other ways. For example, their incomes and education levels are lower than the average; their housing is more substandard. Other noncensus data show that they are also less likely to be aware of available sources than the aged generally. But, there are also some aged Negroes who depart culturally and statistically from the average aged, Negro or white, for their incomes and educational levels are higher, their housing better, and they have effective manipulative skills for utilizing available and creating new resources than the aged generally.

(Another "incidental": Urban renewal has, perhaps, unduly affected a number of aged Negroes [cf. Niebanck, 1965; Niebanck & Pope, 1965]. Among factors affected are those of housing composition, living arrangements, distance from kin, home ownership, to some extent, and social interaction patterns. Urban renewal may well result in additional cultural departures from statistical stereotypes by Negro aged, some of which may be highly undesirable.)

Briefly, empirical findings in social gerontology and related fields contain certain statistical stereotypes from which aged Negroes especially tend to depart. Such literature too often depicts aged Negroes as having extremely weak family structures and assistance patterns, extremely high religious activity and interest (God forbid! Religion is the most important aspect of their lives, according to some investigators), poor or extremely poor health, and almost no organizational participation.

For most aged Negroes with families, the family is the primary source of assistance (to the extent of its ability) and of primary group relationships. When socioeconomic status is controlled, aged Negroes are no more religious than white aged; and their organizational participation, again with SES constant, may even be somewhat higher. Their health is probably better than or no worse than that of whites.

The "laymen's 'statistical stereotypes' " vary, but I think that, within the Negro community, the aged have been thought of in much more favorable terms than the stereotypes which I have heard and read are assigned to the aged by white Americans. While white Americans may have been busy emphasizing youth, Negro Americans have been busier emphasizing survival, and the social roles assigned to Negro aged were delineated and significant (think only—if you will—of the grandmother as described by Frazier [1966]). But, one of the funny things happening along the road to integration, pluralism, or separatism (or wherever we are going) is that of decreasing significance attached to Negro aged by Negroes. This apparent phenomenon is probably a concomitant of the decreasing economic importance of Negro aged for their families.

Too many (even one is too many) welfare workers in particular conceive of their Negro aged clients as "old boys" and "old girls." Such workers tend to degrade such clients and, thereby, fail to establish meaningful and useful worker-client relationships. Many persons believe that aged (and other) Negroes "flock" to the welfare rolls whenever they can. On the contrary, many aged Negroes eligible for such benefits, refuse to degrade (yes, degrade) themselves by receiving welfare. Most of them remain employed labor force members as long as they can.

Other "laymen's 'statistical stereotypes' " could be cited, *ad nauseum*. What is more important than *ad nauseum* citation are two general conclusions about aged Negroes and their cultural departures from statistical stereotypes: 1) obviously, more valid and reliable statistical stereotypes about Negro aged are needed; and 2) morally, we, as social gerontological researchers and practitioners, ought ever be on guard to prevent the unfavorable "laymen's 'statistical stereotypes' " (sometimes supported favorably by invalid research data) about aged Negroes from becoming what Merton (1957) termed "self-fulfilling prophecies."

RURAL–URBAN DIFFERENCES

The rural-urban differences among Negro aged (i.e., sixty-five years of age and over) have received little attention in the literature. But, of course, there are certain differences which yet need to be ferreted out for further consideration in rural and urban programs, planning, and evaluation for these aged.

The focus on such differences within this paper, unfortunately, is highly limited. It is primarily restricted to 1) selected demographic data from the 1960 Census; and 2) selected findings about urban and rural aged Negroes in two Georgia counties, as described by Jackson & Ball (1966).

Most of the demographic data were only available for nonwhites, rather than for Negroes specifically. Since, however, Negroes were 93.6% of all nonwhites, 65+ years of age, in 1960 (91.8% and 95.1% respectively for Negro males and females), the terms "Negroes" and "nonwhites" may be used synonymously.

As can be readily seen in Table 2 below, nonwhite aged in urban, rural nonfarm, and rural farm areas showed little variation by the factors delineated therein. More were married in the rural farm than in the remaining two areas. More males in the rural farm and more females in the urban areas were in the labor force, than were their counterparts.

TABLE 2: Selected demographic characteristics for nonwhites, 65+ years of age, by urban, rural nonfarm, and rural farm areas, 1960 [1]

Characteristic	Urban	Rural nonfarm	Rural farm
% nonwhites, 65+ years of age, in total nonwhite population	5.7	7.4	6.2
Median age, Negroes only	70.8 yrs.	71.5 yrs.	70.8 yrs.
Q	4.2 yrs.	4.6 yrs.	4.2 yrs.
Median school years, nonwhite			
Males: 65-69 yrs. of age	5.3	3.6	3.8
70-74 yrs. of age	5.0	3.4	3.7
75+ yrs. of age	4.4	3.0	3.3
Females: 65-69 yrs. of age	6.1	4.5	4.7
70-74 yrs. of age	5.7	4.3	4.5
75+ yrs. of age	5.0	4.7	3.8
Marital status			
% Nonwhite males:			
Single	7.4	5.4	3.8
Married	64.4	69.3	74.5
Widowed	25.0	23.5	20.6
Divorced	3.2	1.8	1.1
% Nonwhite females:			
Single	4.7	3.6	3.4
Married	29.4	36.8	45.0
Widowed	63.4	58.5	50.8
Divorced	2.5	1.1	0.8
Average family size in same household:			
Husband-Wife, Head 65-74	3.06	3.51	4.09
Head 75+	2.84	3.10	3.61
Other male head, 65+	3.30	3.74	4.24
Female head, 65+	3.20	3.57	4.05
% in labor force			
Males: 65-69 years of age	39.8	34.5	61.6
70-74 yrs. of age	26.1	23.0	47.9
75-59 yrs. of age	18.8	15.0	34.7
80-84 yrs. of age	12.3	9.4	19.4
85+ yrs. of age	8.6	5.5	12.4
Females: 65-59 yrs. of age	22.0	13.7	13.5
70-74 yrs. of age	13.0	7.9	7.8
75-79 yrs. of age	7.9	4.9	5.3
80-84 yrs. of age	4.4	2.8	3.8
85+ yrs. of age	3.8	1.6	1.8

continued

TABLE 2: (continued)

Characteristic	Urban	Rural nonfarm	Rural farm
Median individual income (1959)			
Male: 65-74 yrs.	$1,433	$782	$773
75+ yrs.	$ 859	$601	$620
Female: 65-74 yrs.	$ 688	$550	$545
75+ yrs.	$ 617	$534	$531
% in group quarters	.04	.04	.002

[2] Source of raw data: U.S. Bureau of the Census, *U.S. Census of Population:* 1960. Detailed Characteristics, U.S. Summary. Final Report PC (1) - 1D.U.S. Government Printing Office, Washington, D.C., 1963.

Striking perhaps to some may be the fact that considerably less than one percent of these aged persons were in group quarters of any kind (including institutions) in 1960.

While this table is useful in providing a broad overview of basic social characteristics of its depicted population, its data are obviously much too scanty to assist substantially in planning and evaluating programs for Negro aged. The type of data described by Jackson & Ball (1966) provide a useful, but partial complement to such data.

Using noninstitutionalized Negroes, 65+ years of age, in one rural (N = 70) and one urban (N = 62) Georgia county, they investigated certain rural-urban differences. Their findings should be regarded as tentative, in that the urban sample was somewhat skewed by marital status.

A brief description of the samples: the mean age of the rural and urban respondents, most of whom were Georgia natives, was 74 and 72 years respectively. Approximately 38% and 31% of the rural and urban males, and 70% and 40% of the rural and urban females were widowed. Most respondents had less than a sixth-grade education, and their major lifetime occupations were either as farmers or laborers. The majority were no longer in the labor force, and, for most, their monthly incomes averaged less than $100. These two samples differed significantly (chi-square, $p \geq .05$) by age, sex, marital, employment, and educational status, major lifetime occupation, monthly income, and religious affiliation.

Chi-square results also showed that the rural and urban samples varied significantly ($p \geqslant .05$) by:

1. *Income sources* (essentially more rural than urban were dependent upon welfare funds only);

2. *Health factors* (greater frequency of utilization of services by the urbans; urban males reported the least number of health problems; more rural than urban would first "turn to" their families in case of illness, while more urbans than rurals would first "turn to" a hospital; more urbans than rural placed the greatest responsibility upon a governmental agency for providing them with medical care, while more rurals than urbans placed a greater responsibility for such care upon their families);

3. *Material possessions* (home ownership was higher among the rural than among the urban; some rural respondents had no running water and indoor toilets);

4. *Family and household factors* (rural families were larger; a greater proportion of urban parents received assistance from their children; the rural and urban parents varied in type of assistance desired from children);

5. *Friendship and social contact* (more rural than urban females, and more urban than rural males preferred homogeneous age-group associations; males reported a larger friendship group than did females; more urban than rural males and more rural than urban females felt that their social contact was greater than it was 10 years ago);

6. *Church participation* (church attendance was more frequent for rural than urban females, and for urban than rural males; more of the rural subjects participated in at least one church-sponsored organization than did the urban subjects);

7. *Desirability of a home for the aged* (whereas almost all of the nonwelfare recipients in the samples favored a home for the aged—for others, not for themselves—significantly more of the rural than urban

welfare recipients favored such a home—again, for others, but not primarily for themselves); and

8. *Attitude toward death* (measured very crudely, with a negative attitude being defined as a fear of death, the urban respondents were more positively oriented toward death than were the rural subjects).

These, then, are some suggested variables which may be useful in differentiating between specific rural and urban Negro aged subjects in the "Deep South." In all probability, most of these tentative comparative findings could be replicated in further studies of other Southern, Negro-aged rural and urban groups. Certainly, of course, many other variables need to be compared and tested, if we are to uncover the relevant rural-urban differences among these aged.

Two more points may be of interest. One, whereas both the rural and the urban sample ranked health as the first of three most important problems for the aged, the second and third choices of the rural and urban samples differed. The next most frequent problems for the rural group were inability to work and inadequate income; for the urban, inadequate income and inadequate transportation.

Secondly, these subjects placed "little or no faith" for assistance or adequate program planning for or with them in their local, county, and state governments. "Government" to most of them meant *only the federal government.* This perception is explicable not by unawareness local, county, and state governments, but by the realism of a general non-interest or an active "dislack" of interest in them by those governments.

Therefore, it is incumbent upon the federal government to continue to improve its program, planning, and evaluation for such aged. Moreover, it is even more incumbent upon the federal government to encourage the local, county, and state governments to which these subjects referred (and to all such governmental units in other geographical localities to which they might easily have referred) to begin (or to upgrade if they have begun) to plan and activate realistic and humanistic programs for their aged.

One small, but most significant step in the right direction is that of making certain that all agency personnel having direct contact with Negro aged clients treat them with politeness and courtesy and deal with them efficiently and effectively. Stop referring to aged men and women as "boys" and "girls!"

SUMMARY

The major purposes of this paper were those of suggesting some areas where aged Negroes tend to become "cultural departurers" from statistical stereotypes, and of also suggesting certain variables which may be useful in distinguishing between rural and urban aged Negroes.

Essentially, both tasks were only partially successful, due to the scarcity of available data about aged Negroes, and, no doubt, to the value judgments which I have imposed upon those data.

Given those limitations, however, Negro aged tend to depart from such statistical stereotypes as those which hold that their marital statuses are significantly different from those of white aged; that their life expectancies are typically less than those of whites (they may be longer at the later age periods); that they differ significantly from whites by importance placed upon their families, or that they are more religious, in poorer health, or less active in formal organizations than whites.

Some variables which may be useful in distinguishing between rural and urban Negro aged in southern areas, at least, include those of income sources, material possessions, health, family, and household factors, friendship and social contact, church attendance and participation in church-related organizations, and attitudes toward the desirability of homes for the aged and toward death.

Quite pragmatically, it appears that it may be useful for the minimum age-eligibility requirements for Negroes to receive retirement and other old age benefits to be reduced. It is also necessary for various local, county, and state governments to become more concerned about, and more actively involved in, programs, planning, and evaluation for Negro aged. Social gerontologists and practitioners utilizing their findings have such responsibilities as those of enhancing the validity and reliability of statistical stereotypes about Negro aged, and of working among and for Negro aged to eliminate those valid stereotypes which are undesirable, and of augmenting those which are desirable.

REFERENCES

Eisdorfer, C. Patterns of federal funding for research in aging. *The Gerontologist*, 1968. *8*, 3-6.

Frazier, E. F. *The Negro family in the United States.* (Rev. ed.) Chicago: University of Chicago Press, 1966.

Jackson, J. J. Social gerontology and the Negro: A review. *The Gerontologist*, 1967, 7, 168-178.

Jackson, J. J. Negro aged and social gerontology: A critical evaluation. *Journal of Social and Behavioral Science*, 1968, *13*, 42-47.

Jackson, J., & Ball, M. A comparison of rural and urban Georgia aged Negroes. *Journal of Social Science Teachers*, 1966, *12*, 30-37.

Merton, R. K. *Social theory and social structure.* Glencoe, Ill.: Free Press, 1957.

Niebanck, P. L. Knowledge gained in studies of relocation. In U.S. Department of Health, Education, and Welfare, *Patterns of living and housing of the middle aged and older people.* (Public Health Service Publication No. 1496) Washington, D.C.: U.S. Government Printing Office, 1965.

Niebanck, P. L., & Pope, J. B. *The elderly in older urban areas: Problems of adaptation and the effects of relocation.* Philadelphia: Institute for Environmental Studies, University of Pennsylvania, 1965.

Thornton, R. G., & Nam, C. B. The lower mortality rates of nonwhites at the older ages: An enigma in demographic analysis. *Research Reports in Social Science*, 1968, *11*(1), unnumbered.

United States bureau of Census. *Detailed characteristics, United States summary, 1960.* (Final report PC (1)-1D) Washington, D.C.: U.S. Government Printing Office, 1963.

29:: SOCIALIZATION AND SOCIAL ADJUSTMENT IN FIVE RESIDENTIAL SETTINGS FOR THE AGED

RUTH BENNETT and LUCILLE NAHEMOW

The purpose of this research was to observe socialization patterns in five residential settings for the aged which differed in degree of institutional totality. Socialization, social adjustment, and mental status were investigated to determine if they varied according to institutional totality.

The concept of institutional totality was introduced by Goffman (1960), who defined total institutions as those "symbolized by the barrier to social intercourse with the outside (p. 450)" and which are "encompassing to a degree discontinuously greater than organizations next in line (p. 450)" and act in a way to "break down the kinds of barriers ordinarily separating spheres of life (p. 451)" in the following ways: 1) all aspects of life are conducted in the same place under the same single authority; 2) each phase of the member's daily activity will be carried out in the immediate company of others, all of whom are treated alike and required to do the same thing together; 3) all phases of the day's activities are tightly scheduled, with one activity leading in a prearranged time into the next, the whole circle of activities being imposed from above through a system of explicit formal rulings and a body of officials; and 4) the contents of the various enforced activities are brought together as parts of a single, rational plan purportedly designed to fulfill the official aims of the institution.

Based on a paper read at 7th meeting of International Association of Gerontology, Vienna, 1966. Supported in part by Grant No. CD 00029 of the USPHS, Division of Chronic Diseases.

The concept of totality was extended for this research. Criteria were set up by which institutions could be classified according to level of totality. Using these criteria, the residential settings varied in degree of institutional totality on a ten-point index. A mental hospital, nursing home, supervised apartment residents of a home for aged, a public housing development with special facilities for the elderly received ratings of extremely high, high, medium, and low totality respectively. Results obtained in these settings were compared to those of an earlier study of an institutional branch of home for aged, which ranked in totality between the nursing home and the apartment residence.

Socialization is simultaneously a social process, a social mechanism, and a psychological process. This research is primarily concerned with the psychological process. As a social process, it is one in which normative patterns of a social system are transmitted to newcomers. As a social mechanism, it is an arrangement of positions within a social system whose incumbents act as socializing agents to guarantee the transmission of normative material to newcomers. As a psychological process, it is one in which an individual learns the normative patterns and other cultural material transmitted during the socialization process.

Socialization occurs as soon as a newcomer enters a social system, and it implies learning a new way of life. It is not the same as resocialization during which an individual is given a new orientation to a way of life he either learned or internalized imperfectly. Socialization and adjustment are not identical processes. Presumably, socialization prepares an individual to adjust to a social system; however, an individual may learn very well what is expected of him, yet deviate from these expectations.

Social adjustment consists of three independent processes: integration, evaluation, and conformity. Integration is indicated by participation in activities, volunteering for jobs, membership in informal groups, and friendships. Evaluation refers to opinions of specified aspects of life in a residential setting. Conformity is behavior enacted in accordance with social norms. In this research, social norms were established through participant observation and interviews during which consensus on some items of behavior was found among residents and staff members of the various residential settings.

In earlier research on socialization in a home for aged, newly admitted residents who had been isolated prior to admission were found to be poorly socialized in the home. Socialization was conceptualized as an intervening mechanism between one's experience prior to entry and subsequent adjustment. Thus, individuals who were isolated were thought of as having lost through disuse the ability to interpret subtle cues emitted during social interaction. Those who were not socialized early in their stay were found to be relatively isolated within the home, even after two years had elapsed. Early, as opposed to eventual, socialization was found to be a predictor of adjustment after one month, two months, and six months of residence, indicating the importance of rapid social learning. (Bennett & Mahemow, 1965a)

These findings led to speculations about social settings in which relationships between early socialization and eventual adjustment would or would not obtain. It was thought that socialization might relate better to adjustment in settings in which adjustment criteria were vague rather than explicit. This was because, in situations in which the rules are not spelled out in black and white, the individual must use whatever social skills he possesses in order to learn them and to behave appropriately. On the other hand, in institutions in which everyone is told the rules and regulations explicitly and immediately, socialization would not be a good discriminator of subsequent adjustment.

METHOD

Sample

Interviews were conducted with eleven mental hospital patients, twenty nursing home patients, ten residents in the apartment residence of a home for aged, and twenty tenants of a public housing development. Data were compared to those obtained in our earlier study of one hundred residents of the institutional division of a home for aged. Information on age, sex, race, religion, nativity, and length of education were obtained in all settings. Most respondents were over seventy; those in the institutional settings were about ten years older, on the average, than those in the housing project. The majority of respondents in each setting were female except in the housing project. In all settings, a majority were of the white race. Religious background varied in all settings; Jewish was predominant in the mental hospital and in the institutional and apartment branches of the home for the aged. In all settings at least half were foreign born, and at least half had some elementary education.

Procedure

In each of the five settings, every resident was interviewed at least twice; once within a week of admission and once after a month. Standard interview schedules were used which were constructed for each residential setting. During the first interview background information, mental status, and the individual's initial impressions of the residence were obtained. The second interview requested information on socialization, integration, evaluations, and conformity. While the concepts of socialization and adjustment are equally applicable in each residence for the aged, instruments designed to measure them had to be specifically designed for each residence since rules and informal norms of the group varied. While it is possible to describe conforming people in two different places and compare them to nonconforming people, the specific norms to which they conform differ. The same is true of socialization and, to a somewhat lesser extent, of evaluation and integration. While the measuring instruments used varied from place to place, every effort was made to maintain comparability. For instance, the same number and kind of items were used wherever possible.

However, the extent to which comparability was maintained remains largely unknown.

Socialization was measured by ten-item indices which varied in specific content depending on the setting. In all settings, the indices were made up of two halves: one half contained five questions about relatively fixed rules and daily occurrences; the other half contained questions on less fixed norms and infrequent practices. Both halves were weighted equally. An example of a question about a fixed rule in the state hospital was: Are you allowed to drink here? The correct answer was: No. Any other response or "don't know" was considered incorrect. An example of a question about a less fixed norm in the state hospital was: Are you expected to keep your door open at all times? A correct answer received a score of 1; an incorrect answer got a 0. The possible range was from zero to ten.

The three components of adjustment, integration, evaluation, and conformity were again measured similarly though not identically in all five settings. Integration was measured by obtaining a self-report from each resident, who was asked if he attended any of the specified activities available, participated in any voluntary activities which would be likely to bring a resident into contact with other residents, or met with friends or informal groups. An index of integration was constructed by assigning one point to each activity, job, friend or group named; the points were then added.

The evaluation index consisted of ten questions asking how residents felt about specific aspects of life in each setting. Positive, mixed, and negative evaluations received scores of two, one, and zero respectively, which were summed for a total score. In the institutional branch of the home for aged studied earlier, the conformity index contained four items to determine whether residents acted in accordance with social norms. In the mental hospital, apartment branch of the home, and nursing home it was extended into a twenty-item index. A conforming response was given a score of two and a deviant response was scored as zero. Conformity was not studied in the public housing development since there seemed to be no normative consensus.

Mental status was assessed with Goldfarb's Mental Status Questionnaire. It consists of ten questions dealing with orientation to time and place. One example: "Who is President of the United States?" Ten is the highest possible score and zero the lowest.

FINDINGS

In order to determine where normative information was more accessible, that is, more clear-cut and explicit, preliminary research was undertaken in the form of participant observation and interviews with staff members and old-timers in the five residential settings. The findings obtained showed a curvilinear relation between totality and clarity and complexity of social adjustment criteria.

Residential settings with both extremely high and low totality ratings had in common the fact that adjustment criteria were vague. The criteria of adjustment in moderately total institutions such as the home and apartment residence were clear and explicit and centered around participation in activities and other forms of social integration. The institutions at both extremes on the totality dimension, the state hospital, which was most total, and the housing project, which was least total, had in common the fact that they were not perceived by staff or by residents as being permanent residences (despite the fact that they usually were). It was tentatively concluded that normative information was better disseminated in residential settings which were communities and which served as permanent homes for all residents. (Bennett & Nahemow, 1965b)

Table 1 shows the distribution in percentages of residents in all five settings according to number of items correct on the socialization indices. After one month of residence, the majority of residents in the more total institutions did worse than those in the less total institutions. In both the mental hospital and the nursing home the majority of residents could only answer five or fewer socialization items correctly, while in both the apartment residence and the public housing development 80% of the residents answered six or more items correctly.

TABLE 1:   Percentage of residents of five residential settings for the aged
            according to number of items correct on socialization indices

Residential setting	N	Number of socialization items correct				
		0-1	2-3	4-5	6-7	8-10
State hospital	11	9	27	27	36	0
Nursing home	20	5	15	35	45	0
Home for aged (inst.)	100	12	21	31	25	11
Home for aged (apt.)	10	0	10	10	40	40
Housing project	20	0	0	20	35	45

Thus residents of highly total institutions appear to experience particular difficulty with early socialization, while those in less total institutions are socialized more quickly.

Despite the fact that every effort was made to insure comparability of the socialization scales across institutions, this may not have been achieved. The differences presented in Table 1 may still be due to the items being generally more difficult in the more total institutions. It seems unlikely, however, that the error would be made so systematically as to produce a linear relationship between totality and ease of socialization. In addition, internal analysis of the scales suggest that this was not the case.

If residents of less total institutions were better at learning more difficult items, e.g. those concerning infrequent practices and less fixed norms, a majority of them would know correct answers to those items. Table 2 shows the number of items out of five fixed rules and five unfixed norms to which more than half of the residents gave correct answers. In all settings more of the items about fixed rules were learned by a majority than was the case for unfixed norms. There seems to be no pattern corresponding to degree of institutional totality which would explain these findings. More than half the residents of the extremely total settings such as the nursing home knew correct answers to only two of the five items about unfixed practices, which was exactly the case for those in the least total setting of the public housing development. Thus, it appears that the socialization indices were found equally difficult in all settings by a majority.

The relative ease with which residents of less total institutions were socialized does not appear to be a function of their mental alertness as measured by the MSQ, as is shown in Table 3.

The relatively slight difference in the average mental status score of the residents of a state hospital and those in a public housing project was surprising and may be partly accounted for in two ways: 1) mental hospital patients who scored very low could not be interviewed and therefore were dropped from the sample, and 2) interviewers at the housing project reported feeling uncomfortable asking these simple questions, and it is possible that they did not always press for the answers. In any event, it is notable that MSQ scores did not increase with totality as socialization scores did.

Table 4 shows the correlation between socialization and the three adjustment measures of integration, evaluation, and conformity.

There is a marked curvilinear relationship between the correlations and institutional totality. For all of the adjustment indicators, socialization varies positively with adjustment in the middle range of totality and that is where this positive relationship is strongest.

In all residences for the aged there was a positive relationship between socialization and integration. Either people who are sufficiently sensitive to learn the normative expectations quickly are selected by others as friends, or their friends serve to transmit and clarify the expectations. This appears to be most true for the residences in the middle range of totality in which, it has been noted, the expectations for adjustment were most clear-cut and explicit.

The relationship between socialization and evaluations was somewhat different. In the middle range of totality there was a positive relationship in that those who learned most about the home liked it the best. However, this was not true at the extremes. In the state hospital context those individuals who knew most about the setting after one month of residence liked it least.

As for the relationships between socialization and conformity, there was a positive, though small, relationship between the two in the institutions of the middle range and a negative relationship at the

TABLE 2: Number of items out of five fixed rules and five unfixed norms to which more than half of the residents knew the correct answer by type of residence

Type of residence	N	Number of items about fixed rules to which more than half the residents knew correct answer	Number of items about unfixed norms to which more than half the residents knew correct answer
State hospital	11	3	1
Nursing home	20	2	2
Home for aged (inst.)	100	4	0
Home for aged (apt.)	10	3	3
Housing project	20	4	2

TABLE 3: Mean MSQ scores in five residential settings for the aged

	N	Mean MSQ
State hospital	11	7.33
Nursing home	20	6.20
Home for aged (inst.)	52	8.86
Home for aged (apt.)	10	9.00
Public housing development	20	8.75

*Data on MSQ test were collected on only 52 of the 100 residents.

TABLE 4: Correlations between socialization and the integration, evaluation and conformity components of adjustment after one month of residence in five residential settings for the aged

| Type of residence | N | Correlations | | |
		Socialization & integration	Socialization & evaluation	Socialization & conformity
State hospital	11	.24	-.37	-.57
Nursing home	20	.32	-.05	.12
Home for aged (inst.)	100	.51	.26	.08
Home for aged (apt.)	10	.59	.11	-.09
Public housing development	20	.23	-.16	*

*No data on conformity were obtained in the Public housing development.

extremes. This was somewhat surprising since the concepts of socialization and conformity are often regarded as synonymous.

In some social contexts, while it may be possible to learn the norms adequately, there may be factors which motivate residents to disobey them. In general it would seem that early socialization is a good predictor of adjustment in social contexts where adjustment criteria are clear and where the institution is regarded by both residents and staff members as a permanent home.

DISCUSSION

Socialization was found to be better in residential settings which were low in totality. Socialization seemed only slightly related to mental status. Possibly, use of a more comprehensive psychiatric status instrument would have strengthened this finding. The high degree of socialization found among residents of a public housing development in no way was related to their social adjustment. Normative knowledge, and possibly its internalization, did not appear to be a prerequisite for adjustment in residential settings at either extreme of the totality continuum. It was related positively and significantly only in institutions of the middle range of totality. Perhaps only in the middle totality range is how well you do socially a clear reflection of what you know. It may be influenced by size or degree of cohesion in institutions of the middle range where adjustment criteria were found to be explicit and clearly communicated. This finding was thought to reflect the needs of such institutions which are structured like small communities and which serve as permanent homes for their residents. Perhaps such institutions rely most heavily on an individual's learning and possibly internalizing norms so that he may be able to regulate his own conduct. Thus, an individual who was not socialized early was seriously disadvantaged in adjusting.

At the extreme high and extreme low ends of the totality continuum were a state hospital and public housing development. Neither seemed much of a community, and both were large. Nor is it clear that those who run them think of themselves as working in institutions serving as permanent communities for residents. In such settings many intervening factors may play a role in the relation between socialization and adjustment. There may be a large difference between knowing what is expected of you and doing it.

The factors of personality and pathology may play a greater role in a large and anonymous setting. Those who know what to do may feel less inclined to conform in a setting in which they do not feel personally committed to the community norms. Such residential settings may, therefore, rely more heavily on external agents and sanctions to enforce and uphold norms rather than on individual internalization of norms. Additional research is needed to determine whether the correlation between socialization and social adjustment stems from the value placed on community and the principle of permanency in institutions of the middle range or from some other aspect of their structure. Future research on this problem should involve a comparison of institutions within a single category. Thus, for example a comparison should be made of two homes for the aged of approximately equal size and totality, one of which serves as a community and a permanent residence and one of which does not.

REFERENCES

Bennett, R., and Nahemow, L. Institutional totality and criteria of social adjustment in residential settings for the aged. *Journal of Social Issues,* XXI, 1965b, 44-78.

Bennett, R., and Nahemow, L. The relations between social isolation, socialization and adjustment in residents of a home for aged. M. P. Lawton (Ed.), *Proceedings of Institute on Mentally Impaired Aged.* Maurice Jacob Press, Philadelphia, 1965a, 90-108.

Goffman, E., Characteristics of total institutions. In M. R. Stein, A. J. Vidich, & D. M. White (Eds.), *Identity and anxiety: Survival of the person in mass society.* Glencoe, Ill.: Free Press, 1960.

30:: DEATH RATE OF RELOCATED NURSING HOME RESIDENTS

ALVIN I. GOLDFARB, SIROON P. SHAHINIAN,
and HELEN TURNER BURR

The first admission of aged persons into institutions had been described as a tragic, painful, and stressful experience (Nicholson, 1956) which decreases life expectancy of persons who enter homes for the aged (Lieberman, 1961) or state hospitals (Camargo & Preston, 1945; Kay, Norris & Post, 1956; Whittier & Williams, 1956). Relocation, similarly, has been regarded as emotionally disturbing and harmful.

However, there are actually few studies of the effect of administratively determined relocation of institutionalized aged persons, (Aleksandrowicz, 1961; Aldrich & Medkoff, 1963; Aldrich, 1964; Miller & Lieberman, 1964; Niebanck & Pope, 1965). These studies tend to confirm the belief that relocation of institutionalized aged is associated with a higher death rate than would otherwise be expected. While personal anticipation of relocation does not appear to affect the death rate significantly, for certain groups, described as the helpless, psychotic or near-psychotic, the death rate after relocation exceeds expectancy in the first year, and especially in the first three months (Aldrich & Medkoff, 1963). The higher death rate after movement into an institution has been ascribed to the physical decline and deteriora-

Based upon a paper presented at the annual meeting of the Gerontological Society, New York, New York, November 1966. Thanks are due to Mr. George Kaplan, research aide, for his assistance in preparation of this paper.

tion that precipitated the need for such action rather than to the emotional impact of institutionalization (Goldfarb, Fisch, & Gerber, 1966). For the most part, it has been recommended that once the older person has become acclimated to an institution, has regained a sense of security, and acquired a measure of confidence in his surroundings, he should not be exposed to the possible trauma of yet another change of setting (Nicholson, 1956; World Health Organization, 1959).

An opportunity for studying the effect of forced relocations of aged institutionalized persons presented itself when five of thirteen nursing homes in a follow-up study conducted by the Office of the Consultant on Special Services for the Aged were closed during the first five years of the investigations. (Over 2,000 aged persons in 25 institutions in the New York metropolitan area—nine homes for the aged, thirteen nursing homes, and three state hospitals—were randomly sampled in 1958 (Goldfarb, 1959, 1962) for a longitudinal study by the Consultant on Special Services for the Aged of the New York State Department of Mental Hygiene. A total of 869 aged persons were sampled in the thirteen nursing homes. Of these, 483 were sampled for studies based on direct examination and 386 were sampled for cross-validation purposes and studied by review of records only.)

Four of the homes which closed did so because of inability to comply with architectural requirements of the New York City Fire Department or Department of Hospitals. The fifth case was voluntary, for internal reasons. The closing of the homes should not be taken to mean they provided poor care as compared to those which continued in operation. In fact, as other aspects of the Consultant's Office longitudinal study revealed (Shahinian, Turner, & Goldfarb, 1962), almost all of the nursing homes were found to render a generally equivalent, inadequate, level of care. Differences in the quality of the closed homes as opposed to continuing homes is therefore excluded as a biasing factor in comparisons of the patient groups from the closed and continuing homes.

For all persons originally sampled in the nursing homes of the overall longitudinal survey, the average length of residence in the same home had been about two years. Their year by year mortality, location of survivors, and their condition, have been followed. These data made it possible to compare the course of the nursing home patients forcibly relocated en masse without regard to individual preference or need, with those whose individual circumstances dictated their residence arrangements.

At the time of their closings, these five homes had among them a total of 128 patients who had been sampled and were being followed by the Consultant's Office. Sixty-one of these were in the group being studied by repeated examination and sixty-seven were followed by review of records. Almost all of these relocated patients were transferred to other proprietary nursing homes.

Method of Study

The effects of forced relocation were studied primarily for seventy survey residents of one of the homes which closed—"Home Q." This group were survivors of the original group sampled and directly examined, or whose records were reviewed at the home ten-and-one-half months before relocation, the group had resided there for an average of two years at the time of their examination or record review. They were all transferred about the same time and constitute the largest group of subjects relocated at one time of the 128 patients relocated within the first five years of the survey. Thirty-five of them had been directly examined and information about the other thirty-five had been obtained by review of their charts. The mortality rates for the first year after relocation of these seventy persons, and the thirty-five among them who were examined, were compared to the death rates of groups of residents of the other nursing homes in the Consultant's Office survey for an equivalent year—that is, one which began ten-and-one-half months after original sampling date.

The first comparison group, Control I, consisted of persons who had remained in or never been transferred from their original nursing homes. They were viewed over a follow-up period of as many as seven years after sampling date, which was the most recently completed follow-up period at the time this study was started. Thus, it is a somewhat artificially contrived control group. In effect, it was designed and used to test the relocation effect against a theoretical alternative of what may have happened if, instead, *all* were allowed to remain "indefinitely" in the same nursing home without ever being transferred.

Control II consisted of *all* survivors still in their original homes ten-and-one-half months after the examination date, whether or not they remained continuously in residence thereafter. Thus, Control II is a larger group which includes persons in Control I, the never-transferred group, and also persons who were transferred for various reasons. Control II may be considered as more representative of the total nursing home population than Control I, the never-transferred. They are a representative sample of survivors of a larger sample, the remainder of whom were lost by earlier transfers or death. Strictly speaking, if the test group of relocatees were broken down further by those relocated but never transferred from that placement and those relocated but further transferred from that placement, the former group in this study would be the proper test group for comparison with Control I. However, the relatively small number relocated from a single home at one time and the fineness of breakdowns by certain characteristics prevented dependable statistical comparisons to be made in this way. An exploration like this was made which indicated that results would not be substantially altered or interpreted differently by such methods.

Table 1 shows the number of residents relocated from Home Q and the number in the two control groups.

An examination was made of the relationship of mortality within the first year after relocation, to age, sex, and three measures of physical functioning—physical functional status, motor performance, and physi-

TABLE 1:   The number of residents relocated from Home Q and the number in
            the control groups from the general survey in all other nursing homes

Survey and study groups	Total N	Originally sampled for:	
		Examination N	Records review only N
Original survey group Total of the survey in all nursing homes	869	483	386
Present study groups Relocated from Home			
Q	70	35	35
Control I	176	131	45
Control II	493	287	206

cal independence—to nutritional status, continence, presence and
degree of chronic brain syndrome, and medical and psychiatric
prognosis for life. The predictive strength of these variables for the
institutionalized aged population studied by the Consultant's Office has
been demonstrated (Goldfarb, Fisch, & Gerber, 1966).

Results

Of the seventy relocated Home Q persons, 28% died within the first
year of relocation as compared to 38% of all the never-transferred
(Control I) group over the equivalent year and 27% of the more general
group (Control II). The difference with Control I missed statistical
significance (Chi-Square = 2.9680, 1 df, $.10 > P > .05$).

No consistent or significant differences in mortality between the
relocatees of Home Q and the two control groups during the first year
after relocation was found to be associated with sex, one of the three
measures of physical functioning, nutrition, or continence. Women in
all three groups had comparable death rates, as did the men; persons
with comparable degrees of physical dependence, nutritional status, and
continence status had the same rate of death in all three groups.

Death rates for age groupings were similar for relocatees of Home Q and the larger control group (Control II), but were lower than that for the group of persons never transferred (Control I).

In general, it appears that mortality following relocation was related to functional status, not residence or relocation *per se*. This was evidenced by significant differences in mortality associated with differences in the severity of brain syndrome either as evaluated by a psychiatrist or a psychologist.

Home Q relocated patients with *severe* brain syndrome, as evaluated by a psychiatrist, showed a higher mortality rate (57%) than similarly afflicted and identified counterparts (39%) who resided uninterruptedly in continuing homes (Control I). These patients also showed higher mortality rates than the general survey sample group (Control II) which included persons transferred for various reasons (36%). This pattern is confirmed by the data for number of errors on the Mental Status

TABLE 2: **Mortality the first year following relocation from Home Q and same-year mortality in control groups: by examination findings for chronic brain syndrome**

Type of examination	CBS status on initial examination	Number relocated from Home Q	% first-year mortality		
			Home Q (N = 35)	Control I (N = 131)	Control II (N = 287)
A. Psychiatric	None	5	20	38	18
		12	8	45	22
	Mild	7	–	48	24
	Moderate	16	25	31	26
	Severe	7	57	39	36
	Total	35	26	37	27
B. Psychological MSQ	None-mild (0-2 errors)	11	9	37	12
	Moderate (3-8 errors)	12	17	41	35
	Severe (9-10 errors or non-testable)	12	50	35	30
	Total	35	26	37	27

Questionnaire, a psychological measure for presence and degree of brain syndrome. Although neither of these specific figures for severe brain syndrome patients reached levels of statistical significance, the trend appears to be indicative.

Although adversely affecting the life expectancy of those with *severe* brain syndrome, relocation appeared to have a beneficial effect on persons with *no* or *mild* brain syndrome. This is seen in the case of the twelve relocated patients from Home Q with no or only mild mental impairment at the time of the initial examination. Only one of them died during the first year after relocation, although from the control data more deaths could have been expected. The differences in mortality between these relocated Home Q patients with mild brain syndrome and their counterparts in Control I, the never-transferred, reached statistical significance (Chi-Square = 6.0841, 1 df, .02>P>.01). Thus the data suggest that aged persons with minimal degrees of brain syndrome may profit from forced relocation, and are harmed by long residence in the same nursing home; but that relocation for those with *severe* brain syndrome may possibly be a risk.

Functional status as measured by physical examination and physical

TABLE 3: Mortality the first year following relocation from Home Q and same-year mortality in control groups: by physical functional status and motor performance

Type of physical index	No. relocated from Home Q	% first-year mortality		
		Home Q (N = 35)	Control I (N = 131)	Control II (N=287)
Physical functional status				
No or mild impairment	14	–	27	11
Moderate impairment	12	50	24	24
Severe impairment	9	33	52	38
Total	35	26	37	27
Motor performance				
No or mild impairment	26	15	35	24
Moderate impairment	5	40	43	30
Severe impairment	4	75	45	44
Total	35	26	37	27

TABLE 4: Mortality the first year following relocation from Home Q and same-
year mortality in control groups: by psychiatric prognosis for
remaining life span

Psychiatric prognosis for life	No. relocated from Home Q	% first-year mortality		
		Home Q (N = 35)	Control I (N - 131)	Control II (N = 287)
Less than 3 months	2	50	67	33
3 months to 1 year	14	50	37	33
More than 1 year	19	5	37	23
Total	35	26	37	27

limitations is also related to death rate, as shown by increased death
rates in the moderately and severely functionally impaired.

Psychiatric and medical opinions as to life expectancy were also
significantly correlated with death rate. Table 4 shows that among all
those in the study for whom psychiatrists originally predicted a life
expectancy of more than a year at the time of the initial survey, the
nineteen patients relocated from Home Q showed an exceptionally low
death rate (only 5%) during the first year after relocation.

It was lower than death rates among controls with the same
prognosis—37% and 23%, respectively, for the never-transferred (I) and
the general sample group (II). As in the case of mild brain syndrome,
the lower death rate of the relocated patients with favorable life
prognosis reached levels of significance only in the case of comparison
with Control I (Chi-Square = 7.9092, 1 df, .01>P>.001). Results are
similar using the examining internist's opinion of prognosis for life
expectancy. Patients with good life expectancy according to the
psychiatrist or internist appeared to benefit from forced relocation.

Table 5 shows one-year death rates, in relocated and control groups,
of residents with at least three of the five indicators found in *this* study
to be related to high mortality. These high indicators are: 1) *severe*
brain syndrome; 2) 9-10 MSQ errors or non-testable upon examination;
3) *moderate* physical functional impairment; 4) *severe* impairment in
motor performance; and 5) a psychiatrist's impression that life
expectancy is short—his diagnosis of Brain Syndrome, Chronic, Severe.

TABLE 5: Mortality the first year following relocation from Home Q and same-year mortality in control groups: by multiple signs of high mortality

| Study group | No. | Residents with at least 3 out of 5 signs | | |
		No.	No. died	% mortality
Home Q relocatees	35	6	4	67
Control I	131	27	5	19
Control II	287	46	13	27

TABLE 6: Mortality the first year following relocation from Home Q and same-year mortality in control groups: by multiple signs of low mortality

| Study group | No. | Residents with at least 3 out of 5 signs | | |
		No.	No. died	% mortality
Home Q relocatees	35	14	1	7
Control I	131	31	11	36
Control II	287	98	18	19

Four of the six patients with at least three out of five of these factors relocated from Home Q (67%) died within a year. Only 19% of similarly afflicted patients in Control I and 27% in Control II died within an equivalent year. The increase in mortality reached levels of statistical significance in the case of the never transferred group, Control I (Fisher exact probability test, $P = .0342$). In the comparison with the general nursing home sample, Control II, however, the increase approached, but did not reach, levels of statistical significance. The fact that the *lowest* observed death rate for *severely* impaired patients occurred in the Control I group, the never-transferred, suggests that for severely mentally and physically impaired residents of nursing homes, stability in their environment may prolong life. The converse is shown when multiple indices of *no or mild* impairment—mild or no brain syndrome, no more than two errors on the MSQ, little or no impairment in physical functional status and in motor performance, and a favorable life expectancy according to a psychiatrist—are related to death rate.

An exceptionally low mortality—7%—for relocated patients with three or more indicators that impairment was at most mild (Table 6), compares favorably with the observed death rate of 36% for similar persons of Control I (never transferred) cases and of 19% for Control II, the general nursing home sample. The difference reached levels of statistical significance in the case of Control I (Chi-Square = 5.1100, 1 df, .05>P>.02). The *highest* observed death rate for patients with multiple indications of only *mild* impairment occurred in the Control I group continuously resident in the same nursing home. This suggests that for minimally mentally and physically impaired residents of nursing homes, change in environment may be favorable.

Thus, the greatest contrast is between the group which was "arbitrarily" relocated and those not transferred. Comparison of the arbitrarily relocated with the population which includes persons transferred for personal, often health, reasons (Control II) blurs the difference. Except for the severely impaired, persons in unchanging residence appear to die off faster than their equivalents who were transferred without regard to individual situation. Poor prognosis, multiple indicators of high mortality, and the presence of severe brain syndrome appear particularly lethal to long-term resident nursing home patients who are removed from their environment.

Patients with good prognoses (multiple indicators of low mortality, and the presence of only minimal brain syndrome) appear to benefit from a change of nursing home placement.

Discussion

This study compares nursing home residents relocated as a group for administrative reasons with 1) persons who continued in residence, and 2) persons who continued in residence plus those who were transferred for individual reasons. The effect of relocation on stable residents of nursing homes transferred for administrative reasons is answered in terms of mortality rate during the year following relocation.

Our findings differ from previous studies of the effects of transfer or relocation on death rates of institutionalized aged persons. However, these differences appear to be the result of differences in the samples and the failure of previous studies to take into account fully possible variations in death rate with varying physical and mental functional status.

The study which has the largest number relocated with a good control group (Aldrich & Medkoff, 1963; Aldrich 1964) compares retrospective mortality rates for aged and disabled persons in an old age home with the mortality of residents in the first year after their relocation. Increased mortality after administratively required relocation of patients was attributed by the investigators to "the social and psychological effects of the change (p. 192)." However, our study indicates that persons with *severe* brain syndrome, with or without associated disorder of mood or content, and persons with considerable physical functional impairment are those at risk when relocated. For the relatively well physically, and for those with no or moderate brain syndrome, change of scene may be beneficial.

The findings of our study are consonant with those of Aldrich & Medkoff in that there may be a direct relationship of mortality to psychological stress in persons already physically vulnerable. However, there may be other causes of high mortality in the first few months after transfer, such as inadequate understanding of the physical needs of a new patient, subjection to excessive physical demands, and temporary alteration or discontinuity of supportive medical care.

Summary

In sum, relocation of long-term residents of nursing homes may hasten physical decline in aged persons who are already seriously physically impaired. Physical decline may be augmented by the increase in anxiety it provokes. However, a change in environment may be beneficial to persons physically capable of dealing with the new

demands. These differences in reaction contingent upon initial condition of relocated patients demonstrate the danger of generalizations
about the transfer of heterogeneous groups of aged persons. Other
factors being equal, the death of persons who are grossly functionally
impaired is hastened by transfer, but the longevity of persons who are
physically functioning relatively well is not adversely affected and may
even be benefited by transfer of the persons from one place of
residence to another.

REFERENCES

Aldrich, C. K. Personality factors and mortality in the relocation of the
    aged. *The Gerontologist*, 1964, *4*, 92-93.
Aldrich, C. K., & Medkoff, E. Relocation of the aged and disabled: A
    mortality study. *Journal of the American Geriatric Society*, 1963, *2*,
    185-194.
Aleksandrowicz, D. Fire and its aftermath on a geriatric ward. *Bulletin
    Menninger Clinic*, 1961, *25*, 23-32.
Anonymous. Moving can be killing for the aged. *Medical World News*,
    1962, *3*, 103.
Blenkner, M. Environmental change and the aging individual. Paper
    presented at the 7th International Congress of Gerontology, Vienna,
    June 1966.
Camargo, O., & Preston, G. H. What happens to patients who are
    hospitalized for the first time when over sixty-five? *American
    Journal of Psychiatry*, 1945, *102*, 168-173.
Goldfarb, A. I. Summarization of activities for the year 1958 from the
    office of the Consultant on Services for the Aged. Unpublished
    manuscript, New York State Department of Mental Hygiene,
    Albany, N.Y., September 1959.
Goldfarb, A. I. Prevalence of psychiatric disorders in metropolitan old
    age and nursing homes. *Journal of the American Geriatric Society*,
    1962, *10*, 77-84.
Goldfarb, A. I., Fisch, M., & Gerber, I. E. Predictors of mortality in the
    institutionalized aged. *Diseases of the Nervous System*, 1966, *27*,
    21-29.
Kay, D. W., Norris, V., & Post, F. Prognosis in psychiatric disorders of
    the elderly. *Journal of Mental Science*, 1956, *102*, 129-140.

Lieberman, M. A. Relationship of mortality rates to entrance to a home for the aged. *Geriatrics*, 1961, *16*, 515-519.
Miller, D., & Lieberman, M. The relationship of affect state and adaptive capacity to reactions to stress. *Journal of Gerontology*, 1965, *20*, 492-497.
Nicholson, E. E. *Planning new institutional facilities for long-term care*. New York: Putnam, 1956.
Niebanck, P. L., & Pope, J. B. *The elderly in older urban areas: Problems of adaptation and the effects of relocation*. Philadelphia: Institute for Environmental Studies, University of Pennsylvania, 1965.
Shahinian, S. P., Turner, H., & Goldfarb, A. I. Towards an instrument for rating institutional care for the aged. Paper presented at the meeting of the Gerontological Society, Miami Beach, 1962.
Whittier, J. R., & Williams, D. The coincidence and constancy of mortality figures for aged psychotic patients admitted to state hospitals. *Journal of Nervous and Mental Diseases*, 1956, *124*, 618-620.
World Health Organization. Mental health problems of the aging and aged. Technical Report Series No. 171. Geneva: World Health Organization, 1959.

31:: A SOCIAL WORK PRACTICE PERSPECTIVE IN RELATION TO THEORETICAL MODELS AND RESEARCH IN GERONTOLOGY

LOUIS LOWY

Theoretical models are essential for a practitioner to guide him in deciding when, how, and for what purposes to enter a system. Theories give the practitioner guidelines for intervention, and they also facilitate the setting of goals for the work to be done.

In the helping professions, theories of human behavior have shaped the development of the professions themselves. This can be well illustrated in social work. It has leaned heavily on Freudian theory of human growth and development, which has been primarily concerned with infancy, childhood, and adolescent stages of the human life cycle, but it has largely ignored the later phases of life. Relying upon transposition of such material has been found unsatisfactory, and new approaches by geriatric psychiatrists recently have been introduced (e.g., Berezin & Cath, 1965).

The deterministic aspects of Freudian developmental theories have been partially responsible in social work practice for the notion that personality changes are confined to younger years. This can be illustrated by the fact that until very recently, older clients have been neglected by many caseworkers, as indicated by Kastenbaum in his article, "The Reluctant Therapist," in *New Thoughts on Old Age* (1964a).

Adapted from a paper presented at the 19th Annual Meeting of the Gerontological Society, New York, November 1966.

But even the developmental model in use for younger age groups has left out the qualitative nature of the processes involved in meeting the tasks associated with a particular stage in life. The lack of specificity of the processes involved, the context of the environment, the social structure, the ethnic pattern, etc. make for very sketchy and hazy guidepoints for the practitioner. A greater understanding of these factors can be of considerable aid to social work, both in specifying the tasks to be met and in dealing with the effect of structural factors upon the way these tasks are perceived.

This is particularly well illustrated by Kastenbaum's (1964) theoretical formulations in which he makes the point that the developmental task in later life has something to do with the generation of new meanings. The present and the future situation of the aged person is to be seen not only within the context of his past, but also against his present and his future. The early years of life receive a fundamental impetus from forces of growth and reproduction; the later years have no such intrinsic meaning. Whatever meaning they acquire depends in large measure upon the individual's own interpretation of his immediate and total life situation. Would it not follow that the practitioner is faced with helping the older person in the formulation of his task?

Arriving at an interpretation of the situation as perceived by the older person in it requires a process that engages the older person in a struggle for mastery through which he discovers his own developmental task by restructuring the environment and perceives alternatives from which to choose. May not this process of discovery lead to the development of a mechanism of mastery instead of a mechanism of defense? Is not there an opportunity for the practitioner to find guidelines that may have eluded him in a vain search for developmental tasks with a biased focus on revisions and replacements of earlier modes of life management? Are not these preconceived formulations fitted for life tasks geared toward reproduction, utility, and productivity rather than for the yet unknown tasks arising from situational factors of a later life?

The limitations of a narrow perspective are also pointed to by

Maddox in Chapter 19 of this book. He persuasively argues that the lack of a sociological perspective, by design, colors the results and interpretation of the data in a developmentally oriented theory such as disengagement. Particularly convincing is his argument against the assumptions made by Cummings & Henry (1961) that all individuals have free access to the resources and rewards of their society. There is evidence that older people are largely excluded from such free access in our society. It has been only recently that sociological and anthropological concepts and theories have again found entry into the thinking of the helping professions and into the formulation of diagnostic assessments and treatment.

Theoretical formulations have been powerful agents in the practice of most professions. Social work is no exception. In fact social work, with an insecure knowledge base and a heavy value emphasis, has tended all too easily to latch on to theories that seemed to hold out great promises without always keeping a respectful distance and maintaining a willingness to wait for the evidence. For example, disengagement theory has found readier adherence by social caseworkers than by social group workers who have almost instinctively rejected it because it interfered with their preferred "activity" value orientation.

The power of a theory, and therefore its potential advantage and disadvantages, can be illustrated by the following case. Merton's (1957, pp. 131-160) original formulation about discrepancies between societal goals and accessible means has been further elaborated by Cloward & Ohlin (1960), who have postulated consequences for deviant behavior as a result of differential access by certain segments of the population to the legitimate and illegitimate opportunity structures. Recent social welfare programs such as Mobilization for Youth in New York City and the Anti-Poverty Programs have indeed been shaped and developed largely on the basis of their theoretical formulation.

The merits or demerits of these programs will not be discussed here, for that is not the function of this paper. It can be seen, however, that theories, with or without adequate investigation, can have far reaching impact when action-people take hold of them! For this reason, it is particularly important to be cautious about a theory, such as disengagement, which in its raw form may fit only too well into our American culture orientation with its emphasis on "usefulness" and "work" and which can readily be used to justify further exclusion of the aged from participating in the mainstream of American life.

The introduction of new perspectives—whether sociological, anthropological, economic, or historical—is not only essential to develop theory but also to shape our social policy. In the same way that the theory about opportunity blockage in relation to youth has introduced new dimensions in the developmental theory of young people, or the analyses of situational factors have amended learning theory and have seriously challenged long-cherished notions about the reliability and validity of IQ measurements, new and different light may be shed on the nature of engagement and disengagement of older persons. The factor of exclusion of the aged in the occupational system and in the political system (to use Mogey's [1966, p. 44] formulation) has implications for 1) social policy formulation and implementation, and 2) social work practice.

Thus, for example:

1) In the realm of social policy the recognition of deliberate exclusion of the aged could lead to programs that open up the opportunity structure for older people, some of which have already appeared on the horizon, e.g., social reengagement of older persons through the foster grandparents program. Modern medical science and health practices and their increasing availability through social legislation may lead to healthier aged people with renewed vigor to reengage themselves in the life of their community. Other examples could be cited.

2) In the realm of social work practice, especially casework, the focus upon inevitable decline, defense mechanisms, and adjustmental services could be shifted to a process of discovering developmental tasks and their mastery and to the performance of new social roles made possible by a wider opportunity structure. Social services would become

preventive and life-enhancing rather than curative. Engagement and disengagement could be seen against a situational frame of reference as it is being done in social work diagnosis for other age-groups.

Since cultural values, meanings, and social structures are the matrix for the social processes of all people and therefore also of the aged population, any theory has to take into account the facts and consequences of social and cultural change, which is more accelerated than ever today.

It is precisely such accelerated change and its consequences that not only affect the status and role of the elderly as objects, but also make it possible for the older person as subjects to affect these changes. A perspective that incorporates this into practice may be instrumental in motivating older people toward engaging themselves in our society and produce a different social climate which in turn makes such engagement even more possible. Social movements by the elderly themselves (as Rose [1965, pp. 19-36] has elaborated), and by socially conscious younger people in concert with the elderly, may indeed change social structures that up to now have seemed unshakeable. If we produce a system of social services based on a philosophy of an advancing social standard for the aged (as for everybody else) rather than on a regressive poor-law philosophy of sixteenth-century England, then an analysis of data derived from respondents who have lived through these changes may well yield different interpretations and different theories of the aging process. The collaboration of behavioral scientists and health and welfare activists in the design of such research will add immeasurably to the utility of the findings and produce a "better deal" for our aged population.

The opportunities for collaboration of social welfare activists and behavioral scientists in studies of this type are increasing with the development of social welfare programs in housing developments, Medicare, and the establishment of multiservice centers, etc. Contacts of older people and younger people in foster grandparent programs, home-aides, homemakers, friendly visitors, etc. lend themselves to the design of field studies. Intergenerational family life programs allow for natural observations of the interactional relationships.

Professional social workers, social welfare aides, and behavioral scientists can collaborate as teams in the design and execution of such studies. Careful recording can be made of the observations, discussions, expression of feelings of the actors, i.e., their history during a week or a month or a year, as the days, weeks and months unfold. Needless to say, many older people can and will function in these practitioner and scientist roles.

While there are many obstacles and problems to be solved in designing and executing such studies, many social workers (albeit for different purposes) unwittingly have already been involved in such endeavors in their recording of case histories and observations and in their group recordings. These data are a rich treasure if properly exploited, and they could be further enriched if systematically developed jointly by practitioners and behavioral scientists. For example, we may be able to discern self-concepts of older people as they unfold in recreational programs, in the context of serving others as friendly visitors, in the relationship with their family members, as well as in the way they meet stressful situations. We may be able to learn about fluctuations in their perception of authority through authority figures (such as social workers), the dimensions of morale, their attitudes toward sex, their feelings about their children and grandchildren, their attitudes toward different types of activities, toward political issues, and a host of others. Data derived in the field under natural conditions can then be compared to findings of empirical studies that have utilized other research strategies. Perhaps the day will come when instead of many fragmented research efforts the "principle of coordination" will be applied. Out of a quilt of knowledge-building efforts, a mosaic will then emerge that in turn will lead to further theoretical formulations and further research. Research is not an effort to be given over to the research scientist who turns over his findings to the practitioner for use. The practitioner should and can be engaged as a partner. He should and can contribute actively toward the formulation and design of research. He can be an indispensable link in the chain of theory testing through empirical research and the ultimate accumulation of knowledge concerning human behavior.

REFERENCES

Berezin, M. A., & Cath, S. H. (Eds.) *Geriatric psychiatry: Grief, loss, and emotional disorders in the aging process.* New York: International Universities Press, 1965.

Cloward, R., & Ohlin, L. *Delinquency and opportunity.* Glencoe, Ill.: Free Press, 1960.

Cummings, E., & Henry, W. *Growing old: The process of disengagement.* New York: Basic Books, 1961.

Kastenbaum, R. Is old age the end of development? In R. Kastenbaum (Ed.), *New thoughts on old age.* New York: Springer, 1964.

Kastenbaum, R. The reluctant therapist. In R. Kastenbaum (Ed.), *New thoughts on old age.* New York: Springer, 1964. (a)

Merton, R. *Social structure and anomie.* Glencoe, Ill.: Free Press, 1957.

Mogey, J. Society and the aged. In L. Lowy, & J. Mogey (Eds.), *Theory and practice in social work with the aging.* Boston: Boston University, 1966.

Rose, A. M. Group consciousness among the aging. In A. M. Rose, & W. A. Peterson. *Older people and their social world.* Philadelphia: F. A. Davis, 1965.

Author Index

Aaronson, B.S., 350
Abraham, K., 281, 282, 284, 286, 287, 311
Achebe, Chinua, 361, 363
Adler, A., 254, 273
Albrecht, R., 136, 137, 143
Aldrich, C.K., 72, 90, 94, 256, 273, 525, 535, 536
Aleksandrowicz, D., 525, 536
Ames, L.B., 218, 237, 243, 244
Anderson, T., 111, 115
Arenberg, D., 139, 142
Armitage, P., 172, 199
Arth, M.J., 353, 363
Ayllon, T., 66, 69

Babchuk, N., 490, 500
Bailey, M.C., 90, 95
Bales, R.F., 174, 199
Ball, M.A., 507, 509, 513
Banissoni, F., 374, 394
Barmack, J.E., 51, 60
Barmark, T., 31, 36
Beattie, W., 13, 18
Becker, Howard S., 320, 321, 324, 331
Bellak, L., 220, 243
Bellow, S., 481, 482
Belver, C.G., 60
Bengston, V.A., 27, 35
Bennett, R., 71, 95, 145, 163, 165
Bennett, Ruth, 137, 140, 171, 201, 208, 209

Benny, M., 199
Bereiter, C., 104, 105, 106
Berengartin, S., 31, 34
Berezin, M.A., 27, 34, 296, 297, 305, 311, 538, 544
Berlyne, D.E., 136, 142
Bexton, W.H., 68, 69
Bibring, Greta L., 285, 304, 307, 308, 311
Binstock, Robert, 20, 24, 33, 34, 35
Birren, J.E., 52, 59, 63, 69, 130, 142, 335, 350, 401, 406
Blalock, H.M., 427, 443, 449, 463
Blau, P., 323, 331
Blau, Z., 323, 331
Blendis, L.M., 172, 199
Blenkner, J., 90, 95
Blenkner, M., 72, 95, 536
Blum, R., 6, 18
Bogdonoff, M.D., 322, 333
Boler, D., 165
Borstelmann, L.J., 245, 249
Borstelmann, S., 249
Botwinick, J., 63, 69, 130, 142, 397, 406
Bright, M., 168, 199
Brim, O.G., 320, 331
Britton, J.G., 158, 165
Brodsky, P., 255, 273
Brody, Ealine, 133
Brotman, H.B., 485, 500
Brotman, Herman, 504
Brown, M.I., 446, 463
Buechler, J.S., 172, 199

Subject Index

absolutist fallacy, 102, 104
Acceptance of status quo, 154
acculturation process, 355
Activities of Daily Living scale
    (ADL), Katz's, 93, 130
activity centers, use of, 11-12
activity theory, 108, 298, 339
adjustment, 103, 108, 139, 174,
    337-339, 343, 390
  analysis of, 346
  as morale, 144ff, 161
  cross-cultural, 361-362
  differentiated from socializa-
    tion, 515
  situational, 320
  social, measurement of com-
    ponents, 518
  social, processes of, 201, 515
adjustment indices, 139, 163, 202-
    203, 207, 209, See also
    Cavan Adjustment Scale
adjustment to impending death,
    213, 214-215
adjustment to institutionalization,
    71-72
adjustment to widowhood, as a
    function of age, 487
ADL scale, See: Activities of
    Daily Living
adult socialization, 320, 340-341,
    342, 344-346, 349
Adulthood Isolation Index, 202,
    207
affect, 252, 265, 272
age-related biological changes, 53,
    304
aged, See also old age
  as dysfunctional social ele-

ments, 83, 361, 363
  role of, in Ibo culture, 352,
    353-354
  role of, in Yoruba culture, 353
  rural-urban differences among
    Negro, 507-512
Aged Services Project, 118
aging, anthropology and the study
    of, 352-354, 362
  as biological process, 318-320,
    325
  as a developmental process, 169,
    317-323, 325, See also:
    Processes, developmental
  attitudes toward, 48, 154, 287,
    368
  definition of, 3-4
  effect of environmental change
    on, 72-77
  Freudian attitudes toward, 297,
    309-310
  process of, 279-280, 309, 334ff.,
    342, 446, 463
  social policy, 3-18, 20, 33, 54,
    334, 349
aging in prison, early stage of
    adult life cycle, 468-470
  late stage of adult life cycle,
    472-474
  middle stage of adult life
    cycle, 470-472
  optimism of inmates about,
    467-468
  study of inmates' impressions
    of, 466
aging subculture, 109, 110, 336,
    341, 342-344, 348
Agitation, 155, 163